Questioning Sociology

Questioning Sociology

A CANADIAN PERSPECTIVE

EDITED BY

George C. Pavlich / Myra J. Hird

OXFORD
UNIVERSITY PRESS

OXFORD
UNIVERSITY PRESS

70 Wynford Drive, Don Mills, Ontario M3C 1J9
www.oup.com/ca

Oxford University Press is a department of the University of Oxford.
It furthers the University's objective of excellence in research, scholarship,
and education by publishing worldwide in

Oxford New York

Auckland Cape Town Dar es Salaam Hong Kong Karachi
Kuala Lumpur Madrid Melbourne Mexico City Nairobi
New Delhi Shanghai Taipei Toronto

With offices in

Argentina Austria Brazil Chile Czech Republic France Greece
Guatemala Hungary Italy Japan Poland Portugal Singapore
South Korea Switzerland Thailand Turkey Ukraine Vietnam

Oxford is a trade mark of Oxford University Press
in the UK and in certain other countries

Published in Canada
by Oxford University Press

Library and Archives Canada Cataloguing in Publication

Questioning sociology: a Canadian perspective / edited by George C. Pavlich
and Myra J. Hird. Includes bibliographical references and index.

ISBN-13: 978-0-19-542273-3
ISBN-10: 0-19-542273-2

1. Canada--Social conditions--Textbooks. 2. Sociology--Textbooks.
I. Hird, Myra J. II. Pavlich, George Clifford

HN103.5.Q84 2006   301   C2006-903841-4

Cover Design: Brett Miller
Cover Image: Thomas Francisco / Getty Images

1 2 3 4 –10 09 08 07
This book is printed on permanent (acid-free) paper ∞.
Printed in Canada

CONTENTS

PART 3:   CRITICAL IMAGINATIONS AND CANADA   207

ACKNOWLEDGEMENTS

The editors wish to thank all the contributors for their insight and collegiality—the product is fitting testament to their enormous creativity and talent. We would like to acknowledge the thoughtfulness, support, encouragement, and assistance of Lisa Meschino and Lisa Proctor of Oxford University Press. Thanks also to Dorothy Turnbull for her unparalleled copyediting of the text.

George Pavlich would like to thank Myra Hird for her insight and a friendship of many years. I dedicate my efforts on this text to an extraordinary person, my mother Tally Pavlich. Finally, to Carla Spinola and Seth Pavlich I offer the gratitude of one who is lucky enough to be part of your lives.

Myra Hird would like to thank George Pavlich for his patience and friendship. I thank Anth, Inis, and Eshe for both the journey and destination.

INTRODUCTION

SOCIOLOGICAL QUESTIONS

George C. Pavlich and Myra J. Hird

Sociology bears a variety of reputations. Ardent critics dismiss it as a disreputable discourse of hot-headed radicals, protesters, discontented do-gooders, old-fashioned social democrats, politically correct moralists, or bleeding-heart liberals. Sociologists, so the criticism goes, never see the good in anything. Such critics often trivialize the sociological endeavour, viewing it as little more than a jargon-filled restatement of the 'obvious'. Or, as in the infamous dinner party joke:

> Q: *What do you get when you cross an organized crime boss with a sociologist?*
> A: *An offer you simply cannot understand.*

The ensuing laughter masks an unspoken disdain for the idea that critical commentary on social matters can ever lend itself to systematic discussion, let alone legitimate disciplinary 'science'. This posture denies that anyone learned in the ways of sociology's imaginations speaks with any kind of authority.

Yet sociology does have its fair share of supporters. Some see in it a refreshingly relevant counterweight to the humdrum of academic pursuits that ignore or even deny the importance of the changing human worlds we inhabit. Others see in sociology a vibrantly systematic, even scientific, way of coming to grips with what it means to live with others and of thinking carefully about how best to do so. Sociology provides supporters with a vocabulary through which they can explore questions beyond the immediacy of individual lives. Using that vocabulary, they can move beyond the self-absorbing obligations of everyday existence. The different critical languages within sociological archives appeal to many people. This is especially true for the approaches that speak to and seek to change wider injustices.

A BOOK OF QUESTIONS

The chapters in this book invite you to consider several different sociological languages that you can use to think about social relations among subjects in Canada. The authors will expose readers to a variety of sociological approaches, encouraging you to think critically about these approaches. They will entice you to use that critical knowledge to consider the effects of various social relations in Canada. In this way, we hope to help readers to develop what a leading sociologist, C. Wright Mills, calls a 'sociological imagination'. This imagination, described below, is not uniform. But continuous questioning is its life-source. And each of the chapters addresses questions that tap into important aspects of our collective lives.

We have divided the book into three parts. The first part tackles questions that start with us as individuals or selves. In various ways, each chapter explores how our relations with other people actually create things that we often take to be unique to ourselves. The second part deals with sociological imagin-ations that focus attention on collective relations among people as 'social' relations. The final part of the book responds to critical questions on specific aspects of Canadian society. These essays reflect a variety of critical sociological imaginations as they grapple with important issues facing many Canadians today.

SOCIOLOGY?

But what exactly *is* sociology? As with other disciplines, this sort of question elicits almost as many responses as the number of texts in which it is raised. Rather than adding another static response to the question, we will not frame sociology as a field definable by a fixed object of study, a core set of theoretical texts, or a required theoretical approach, or even as a discipline held together by the use of one (scientific?) method.[1] Instead, we will position sociology as an ever-evolving craft, a changing process of assembling and linking concepts in ways that allow people to reflect on their lives as participants within and contributors to their associations with others. This formulation allows sociology to emerge as a changing yet systematic attempt to create, assemble, or reassemble concepts by which we may examine the assumptions that shape our social being at given moments in history.

This view echoes the work of C. Wright Mills, who saw sociology as providing the space to create a uniquely sociological imagination. For Mills, the socio-logical imagination may be described as a 'quality of mind' that seeks to 'achieve lucid summations of what is going on in the world' (1959, 5). As the basis of soci-ology, this frame of mind promises 'an understanding of the intimate realities of ourselves in connection with larger social realities' (15). It enables the sociologist to make imaginative leaps and connect the most intimate of personal 'troubles' (experienced by specific individuals) to the most general structures that shape a given society. These leaps enable us to develop broader understandings of our-selves by connecting our self-identities to wider socio-historical formations. The understandings help us to address the social patterns 'of which we are at once creatures and creators' (164).

This introduction explores various facets of the sociological imagination in four related sections. The first section uses hypothetical examples to describe key characteristics of this imagination, while the second situates sociological thinking against other disciplines. The third section outlines three influential theoretical approaches in sociology often used to help create sociological imaginations. In the

fourth section, we discuss the basic role that questions play in formulating a sociological imagination. Reflecting a central theme of this book, this final section
shows how fundamental questions can arrest everyday views of the world and
open us up to a sociological imagination.

SOCIOLOGISTS AND THE SOCIOLOGICAL IMAGINATION

What sort of thinking is distinctive though not necessarily exclusive to sociology? In responding to this question, and to elaborate on Mills's 'frame of mind',
it is helpful to differentiate between two of the many possible ways of thinking
about the world: namely, the *everyday* approach and the *sociological* approach.[2]
Typically, we rely on everyday, taken-for-granted assumptions to help us negotiate our lives. I may, for instance, feel hurried because I am late for an appointment. This perception encourages me to drive faster or speed up my walking
pace. In such circumstances, we seldom stop to consider the underlying notions
of time or the actions that flow from our common impressions of time. We do
not ordinarily question assumptions behind notions of 'being in a hurry' or
'keeping an appointment.' For instance, we seldom examine how the idea of
'hurry' relates to socially established conventions of time or how these ideas are
ingrained in the sorts of individuals that we are. The common sense meaning
maps we use to guide us through life, once learned through socialization,
become taken-for-granted frameworks. They condition our everyday thinking
and actions.

To take a related example, I might ask someone, 'Excuse me, do you have the
time, please?' Ordinarily, I do not expect that person to engage me in a philosophical discussion of time or deliver a lecture on how global time standards
came to be established. In our everyday thinking, when we ask someone what
time it is, we expect an answer like, 'Oh, it's is a quarter past five.' I would then
probably thank the person, and through the interaction, both questioner and
respondent embrace a shared common sense view of time.

However, suppose the respondent happens to be a sociology major conducting fieldwork and responds thus: 'What do you mean, "do I have the time?" What
is time? In what sense can one have it? Do you mean to imply that I, as a human
being, can own the time?' This response would likely strike one as facetious if not
downright rude. But it would also disturb the everyday common sense meanings
ascribed to time in a given context. Through this different interaction, the sociology major may prompt you to consider alternative possibilities. You may, for
instance, think differently when understanding and responding to your 'world'.
Were this to happen, the questions would have encouraged you to examine
assumptions grounding your common sense ways of acting around time. In the
process, you might begin to experience a 'quality of mind' that is akin to Mills's
'sociological imagination'.

The same point can also be made through an even simpler example. Suppose
I want to hang a picture on the wall and so reach for my hammer. In this situation, I typically do not raise questions about the nature of the hammer's existence: Is it real? What is the true nature of a hammer? Who defines what a

hammer is? I simply want to use it to drive a nail into the wall. However, there are moments when I might reflect on the being of the hammer. Let us suppose that after repeated and accurate swings of the hammer, the nail fails to make any impression on the wall. I might hold the hammer up to scrutiny and ask, 'What is this confounded thing, and what's wrong with it?' The questions explicitly focus my thoughts on the hammer's existence and prompt me to adopt an attitude beyond ordinary ways of existing. Again, events interrupt everyday patterns of thought to provoke fundamental questions, paving the way for reflective frames of mind to surface.

In sum, these examples suggest several distinct qualities of mind. First, there are our everyday, common sense patterns of thought (for example, seeking the best time to arrange a meeting or thinking about how to attach the nail to the wall and hang the picture). This is our usual, familiar attitude when we approach our worlds. When we think in this way, we simply take for granted concepts of time, the hammer, and so on to accomplish an activity. Second, and by contrast, are the moments that arrest our everyday, common sense thought and action. These moments often involve reflective thinking. Here we question the activities, tools, and concepts that engage us. The challenging response of the sociology major and the hammer's failure, for example, provoke me to think about my assumptions of time and the hammer's existence.

This second mode of thinking encapsulates the 'quality of mind' from which a sociological imagination may develop. It requires an imaginative leap in which we, subjects of given social contexts, suspend our everyday understandings. We do so in order to reflect on our typical patterns of thinking and acting with others. This reflective jump forms the basis of sociological ways of thinking, speaking, and writing. It appeals to theoretical languages different from those of common sense. There are many theoretical languages within and between disciplines to assist in such a task—the languages of economics, criminology, psychology, and women's studies, for example. However, sociology's traditions provide a unique vocabulary of collective (social) concepts. These concepts are designed to help participants negotiate being both participants in and analysts of a given social context.

It is clear that becoming a sociologist in this sense requires a particular sort of preparation. Specifically, one develops a reflexive imagination from concepts that either draw on or extend existing sociological (and related) traditions. To think sociologically involves becoming a specific kind of subject in a given social context. We remain participants in ordinary life; we do our shopping, play sports, visit friends, go to work, and so on. But beyond all that, we must learn to scrutinize particular aspects of our lives from a different vantage point—collective, socio-historical, or critical, for example. The process of learning to become a sociologist is very much about learning how to become someone who imagines collective life differently from those who never venture beyond the everyday. And the basic tool for negotiating a sociologist's identity, the passage from everyday to reflexive thinking, is none other than the difficult, arresting, provocative, yet always elusive *question*. Thus, sociological thinking most often starts at moments of astute questioning. Such questioning challenges the limits of ordinary, common sense frames of meaning. It leads us beyond the vocabulary and grammar of everyday thought to the conceptual languages of sociology. But how does such thinking relate to other disciplines?

THE SOCIOLOGICAL IMAGINATION AND OTHER DISCIPLINES

Suppose you are having coffee on the deck of a friend's small urban back garden. Dew glistens on the green leaves of a maple tree, reflecting the bright morning sunlight. The tree is undoubtedly the outstanding feature of an otherwise bleak garden. Your friend's mood is glum as she reflects on her inability to pay mounting bills and debts. She rents a small house in a barely affordable and somewhat undesirable suburb. As a single parent, she supports two children and spends a great deal of time trying to find a job that will enable her to meet her responsibilities.

She speaks of her inability to afford even the basics, like groceries, water, and electricity. Your friend has come upon hard times of late, and she says she now knows what the term poverty means. She even confesses to thinking about pilfering some 'good food' and has pondered ways of committing benefit fraud. Each time, however, she has thought better of it and let her life take its increasingly strained course. She has become frazzled by her predicament and blames the changing times: she points to increasing calls for the reduction of social assistance and the rising cost of heat, water, and electricity. Unable to find a job that will allow her to tend the children as she wishes, she has become dependent on social services and is perturbed by the identity this has thrust upon her. She stares meaningfully into her cup and sighs deeply. You place your hand reassuringly on her shoulder.

There are many ways to analyze this snippet of life. In the academic world, different approaches are often used to distinguish specific disciplines from others (engineering, anthropology, medicine, history, and chemistry, for example). However, the boundaries between disciplines are never clearly defined; their borders are often contested, they change over time, new disciplines are created, others are merged, and explicit calls for interdisciplinary work often arise. However, universities still distinguish between disciplines, though in different ways. They usually isolate social sciences and humanities from the natural sciences, the former seen as focusing on the human dimensions of a situation. Referring to your friend's situation in the foregoing example, a so-called natural science like plant biology might focus attention on the species of the maple tree, explaining how energy from the sun helps to sustain the life of the tree with its bright colours through photosynthesis. The physicist might examine the properties of the sun's refracted light through the prism-like bubbles of liquid. A chemist might seek to establish whether the liquid on the leaves is water or some other translucent substance secreted by the tree. The physiologist might collaborate with medical colleagues, and indeed the chemist, to study the potential effects of coffee on the human body.

Within the social sciences, the economist might describe redistribution of money in free market contexts, explaining your friend's current plight as the result of basic adjustments in previously more regulated markets. Psychologists, in contrast, might discuss the elements of mind that create your friend's depressed mood and prescribe treatments for her 'frazzled' state. Those of a more psychoanalytic bent might examine what lies buried in her expressive sigh or your comforting gesture. Feminist psychologists might identify the effects of patriarchal power relations that disproportionately disadvantage women. Political scientists would probably point to underlying changes to previous welfare state formations or to current pressure on the state from neo-liberals to sell off many public services, such as water and hydro facilities, to private enterprise. Classical criminologists might zero in on the cost/benefit, rational calculations that your friend makes before contemplating theft. They would undoubtedly note her free choice to obey the law rather than risk punishment if she breaks it.

Sociologists, however, are likely to approach the setting in the back garden through a rather different set of perspectives. The use of the plural form of 'perspective' is deliberate here, for there is little consensus on the exact way in which sociology ought to proceed. However, the approaches and practices of sociologists do differ from those of, say, economists or political scientists. Without suggesting that there are absolute distinctions among the disciplines, one might say that sociology tends to be involved with naming, understanding, and critically evaluating collective patterns through which people live their lives. These patterns are often referred to as the *societal* aspects of contexts.

Yet, as noted earlier, sociological imaginations are generated from many different theoretical approaches and employ a variety of practices ranging, for example, from surveys, laboratory experiments, and statistical analysis to participant observation, interviews, interpretative analysis, theorizing, critique, and political engagement. The sociological imaginations of this book's chapters, however, tend to draw on three main traditions. Most of the essays draw simultaneously—in some measure at least—on aspects of all these traditions and in various ways. However, some also draw on other theoretical orientations, which are beyond the purpose of this introduction to address.

THREE SOCIOLOGICAL APPROACHES AND IMAGINATIONS

Subjective troubles

Some sociologists develop a sociological imagination from theoretical traditions centred on how we interact with other subjects. These interactions create meanings that shape our views of the world and so affect how we act. The sociological traditions are concerned with interpreting and explaining social relationships— they deal with the meanings and actions that these relationships generate. Max Weber, a key figure in developing this approach, defines social relationships thus: 'The term "social relationship" will be used to designate the situation where two or more persons are engaged in conduct wherein each takes account of the behavior of the other in a meaningful way and is therefore oriented in these terms'(1962, 63). He distinguishes between behaviour (say, a random movement of your hand) and socially meaningful behaviour (a wave of your hand). He calls the latter 'social action'. For him, sociology is exclusively concerned with social actions and relationships.

Weber-inspired sociological imaginations thus focus on social actions, shared meanings, and relationships among subjects. Such sociologists focus on *intersubjectively* created meanings that guide people's actions.[3] With reference to the example above, they would focus on how you and your friend interact using meanings that both of you understand. They would want to examine what sorts of meanings allow you to interact with each other and the world around you. They might also ask how processes of socialization (that is, how you were taught the meaning horizons of a given society) have helped to create you and your friend as particular kinds of individuals (subjects) capable of functioning in *this* society.

To develop this sort of imagination, sociologists are likely to ask the following sorts of questions: Why do you behave and think in the ways you do? How do social interactions shape one's world view, and how does that world view affect the ways people subsequently behave? How do the meanings by which you make sense of the world lead you to act more or less predictably? What wider social history makes possible the thoughts and actions that colour your friend's and your social worlds? How do you come to interpret images, actions, gestures, and words in particular ways?

Such approaches foster a sociological imagination that focuses on subjects (selves) as both creators and creatures of social interactions. As a result, an important aspect of this imagination is reflected in the question: in what ways have you and your friend come to identify yourselves as very specific sorts of subjects at this moment in time? There are many different ways in which people can identify themselves and each other as subjects. For example, imagine a thirteenth-century peasant magically transported to your friend's back yard. This subject, who hails from a radically different social context, would not understand the meanings you and your friend assume as you effortlessly communicate with one another. Would the kindly peasant of yore have even the vaguest sense of the background political context of social welfare or privatization or even a concept of the city? This person might not even see himself or herself as an individual, as someone with private thoughts, capable of feeling 'stressed' the way your friend is. The peasant is a creature of a very different social world, understood and shaped by an entirely different social context. Consequently, the peasant's view of the world (and understanding of his or her location within it) would be very different from current beliefs.

The peasant example challenges the idea that individual subjects are essentially and universally the same. At the very least, it indicates that subjects can and do assume very different forms. Their understandings of themselves and their worlds vary greatly depending on the social contexts from which they emerge. Hence, Weber-inspired sociological imaginations require us to shelve the everyday view that I am essentially (i.e., at my core) a constant, unchangeable, and absolute individual. These imaginations draw on a theoretical tradition that views subjects as malleable creators (agents) and creatures (products, effects) of a given social history and context. Viewing subjects as creatures of ongoing social interactions focuses attention on how we as subjects are shaped by our interactions with others. It also leads to specific questions, such as those in the first part of this book, based on the possibility that various images of the self (as free agent with a particular sexual orientation and ethnicity) are produced out of social interactions within a socio-historical context.

However, the essays in Part 1, as well as many other chapters, also draw on what may be loosely termed 'post-structuralist' approaches.[4] Although difficult to define in outline, this set of approaches expands on and responds to a so-called 'structuralist' view. In sociology, structuralism takes various forms but holds that systematic inquiry can discover regular, recurring, and ordered patterns of social behaviour (for example, the micro-rituals of crossing streets at traffic lights, the way students file into lecture halls, the ways that the education system feeds into economic and political systems). Structuralists describe these patterns as *social structure*, which are thought to create individual human subjects. For structuralist thinkers, if individual subjects appear to have a stable nature—a core—it is precisely because of the relative stability of primary social structures.

Post-structuralists agree that subjects (e.g., people, I, you, me, he, she) are created identities but challenge the view that social structures exist in any absolute way. For them, subjects are always products of unpredictable and changing (thus not regular) historical contexts. From this perspective, any attempt to 'discover' regular social patterns cannot succeed; any such claims are mere beliefs, artificial impositions. All things (including language, knowledge, images of truth, the sociologists, the subject) are located within ongoing and non-necessary flows of history. Jacques Derrida and Michel Foucault are key French theorists often associated with post-structuralism, although they do not identify themselves as post-structuralists. Derrida's work in part indicates that language is assembled and used in very different ways: in current practices in our contexts, language is used in such a way as to create particular images of the subject (Derrida 1976). For example, the use of the first person as the subject of language often imparts the impression that individuals are absolute beings with a core essence (for example, the statements 'I am rational', 'I am happy' use language in such a way as to create images of a unified or fixed 'I').

Foucault also rejects the idea of a stable subject, but he emphasizes power relations as the key to understanding how particular images of individuals and selves are created (Foucault 1978; 1980a). In addition, both theorists challenge the idea that there are universal truths to discover; for them, truths (say, about subjects and social structures) are always the result of hard, truth-producing 'work' in particular contexts. Some feminist writers modify this approach to accommodate distinctive ways of redressing the plight of women in contemporary societies (Weedon 1999). The sociological imaginations of Part 1 tap post-structuralist traditions to question various everyday senses that people have of themselves as 'selves', free beings, sexual beings, citizens, and political agents.

Imagining the social

A second tradition used to generate sociological imaginations views collective life as a distinct object in its own right. Imagine the idea this way: While walking home from university you happen to glimpse a fair-sized flock of Canada geese flying overhead. You are struck by the overall patterns created as the geese dart and fly their various courses. One can focus attention on the antics of a particular goose, on the interactions of a smaller grouping, or indeed on the changing shape of the whole flock. The sociological tradition referred to in this section focuses on the whole flock. Furthermore, it argues that when thinking sociologically, one should explain the shape of the whole by referring to groups of geese and their characteristics, not by referring to an individual goose (that would be the subject matter of an individual-orientated discipline like psychology). Thus the collective whole must be explained through the component (social) groupings, and this would in turn indicate why individual geese act as they do.

The famous sociologist Emile Durkheim observed that society could be seen as an entity in and of itself, made up of social facts. For him, sociology should explain society by focusing explicitly on these underlying social facts. Durkheim (1938) regarded sociology as a unique science and saw its role as explaining individual behaviour through the relations among social patterns that create particular kinds of people in the first place. That is, sociologists can explain why one acts as one does by turning not to psychological or economic factors but specifically to *social* facts.[5] These facts are actualized through individuals and the interactions among individuals. But for Durkheim, they exist independently of any one individual; that is, they are detached from and then serve as a constraining force over a particular individual's actions. A Durkheimian sociological imagination would tend to use scientific methods to explain human behaviour by studying how social facts are related to one another. Thus a Durkheimian sociologist explaining why a person committed a criminal act would not look to, say, the psychological or genetic make-up of the offender. Instead, he or she might try to explain the social facts of crime in relation to other social facts (for example, identify general crime rates and then relate them to poverty rates or economic growth rates to explain the emergence of particular individual crimes).

Developing this sort of imagination, Durkheim-inspired sociologists might ask this in regard to the friends sharing coffee on the deck: can the social fact of increasing poverty be explained by wider economic (e.g., free market) and political (e.g., the decline of the welfare state) changes? How can scientific methods be employed to study the social facts of this situation? For instance, what social facts lie behind this particular woman's reliance on social welfare? Is the fact of growing social inequality in Canadian society related to the facts of free market economic arrangements or to class, gender, and ethnicity? What scientifically based policy recommendations and interventions might help to change society for the better?

The chapters of Part 2 develop various sociological imaginations around the theme of the 'social'. Though diverse, many of the essays also implicitly embrace the post-structural idea that the social does not exist absolutely; if it exists at all, it is because of given 'systems of truth' located within a given history. These essays suggest an imagination directed to showing how the social as a concept could generate more fair, public-spirited, compassionate, gender-equal, non-imperialist, and just ways of associating with others.

Critical sociology

A third, well-established critical sociological tradition gives rise to various critical imaginations. These imaginations seek to understand the injustices of given contexts, the underlying objective being to find effective ways of bringing about incremental or indeed revolutionary social change. Many budding sociologists have had direct experience of what it means to be poor, to witness the destruction of beautiful environments for short-term monetary gain, to bear the brunt of coercive control, or to be on the receiving end of discrimination based on ascribed gender, ethnicity, sexual identity, age, 'deviance', eccentricity, and so on. Seeing the unequal chances that individuals have to live a preferred life, the glint in the eye of a downtrodden child, the ruthless effects of social exclusion, discrimination, and intolerance, some seize on sociology to make sense of—and to fight against—social injustice. For these people, sociology serves as a theoretical awakening, a means of explaining experiences of injustice and directing political action in search of social change.

There are many different sociological imaginations of this ilk, but most tend to assume a macro (wide) focus and might approach our backyard example through questions like this: What social patterns and structures have created the conditions in which your friend must now negotiate who she is and what to do in her day-to-day life? How is her individual situation a product of wider power formations that advantage some people (e.g., the wealthy) and disadvantage other groups (e.g., the lower class, women, the young, the elderly, ethnic minorities)? What collectively shaped ideas, decisions, and actions make it possible for some people to own property and permit others to rent from them (such as a capitalist society based on private property ownership)? What socio-political decisions create conditions for and frame the type of life your friend now lives? How are these decisions made, by whom are they made, and what sort of effects do they have? How have the economic arrangements of the day favoured the wealthy or powerful at the expense of the poor or oppressed? In whose interest is it to continue the free market policies that entrench a particular brand of capitalism? What sorts of institutions have been created to develop, enforce, and monitor wider decisions as policies? What can be done to change the present society and bring about a different (fairer, more just, equal) society (Marx and Engels 1948, 1970)?

The chapters in Part 3 mobilize aspects of this tradition but with the aim of developing a sociological imagination that deliberately examines the ways in which sociological knowledge can speak to power relations by naming and indicating the effects of particular 'truths' in everyday life. They too implicitly tap post-structuralist themes; specifically, the chapters imply that power and knowledge emerge as closely connected processes (that is, truth is produced through power relations, just as knowledge helps to set up particular power relations—see Foucault 1977b; 1978; 1980a). What is taken to be true in any social context is a socio-political achievement, not an independent discovery. As such, critical sociological imaginations are particularly concerned with ensuring that knowledge that challenges current social forms be given a legitimate voice. Without critical analysis, there is little to challenge current social forms with all their injustices, inequalities, and so on (Pavlich 2000, 2005). Tyranny is never far away when critique is not allowed, and this is precisely why the authors of the final chapters call for new knowledge-producing environments—environments that encourage rather than stifle and silence critical imaginations.

WHY THE QUESTIONS?

To sum up for the moment: We have noted several approaches that inform the sociological imaginations of this text. In general, one might say that most sociologists are involved with naming, understanding, critically evaluating, and/or seeking to change the collective patterns and groupings in which people live their lives. These are often referred to as the *societal* aspects of life. Is there one sure way to develop this imagination? As Mills makes clear, there is no hard and fast blueprint. However, we have already noted one basic tool for the task: the ability to raise fundamental questions about our collective being.

Even a cursory glance at this text reveals an emphasis on questions. Indeed, the title *Questioning sociology* conveys that message from the outset. In the introduction, we have tried to communicate a sense of sociological thinking by posing questions. And each chapter develops from a specific question. Despite their differences, all the chapters adopt a questioning, interrogative stance. In each case, various aspects of the sociological imagination emerge as a result of responses to questions that require analysts to *reflect* on collective issues.

The practice of *asking questions* that leads beyond the limits of everyday common sense is thus a basic methodological resource for sociological thinking. That is, sociological thinking occurs at moments when we suspend our participation in everyday, common sense ways of understanding and acting in the world. It starts by reflecting on those understandings and actions. Instead of using common sense meanings to negotiate our way through life, sociologists look to other (sociological) meaning horizons. Developing a sociological imagination is very much like learning a different language, a new vocabulary, syntax, grammar, diction, style of expression, and so on. This language may be related to everyday life, but it involves a specifically reflective, *questioning* orientation that leads us beyond the limits of familiar common sense understandings.

Yet sociology explores ideas and actions in a language that is neither homogeneous nor complete: it is always evolving and changing. Since sociological thinking reflects on moments in history, and since these moments are constantly changing and never beyond question, sociology itself must remain open to new ways of exploring social life. In particular, sociological qualities of mind require us to go beyond the limits of given everyday ways of communicating. They require us to question the objects, concepts, and images that are simply assumed in ordinary life.

Thus, learning to think sociologically is an endless process because there is no final or finite language one can learn. Sociology does not have one canon or doctrine that all sociologists must observe. Instead, the languages of sociology are multiple, dynamic, and forever developing through new ideas, texts, presentations, and so on.

However, sociology's methodological reliance on questions is even more basic than that. For example, underlying all versions of the sociological imagination is a question that many sociologists must face: what methods are appropriate to address the collective aspects of our lives? Can the scientific methods of natural sciences such as physics and chemistry be transposed to a different context to explain social facts?[6] Or is the subject matter of sociology so different that it requires its own unique methods of analysis? If so, in what ways are the objects of sociology different from those of the natural sciences (say, sexuality versus gravity)? What methods can best address such objects? Is sociology a discipline that must remain committed to studying its objects using scientific methods (Durkheim 1938)? Or should it interpret social meanings with the greatest possible conceptual precision (Weber 1968)? That is, should sociology only aim at describing a 'taken-for-granted' reality? Or should it, in contrast, offer a critical view that judges a given society against a justified image of an ideal, advanced, equal, or rational society? Should sociology, for instance, not only name the social structures responsible for your friend's poverty but also suggest ways by which those structures can be changed to bring about a better society (Marx 1970)? The last question implies that societies are able to change over time. It also supposes that sociological analysis can help point both to appropriate directions for change and to the mechanisms for achieving such changes (for example, through revolution: Marx and Engels 1948, 1970).

The basic point is that while sociologists use particular kinds of questions to arouse the sociological imagination, they also make abundant use of questions to reflect on their own practices. The reign of the question is therefore basic to developing a sociological imagination. Were sociology to have a motto, it would surely be something like this: 'Question, Question, and Question Again!'

Notes

1. Indeed, as Anthony Giddens puts it, 'Like all other social sciences . . . sociology is an inherently controversial endeavour. That is to say, it is characterized by continuing disputes about its very nature' (1987, 2–3).

2. As in earnest dinner conversations with good friends when people argue over the world's plight and try to solve its most intractable problems, sociology often does examine pressing issues. However, unlike ardent, spontaneous meal-based debates—and perhaps even before August Comte's *Cours de philosophie positive* (published in 1838) put the term 'sociology' into wider circulation—sociologists have historically positioned their discussions as systematic analysis. Indeed, Comte termed sociology the royal science—indeed the queen of all sciences—because unlike others such as physics and chemistry it dealt with the very basis of collective being: human morality. Thus it was logically prior to all other sciences—because without stable social moorings, without peaceful social arrangements, all else in human society becomes impossible. Could computers ever be invented, understood, developed, and deployed in a society incapable of preventing its members from annihilating each other? First things first, according to Comte, and sociology's promise to explain peaceful, rational co-existence places it among the first of sciences.

3. See Weber (1968) and Berger (1973).
4. For a more detailed discussion of post-structuralism, see Seidman (1998) and Calhoun (1995, 113–16).
5. For Durkheim, '*A social fact is a way of acting, fixed or not, capable of exercising on the individual an external constraint; [or again] every way of acting which is general throughout a given society, while at the same time existing in its own right independent of individual interpretations*' (1938, 13; emphasis in the original).
6. Some say that this question betrays a deep-seated insecurity about the relative status of *social*—as opposed to *natural*—sciences. Disturbed by the charge that sociology is not a 'real' science, or that it is always a depraved cousin to its natural ('hard science') counterparts, many sociologists respond by clinging inveterately to 'science'. They try to be more scientific than any other scientist. No doubt this obsession has its own sociological pedigree, and its legacy *has* yielded many taxonomies, classifications, and descriptions of the seemingly obvious. Visit the far reaches of an older library and find the spot where sociology texts are filed. Look for the dusty tomes of yore that if ever pried from long-forgotten shelves would herald the functions of this or that social system or more ambitiously posit the absolute nature of all social existence. You will see that this 'science' has fallen prey to the ravages of time, its claims to final truth clearly exposed as rooted in a given time and place.

PART I

SUBJECTIVE TROUBLES

The first part of this book deals with developing sociological imaginations that question how we identify ourselves as particular kinds of people. It tackles questions of the self, the 'I', which seems so immediate to us, as a product of complex relations with others. In various ways, the chapters in Part 1 challenge the view that 'I' (our sense of self) is a primitive, fixed, primary being that exists before social interactions. Each chapter points to different means through which this 'I', or the self, is created by broader social relations with others.

George Pavlich's chapter, 'Am I Free?', for example, challenges the everyday view that selves are naturally free (that is, I am different from a stone or a flower because my nature as a human being is not fully determined—I am free to choose, within wide limits, how to act). Pavlich taps into this view by noting the extent to which Canadian society is based on images of individual freedom. Its founding liberal philosophy assumes that individuals are by nature free and that state power always curbs that freedom. In contrast, he formulates a sociological imagination that views freedom beyond everyday images that take the 'I' to be naturally free. He argues that neither the individual nor freedom exists in absolute terms. As well, he notes that power and freedom are not necessarily opposing ideas. Drawing on Foucault, he invites us to imagine that power is sometimes exercised precisely by enforcing 'free' individual identities. This is especially the case for liberal democracies in which governments claim the right to govern in part because they guarantee individual freedoms (freedom of speech, assembly, religion, and so on). However, if power is exercised by compelling each 'I' to be free in specified ways, then we are forced to reconsider what we mean when we say 'I am free.' In trying to be free individuals may well be endorsing a freedom that effectively allows them a narrow choice—namely, that of choosing their own chains.

Chapter 2 considers the most fundamental of human questions, 'who am I?', by invoking a particular sociological imagination. Dawn Currie and Deirdre Kelly draw on empirical research conducted to expose girls' experiences of peer relations. This research provides a basis for exploring how an individual's sense of self is sustained by various complex interactions among the social, political, economic, and cultural structures that surround the individual. Responding to the question 'who am I?', Currie and Kelly focus attention on how adolescent girls are actively involved in developing identity projects in social contexts, described as a search for selfhood. Here they work out who they take themselves (the 'I') to be. Based on 28 interviews with girls between the ages of 12 and 16, the research challenges two divergent strands of thinking: not only mainstream sociology and its failure to investigate identity projects of non-dominant groups (mistaking dominant identities for the norm) but also the view that girls are simply passive victims of 'adolescent femininity'. Currie and Kelly instead analyze the words of adolescent girls that describe the numerous pressures to 'fit in', to conform to conservative and traditional notions about how girls should dress, talk, act, and relate to others. Although these pressures are both intense and relentless, the researchers are clear that adolescent girls are active agents too. They make use of opportunities to resist wider relational structures and pressures. While girls who resist do not necessarily create entirely 'free' subjectivities, they are at least able to construct alternative, sometimes oppositional, understandings of themselves.

Myra Hird's chapter, 'Am I a Woman?', takes up the discussion of gender in Currie and Kelly's chapter in a different way. Hird argues that sociologists often champion the idea that gender profoundly shapes an individual's experience of the world. From this vantage point, whether an individual is identified as a woman or a man has significant consequences for the way other people relate to that individual, their occupation, family life, salary, health, intimacy, and so on. Many feminist sociologists share this view of gender. They often accuse sociology in general of ignoring or at least downplaying the significance of gender in determining an individual's life course. However, Hird invites us to consider questions of gender in another way. She notes that sociologists tend to separate the term 'gender' from 'sex': gender refers to socially constructed elements of personhood (femininity and masculinity), while sex refers to biological characteristics (what makes us either female or male). Her chapter challenges this distinction by arguing that our assumptions about sex as something natural limits the ways by which we are able to analyze gender. Sex is also a socially generated category. Indeed, Hird maintains that the so-called 'opposite' sexes are actually more similar than they are different. On that basis, she invites sociologists to develop ways of analyzing gender that do not inadvertently reinforce gender discrimination.

The following chapter, by Barry Adam, explores another dimension of the 'I' and the self by responding to the question 'why be queer?' In his formulation of a sociological imagination, Adam details the complex mechanisms through which social relations within Western society define, manage, and regulate sexuality. He begins by outlining a complex history of social processes that led to the 'invention of homosexuality as a juridical and medical category'. The processes also generated a negative bias—a *homophobia*—against those who identify as lesbian, gay, bisexual, and transgendered people. Dominant institutional structures within society, such as the law, medicine (especially psychiatry and psychology), and educational and public policy arenas, encourage us to identify as selves who align with prevailing gendering practices. Despite the considerable costs of defining oneself as queer, Adam convincingly challenges 'the ugly taskmaster of homophobia'. He argues against its tyrannical social censures that fail to comprehend the benefits to be gained from diversity in all its forms. He concludes by noting that if all selves were to reject homophobia, those selves' personal horizons would be greatly expanded and enhanced. This in turn could potentially help many more people to be 'at peace with themselves'.

Stephen Katz's chapter concludes Part 1 by responding to a recurring theme in the book: 'is the self social?' He does this by analyzing several major sociological approaches that focus on the relation between self and society, between inner lives and broader relations with others. Echoing C. Wright Mills's attempt to connect personal biography with history, Katz develops a sociological imagination by engaging several sociologists who argue that the self is socially produced. Drawing on Georg Simmel, George Herbert Mead, Irving Goffman, and Harold Garfinkel, he examines different views on how self-identity ('I' and 'me') is produced through interactions with others. He also examines recent developments in the sociology of emotions to show how collective norms of seemingly individual emotions (love, for example) create shared meanings about selves capable of such emotions. Sociological analyses of emotions allow us to glimpse how subtly the self is socially produced. Similarly, research on identity and aging tells us that different visions of self are considered normal during specific stages of life. Such norms reflect prevailing images of normality and abnormality, deviance, and difference. And that is crucial to self-definitions in contexts where selves are encouraged to define themselves in relation to 'others'.

Chapter 1

Am I Free?

George C. Pavlich

INTRODUCTION

Many people bandy the term 'freedom' about as if its meaning were so obvious that it merits little further attention. After all, inhabitants of a country like Canada live in a 'free society', part of the 'free world'. People go about the business of everyday living without undue interference from the powers that be. We exercise many free choices in the course of each day—whether or not to eat breakfast, which cereal to eat, how to style our hair, what clothes to wear, whether to attend classes or work, which mode of transport to use, what route to take, and even whether to protest against the government on a given issue. Indeed, the number of choices we have to make on a daily basis as members of a 'free society' is vast.

Over and above these personal choices, free societies provide formal guarantees for particular freedoms, such as those enshrined in the Canadian Charter of Rights and Freedoms. These laws are designed to protect 'fundamental freedoms', including freedom of religion, conscience, expression, peaceful assembly, and association. Other laws aim at protecting individual privacy from unfair intrusions by the state or other parties into one's personal affairs. These legally underwritten freedoms are part of a wider democratic political system, a system that relies on citizens being free to cast votes for the parties of their choice. Such freedom is key to any liberal democracy. Compromising its tenets threatens the integrity of the entire system. Similarly, capitalists champion the importance of free markets to economic well-being. The emphasis on freedom is evident in cultural contexts as well, with artists, writers, musicians, and dramatists fervently championing freedom of expression. Clearly, freedom is a prominent feature in the everyday, political, legal, social, economic, and cultural spheres of our lives.[1]

Does this mean that I am free? One cannot deny that we do exercise degrees of free choice, but in what sense does this mean that we are free? Certainly, we are not free to do exactly as we please under any circumstances. Nor can we fully decide how to live without external interference.[2] So perhaps we need to rephrase the question in more precise terms: in what way am I free when I exercise the choices available to me (or perhaps required of me) as a member of this society? This chapter explores this question by examining two responses that have inspired influential sociological approaches.

First, it examines a popular liberal view that individuals are 'born free' or that freedom is a natural aspect of all individuals. In this view, free individuals can only live according to their true nature when they live in free societies in which formal power is held in check. Here, individual freedom is taken to be the opposite of political power; indeed, it is thought only to exist when the state's power is reined in. This 'liberal' view makes a number of assumptions about society, including the notion that a 'free society' nurtures and encourages individual freedoms by reducing and limiting state (and other) powers. From this perspective, sociology—as a science of society—could seek to preserve individual freedom by discovering the real nature of a free society and offer recommendations on how best to achieve it.

Against this position, let us consider a second viewpoint, espoused by the influential French thinker Michel Foucault. Foucault challenges the main assumptions of modern liberal thought and argues that individuals are not born free. Rather, he holds that *power* creates both individuals and particular freedoms: neither individuals nor freedom can be regarded as natural entities. From this vantage point, who we are as individuals, our pleasures, our desires, our likes, and our freedoms are all produced by power. Power shapes both the sort of individuals we want to be (our identities) and the freedoms that we hold so dear.

In this view, individual freedom can never exist when power is held in check. Instead, no aspect of our relation with others is beyond power, and no social relation (including social freedom) is without power. A free society is itself structured and fashioned by power. Foucault's alternative view of freedom, individuals, power, and society has important implications for the role of sociology, especially a critical sociology that seeks to expose the dangers of given power formations. It also offers a unique response to the question 'am I free?'

SOCIOLOGY AND LIBERAL IMAGES OF FREEDOM

Man is born free; and everywhere he is in chains (Rousseau 1983, 165)

This brilliantly succinct statement, the first line of Jean-Jacques Rousseau's famous work *The social contract*, implies many of the founding assumptions of liberal sociology's approach to freedom in modern society. In this statement, and throughout the rest of the book, Rousseau regards freedom as a natural condition for human individuals.[3] To grasp the main idea, think of individuals born on a desert island. Left to their own devices in an ideal state, without constraining interventions by formal powers, these people would—according to Rousseau— grow up and live as natural, free, and sociable beings in a free society. They would be free to choose social rules under which they were prepared to live. Rousseau argues that modern industrial societies constrain rather than liberate individuals from the shackles of past societies (hence he finds people 'everywhere in chains'). As a result, individuals, free by nature, do not live in societies that allow them to live the free lives that their natural inclinations demand. Rousseau has much more to say on a wide variety of issues, but he formulates a liberal position on the freedom of individuals in modern society that has inspired influential sociologists. Many sociological works—including those of Durkheim and Weber—may be silhouetted against this view to the extent that they are all concerned with enhancing freedom by seeking to reconcile free individuals with tolerant, liberated societies. Let us explore this wider liberal backdrop on freedom in greater detail before turning to Foucault's alternative view.

Human beings are inescapably free

As should be clear, a classical liberal response to the question 'am I free?' would be this: yes, as a human being you are by your nature (i.e., make-up) a free being. A snail does not have the ability to choose how to act; that is predetermined by its surroundings. Further, so this perspective goes, a lion is born with instincts that largely dictate how it lives its life. It may learn hunting skills and could be a better or worse hunter, but instincts require it to hunt for survival. Lions cannot be held responsible for their actions because they do not make free moral or political choices. If a lion eats an antelope, we do not say that it is immoral (implying that it can be held responsible for its actions) for it is following its instincts. Similarly, a rose grows in direct accordance with its predetermined genetic disposition and the environment in which it is placed. An acorn does not decide whether or not to grow into an oak tree. Instincts and the physical environment in which they exist determine the fate of lions, roses, and acorns. None of them makes strictly moral choices; they do not have a capacity to rationally choose how to exist or to decide on the most ethical ways to behave.

Human beings are said to be different precisely because they are born with a free will and an ability to make rational decisions on how to live their lives. From this viewpoint, people have a unique ability to exercise choices over their being; they are not completely driven by basic instincts or by their environment. As free-willed beings, we must choose life courses from a range of possibilities. The choices include such physical things as how to grow (through diet, exercise, and so on) and whether or not to reproduce but also extend to questions about the sorts of people we want to be (such as reliable, compassionate, selfish, courageous), what career to pursue, and so on. Individual human beings are seen as unique in having the ability to choose, within the limits of certain physical constraints, how to live. Our fate is not predetermined in the way that the fate of plants and animals is; we are born with an ability to choose particular life paths. Freedom is therefore part of our special make-up—it is our distinguishing essence. For liberals, to be human is to be free to choose how to live one's life.

Before and after the Second World War, a group of influential philosophers associated with so-called 'existentialist' ideas expanded on this view. Most notably, Jean-Paul Sartre (1964, 1970) and Albert Camus (1991) described the cold, harsh realities facing us as agents of freedom in our everyday lives. Their work explores this unique aspect of what it is to be human, describing the terrible anguish involved. They insist that no matter what situations we find ourselves in, no matter how constrained or seemingly hopeless, human beings are always in some measure free.[4] Consider the case of a downtrodden person who is horribly exploited by a master as in past times when 'masters' who 'owned' slaves often treated them very poorly. Let us say further that the case involves a slave who is tied up and about to receive another lashing from her/his master. Even when restrained, the slave is free to respond in different ways, to imagine the situation in different ways: as a painful example of injustice, as a good reason for plotting revenge on a master, as part of the inevitable fate of a slave. Or the slave might let his or her mind wander in a dream world of sumptuous feasting. Any number of possibilities could be entertained. For existentialists, this sort of situation provides evidence that human beings are always and inescapably *condemned* to be free. Our lives are inevitably and irreconcilably undetermined—and hence free. Foreshadowing existential thought, Rousseau notes that 'to renounce liberty is to renounce being a man, to surrender the rights of humanity and even its duties' (1983, 170).

The idea of being condemned to freedom is beautifully characterized in Jean-Paul Sartre's philosophical novel *Nausea* (1964). The book chronicles the life of an ordinary man who is forced to confront a life of freedom. Through the narrative, Sartre tries to show how being condemned to freedom does not mean that we are therefore bound for 'easy street'. On the contrary, freedom is a terrible burden to bear because with freedom comes responsibility. That is, we may chose freely, but we are also responsible for the choices we make. Sartre sees this as condemning us to a life sentence of freedom. He describes the sheer burden of having to make choices and be held responsible for them in a world that is ultimately meaningless. Because we are free, we are free to shape meaning, but—and here is the catch—we can never be certain that the choices we make are the best, right, just, fair, or correct ones. That imposes a tremendous anguish on our lives, an existential *angst*, because we make choices never knowing whether they are moral or not. And then we are held accountable for those decisions. As we recognize this grave situation, this terrible fate, we are struck with awful feelings of anxiety, a pitiable nausea. We try to overcome the nausea by doing everything in our power to deny our freedom, trying to hide behind the illusion that we have done things out of necessity (i.e., we had no choice).

This thinking has been incorporated into sociology in various ways, including through an existential sociology in the 1970s (Douglas 1970; Douglas and Johnson 1977). This approach worked from the assumption that we are free to choose the social meanings that we do, focusing attention on the social effects of individuals being condemned to freedom. Existential sociology explored collective patterns generated by the anxiety facing individuals as they try to give their lives meaning in a meaningless world. Closely related to this approach was a so-called ethnomethodological approach in sociology. It analyzed the logic of the 'methods' (*methodology*) that people (*ethno*) use to create meaning in the ever-changing social environments in which they find themselves (Hilbert 1992; Garfinkel and Stoller 1967; Garfinkel 1986).[5] Despite their differences, these sociological approaches assume that individuals are fundamentally free and note that such freedom includes an ability to create meanings (see chapter 5). Meanings are shaped and mediated by meeting with other subjects in social contexts. Such socially structured meanings inform the way people decide to act. In turn, the multiple ways that people act, when considered as a whole, create the shape of society at a given point in time. From this vantage point, society and its meaning horizon emerges from at least relatively free choices made by individuals in specific contexts.

Power as the inverse of freedom?

> Being free stands opposed, classically, to being in someone else's power, being subject to the will of another (Ivison 1997, 1).

Rousseau offers a characteristically liberal critique of modern society by suggesting that in society people are 'everywhere in chains'. He worries that individuals have been trapped in power networks that restrict their free nature. In a characteristically liberal conception, power is seen as the opposite of freedom: where there is freedom, there is no power. Conversely, where power operates unhindered, where it constrains absolutely, there is no freedom.[6] This formulation no doubt implies a very specific conception of power: namely, power is identified with political institutions that limit individual freedom.

This image of power is perhaps most clearly developed in Thomas Hobbes's famous work *The leviathan* (1989). In this text, Hobbes accepts that individuals are born with absolute freedom and are thus potentially able to do anything within their grasp. With such absolute freedom, they can choose to help one another, but they can just as easily decide to kill one another to maximize their self-interests. In a 'state of nature', in a natural condition where individuals are absolutely free to do whatever they please, Hobbes describes a horrific 'war of each against all' in which life is 'nasty, brutish and short'. Now, as egoistic and rational beings who pursue pleasure and turn away from pain—who pursue their self-interests—individuals band together to form a 'social contract'. In this contract, they promise to yield selected freedoms to a sovereign power (the state). In turn, they receive protection and the security to live life without the constant threat of death, terror, theft, and so on. The sovereign has absolute power to enforce the social contract enshrined in formal rules called laws.

This intriguing and important analysis presents a view of power as a way of limiting, constraining, and checking individual freedom. Power emerges as something possessed by a sovereign (state, parliament, king, queen, and so on), which is exercised over all citizens. The sovereign wields power over others, restricting their actions, forcing them to act in particular ways, and thus confining their natural freedom. In this framework, power limits, stops, prevents, or coerces (Wrong 1988). The point is that where power operates, natural freedom is limited; power and liberty are thus inversely related.

What does this mean for the question 'am I free?' Clearly, this view of power means that I am only free when power is held in check, when a sovereign power does not interfere with my choices. In contexts where a sovereign does exert power, even if that power is considered legitimate (for example, exercised through the democratic rule of law), my freedoms are constrained when power is exercised, when an overarching power can determine how I should act. So we are never really free in the presence of a power over us. According to this view, we need domains of freedom where sovereign power is disallowed. Liberal thinkers have long pondered and tried to develop such domains, from the early images of 'public life' (Sennett 1992), to 'civil society', to images of the 'social' or 'community' as domains free from state power (Habermas 1971). Sociology has been involved in various attempts to develop free societies that regulate themselves as far as possible, beyond the coercive interventions of sovereign powers.

Individuals and a free society

This raises a further question: what sort of collective grouping (society) can we imagine that limits state power and maximizes natural individual freedoms? As we have noted, a recurrent dream within sociology has been to reconcile the natural state of individuals with appropriate social groupings; or to put it differently, sociologists have aimed at discovering a free society that would transparently reflect the individuals comprising it. How could this be achieved? Let us take Durkheim's (1984 [1893]) specific suggestions in his famous text *The division of labour in society* as a case in point.

As a sociologist, Durkheim does not deny that there is a biological (natural) component to 'individuals'. However, he insists that sociology is concerned only with that part of the individual that has to do with society. For him, people only come to exist as 'individuals' and moreover as free individuals in modern societies. The type of society into which people are 'socialized' largely determines whether they will live as free individuals or not (1984 [1893], 238–9). The type of society, in turn, is determined by the ways in which labour is organized in a given context (that is, the ways that tasks are divided up and apportioned by a group: how food is collected, how children are tended, how food is prepared, and so on). He argues, for instance, that pre-modern societies are of a type held together by 'mechanical solidarity' (1984 [1893], book 1, ch. 2). Necessary tasks are relatively simply structured, strictly regulated, and broadly divided (often between men and women, tribal elders, and others) through rules and customs. In such societies, individuals are not clearly identified apart from the roles they play as members of clans, tribes, and so on. A member of a group is not identified beyond the social functions, duties, and roles defined by customs and laws. In that context, it makes little sense to suggest that individuals are naturally free, since individuals are not clearly distinguished in context.

In contrast, Durkheim argues that modern capitalism—with expanding populations and industrialized forms of production—produces a type of society in which labour is divided in new and complex ways. In particular, tasks are broken down into discrete components, become specialized, and require many individuals to work in concert to get the overall job done (for example, to get a tomato onto my dinner plate requires numerous people who expend labour on diverse tasks, including developing seeds, growing plants, distributing the product to supermarkets, and selling it). This type of society is held together by an interdependence of function. Durkheim regards this bond as a resilient social 'glue', which he calls 'organic solidarity'.[7] Members of the society are required to per-form specialized labour tasks, and this makes them highly dependent on one another for their survival. For example, a housekeeper may place her or his money in the bank, but the manager of the bank may rely on the housekeeper to prepare food; both rely on others to produce the food, and so on. This mutual reliance on diverse labour functions makes it possible for modern societies to develop a 'cult of the individual'. This encourages members to regard themselves (or identify) as 'individuals', as free beings, who collectively make up society. The shift to modern societies brings with it a particular conception of freedom and individuality. It even allows the idea of individual freedom to dominate.

This sort of analysis raises several important issues for sociology's attempts to develop a free society that maximizes the individual's freedom. First, Durkheim is clear in condemning modern society for not adequately capturing or reflecting natural individual capacities. In a section of the book entitled 'The forced division of labour' (1984 [1893], book 3, ch. 2), he offers a critique of modern society, arguing that it has not allowed a division of labour to develop *spontaneously* in line with the natural development of human beings. His point is that a healthy society should develop according to the innate make-up of human beings and their needs and desires at a given moment in their historical evolution. In other words, societies should not be artificially forced in one direc-tion or another.

He explains in part why modern society is not a healthy one by arguing that it has put in place a 'forced division of labour'. Because it did not develop spon-taneously, this forced division of labour has created artificial inequalities and injustices. It constrains people in ways that do not promote their well-being and indeed even promotes a situation in which people find themselves without clear images of what norms to follow. This generates a condition of normlessness or 'anomie', as he calls it, in which individual freedom runs rampant without clear or comforting limits. For him, this is the 'disease' of modern life.

In contrast, a free society is one that develops spontaneously to accommodate the natural capacities of individuals; it would seek harmony *through* rather than *at the expense of* individual freedom. Now, if the reconciliation of individuals and society is to be based on freedom, social structures must be allowed to develop spontaneously, to emerge from patterns of interaction freely chosen by the indi-viduals that make up a particular grouping. Echoing Rousseau, the theory holds that individuals must be allowed to associate freely, to choose their normative arrangements. Only then can social structures develop out of free individual interactions.

Second, because individuals are free, their natural condition is said to have a history. That is, the nature of individuals is not a closed book—precisely because they *are* free beings. To say that an individual is naturally free is to say that what we take to be 'free' is conditioned by several factors. One of these factors, and an important one, is society. The ways in which people gather in a society, then, can have important effects on the ways that individuals choose to see themselves. The Durkheimian sociologist focuses on exactly how society shapes individual being.

Third, and with the previous two points in mind, the role of sociology becomes that of defining and recommending how to achieve a free society. This raises questions about what kind of science sociology is and about the sorts of methods that might be appropriate to its unique (i.e., free) subject matter. That is, if sociology is to study the collective life of free individuals, then are the scientific methods used in a science like physics applicable? For so-called 'positivist' sociologists, including Comte and Durkheim, empirical methods of observations of the kind used in physics are directly usable within the context of sociology. As noted in the introduction, this approach assumes that 'social facts' can be treated as 'things' as if these facts were governed by their own natural laws. In contrast, followers of what has become known as a hermeneutic tradition argue that sociology must use different methods of interpretation because individuals, unlike physical phenomena, are capable of exercising free choice. The debate is complex, but it is sufficient here to suggest that sociologists have remained divided on which methods to use when trying to explain or understand society (Giddens 1987). However, most liberal sociologists would not dispute that the aim of sociology is to discover how society works. Specifically, they want to explore how a *free* society works and in much the same way that physicists try to discover the real workings of physical phenomena.

The assumption is that societies, like physical phenomena in the world, are ordered (that is, come to exist in the ways that they do) by underlying laws that can be discovered through scientific inquiry. And the aim is to obtain valid and true knowledge of how free societies really operate. Armed with that knowledge, sociologists can make recommendations to a given society on how it might improve or make progress toward becoming a better, freer society. From this viewpoint, the work of a sociologist can be seen as akin to that of an engineer designing a bridge: both work on the basis of scientifically established principles of truth.

AN ALTERNATIVE VIEW OF INDIVIDUAL FREEDOM

We have so far examined a liberal sociological view of freedom and society. We saw how some social thinkers regarded freedom as natural to individuals but limited by power. Although it is deeply influential in sociological thinking, there are certain problems with this approach. For example, is freedom the same everywhere? Is freedom difficult to define precisely because it always emerges in the context of given social, economic, political, and cultural environments? And if freedom is relative to context, is it really the opposite of power? Or do particular forms of power imply particular kinds of freedom? As well, is the individual a static thing like a tree? Or does modern society and its unique power formations actually create individuals? If freedom is relative to context, and if individuals are socially created, then what does it mean to say that 'individuals' are born 'free'? These questions have encouraged social thinkers like Michel Foucault to develop alternative understandings of freedom, power, the individual, and society. This alternative framework also suggests a different way to understand the role of sociology.

Is freedom relative to context?

For writers like Michel Foucault, freedom is *not* something static—always the same—regardless of where it is found. The statement 'I am free' is always uttered in a specific context. It is not independent of, outside, or impervious to a given social history. That is, all kinds of freedom, including those that are held so dear in Canada today, have a very specific history. Just as it may be possible to trace your family tree, so it is possible to trace the family of ideas that give life to our various uses of the term 'freedom'. Following this logic, one may use the term 'freedom' to describe our ability to shop 'freely' within the limit of a budget when visiting a local mall. But we are surely using the term very differently from the way that people who aim to revolutionize societies for greater individual freedom do. The meaning of the term freedom is dependent on the context in which it is used. Freedom is not a universal concept with a single meaning regardless of the time and place; rather, it is very much the product of differing historical contexts.

Developing this argument in more detail, the sociologist Zygmunt Bauman (1988, 28–48) offers a most interesting history of the various ways in which freedom has been used in different sorts of societies. One of the oldest ideas linked freedom to a very specific act in classical antiquity. In this social context, freedom was conceptualized not as a natural, unchanging characteristic or social condition but rather as an act: namely, the act of releasing a slave from bondage. The released slave was referred to as a 'freedman' or *libertinus*. Slaves did not choose to be liberated, since removing the ties of slavery was a decision made by powerful masters. These masters owned slaves in much the same way that one might today own a car or a washing machine; it was they and they alone who could decide to release a slave from their direct control. As Bauman puts it, 'Freedmen had to be *made* free' (1988, 30). Their release, which was called *manumission*, changed the status of a slave from that of a chattel (i.e., personal goods that a person can own) to something slightly less than the full humanity granted to slave masters. Here, freedom has a very specific meaning. Significantly, the active agent is not the slave being released but the master who granted manumission.

Images of freedom as a granted privilege can be read into much of Western history. It recurs in the teaching of the early Christian church, specifically in the work of the theologian Pelagius. Bauman describes how for Pelagius, freedom was something granted: 'God *made* humans free; having been so made, humans could choose between good and evil according to their will. It was up to them to live toward salvation or doom; having been made free, having been given the gift of free will, they bore entire and sole responsibility for their deeds' (1988, 31). What these examples suggest is that freedom is used in radically different ways as a direct response to specific social conditions. The meaning of freedom differs in each context. Yet in both contexts, freedom is permitted only to the extent that it suits the powerful and does not threaten the social order of the day.

In the Middle Ages, freedom was more closely related to power struggles and associated with conquest. Free people were those with the strength to enforce their viewpoints: freedom was a spoil for victors. In this context, freedom came to mean the ability to withstand or be exempt from the specific demands of a stronger power. Bauman usefully cites the *Magna Carta Libertatum* (Britain's early 'great charter of freedom') as a relevant case in point. Its use of freedom reflected a particular social situation wracked by the growing threat of civil war that allowed a powerful group of barons to demand certain freedoms from the monarch, which were detailed in the Magna Carta. Among these freedoms was the well-known *habeas corpus*, which prevents the monarch from arbitrarily detaining or imprisoning subjects without the judgment of their peers in law.

During the late Middle Ages, from about the twelfth century onwards, freedom was not only granted to individuals and wealthy barons. It was also sometimes extended to groupings such as towns. Freedom could be granted a town to exempt it from taxes, restrictions on trade, and so on. Or a town's freemen (usually the wealthy) might be granted self-government and release from certain obligations to landed barons and even to the monarchy. The freedom awarded to towns or cities emerged as an important social change in which social patterns previously seen as natural and therefore inevitable were suspended.

One could go further with the historical analysis (for example, explore the ways that freedom was ascribed to individuals), but our observations so far are sufficient to explain why some theorists do not see freedom as a universal concept. Yet if freedom is relative to context, then we can raise two important questions. First, how can one say that individuals are always born free as if freedom were something universal? Second, is freedom always the opposite of power? In other words, is the freedom that we hold dear in Canadian society always outside of state power, or does the state—or law—help to shape the sort of freedom available to us as members of this society?

Power's creations: Individuals, freedom, and the free society

When we turn back to the first question, the notion that freedom is innate and universal to all individuals becomes problematic. If we cannot provide a definition of freedom that applies in all times and places, then how can one say that individuals are born free? Worse still, it may be that the very idea of an individual cannot be that of an unquestionable, primary being; instead, the individual could very well be seen as one of the products of modern society. Durkheim implies this view to some extent, but some—following Marx and Engels (Marx 1976, 205)— take the point even further. For them, not only is freedom located in history, but so too are the individuals whom the earlier theory held to be naturally free. If this logic is correct, then I am not naturally and for all time an individual, as common sense might dictate. Rather, social relations at a given point in history create the very *idea* that we are 'individuals'. As Marx puts it, 'The human being is . . . an animal which can individuate only in the midst of society' (1973, 84).

This is a profound statement: it means that each of us, with our different identities—from the clothes we wear to our images of self, from the pleasures we enjoy to the dislikes we avoid, from our most intimate thoughts to our most public expressions—are creations of a given social context. Change the social context and from this viewpoint you change the subjects (e.g., individuals) who inhabit them. The individual is thus not a primitive or primordial concept, one that cannot be opened to scrutiny.

But what specific mechanisms in society create individuals? Many different theories have been offered to answer this question. Michel Foucault (1977b; 1978; 1980a) argues that power relations create individuals. This is not the place to detail Foucault's intricate and complex images of power.[8] However, it is important to note that for Foucault, power needs to be understood in terms of relations among people—it is not something that is part of any entity (e.g., an individual, a king, a corporate tycoon, a prime minister, a parliament). According to him, nobody possesses power in any absolute sense; some may be able to exercise it more effectively than others in a given collective arrangement. Power is exercised in a play of forces that may always also be resisted.

In short, power for Foucault is not something absolute but a changing set of techniques and tools that involve actions by a subject (either a single one or a group) on the actions of other subjects. It operates from the 'bottom up'—from the local-level 'petty clashes of will'—and these clashes of will cumulatively make up wider power blocs that in the end constitute society at a given moment. But Foucault insists that power is not primarily repressive and constraining: it is also productive. Furthermore, it is everywhere. It is endemic to all forms of social being: wherever subjects assemble in groups, there is power. Power is one of the key ways through which we interact with others, help to define them (say, as friends) and the world around us, and conceive of ourselves as particular kinds of individuals. Power relations are thus much more local, creative, and intimately entwined with our very being than is ordinarily conceded by grand, top-down theories of power (Foucault 1978, 92–8).

In this sense, power does not so much restrain, constrain, and limit what individuals can do: it actually *creates* them. Foucault's deeply influential book *Discipline and punish: The birth of the prison* (1977b) describes, among other things, how a new technique of power—discipline—emerged with the rise of modern societies and helped to create specific kinds of 'normal' individuals. For him, discipline is a form of power that effectively creates 'normal' individuals, separates them from 'abnormal' cases, and locates them as the basic units of normal societies. It is worth noting that Foucault saw disciplines like sociology (as well as psychology, criminology, and education) as forms of knowledge that constitute an important part of modern society's attempt to create normal individuals. But his basic point is this:

> The individual is not to be conceived as a sort of elementary nucleus, a primitive atom, a multiple and inert material upon which power comes to fasten, or against which it happens to strike . . . In fact, it is already one of the prime effects of the power that certain bodies, certain gestures, certain discourses, certain desires, come to be identified and constituted as individuals. The individual, that is, is not the *vis à vis* of power; it is . . . one of its prime effects. (1980a, 98)

So individuals are the products of power relations and the power blocs that emerge out of local contexts at a given moment in history. Further, we as the bearers of freedom may well be condemned to be free (as Sartre pointed out) but not so much by nature as by the historical power relations that have created us as individuals who are 'obliged to be free' if we are to be 'normal' people in this society (Rose 1999).

From Foucault's perspective then, power relations generate particular kinds of free individuals in much the same way that their freedoms imply circumscribing power relations. Power and freedom imply one another directly in ever-changing and tense relationships. This is why Foucault argues that there is no power relation without freedom—it is not possible for an agent to structure another subject's actions (i.e., exercise power) without the subjected having some measure of freedom. He insists that by definition power must involve freedom (1982). If subjects are stripped of any capacity to resist in a given situation, then they are not engaged in power relations. In short, Foucault argues that we must be free at least to resist, to be able to taunt or react to attempts to structure our behaviours: 'Where there is power, there is resistance' (1978, 95).

Now, in view of this alternative formulation, in what sense might one claim to be free? Clearly, from Foucault's vantage point we may deem ourselves to be free but not in the ways implied by liberal thinkers. It is not that individuals are naturally free (i.e., regardless of historical circumstance) or that free beings necessarily exist outside of power relations. Rather, the very claim that 'I am free' must always be understood from within given historical contexts. The 'I' is a historical product of power relations in a given society, and the freedom ascribed to that 'I' is similarly created.

This approach suggests at least two issues. First, the obligations and compunctions to be 'free' in a certain way are the demands made of us as subjects in a 'free society'. To live as a normal individual in a free society is to be required to meet the obligations imposed on free individuals. Marx (1976, 301) notes of nineteenth-century individuals that they may be free to choose their religion but are not free to choose whether to be religious or not. In our times, we may choose to own various sorts of property (land, cars, books, TVs, videos, etc.), but this society does not permit us to choose not to accept private property relations. I cannot—without facing significant sanction—take another person's TV on the grounds that I choose not to believe in private property.

Free Canada requires its subjects to be free in particular ways, to perform rituals and engage the world as very specifically defined free individuals. To do otherwise is to risk the sanctions imposed on those deemed incapable of making 'rational' or 'proper' free choices, such as the insane, children, or the dangerous (Rose 1999). Freedom in this sense is an important mechanism through which given power relations operate. Power is exercised through our claims to be free: to say 'I am free' is to endorse the 'free society' that has created both the 'I' and the 'freedoms' that 'I' hold so dear.

There is, however, a second aspect to freedom in 'free societies'. History is always open-ended, and the limited freedoms espoused by a free society may always be opposed or challenged. There is always the possibility of resisting, of standing up to the freedoms offered by society: one may imagine new forms of freedom, and it may involve a more fundamental freedom than is offered by any given society. The point is not that it is possible to arrive at a natural state of freedom to escape power. Rather, we can draw on our current free identities to locate dangers within them and then to imagine and work toward different forms of freedom. But it is important to recognize that such freedoms will themselves always be relative to specific power relations and social formations. This is inescapable. Yet we can escape the limits of given power formations and the types of societies they structure. If one sort of freedom supports existing social patterns, there is also a freedom that allows us to imagine different and alternative social relations, subjects, and freedoms. In this sense, we might want to say that a 'free society' is never a static entity; on the contrary, a free collective entity is always open-ended, always open to the practice of imagining and exercising freedom in new ways.

And how are we to imagine alternative social realities, subjects, and freedoms? How are we to envisage different images of our individual identities, societies, and freedoms? What allows us to express or imagine our freedom in new ways? This is where a critical sociology of the kind described in the introduction comes in. A critical sociology is of a very different order from that of positivist sociologies that aim to discover the true nature of a society. Perhaps the role of a critical sociology is little more than an attempt to bear witness, to expose, to name, and to resist specific dangers that cloud given forms of power. It questions common sense definitions of issues and names issues in new ways.

So a critical sociology might question taken-for-granted, common sense understandings of what it means to say 'I am free'. By locating these understandings in historical perspective and reflecting on the assumptions of such freedom, it is possible to entertain alternatives that could alter the ways we see the world and thus the ways we act.[9] Through modest attempts to reflect on the assumptions of liberal conceptions of freedom and draw on elements of Foucault's alternative conceptions, this chapter may be seen as an example of how critical sociology can be mobilized to explore the limits of our freedom today.

CONCLUSION: AM I FREE?

Responding to the question 'am I free?', this chapter has explored a liberal vision that has influenced several sociological approaches. And its response is clear: yes, we are all born free, but there may be social conditions that constrain us and stifle our natural freedom. If we want to live according to our nature, then we must preserve and try to understand our lives as free beings. From this vantage point, we should try to ensure that we protect as many of these natural freedoms from being taken over and destroyed by power. Indeed, legitimate governments should see their main role as nurturing and preserving individual freedoms in free societies that are—as far as possible—spontaneously (naturally) ordered. Sociology emerges in this story as a science seeking the true nature of a free society and recommending ways for our societies to strive for this ideal. It is enlisted as one of many attempts to widen the natural freedoms available to us.

From an alternative, Foucault-inspired perspective, our question is rather more difficult to answer. Yes, in one sense I am free, but I am free in a very limited way. I am certainly not 'naturally' free if that means that I exist outside of a social history. In this framework, 'I' am a creation of power relations that have fashioned me as an individual in a particular society, and the freedoms that are granted to me are neither universal nor natural. Instead, the idea that I am naturally free is generated by modern societies and their underlying power formations. When I claim to be free, I do not so much assert my freedom from power as accept a given form of power. In other words, individual freedom is not outside of power but rather one of its products. As freedom is always relative to context, a free society embraces only the finite possibilities of what it is to be free. For Foucault, this is neither good nor bad, but any conceptions of freedom do contain dangers for those who are subject to them.

Here, perhaps, we glimpse a sense of a different kind of freedom that is not tied to a given image of the individual or a free society. That is, there is a form of freedom that liberates us from thinking about ourselves as free in ways defined by given contexts; we are free to imagine new ways of thinking about freedom and new ways of practising being free subjects (but always from within a given context). In turn, this implies the possibility for a critical sociology that continually names dangers within existing images and practices of freedom, pointing to new possibilities for freedom.

This chapter has presented various approaches to the question 'am I free?', leaving you free to decide which of them, if any, best answers the question. The point to underscore here is that in working your way through these frameworks and in challenging everyday common sense to make your way through the issues at hand, you begin to glimpse the practice of thinking sociologically. The fact that this text provides you with no firm answers but instead encourages you to think through questions for yourself implies a freedom that should be cherished as one of the best aspects of a critical sociology. By engaging critical sociology, you may not be able to say with absolute conviction whether you are free or not, but you will be able to say that you have exercised a freedom to think otherwise than you normally would. The challenge is to keep that spirit alive and never allow thought to be closed off as something that must not be questioned.

Questions to Consider

1. Are we born free? What kind of society do you think is most capable of accommodating your response?
2. Does Canadian society create, reflect, or constrain individual freedoms?
3. Are power and freedom opposing concepts?
4. If, as Foucault suggests, we are partly governed through the freedoms we hold so dear, what does it mean to use our freedom to challenge government decisions?
5. Suppose you are explaining why you believe Canada to be a free society to

someone with a completely different world view. Suppose further that they respond by saying: 'How can all this talk and practice of individual freedom lead to anything but selfishness and anarchy with no concern for the collective good?' How would you respond?

Notes

1. As well, both the images of freedom and the actions performed in its name are distributed differently in society. Not everyone has the same ideas, if any, on the actual nature of freedom. Those who do reflect on its meaning harbour many different ideas of freedom, ranging from those of the radical freedom-fighters seeking the end of oppression in all its forms to those of the free marketeer in search of maximum freedom to invest or move capital from one venture to the next. Also, not everyone enjoys the same sorts of freedoms: the choices available to the solo parent on welfare are markedly different from those of an executive with access to the corporate jet. In short, freedoms are quite different for the rich as opposed to the poverty-stricken, women, people from minority ethnic groups, and so on. The point is this: while images and practices of freedom circulate through our society, they do not circulate in uniform, equal, or even necessarily just ways.

2. This statement echoes Miller's common view that freedom 'is a claim to throw off the chains that enslave us, to live our lives as we ourselves decide, and not as some external agency decides for us' (1991, 2).

3. It is important to note that Rousseau uses the exclusionary term 'man' and does not appear to intend to include women under the rubric. As well, it would seem that men of peasant backgrounds, those who were not clerics, aristocrats, or relatively well-off commoners are similarly excluded. However, subsequent liberal theorists, especially feminist writers and socialist thinkers, broadened the idea to include all human beings (see Birke 2000; Squires 2000; Weedon 1999).

4. As Sartre notes, for human beings, 'to be is to *choose oneself* . . . freedom is not *a* being; it is *the being* of man' (1970, 151).

5. These approaches grew out of a phenomenology that tried to understand 'society' by understanding the meanings generated by individual actors and the choices they make (Berger and Berger 1976; Schutz and Wagner 1970; Schutz 1967).

6. Elsewhere he states, 'the larger the state, the less the liberty' (Rousseau 1983, book 3, ch. 1, 210).

7. Durkheim uses the term 'organic' to suggest that these societies are held together by their functional interdependence in much the same way as an organism such as the human body. Think of it this way: your heart has various functions (pumping blood through the body via a systems of valves) while the lungs oxygenate the blood and the brain sends signals to vital muscles. The heart, lungs, and brain all perform identifiable functions, but the entire body requires that all of these functions be coordinated if it is to exist in a healthy state. In an analogous way, society (the whole body) is made up of many different interdependent functions (the banking system, commercial systems, education systems, etc.). These functions must be integrated and coordinated for society to exist in a healthy state. Social solidarity is assured because many functions must be coordinated for people to survive.

8. The interested reader might consult any one of many secondary sources, including Smart (1985), Moss (1988), and McNay (1992; 1994).
9. Interested readers may want to turn to Bauman (1987; 1992; 1997) for an excellent account of the interpretative possibilities of a sociology that faces post-modern conditions.

Chapter 2

Who Am I?

Dawn H. Currie and Deirdre M. Kelly

INTRODUCTION

Historically, sociologists have not shown much interest in the study of identities as social projects. As post-colonial and anti-racist feminists have argued, this neglect reflects the fact that socially dominant groups tend to (mis)take their own identity for a naturally occurring 'norm' for humanity. Thus it has primarily been those designated as 'other'—women, people of colour, sexual 'deviants'—who have questioned how we become 'who we are'. During the 1950s, Simone de Beauvoir reminded us that women are (man-) made, not born. Within a growing liberation movement, women were among the first to ask 'who am I?' and 'what can I become?' Their need to do so comes from a context of what Bartky (1997) calls women's psychological alienation: the social definition of what it means 'to be a woman' has been authored by male 'experts'. Women themselves were denied control over the production of their identities as women. Because this alienation robs women of self-determination, they have been denied the exercise of what constitutes us as social subjects in liberal Western democracies. Thus the movement by women to claim selfhood presented a direct challenge not simply to femininity as a seemingly naturally occurring identity but to the power of men, as the dominant group, to name our identity as women.

In this chapter, 'Selfhood' refers to a specific form of identity; it informs our sense of what we 'are' and therefore what it is possible for us to 'do' and to 'become'. It captures the meaning that our social presence has for us and thus sustains a degree of predictability in our encounters with others. For adults, much of the routine 'work' entailed in reconstituting our Self occurs at a level below ordinary consciousness. During adolescence, however, figuring out 'who' we are and 'who' we want to be becomes an urgent task. As a time of physiological maturing, adolescence coincides with heightened awareness of the gendered and sexualized nature of our social identities. This awareness is not limited to the teenagers themselves, however, and much public concern surrounds the gendered and sexualized self-expression of teens. For example, in reaction to what is seen as the overtly sexual dress of schoolgirls, there is much discussion about dress codes for public school.[1] Lost in much of this debate is what the often extravagant displays of Selfhood mean to the youth themselves. Recognizing this gap in the discourse, our research explores the identity projects of girls between the ages of 12 and 16, and in this chapter we draw on interviews with 28 girls.[2] The fieldwork explores, quite simply, how girls talk about their social presence at school. Because we see the girls as playing an active role in this presence, we refer to their identity projects as 'doing girlhood'.[3]

Academic interest in adolescents has a long history in sociology.[4] However, for the most part, our everyday understanding of adolescent Selfhood has been influenced by developmental psychologists, many of whom take up Erikson's view of adolescence as a time of 'stress and storm' (Erikson 1968). This view emphasizes adolescence as a time of 'risk', especially for girls: what girls risk is a lowering of their self-esteem, setting the stage for such problems as disordered eating, hatred of the female body, depression, and self-inflicted harm. Feminists link this process to recognition on the part of girls that femininity requires adoption of a subordinate gender identity valued for passivity and compliance (see for example Pipher 1994; Brown 1998; Brumberg 1997).[5]

While we do not dismiss the importance of research on adolescent problems, one purpose of our work is to challenge the view of girls as victims of adolescent femininity. Our analytical focus is girls' agency, evidenced in their identity projects as a search for Selfhood. These projects show us many ways by which girls successfully navigate the perils of adolescence. In our study, we are drawn to girls who defied powerful pressures to conform to gender norms that rob girls of self-determination and threaten their self-esteem. By focusing on agency, we recognize that identity projects are an expression of the operation of power. On the one hand, girls play an active role in defining who they are and whom they want to become. On the other hand, extensive research shows how 'doing gender' engages us with forces that do not simply shape 'who we are' but also limit our capacity to 'be otherwise'. Understanding girls' search for Selfhood requires recognition of both the pressures on youth to take up conventional ways of being and their ability to resist processes that reconstitute girls' subordination to boys. As feminists, we are aware of the former but are interested in the latter; our goal is to better understand how power operates as a positive rather than a necessarily negative force in girls' lives. Ultimately, we are interested in whether girls' agency can potentially transform girlhood as a social identity for young women.[6]

In order to understand agency sociologically, our work explores the ways that girls' subjectivities are constituted through discourse. Following Gee (2002), 'discourse' in our work refers to ways of thinking and talking that bring social reality into 'existence'. However, discourses involve more than language. They 'coordinate language with ways of acting, interacting, valuing, believing, feeling with bodies, clothes, nonlinguistic symbols, objects, tools, technologies, times and places' (25). Gee differentiates Discourses (capital D) from discourses (little d): while Discourses are equivalent to social languages employing referents that are recognized beyond the immediate context of their use, discourses refer to everyday language-in-use or stretches of language that make up conversations or stories (17). In our work, we view the cliques that characterize school cultures as social groupings that sustain particular discourses about girlhood; they may draw on Discourses but not necessarily. We therefore characterize peer cultures as 'semi-autonomous' spheres of cultural production.

DOING GENDER: UNDERSTANDING GIRLS' AGENCY

In our research, girls' agency is apparent through their self-expression and self-directed actions. A focus on girls' agency rather than on their victimization helps us as feminists to understand how girls exercise control over everyday life at school. However, girls' self-expressions cannot be read as simply 'choices' about 'who I am'; rather, girls must choose between being deemed 'OK' or 'normal' by their peers rather than 'weird' or 'different' (Jones 1993, 5). Twelve-year-olds Sally and Marie described this pressure to Shauna Pomerantz, our interviewer and research collaborator, by mimicking classmates:

Sally: 'Why are you doing this?' 'Why don't you have that?'

Marie: Clothes, acting—

Sally: 'You're so dorky!'

Marie: 'You don't go out for lunch'—that kind of thing.

Sally: 'You don't have a lot of money.'

Hearing girls talk this way draws attention to the lived complexity of the peer cultures in which adolescents 'make themselves' as self-conscious projects.

For girls like Sally and Marie, fitting in at school was a source of constant stress. They described pressure not simply in terms of avoiding negative peer labels but also in terms of their desire to keep up with the trends that made girls 'popular' at their school. The problem was that 'styles change all the time. Like now there is flares and then there was capris and then no tank tops and that went away and platforms was the big thing one year. . . . It changes so much, and you run out of money.' As we see here and in other interviews, socio-economic class is implicated in how girls are able to 'do gender' at school. Thus Bettie (2003) argues that it is useful to conceptualize class not only as a material relation but also as part of the girls' performance of gender. In her research, 'group categories at school require[d] different class performances, and students engage[d] in practices of exclusion based on authentic class performances' (53). In our study, girls like Sally and Marie, both from 'middle-class' families, worked very hard to maintain the kind of self-presentation that made the popular girls at their school the envy of many of their peers.

Given the pressures for conformity, it interested us that some girls actively embraced identities that girls like Sally and Marie worked so hard to avoid. During exploratory focus groups with young university women,[7] we were encouraged when 18-year-old Stephanie exclaimed that during high school, 'We called ourselves "geeks" and we accepted that. We thought it was good. . . . One of my friends put up a web page and it was called the Geek Ring.' Excited by this 'confession', 19-year-old Myra added, 'Like my friends and I like we called each other geeks. And I don't mind being called a "geek". We even got our physics teacher to make buttons that said "The geeks shall inherit the earth!"' In the past, the identity as a 'geek' would have marginalized young people among their peers (Milner 2004). What gave these girls the ability to defy harsh judgments from other youth? Their ability to embrace 'geekiness' challenges the image of girls as lacking self-esteem as they turn negative judgments inwards. For us as feminists, it signalled girls' power to escape conventional gender norms and suggested that girlhood can be rewritten. Consequently, we were drawn to interviews with girls who consciously constructed identities that made them distinct from rather than similar to the popular crowd at their school. However, in order to understand how they were able to do so, we first needed to explore the power of popular girls. As we shall see, the power of popular girls reflects group affiliation and peer dynamics, both governed by girls' dress and physical appearance as strategies to gain attention, especially from boys.

Popular girls and the power to 'squash people'

As explained by 15-year-old Emily, group affiliation is central to one's social identity at school because 'most people don't define us for who we are but for who we hang out with.' Within this context, being identified as a member of the Popular crowd was desirable; according to 13-year-old Vikki, the Popular crowd were the 'cool kids' who 'go out and *do* stuff'.[8] In the words of GG, also 13, if you're not Popular 'you're just one of those *other* people.' However, becoming Popular and maintaining membership in the Popular crowd was not easy. As 16-year-olds Christine and Kate explained, 'There's so much gossiping and like backstabbing, whatever. You know, [some] people don't like [other] people. Then those people who aren't liked don't even know it [but Popular girls] look down on them as if they're not worthy of walking past them, or whatever. That's just like "Eew".' Fourteen-year-old Riva had first-hand experience of this kind of treatment:

> We were really good friends. Then the next day—if she is with somebody else, she kind of ignores me. And if I ask her something she gives me a one-word answer and she goes away. Stuff like that just kind of makes you upset. They're [Popular girls] just so two-faced, and they just treat you however they feel like treating you at that time. And that kind of brings you down.

According to Riva, the ability of Popular girls to make other girls feel bad about themselves reflects their social 'power':[9]

> Like they're not like physically mean to anyone. Like they don't push people around, really. But it's just like emotionally. Like how others might react to stuff they say 'cause it seems like they have so much power. So, like when they say something mean to you, you just feel like that—everyone feels like that because they are supposedly so great.

Although many girls did not like this mean behaviour, especially when they were the target, like Riva most simply accepted the dynamics of Popularity: 'I don't even know why they're popular. But that's the way it is.' In fact, 15-year-old Brooke, a member of the Popular crowd at her school, explained it as simply 'high schoolism'. Our first task, therefore, was to demystify Popularity: what makes girls 'popular' when they are not even well-liked? How does 'Popularity' in the sense used in this chapter operate as power?

Despite the fact that the girls in our study were drawn from a broad range of schools, their explanations for Popularity were consistent: above all, 'you have to be cool. And it's hard to say what cool is, but you have to like wear the right clothes and talk the right way' (13-year-old Liv).[10] 'You know, they're all like "Oh, I'm so fat," and they diet and stuff like that. And then they just get more skinny. And, yeah. I guess that's their whole image' (13-year-old Vanessa). According to 14-year-old Anna, to be Popular 'you have to hang out with the right crowd every day, even though you want to hang out, I don't know, with somebody else.' And you have to 'keep up' your reputation because 'it's like if you do even one little thing wrong, it gets talked about everywhere' (14-year-old Vera). Virtually every explanation emphasized that Popular girls are pretty, 'tall, skinny. They tend to wear a lot of like low-slung jeans, tank tops that bare their belly a lot. . . . Not all of them are blond but [they] all have long hair.' The result is that if a girl sought Popularity, she would have to look and 'be' a certain way. According to Liv, it is a combination of dress and attitude: 'It's the clothes that they wear and their personality. Like if they don't go out with anybody or they don't *want* to go out with guys yet, then they're not considered "cool".'

Sally and Marie claimed that 'the right attitude' helps to gain attention from boys. Brooke agreed: 'Basically, the more guys you know, the more like popular you are.' When asked how to maintain Popularity, she replied, 'Date a certain guy. Not date certain guys. You know. Just hang out with the *right* people, basically.' Across all schools, girls claimed that having attention from boys is a source of power. However, gaining attention from boys 'the *wrong* way' could earn even Popular girls the derogatory label 'slut'. The wrong way was often—but not always—through sexualized appearance rather than overtly sexual behaviour. Fourteen-year-old Amelia described a classmate as a 'slut' because 'she goes out with guys, and the way she dresses. She usually wears like these really, really short denim dresses with a denim tank top on and stuff like that, right? She wears lots of make-up and stuff. She tries to make herself pretty.' Shauna asked Amelia about trying to 'look pretty' since it was a common activity among the girls:

> Like me, right? I'll probably put like a little bit of eye shadow on and stuff like that. Like just a little bit, you can barely see. *She* puts on this really whole bunch of blue, and she'll put like this weird colour lipstick on and lots of black mascara and stuff like that, right? She just looks like a slut by the way she dresses.

What Amelia's response tells us is that the line between everyday practices of girlhood and 'being slutty' is very fine. In fact, despite the dire consequences of labelling, the criteria employed by girls appeared to be contradictory: 'Like, low-cut tops and uhm, I don't know. . . . I think that low-cut tops are bad but I don't see anything wrong with showing your stomach. There's nothing revealing about it' (Liv). To us, distinctions seemed to rest on girls' sexual agency. For example, Amelia elaborated:

Amelia:	She thinks she's pretty and stuff like that, right? And she'll walk past a couple of Grade 10 guys, and then she'll look back and I'll see them glancing at her and stuff like that. Or she'll stand there, and she'll start talking to someone else. A whole bunch of guys will be just staring at her, right? It's disgusting.
Shauna:	Which part is disgusting?
Amelia:	Just *her*. The way she dresses.

As suggested here, what underlies Amelia's reaction are unspoken expectations about just how much agency girls can express in their pursuit of Popularity. It also shows that girls without the 'right looks' might use their sexuality to gain access to the Popular crowd, a tactic described by Brooke. She claimed that 'with girls—like you can't really get *rejected* from a guy. I mean, like. . . You know. Like if you're not popular, and if you're not pretty or whatever, then you can—like you can get with someone and become "easy", kind of.' Brooke called this strategy 'getting in the back door': 'it's a way you get, uhm, kind of *known*. It's a way, a back door into getting into certain groups of people. Because then, if you hang out with like a popular guy, then you'll hang out with all the guys' girlfriends.'

However, getting 'in the back door' may not be as straightforward as Brooke made it seem. Among other things, Popular girls actively distanced themselves from other girls:

> Like the Popular girls walking down the hall, they don't look at anyone. They don't smile at anyone. They don't say 'Hi' to anyone, for some stupid reason. . . . It makes other people feel like they're less of a good person, or whatever, which is just totally not true. And like, makes them feel small. . . . I see someone saying 'Hi' to a Popular girl and they just kind of like 'Hi' and roll their eyes at them and walk away. That's mean. (Riva)

In fact, Vikki claimed that some teens were afraid of Popular girls: 'She doesn't seem like a bully, but there are some things that she's done that are really nasty. So a lot of people are scared of her. So she kind of finds she's like on top of the Popular people.' Liv, a member of the Popular girls at her school, did not try to hide her nasty treatment of other girls from us. In fact, she bragged, 'we're kind of at the top, like the most popular, most known people. But that doesn't mean that we get along with everybody. Like I know a lot of people that don't like me. And I know a lot of people I don't like. . . . Basically, if someone bugs me I do something about it. And sometimes I hurt them.' It was this kind of attitude and behaviour that made Vanessa claim that Popular girls act 'superior than you sometimes because they sort of have that power. They feel that they can do whatever they want and say whatever they want.' As a consequence, Popular girls made girls like Vanessa feel insecure: 'So you kind of feel like you're sort of—like you want to be part of the conversation, but you don't want to let yourself out totally in case you do something stupid or say something stupid. You know, embarrass yourself.'

Given so many negative descriptions of Popular girls, we were curious about how they maintained their high status. Part of the answer lies in the fact that Popular girls were not often challenged by other girls. Like Riva, many girls did not want to be their next target. While Riva claimed that she didn't 'feel intimidated by them or anything', she also indicated that 'I don't really want to make enemies with them. That's like a big thing 'cause if they make up something, it goes all around. Like everyone knows.' Similarly, 15-year-old Kate maintained:

> They have the power to set trends because they can afford it. They have power to squash people because they have support. One [Popular] girl I know, she has the worst personality I have ever seen. She like totally runs over people, and no one will say anything because if you say something to her you will totally get like put down by everyone else. . . . I do not like being around [those] people because I don't like the attitude, but I'll be friendly upfront. You know, be civil. I just won't hang out with them.

The association of meanness with Popularity was so strong that 12-year-old Eve claimed that 'you have to put people down to make yourself really popular.' Similarly, Vikki maintained that boys are attracted to the kind of girls who were described to researchers as 'mean':

> They can be bitchy. They can be all that. . . . And so guys like that 'cause they think that those girls are 'all that stuff' and [that] they are really cool and [that] we like them. And they're all sexy and whatever. . . . Like sometimes, you know, you see in the movies when girls are all like bitching at the guys. You'll be like 'blah, blah, blah' and the guy will just go into the kiss sort of thing 'cause he gets turned on by the girl getting like so—all in his space. She's just sort of 'there'.[11]

Even while they disapproved of Popular girls' meanness, they knew that being associated with Popular girls could reap 'benefits' among their peers. Although she 'didn't know why', Riva explained that 'when like one of my popular friends or whatever is paying me a lot of attention in front of a lot of people, you feel important.' Given that type of benefit, many girls aspired to be among the Populars. However, not all girls wanted to be Popular. In our study, a number of girls actively resisted the pressures to 'be' and act in ways that might earn them membership in the high-status Popular crowd. In this chapter, we designate these girls as 'alternative'.[12] They interest us because their ability to resist conventional norms suggests different ways to 'do' girlhood; it directs us to girls' exercise of power as a positive rather than a negative force.

Alternative girls and the power to 'be who you are'

Popular girls were not well liked by the girls we designated as 'alternative'. As two 14-year-olds put it:

> Grover: We call them 'bun' girls . . . [because] they used to all like wear hair buns and like, tight jeans and stuff like that.

> Sandy: But not just—they wear these really tight tank tops. And they all look the same. But it's not, you know. I mean it's also just the way that they act too. It's not just how they dress. They all act like 'Aaahhh'. Ditzy like.

Sandy complained, 'They're like "eeeaah" and like act stupid when they're really smart or something.' Fifteen-year-olds Zoe and Pete also found Popular girls annoying. For Zoe the problem was that 'they're always the same, sort of. Like they talk the same, they always dress the same. And it gets annoying after a while.' Agreeing, Pete claimed that 'their main goal in life—at least it looks like to me—is to be "cute". It's all they care about.' Pete directed her annoyance to 'the way they live their lives through an image that kind of pisses me off'. She described this image as 'skinny. The whole "girl thing." The whole skinniness—being skinny, thin, pretty, make-up. Uhm. Lots of money. . . . Kind of living their life for a guy—that kind of annoys me too. . . . I think it's just totally wrong to live your life like that.'

Among other things, these kinds of comments illustrate how dress is one of the most visible, hence culturally encoded, representations of gender. It is also one of the most 'policed' aspects of girls' self-representations. Sally and Marie found the pressure to 'be' a certain way in order to win acceptance stressful; this stress came from the uncertainty caused by constantly changing 'rules' about how to dress for school and harsh judgments about 'mistakes'. While the 'ordinary' practices of looking pretty and attracting boys were accepted, 'excessive' sexual agency earned disapproval. Errors could be costly: being labelled 'slut' was a devastating experience. Once labelled, a girl faced rumours and loss of reputation that could be difficult if not impossible to counteract (White 2002).

Because of the stress involved in having to look 'a certain way', many girls claimed that freedom from such pressure made school easier for boys. Marie, for example, claimed that 'the social pressure isn't as big on the boys, between boys. Like the pressure of dressing "this way" or looking "this way" or acting "this way" or having "this"'. This sense that boys have more freedom led Grover and Sandy to conclude that school is more complicated for girls:

> Grover: If you're a girl, it seems like it's more like—girls strive more to be popular and, like guys, they're just like, 'it's high school.' They don't really care.

Sandy: . . . Like if you talk to a guy friend, like—just that the way they think is more, oh, you know, 'I am just having fun with my buddies.'

Grover: Like relaxed.

Sandy: Like they don't have to like, they don't stress out as much. They're more like carefree and less worried.

Sally and Marie referred to these complications of girlhood as 'peer pressure': pressure for girls to be pretty but not 'self absorbed' about their appearance; to be envied by the 'right people' but not a social 'snob'; to be independent but not a 'loner' or an outcast; and so on. It is significant that the 'alternative' girls in our study rejected these rules.

Despite the stress associated with the 'right' styles, dressing for school was also seen by some girls as a fun side of being a girl. For example, 13-year-old Rose exclaimed that she *really* liked dressing up. She saw it as a specifically female mode of expression: 'If you're a guy and you told some of your friends that "Oh yeah, I thought I'd wear this today because I *really, really* like it, I really like these pants," they'd probably be going—[breaks into laughter]. But if you're a girl, they'd just be like, "Oh, cool!"' For our 'alternative' girls, the fluidity of meaning surrounding dress opened possibilities for oppositional self-presentation (Gleeson and Frith 2004). Fourteen-year-olds Gauge and Spunk ridiculed the conformity of the Popular girls. According to Gauge, 'They're sheep and we're like penguins. Sheep [pause] all do the same things, and penguins are cooler [both laugh together].' However, being 'penguins' earned Gauge and Spunk the label 'weird' among their peers. They attributed this label to the fact that their group is 'outgoing and doesn't listen to pop music'. Importantly, they rejected the rules that governed other girls' dress at school. These rules entailed 'tight jeans obviously. Always. Always. And, I don't know. Just brand names. A shirt that has a brand name on it is "cool"' (Spunk). At the time of their interview, Gauge was wearing a skater T-shirt and baggy pants, while Spunk was dressed in black and sported a shaggy haircut. Spunk called herself 'punk rock': 'I don't know. It's mostly—that's what people call me. I wear a lot of black and I have a lot of chains and I have a dog collar and—I don't know. I just like that kind of stuff.' Both girls talked about themselves as 'alternative-looking'. Significantly, Gauge and Spunk were among the girls in our study who had taken up skateboarding, a physical activity that until recently has been dominated by boy skaters. Their case illustrates that dress does not simply signal 'girlhood' as an identity label but shapes what it is possible for girls to 'do' (Kelly, Pomerantz, and Currie 2005; Pomerantz, Currie, and Kelly 2004).

Like Gauge and Spunk, Sara was proud of the fact that other young people positioned her as 'weird' or 'different' within peer culture. This designation gave her a sense of versatility not afforded the 'sheep' identified by Gauge. Describing herself as a 'chameleon', Sara maintained that:

I suppose you could call me 'alternative' [but] my style varies. I can sometimes be very mainstream, sometimes I can be like more dark, and sometimes I can be punk. Uhm, right now I'm wearing plaid [laughs]! Plaid pants and a black studded shirt. I'm also into like studded belts and studded collars, and I have a bike chain around my bracelet. . . . Yeah, I'm really into safety pins. Uhm, I'm not really sure. I guess purple is my favourite colour. I wear black a lot. Uhm, I have spiked whore boots [laughs]. Like up to the knee, with big platforms.

For girls like Sara, dress was an expression of resistance to the pressure for conformity and an opportunity to 'play' with gendered norms. What made their transgression possible?

So far, we have seen that the most powerful girls at school were those designated as Popular by their classmates. In our study, the designation of Popular was associated with what Connell (1987) calls an 'emphasized femininity': a form of femininity, defined at 'the level of mass social relations', that is based on women's compliance with their subordination to men and 'oriented to accommodating the interests and desires of men' (1987, 183). Emphasized femininity is the most culturally valued form of femininity, reflected in the prevailing beauty standard for womanhood.[13] While girls repeatedly claimed that Popular kids had money—to buy the right clothes, do cool things—Popular girls were also described as pretty, thin, and attractive to boys. For them, emphasized femininity was a route to social approval, hence their avenue to power. However, because physical appearance, combined with the 'right' dress and attitude, can earn individual girls Popularity, this power can seem to be a personal accomplishment rather than a social attribute. Sociologically speaking, the power of Popular girls comes from group dynamics and operates to regulate statuses in a competitive social hierarchy. Given the potential risks of transgressing the norms that regulate status in this hierarchy, what gives the girls we designated as 'alternative' their power 'to be otherwise'?

As feminist researchers, we were aware of the ways in which emphasized femininity is implicated in the lowered self-esteem of many girls. Admittedly, it was our hope that these girls would cite feminism in their resistance to normative femininity as the desired route to girls' social presence. However, for the most part, our desire was not fulfilled. While 15-year-old Gracie expressed pride in exclaiming, 'I am a feminist,' it was far more common for girls to distance themselves from feminism, as did Sandy: 'I wouldn't say I was a feminist. I mean, I am *for* it.' Whether embracing or actively resisting the conventions of emphasized femininity, the most forceful discourse we heard in girls' talk was that of an individualism that allowed girls to claim to be 'unique'. By individualism we refer to the way that girls expressed their sense of Self through continual reference to 'being yourself'. Across interviews, the notion of 'being yourself' was employed to signal the authenticity of girls' self-representations. It allowed girls to claim what Gee (2000–1, 111) calls a 'core identity' that gives each person a 'unique trajectory' through discursive space. This trajectory and the speaker's own narrativization of it are what constitute her (never fully formed or always potentially changing) sense of what we call 'Selfhood'. As a taken-for-granted category, 'being myself' foreclosed discussion that might otherwise draw attention to the instabilities and inconsistencies that typify any individual's self-construction. This individualism was expressed when Sara, for example, claimed that 'popularity is not important to me, but just being acknowledged. Being known as *a person*. Like *Sara*. When I die, what are people going to look back and see? "Oh yeah. That girl that I went to school with." Or, am I going to be, you know, "this character who had *personality*"?' Similarly, 14-year-old Beverly emphasized, 'I want to be known as, like, who I *am*.'

This ability to be 'unique' rather than 'feminist' was not entirely disappointing to us. Individualism enabled some girls in our study to resist the social pressures that were so stressful for Sally and Marie. Fourteen-year-old Onyx reasoned that 'if you keep adjusting yourself to fit in', you could lose yourself, a problem that she saw as 'the centre of teenage problems':

> Not finding yourself again. Not knowing what you're worth. Thinking that you are only good if someone else finds you to be their—be who they think you should be. And I think this is a time when, this is a big time for kids like our age to either go one direction or the other.

In like fashion, Grover's self-confidence was expressed through a discourse of 'being yourself':

> I know who I am and I am confident with who I am. . . . I think you should just let someone, you know, express themselves the way they want to be expressed. And I am against people, you know, saying 'You shouldn't look a certain way' like that because, you know, 'it's not pleasing', 'it's degrading', or something like that.

This notion of authentic Selfhood enabled Gracie to claim that your own opinion of yourself is what matters most ''cause if you don't think high of yourself, then it doesn't really matter what anyone else thinks because you still won't feel happy.' Knowing 'who I am' allowed Onyx to assert, however tentatively, 'I think I know what I want. Well, I have direction. I mean, I know how I am going to get there and what I am going to have to do.' Included in what she wanted was 'to go on to university and become—I'm not sure what yet, but I have choices and I'm trying not to limit them.'

The search for authentic Selfhood was an important theme in interviews with girls who rejected the emphasized femininity that made 'bun girls' popular. According to Onyx, 'They think they are real but to everyone else they look fake. . . . They are not really their *own* person.' Grover and Onyx were adamant that 'we're not bun girls!' In contrast to the fakery exemplified by bun girls, claiming a 'real' Selfhood enabled Grover and Onyx to position themselves outside the male-centred culture at their school. It enabled girls to claim identities that are devalued within practices of emphasized femininity. Like other alternative girls, Onyx reasoned that 'I think everyone's unique, and if you change that you wouldn't be unique anymore. You'd just be like wanting to be something else. And that's not *you*.' To be sure, we are not claiming that the Popular girls would not use a vocabulary of authentic Selfhood. However, as practised by our 'alternative' girls, a discourse of authentic Selfhood signals possible awareness of the socially constructed nature of femininity. It thus opens up the search for Selfhood to critical introspection:

Sandy: Well, I guess 15, 16 is kind of like—

Onyx: The age where you separate yourself from maybe other people.

Sandy: Yeah. You're more like—I think it's more like you're independent, especially from your parents. I think you become more like—like you think the way you want to more and like, you know, you're more social. And I don't know. You just kind of know yourself better than when you were younger. . . . You know yourself and you've been around longer, so like you just make better decisions and—

Onyx: It's like between wanting to be a woman and realizing that you are one. Maybe that's what this age is all about.

This ability to reflect on 'realizing you are a woman' is important: like other girls, Sandy described 15 as 'the "breaking age" of like where you are trying to figure out like who you are. And what you want to do. And stuff like that.' It encouraged us that despite their descriptions of life at school as complex and stressful, Sandy and Gracie celebrated girlhood as giving them freedom to explore 'who you really are' with girlfriends:[14]

Sandy: You think it seems like—not like this is true—but it seems like you [girls] think more, and like you care more about things and you're more—you try to be more involved. Maybe.

Gracie: I think probably it's better being a girl because you can be like more 'who you are' because the guy, you have to—I don't know, you can't really talk about things that much. And with girls, like your friends are usually like really important to you. And you can always just talk to your friends if you want to. And I don't think that it is the same for guys. I mean, they have friends, but they can't be, like call their guy friend up and be like 'Oh, I have a problem.'

Whether or not these girls are 'correct' in their perceptions about boyhood, given that they both believe that 'girls have a lot more stuff to deal with,' the freedom they associate with being able to be 'yourself' is important. In this sense, 'authenticity' within girls' identity projects opens up ways for girls to think about new possibilities for 'doing girlhood'. To us, this kind of talk about girlhood gave girls the ability to reflect on and actively resist conventions that reconstitute a femininity based on the approval of boys and the envy of other girls rather than on a girl's own actions and accomplishments beyond 'looking good'. This way of talking gave girls the power to 'do girlhood' in new ways. Does it also signal the power for girls to rewrite girlhood as a social rather than a personal identity, an act we would associate with transformative agency?

TRANSFORMING GIRLHOOD? FROM PERSONAL TO SOCIAL CHANGE

How individual actions can effect social change has been a central question in sociology since its inception. Until fairly recently, sociologists framed their answers through debates over the relationship between agency and structure. In large part, debates revolved around the problem of how structures—operating through the social institutions that are the focus of sociological inquiry—determine what individuals do, how institutions are created and maintained, and what limits, if any, structural constraints have on individuals' capacity to act independently. Beginning with Durkheim, a longstanding argument has been that sociology should be concerned only with social structures as the enduring, ordered, and patterned social relationships into which individuals are born. Because these social structures pre-date any individual (and continue after she or he is gone), they determine the characteristics and actions of individuals—whose personal desires and actions are insignificant, sociologically speaking. Such an approach—that maintains that social relations, not individuals, are the proper objects of analysis—is apparent in sociology. One problem with that approach is that it considers social structures, not people, as sites for the operation of power. Its critics reject a sociology within which people disappear, arguing that sociology should study the way by which individuals create the world around them. In the extreme, some even argue that there is no such thing as social structure (Abercrombie, Hill, and Turner 1984). Until fairly recently, sociologists tended to emphasize either social structures or the agency of human actors in their explanations of how power works as social change.

More recently, sociologists such as Anthony Giddens have attempted to offer a 'third' way of thinking about these issues. Giddens (1984) employs the concept 'structuration' to signal the mutual dependency rather than opposition of human agency and social structure. He maintains that social structures should not be seen as barriers to individual action but rather are implicated in an individual's ability to act: the structural properties of social systems provide the means by which people act, but they are also the outcome of those actions. In fact, Giddens maintains that all competent members of society are expert 'sociologists' because they are vastly skilled in the practical accomplishments of the social activities in which they engage (26). He uses the term 'reflexivity' to refer to the way in which individuals monitor their aspirations and behaviour in response to the ongoing flow of social life (3).

Following Giddens's view, the notion of *reflexive modernization* has become one of the most influential ideas in contemporary sociology. While the term 'reflexivity' has been taken up in various ways, writers agree that there is something distinctly new about the contemporary period of modernization that has enhanced the reflexive nature of social life through the proliferation of communication technology and easier access to knowledge.[15] These developments have enlarged our agency by expanding the individual's capacity to orient themselves in the social world: today we have the ability to reflect on and hence monitor our social presence to a degree not possible in previous societies. As a consequence, we no longer passively accept our destiny as prescribed by the traditional patterns into which we were born but instead construct our own ways of being in the world. Thus our personal histories are not predetermined by conventions surrounding age, gender, class, race, and so on because our biographies have become personal projects characterized by mobility and flexibility as we continually reinvent ourselves. In short, these writers characterize our biographies as lifelong projects of self-production. People in post-industrialized nations are free to choose much more about their lives than was even thinkable in the past—for example, they actively choose their occupations, whether to marry and have children, to alter their sexed and racialized bodies, and so on. By claiming that gender, class, and family 'roles' no longer have a determining influence on individuals, these writers describe Western societies as 'detraditionalized' (Adkins 2002).

At first glance, these kinds of arguments may have intuitive appeal: our contemporary culture is characterized by a rhetoric of free choice embracing everything we do, from participating in democratic elections to reshaping our bodies. However, the notion of reflexive modernization is contentious among feminists. As Adkins (2002) notes, one problem is that while theoretically emphasizing individual agency and power, proponents of the notion of reflexive modernization fail to illustrate empirically how and whether individuals are truly free from the constraints that accompany being socially designated as 'women'. Nor do they consider the social distribution of the resources that make the notion of personal 'choice' meaningful (Hennessy 1995). For the most part, writings about reflexive modernization do not distinguish between the cultural sphere, dominated by messages urging us to make ourselves through commodity consumption, and the social sphere, which engages us in 'larger' economic and political projects. McNay (2004, 171), for example, points out that while women have undoubtedly benefited from greater social, economic, and political freedom since the 1960s, employment is still characterized by gender segregation and unequal pay.

For the most part, the ungrounded claims of reflexive modernization ignore the lived experiences of women. According to many feminists, the thesis is itself gendered because men, more than women (and then only *some* men), have benefited from the kinds of 'freedoms' posited by reflexive modernization writers. Notably, women have not been 'freed' from having to subordinate their individual aspirations and biographies to the needs (and desires) of others. These feminists question whether femininity has in fact been freed from traditional constraints. Within this context, we return to our opening questions: What enables some girls to escape or at least actively resist conformity to the emphasized femininity associated with women's subordination? Do our alternative girls provide an illustration of how young women today reflexively control notions of 'who we are' and 'who we can become'? Does their reflexivity signal that girlhood itself is being rewritten on a grand scale?

Individualism and the limits of reflexivity

As we have seen, most of the girls in our study would agree with 14-year-old Grenn: 'You're supposed to be a certain way. The other girls expect you to be that way. You go against them, then they *hate* you.' To be sure, girls' search for Selfhood entails many factors that go beyond school culture and thus are invisible in our interviews. We acknowledge that mothers, fathers, sisters, brothers, teachers, and numerous other people play an important role in the identity projects of young girls; this role cannot be heard in our text. What *can* be heard is a neo-liberal discourse of Selfhood, a discourse that rhetorically values autonomy and self-determination.[16] For the most part, this discourse, more than the discourse of feminism, enabled girls to position themselves against conventional femininity. This positioning was accomplished by taking up 'me, myself, and I', an empty signifier in everyday discourse. For girls like Sara, this sentiment of being 'me' enabled her identity as 'alternative': 'I'm *me*, and if they [other kids] don't like me, then they can kiss my ass.' This is not to claim that Popular girls—the girls who strive to win approval by remaining within the confines of emphasized femininity—may not espouse Selfhood. Rather, we hear 'me, myself, and I' as part of a struggle for girls to gain a voice independent of conventional definitions espoused by others. While girls may experience and describe this manner of speaking as an expression of 'authenticity', we view it analytically as providing a discursive space through which Selfhood is constituted.

It was significant for us that during interviews the invocation of 'Self' did not require elaboration, as did other terms (such as 'bun girls') used by girls to describe identity projects. However, the seemingly obvious 'Self' evoked by these girls is not an essential and transcendent form of social being but rather a historically specific and culturally limited way of asserting one's social presence, a presence that requires repeated practices of self-production (Nelson 1999). What remains hidden in girls' talk of authenticity but nevertheless gives shape to projects of self-construction are 'larger' economic, political, and institutional processes (Byrne 2003; Connell 2004). Once we recognize Selfhood as a culturally specific way of achieving and maintaining a social presence, we can link it to the competitive individualism of our contemporary consumer culture. Within this context, we should not be surprised that socially approved identity projects require the display of the 'right' symbolic capital such as clothes, make-up, and attitude. While dress and self-presentation were also important to the girls we designated as 'alternative', their identity projects were characterized by self-conscious rejection of symbols associated with the rules of conventional girlhood, the symbols of what we have called emphasized femininity. In theoretical terms, these girls refused to reiterate 'good girl' displays of middle-class priority (see Nelson 1999). This refusal was no minor accomplishment: the pressures on girls to conform are considerable, and their actions transgressed the norms of middle-class youth culture. The question that remains is whether their transgressions signal the transformation of girlhood as a social (and potentially feminist) project rather than a personal project.[17]

In seeking the answer, we were drawn to the reflexivity that empowered the 'alternative' girls and enabled them to sustain difference in a context demanding conformity. Such reflexivity requires a sense of control, illustrated by 13-year-old Jessica: 'If I don't like the way something is going, I'll work hard to change it. Like, if I know I should be studying but I just can seem to get around to it. I'll work really hard to, you know, "hit the books". Like, studying isn't a fun thing, so I try to avoid it. But when it really comes down to it, you got to really put your mind to it and really got to stick to it, otherwise it's just useless.' Jessica closed her interview by telling Shauna: 'But I guess I [used to] listen to other people's opinions first, and then I would make up my mind. And, you know, I really didn't like that, and so I try to have my own opinions and stick to it. And, you know, I think that's worked pretty well.'

In the final analysis, this kind of talk about 'Self' as an 'object' of introspection reminds us that girls, potentially, are able to reflect on and actively negotiate the (immediate) conditions of their gendered performances of girlhood. The problem remains, however, that although it allows this kind of reflexive thinking about Selfhood, the individualism required for them to do so can limit the transformative potential of girls' agency. This is because the ability to 'speak' oneself into an 'alternative' existence requires the speaker's belief in that ability. The alternative girls in our study felt that belief in gender equality was a condition of self-mastery. Such a belief might seem to render feminism redundant in their eyes. According to Sara, for example:

> We're equal, as equal as we're going to get. And it's just the way that you carry yourself. And they think—I think they [classmates] have less self-esteem and they feel that they don't have that much power and that's what makes—that's why they think they should be feminist, because they feel that men have more power. I don't feel that men have more power, and so I don't think I should have to be a feminist.

Despite these claims, when Shauna asked about sexism at school, Sara was able to describe everyday examples, which she simultaneously discounted: 'It bothers me a little bit, but I think they're [the guys] being jackasses. And it has nothing to do with the truth. It's just the way they feel. And we can't change the way they think. Uhm. We can prove them wrong.' This kind of thinking allowed many girls in our study to claim that while feminism might have been necessary 'in the past' when women faced barriers to their self-determination, it is no longer needed. Fifteen-year-old Pete was among the girls who maintained that 'sometimes feminism is brought too far':

Like there is, yeah 'I want to be equal to the men. Get paid the same wage for doing the same job.' And there is 'I'm going out and be a firefighter just for the sake of having women on the force.' . . . Some things aren't—don't make sense, just don't click with me.

At first, we tended to attribute this kind of reasoning simply to girls' (mis)understandings of feminism. However, Gauge's remarks illustrate the way some girls saw feminism as contrary to self-expression:

Some of it's silly. I mean, like, you're not allowed to wear tight clothes. You have to wear baggy sweaters and absolutely no make-up and your hair has to be, like, just *normal* and— . . .You've just got to be *who you are*. You shouldn't, you know, just try to be someone you're not just based on things what people [feminists] say.

Here Gauge consciously placed herself against discourses of feminism. While this move supported her search for a unique and 'authentic' Self, it placed her outside discourses that help to make visible the socially constructed nature of girlhood. As a result, because Gauge accepts the status quo as a condition of her possibility, she is also open to 'common sense' gender essentialism (Marshall 2000). By essentialism, we refer to the belief that there is something inherent in 'being a girl' that lies beyond an individual's control. Essentialism led Pete and Zoe to claim that their lives are emotionally complex and therefore 'less logical' than life for boys:

Pete: Guys seem to be more logical at this age. They kind of see things for what it's for. And girls seem to be more twisty about it and—

Shauna: 'Twisty'?

Pete: Like they kind of turn things less logically, and they're into their feelings. And they kind of consider a lot of different areas that affect whatever it is they're trying to decide or see.

Zoe: Yeah. It's true because at this age we are all into how we feel. And they're—the guys— aren't like that.

For 14-year-old Vera, girls' emotionality was a plus because it meant that 'we can just let everything out.' Not all the girls shared this sentiment: we found it discouraging, for example, that Marie invoked essentialism by saying more than once that the emotional flux of girlhood is 'a PMS kind of thing'. While Grover and Sandy discussed masculinity as 'constructed', they nevertheless echoed Marie's claim that gender differences are 'natural':

Sandy: I think maybe for guys they have to like act more like 'manly' and stuff, even if they are kind of more sensitive, they just pretend not to be.

Grover: Yeah.

Shauna: Why do you think that is?

Sandy: Because they will be made fun of.

Grover: Yeah. Laughed at.

On this basis, Sandy and Grover claimed that it was better to be a girl:

Sandy: Because you are allowed to be like—

Grover: Be sensitive and allowed to have emotions.

Sandy: Like it is a natural thing, you know what I mean.

Despite the girls' claims of personally constructed Selfhoods, this gender essentialism about girlhood was widely shared and disappointing to us, given the girls' seeming sophistication about so many other aspects of peer interaction. It is tempting, of course, to view their reasoning as evidence of what Pete called girls' 'twisty' thinking; instead, we heard gender essentialism as signalling how difficult it is for girls to understand the socially constructed nature of their gendered identities in a culture of individualism that conflates 'girlhood' with the female sexed body. On the one hand, the girls' invocation of gender essentialism legitimated their claims to authentic femininity. On the other hand, it indicated that extending the boundaries of girlhood to include the 'alternative' does not necessarily signal transformation of gender norms.[18] In short, traditional expectations for girls (and women) are being reconfigured rather than eliminated.

We would not discourage girls from believing, as Jessica put it, 'We can do whatever we want to do if we just put our minds to it. Like there's nothing to stop us from doing what we want to do . . . we've come such a long way from, you know.' Such thinking informs Jessica's claim that being a girl is 'great . . .'cause you can prove to people that girls aren't wusses and they can be strong.' After all, it is this kind of enthusiasm for girlhood that attracted us to these girls in the first place. Our purpose has been to understand, sociologically, the conditions through which girls can claim the kinds of identities described in this chapter. In our larger study, we have been able to explore more fully the economic, cultural, political, and institutional context of girlhood as self-construction, whereas in this chapter we have focused on school-based youth cultures. These cultures interest us in that they offer adolescents a 'semi-autonomous' sphere of identity production that sustains particular 'ways of being girls' (and boys). We use the term 'semi-autonomous' because we recognize that while youth experience a degree of 'freedom' from constant adult supervision, their peer cultures are mediated by dominant institutions such as commercial media and school. One purpose of our study has been to explore the extent to which feminism, as well as other public discourses about social justice, also mediate youth culture. While we would not advance grand claims about youth cultures as microcosms of either social reproduction or social change, we question the value of sociological theory that neglects them when discussing the 'detraditionalization' of social life. With Dorothy Smith (1987), we call for a sociology that retains the presence of social actors, making visible the ways in which our identity projects, as an everyday activity of claiming a social presence, express the operation of power. Smith differentiates this kind of sociology *for* people from a sociology *about* people. It is our belief that such a sociology *for* people can deepen the reflexive engagement of individuals as they actively construct identities and biographies that, to borrow from Karl Marx (1975 [1852], 103), are of our making, albeit not under conditions of our choosing.

THE GIRLS (IN ALPHABETICAL ORDER)

Amelia: 14;   white; from a working-class family; now living with her mother but has been in foster care; describes herself as lonely; calls her style 'grungy'.

Anna: 14;   Filipino-Canadian; from a working-class family; lives with her mother, father, and little brother; into computers as 'anime freaks'.

Beverly: 14;   Chinese-Canadian; came from Hong Kong when she was 10; from a working-class family; lives with her mother, father, and older brother.

Brooke: 15;   white; from an upper middle-class family; member of the Populars.

Christine: 16;   white; from a working-class family; into sports.

Emily: 15;   white; from a middle-class family; hangs out with the skaters at school.

Eve: 11;   Chinese-Canadian; from a middle-class family.

Gauge: 14;   white; from a middle-class family; lives with her mother, father, and sister; a skateboarder.

GG: 13;   'GG' stands for Ghetto Girl, her self-selected pseudonym; white; from a middle-class family.

Gracie: 15;   white; from a middle-class family.

Grenn: 14;   white; from a working-class family; a skateboarder and anime fan who describes herself as 'alternative'.

Grover: 15;   Latina; from a middle-class family; attends a Catholic co-ed school.

Jessica: 13;   white; from an upper middle-class family; attends a private school for girls.

Kate: 15;   white; from a working-class family; into sports.

Liv: 13;   white; from a working-class family; lives with her mother and sister; a cheerleader and member of the Popular crowd at her school.

Marie: 12;   white; from a middle-class family; wants to be a Popular.

Onyx: 14;   Chinese-Canadian; from a middle-class family; her friends call her 'the seducer'.

Pete: 15;   Chinese-Canadian; from a middle-class family; a skateboarder.

Riva: 14;   Iranian-Canadian; from an upper middle-class family.

Rose: 13;   white; from a middle-class family; a Buffy and anime fan; sports a 'neo-punk' style.

Sally: 12;   white; from a middle-class family; wants to be a Popular.

Sandy: 15;   Chinese-Canadian; from a middle-class family.

Sara: 14;   Jewish; from a middle-class family; sports a punk/goth style; drummer in an otherwise all-boy band.

Shale: 13;   white; from a middle-class family; a Buffy and anime fan; a self-identified bisexual; a practising wiccan.

Spunk: 14;   white; from a middle-class family; lives with her mother and sister; a self-identified bisexual wiccan who just started skateboarding.

Vanessa: 13;   white; from a working-class family; into computers as well as sports and dance.

Vera: 14;   Chinese-Canadian; from a working-class family; lives with her mother, father, sister, brother, and grandparents; into computers as 'anime freaks'.

Vikki: 13;   white; from a middle-class family.

Zoe: 15;   First Nations/white; from a middle-class family; a skateboarder.

Questions to Consider

1. In this chapter we explored the importance of dress for adolescent girls at school. To what extent are the girls correct in claiming that the pressure to 'look' a certain way makes life at school harder for girls than for boys? Do boys experience similar pressures? Why is self-presentation so important to youth?
2. Thinking about your experiences of high school, can you remember any situations when different standards were used to assess the performance or behaviour of girls versus boys? If so, how were these different standards justified? At the time, did you agree with the practice? Has your thinking been challenged since you became a sociology student?
3. In this chapter we discussed 'emphasized femininity' as a form of femininity associated with popularity for girls. Is there an 'emphasized masculinity' that is similarly valued for boys? What performances of masculinity make boys 'popular' among their peers?
4. Adults often 'explain' what they find puzzling or difficult about teenage behaviour as a consequence of 'peer pressure'. How might a sociologist discuss these concerns with interested parents/adults?
5. How does the cultural importance of 'being myself' prevent us from understanding our world sociologically? To what extent is 'individuality' historically and culturally specific to contemporary commodity-based societies?

Notes

1. See for example Alphonso (2004).
2. We describe the backgrounds of the girls who participated in our study at the end of the chapter.
3. Following Butler (1990), we prefer the notion of 'doing gender' to that of 'having' a gender identity. Butler's performative approach suggests that gender does not exist prior to its expression and thus implies that gender is much more unstable—hence changeable—than implied by socialization theory which posits that we internalize gender scripts during infancy/childhood that stay with us throughout our lives.
4. We have in mind the work of Hollingshead (1949), Coleman (1961), and Hebdige (1979), among others.
5. 'Feminism' defies a succinct definition. In this chapter, 'feminism' signals a commitment to the goals of the women's liberation movement. That is, feminist work is unified by its commitment to the accomplishment of gender equity, despite theoretical and political disagreements over how to accomplish this goal. In our research, one important differentiation is the one between the 'second wave' that brought feminism into sociology

(through notions of gender roles and gender socialization) and 'third wave' feminism that positions itself against many of the central tenets of conventional sociology. For an overview of the schools of feminist thought, see Beasley (1999); Lorber (2005); Jaggar and Rothenberg (1993); and Mandell (2005).

6. Here we draw attention to a large literature on masculinity and boyhood, which has also been the subject of much feminist research and debate. See for example Connell (2000); Kenway, Willis, Blackmore, and Rennie (1998); Martino and Meyenn (2001); Martino and Pallotta-Chiarolli (2001); Renold (2004); and Titus (2004).

7. In order for us as adult researchers to better understand young women's experiences of public school, we conducted focus group discussions with young female university students before we began our fieldwork with younger girls.

8. The girls ascribed two meanings to the term 'popular'. They used it in the common sense way to signal being well-liked by peers. However, they also used the label 'popular' to identify the powerful girls who belonged to a high-status clique. In this chapter, we are interested in the latter notion of 'popular', and in our discussion we signal this definition by capitalizing the term.

9. While our chapter discusses the dynamics of girls' social groupings, we acknowledge that power operates through boys' social networks as well.

10. 'Cool', like the term 'Popular', indicates a status that is achieved by embodying certain ideals of femininity; its analysis is beyond the scope of this chapter. Popular girls had to look 'perfect', 'like all the movie stars and stuff like that'.

11. A number of Hollywood blockbusters have featured mean yet popular girls who rule their schools and are highly desired by boys: *Mean girls* (2004; based on the best-selling book *Queen bees and wannabes* by Rosalind Wiseman) and *She's all that* (1999). An earlier generation of such movies includes *Clueless* (1995) and *Heathers* (1989).

12. By including these girls in the category of 'alternative' we do not intend to create a dichotomy between 'regular' and 'alternative' girls.

13. Our use of 'emphasized femininity' corresponds to what others might call 'conventional' or 'traditional' femininity. To Connell's description we point out the way that emphasized femininity is based on white, middle-class expectations for 'good girls'.

14. For a discussion of girls' friendships, see Hey (1997).

15. While writers following Giddens emphasize the conscious nature of reflexivity through a focus on what they call our practical consciousness, Giddens (1984) discusses the ways in which human knowledgeability is always bounded and the way in which the flow of action continually produces consequences that are unintended by actors (27). For a discussion of the various meanings of reflexivity, see Adkins (2002).

16. We use the term 'rhetorically' to differentiate neo-liberal notions of autonomy and self-determination from feminist notions.

17. In Currie, Kelly, and Pomerantz (in press) and Pomerantz, Currie, and Kelly (2004), we maintain that these girls embody a feminist subjectivity and praxis even though many reject a feminist label.

18. 'Alternative girlhood' as an act of transgression in fact takes its meaning from emphasized femininity; it thus confirms rather than displaces traditional rules for girlhood.

Am I a Woman?

Myra J. Hird

INTRODUCTION

Am I a woman? This seems at first blush an easy question. Of course I am. When I want to use a public washroom, I head for the door with a picture of a stick figure wearing a dress. When I complete a boarding card at the airport, I tick the 'F' box. My family, friends, colleagues, and strangers *treat me like* a woman. So I must be a woman. Moreover, in sociological terms, I *must* be a woman in order to make sense in society. If I'm not a woman, and I'm not a man, then what am I? How would people know how to treat me? How would I understand myself? How would I understand, relate to, and interact with others?

The aim of this chapter is to consider the importance of the concepts of sex and gender in Canadian society. To do this, let us 'work on' the title of this chapter in two ways. First, we might consider the chapter's title question as it is perhaps most commonly understood: the difference that sex and gender make to individuals and society. From a sociological standpoint, sex and gender *matter* (meaning that sex and gender are important) a great deal socially, economically, politically, medically, and culturally to individuals in Canadian society. As Canadian sociologist Roberta Hamilton (2004) shows, people experience different realities depending on their gender. Take work, for example: women continue to receive lower pay than men for equal work, various jobs continue to be gender-segregated, women continue to do the bulk of non-paid work in society (the famous 'third shift'), and so on. We could add to this by explaining how sex and gender interact with other important characteristics by which society is divided, such as race, education, ethnicity, age, sexuality, nationality, and (dis)ability. For example, as sociologists we would want to consider the ways in which poor indigenous women with limited education experience the criminal justice system compared to the ways that middle-class, well-educated white women do. To take another example, there was much debate, anxiety, anger, fear, and anticipation as members of Parliament prepared to vote on the legalization of 'same-sex' marriage across Canada, and the new Conservative government promises to revisit the debate. From this perspective, sex and gender *do* matter because Canadians experience different levels of ongoing opportunities depending on their gender.

However, there is another way to interpret the title question, and that is by pondering whether 'am I a women?' refers to 'fleshy materiality' or to what is commonly termed 'nature'. In this sense, asking whether sex and gender *matter* is asking whether these concepts are grounded in some sort of universal, natural, and immutable reality. This is a much more complicated question, and I devote the rest of the chapter to exploring the answer.

In order to tackle the second interpretation of the chapter title, we need to consider how the terms 'sex' and 'gender' have been used in society. We typically take sex and gender for granted, as an important and indelible aspect of our personal identities, 'locked in the mysterious recesses of the body' (Weeks 1995, 47). Indeed, we tend to think of the relationship between sex, gender, sexuality, and identity thus:

Sex (female)→gender (woman)→sexuality (heterosexual)→identity (businessperson, wife, mother)

In everyday language, sex is defined as the anatomical differences (usually understood as genitals but may also include chromosomes, hormones, and gonads) between females and males. These differences are seen as natural and immutable. In other words, they are 'givens'. So even though we don't see people's genitals in everyday public situations, we act as though we do. Gender refers to all of the behavioural practices such as clothing and mannerisms that correspond to one or the other sex. So, for instance, female 'sex' is thought to produce proportionally smaller bodies that express emotions (other than aggression) more frequently. Male 'sex' is thought to produce proportionally larger bodies that show more aggression. We start with sex, which produces gender, which in turn leads to our sexuality. Sexuality is typically seen as a constitutive feature of our personality, comprising our desires, our pleasures, and the sexual acts we engage in (see chapter 5).

The formula I have just described is a feature of a distinctly *modern* understanding of subjectivity, of how we define ourselves as social beings. We might be surprised to find that individuals did not always define their sex, gender, and sexuality in the same ways that we do now (see chapter 5). There is no single way of thinking about these concepts or what is 'normal' and 'abnormal' about them. And this is an important sociological point: sociology is more concerned with exploring how certain societies come to understand certain social practices, like femininity and masculinity, as 'natural' and 'normal' or 'unnatural' and 'abnormal'. It is *not* concerned with supporting beliefs that some kinds of gender practices are 'good' and others are 'bad'. We leave that to the politicians and moralists.

The fact that we think of sex and gender as fixed, essential parts of our individual 'natures' leads to the commonly accepted notion that individuals and societies constitute separate entities. And the moment that individuals and societies are so separated, and society is discussed as though it is a sort of 'super' individual in itself, sociologists get agitated. Our disquiet comes from the knowledge that this kind of separation between the individual and society often leads to biological and psychological determinism—two ways of thinking that have devastating consequences for people's lives.

So one of the major arguments of this chapter is that what we think of as being a 'given' about our identities is, from a sociological perspective, actually a complicated *outcome* or *product* of our understandings of sex and gender. This means that it is worth our while to explore the ways in which we understand sex and gender. It also means that from a sociological perspective, the way in which we think about sex and gender is changeable. Sex and gender are not 'natural' or 'immutable'. Rather, they are social creations and thus infinitely changeable. This is good news for those of us whose identities change and evolve.

DIVIDING 'SEX' AND 'GENDER'

You might find that the terms 'sex', 'gender', and 'sexuality' are often written about simultaneously or at least interchanged in confusing ways. Until recently, sociologists regularly differentiated between the terms sex and gender as I outlined above. 'Sex' referred to the anatomical, biological differences between females and males. 'Gender' referred to the ways that society constructs differences between women and men. The sex/gender distinction was in fact a post-war Anglo-Saxon invention. The separation of these two terms served a number of functions for sociologists—for example, it provided a convenient way of naming and challenging the hierarchical relationships that subordinate women to men.

However, there is considerable debate now as to whether this sex/gender distinction continues to be of value. Delphy offers an interesting counter-position: rather than seeing sex as the baseline against which gender can emerge through social relations with others, she argues that 'gender . . . create[s] anatomical sex' (1994, 144). Her point is that what is often posited as 'natural' is in fact a social construct. In particular, the so-called 'natural' difference is almost entirely based on one specific aspect of biology: sexual reproduction.[1] Under the rubric of sexual reproduction, an entire orchestra of 'biological facts' is brought into play to fix the notion of biological sex differences. Thus, as we shall see, chromosomes, hormones, and genitalia have been variously 'constituted as embodying the *essence* of sex' (Harding 1996, 99; emphasis in the original).

So despite a largely taken-for-granted status, sex differences actually depend on three interrelated assumptions (Hood-Williams 1996). First, the biological distinction between women and men assumes that a distinction can be made between biology (sex) on the one hand and culture (gender) on the other. Secondly, it is assumed that while gender is changeable, sex is immutable. Finally, and most importantly for our purposes, this binary depends on the idea that biology itself consistently distinguishes between females and males. Nature, as I hope to argue, offers a different picture that challenges these assumptions. Considering that sexual difference is only one aspect of human biology, it should not be surprising that nature actually offers shades of difference and similarity much more often than clear opposites. With this in mind, we could say that modern societies have created and imposed the current template of sexual difference.

Recently, a number of studies have shown that prior to the eighteenth century, women and men were considered to share one 'sexed' body (Daston and Park 1998; Laqueur 1990; Oudshoorn 1994; Schiebinger 1993). As the superior form, male bodies contained the heat necessary to 'display' the penis and scrotum externally; lacking heat, female bodies bore their penis and scrota internally. The leading medical and philosophical scholars detailed the anatomical equivalence of vagina and penis, labia and foreskin, uterus and scrotum, ovaries and testicles.[2] Countless drawings, often based on dissections, depicted the vagina as an internal penis. Only as a result of considerable controversy and political upheaval did the contemporary 'two-sex' model eventually dominate scientific discourse (Laqueur 1990).

During the sixteenth, seventeenth, and eighteenth centuries, what we would term gender held the same definitional status as our modern understanding of sex. Men were defined by the characteristics of heat, strength, and rationality, while women were characteristically defined as cold, weak, and emotional. These were characteristics of degree, with men and women sharing one axis. This afforded a fluidity of movement across the gender continuum, with a large number of possible variations. For instance, medical literature during this time contains many accounts of individuals changing sex.[3] Most of the accounts detail legal changes of women into men. They often reflect the courts' belief that a body would always attempt to become more 'perfect' (i.e., male).[4] Through the movement of the penis from interior to exterior, the body could express the gender characteristics that most suited the individual's disposition and behaviour. Since men enjoyed greater social and economic privileges, magistrates were more concerned with maintaining the gender boundaries than with the 'authentic' sex of the individual.[5] Today, we might think that changing sex is impossible, that individuals are born either female or male. We might be surprised then to find that scientists today also believe that people can change their sex.

This bit of history is not intended to demonstrate the advance of modern understandings of the body over previous ones. The point, rather, is that these analyses suggest that objects do not express meaning in and of themselves: they are made meaningful through their interpretation. So, for example, it is through our historical interpretations that we continue to superimpose dichotomies onto a world that is really marked by diversity. Renaissance drawings depicting the vagina as an 'interior' penis reflect dominant beliefs, not accurate observation. These beliefs literally determine how the body is seen and understood. Therefore, it is not that we now know the truth of the body: rather, gender discourses *are already at work* in any discussions of sex—before they begin.[6] In short, like gender, sex is an invention.

The ambiguity of sex[7]

People with intersex conditions provide us with a valuable opportunity to explore the relationship between sex and gender as well as the way that difference is created through meanings and categories. In this section, I hope to argue that the sex/gender binary is particularly problematic for people with intersex conditions, with very real political, social, and personal implications. Chase (1998) estimates that one in every 100 births shows some morphological 'anomaly'. This is observable enough in one in every 2,000 births to initiate questions about a child's sex.[8]

So what is intersex? This umbrella term refers to a wide range of conditions present at birth. One is Androgen Insensitivity Syndrome (AIS), which is most often a genetic condition in which a person born with XY chromosomes does not respond (in complete cases) to the androgen hormone, producing the female genitals, undescended or partially descended testes, and usually a short vagina with no cervix. Congenital Adrenal Hyperplasia (CAH) refers to a condition in which the adrenal glands make higher levels of hormones that have the effect of enlarging the clitoris and labia.[9] Children who have hypospadias are born with the urethral opening somewhere on the underside, rather than the tip, of the penis. In some cases, the urethral opening is absent, and urine exits the bladder behind the penis. Children with Klinefelter Syndrome inherit an extra X chromosome from their biological mother or father. In these cases, the testes appear to be small and firm. At puberty, children with this condition do not tend to grow as much body hair and may experience breast development (for a more detailed list of intersex conditions, see www.isna.org).

The New Zealand-born sexologist John Money founded surgical sex 'reassignment' of infants with intersex conditions in the United States, and his protocols remain standard practice today. Money's extensive published work testifies to the discursive gymnastics required to sustain a two-sex model. It also details the profound impact this reductionist model has had on the lives of people with intersex conditions.[10] Money developed a vocabulary that combined biology and sociality, allowing the medical community to sustain the belief that 'sex' consists of two exclusive types, despite *their own evidence* that this is not the case.

According to Money, core gender identity results from the child's interactions with parents as well as a child's perception of their own genitals (1985, 282). We might expect that the emphasis on gender identity as *socially* acquired might lead Money to conclude that anatomy is not destiny, especially since he is studying children with *variable* genitalia who nevertheless identify as either girls or boys. But Money does not do this. Instead, he reasserts the importance of aligning sex and gender. He notes a 'critical period' of parent/child interaction that cements an earlier in-utero period when hormonal activation of the brain sets the direction of neural pathways in preparation for the reception of 'post-natal social gender identity signals' (Raymond 1994, 47). On this basis, Money argues for surgical intervention as soon after birth as possible *for the child's psycho-social well-being* (Hird and Germon 2000). In other words, surgeons believe that they 'merely provide the right genitals to go along with socialization' (Kessler 1990, 17).

Whether genitals, hormones, or chromosomes should 'determine' an infant's sex is much debated.[11] For the most part, the 'abnormal' appearance of a newborn's genitals is the factor that initiates medical intervention. Thus genital appearance is privileged over hormones, chromosomes, gonads, and internal reproductive structures (Hausman 1995). Garfinkel and Stoller argue that the 'natural, normally sexed person [as] cultural object' must possess either a 'vagina *or* a penis' and when nature 'errs', human-made vaginas and penises must serve (1967, 122). A newborn with ambiguous genitalia is thus considered a 'social emergency' (Pagon 1987), and surgeons are roused from sleep to decide the child's 'best sex' (Feinberg 1996).

Chromosome tests are also used to determine the genetic make-up of the child: if they reveal an XX configuration, genital surgery is usually performed without delay (Kessler 1990). When tests indicate the presence of a Y chromosome, surgery may be delayed while further tests determine the responsiveness of phallic tissue to androgen treatment. Such treatment enlarges the penile structure to the point at which it can pass as a *real* penis:

> Since ... reproduction may be disregarded, the most important single consideration is the child's subsequent [hetero] sexual life. ... If there is little or no penile growth the male sex will be out of the question and the female sex should be chosen; with good penile development the male sex may be appropriate (Dewhurst and Gordon 1969, 45).

The old trope proves true as penis size ultimately dictates whether the child is reconstructed as male or female (Griffin and Wilson 1992; Pagon 1987). Surgeons consider the condition of a micro-penis so detrimental to a male's morale that reassignment as female is *justified on this basis alone*. The implication here is that *male* 'sex' is not only or most importantly defined by chromosomes or by the ability to produce sperm. Rather, masculinity is determined by the aesthetics of an *appropriately sized* penis:

> If the subject has an inadequate phallus, the individual should be reared as female, regardless of the results of diagnostic tests. In the patient with an adequate phallus, however, as much information as possible should be obtained before a decision is made (Griffin and Wilson 1992, 1536).

Consequently, it is common for infants with an XY chromosome configuration to be assigned and raised as female.

Further illustrating that nature does not itself provide sufficient material from which 'sex' can be read, the medical literature and the treatment protocols openly privilege maleness and devalue femaleness. Delays in 'corrective' surgery beyond the neonatal period to reduce (or remove) the phallic tissue of an XY infant is to invite 'traumatic memories of having been castrated' (Kessler 1990, 8). Clitoroplasty, on the other hand, is undertaken when the child is anywhere between seven months and four years of age and sometimes as late as adolescence.[12] Further, little attention is paid to aesthetics in the creation of a vagina. The main requirement is that the vagina be able to accommodate a penis.[13] Scar tissue is often hypersensitive, resulting in extreme pain during intercourse. Because scar tissue lacks elasticity, a daily regimen of dilating the vagina is required to prevent it from closing. The vagina is often constructed from bowel tissue, which lubricates in response to digestion rather than arousal (Laurent in Burke 1996).

The high-profile case through which Money first argued for the necessity of surgical intervention illustrates many of the contradictions in the modern two-sex model of sexual difference. David Reimer and his identical twin brother were born in Winnipeg, Manitoba, in 1965. After a bungled circumcision during infancy, David eventually found himself in the hands of Money's surgical team, who reassigned him as female. David's case was particularly important because he happened to have an identical twin brother. Money argued that if David 'lived' the experience of femaleness, then sociality, not chromosomes, determine gender identity. While Money repeatedly detailed David's success in living as woman, interviews with David after he became an adult reveal that this success was greatly exaggerated (Colapinto 2000). Despite Money's assurances that 'Brenda' would live comfortably as a woman, as an adult David lived with his wife, three adopted children, and a reconstructed penis, adamant that he was a man. In 2004 David committed suicide.

While David and Money would seem to disagree on just about every fact of this case, they concur as to the constitution of femininity and masculinity. Money argued that the identical twin brother was 'male' because he preferred playing with 'cars and gas pumps and tools' while David was 'female' because of his preference for 'dolls, a doll house and doll carriage'. David himself says that he 'knew' he was not a girl because, among other signs, he did not like to play with dolls, preferred standing while urinating, and daydreamed about being a '21-year-old male with a moustache and a sports car, surrounded by admiring females' (Colapinto 2000, 69). The various psychiatrists who eventually examined David used similar markers to define his 'underlying' masculinity. One psychiatrist, for instance, described seeing David 'sitting there in a skirt with her legs apart, one hand planted firmly on one knee. There was nothing feminine about her' (70). Paradoxically, at the same time that the medical community strongly requires a biological definition of the gender of a person with an intersex condition, the surgeons, endocrinologists, and psychiatrists themselves clearly employ a *social* definition.[14]

A growing political intersex community identifies many of these problems: the variability of sexual identification, the a priori assumption of feminine and masculine behaviour, the phallocentric bias in sex reassignment, and the problem people with intersex conditions often experience with belonging in a society that demands gender differentiation.[15] The Intersex Society of North America (ISNA) and its associated support groups around the world are currently lobbying to abolish all unnecessary surgery. They want to ensure that any surgery still performed is with the full understanding and consent of the individual involved. In making these demands, ISNA necessarily keys into the wider debate about the so-called nature of sex.

The modern medico-psychiatric response to intersex reinscribes the normative belief that 'sex' creates 'gender' (Hird and Germon 2001). This reinscription takes place '. . . in the face of overwhelming physical evidence that this taxonomy is not mandated by biology' (Hausman 1995, 25). Thus Money refigures the natural provision of more than two sexes as an aberration—a 'handicap' and 'birth defect of the sex organs' when manifested in an individual, which surgery will 'repair' (280). What encourages the medical community to favour extremely intrusive surgery for anatomical conditions that these doctors themselves admit present no functional or medical dangers? The *authenticity* of 'sex' resides not on or in the body but rather results from a particular nexus of power, knowledge, and truth. As Garfinkel and Stoller argue, surgeons can substitute for nature when they 'provide what nature meant to be there' (1967, 127). That something as natural as sex can be or indeed needs to be produced artificially is a paradox that appears to have escaped the medical fraternity (Hird and Germon 2001; Kessler 1990).

That people with intersex conditions might experience sex in different ways challenges both the thinking of the medical community and feminist theory to the extent that both are predicated on the sex/gender binary. In order to surgically assign an individual as a female requires us to have a prior notion of 'femaleness'. As we have seen, from a medical standpoint femaleness seems to be largely defined in terms of heterosexuality—the ability of a person to 'accommodate' a penis with a vagina and the ability to bear children. Moreover, any definition of woman in terms of gender that retains any corporeality must be able to define that corporeality, and this is exactly where the problem begins in definitions based on sex (Hird and Germon 1998). A woman with an intersex condition may have any combination of partially or totally surgically created vagina, labia, and/or breasts. She may or may not be able to sexually reproduce. If being female does not entail the possession of particular anatomical parts, then the artificial creation of these body parts is inconsequential. But our current assumptions about the constitution of 'sex' struggle with such a reality. According to Raymond's criteria for womanhood (quoted above), one criterion is the presence of 'female' chromosomes. I do not agree that 'we' know we are born with XX or XY chromosomes. How many readers have actually had their chromosome configuration checked? There are likely to be many more individuals with 'ambiguous' chromosome configurations than we currently identify.[16] The overwhelming odds are that the adult(s) present at our birth took a cursory look at our genitals and defined our sex—'it's a girl!' or 'it's a boy!'

The variability of gender

If people with intersex conditions raise sticky questions about the extent to which sex is 'fixed', at least they have not *chosen* their bodies in the way that 'trans' people[17] are often claimed to have done.[18] Indeed, trans people focus on the assumption that one needs a particular relation to patriarchy to 'know' oneself as a woman. As the introduction to this chapter suggests, some feminist scholars, sociologists, and members of the public particularly value the *experience* of living in the world as a female or a male and cite this as a *criterion* for 'authentic' embodiment. Trans women claim gendered status as women on the basis of 'knowing' themselves to be women even though they lack the accepted corporeal signs designated as 'female'.

Like many, Janice Raymond is concerned that trans people seem to be claiming an identity that has not been 'earned' the old fashioned way—through lived experience. Trans people are individuals who have spent their childhood, adolescence, and often much of their adult lives within the bodies of one sex. At some point in their lives, trans people begin to live as the 'opposite' sex, often with the aid of hormone therapy and surgery. Raymond's *Transsexual empire* argues there are 'authentic' and 'inauthentic' women:

> We know who we are. We know that we are women who are born with female chromosomes and anatomy, and that whether or not we were socialised to be so-called normal women, patriarchy has treated and will treat us like women. Transsexuals have not had this same history (1994, 114).

Christine Jorgenson's sex change operation in 1953 propelled trans onto the modern public stage. The trans narratives of that time adhered strongly to the 'woman-trapped-in-male-body' trope. Bolin (1994) argues that this narrative was performative, created out of necessity to forge an 'origin story', which was required by the medico-psychiatric community that regulated access to surgery. That is, medical practitioners, psychologists, and trans individuals alike crafted a 'transsexual identity' based on the sustained desire for surgery (Billings and Urban 1982; Bolin 1994). Many trans individuals were also keen to differentiate themselves from pathologized gender identities such as transvestism or from pathologies such as pedophilia. Thus trans was emphasized as a temporary identity, a pit-stop before permanent womanhood.

Given feminists' commitment to illuminating supposedly innate 'feminine' behaviours as socially constructed requirements of patriarchal society, trans narratives unsurprisingly raise suspicion and rancour. Raymond's critique has been echoed by a number of feminists. For instance, Jeffreys (1990; 2003) offers a critical review of early autobiographies by Roberta Cowell and Jan Morris, whom Jeffreys claims are 'typical' trans stories. Jeffreys argues that transsexual women choose to 'imitate the most extreme examples of feminine behavior and dress in grossly stereotypical feminine clothing' in preference to feminists who supposedly dress 'in jeans and t-shirts' (1990, 177, 178). Jeffreys criticizes trans women for what she argues is an inability to understand supposedly 'feminine' behaviours and characteristics that women must adopt in order to avoid punishment from patriarchy. She maintains that what transsexual women consider individual attributes are really political signifiers of women's oppression. By donning stereotypical clothing and behaviours, trans women, for Jeffreys, collude with patriarchy and further contribute to women's oppression.[19]

Jeffreys's suspicion about sex reassignment as 'transgressive' is grounded in a feminist perspective, but scholars more generally share this scepticism. Those opposed to sex reassignment surgery argue that the medical fraternity colludes with society to perpetuate the cultural imperative of the two-sex system. For example, MacKenzie (1994) argues that surgery maintains the current artificial distinctions based on sex rather than challenging them in any way. In *Sex by prescription* (1990), Szasz suggests that trans is a 'condition tailor-made for our surgical-technological age': the desire to experiment with new technology ensures that critical reflection on the efficacy of sex-reassignment is minimized (1990, 86). A number of scholars argue that trans is a conformist, inauthentic gender expression, invented by a modern medical community keen to experiment with new technology (Sagarin 1978; Socarides 1970; Szasz 1990). In *Changing sex*, Hausman (1995) similarly argues that trans is a product of a modern belief in technology as societal saviour. For Hausman, trans symbolizes a literal (embodied) privileging of gender identity over the sexed body (Hemmings 1996). For this reason, Hausman calls for a return to 'bodies' and 'sex' rather than what she sees as the transformation of gender identity. In Hausman's view, medical discourse creates the transsexual, to the exclusion of trans people's own subjective accounts. She argues that trans people's active participation is limited to their demands for sex reassignment surgery.

This scepticism is not limited to academia. Witness the outcry that ensued in 1995 when Kimberley Nixon, a trans woman, attempted to train as a volunteer counsellor for female sexual assault survivors at the Vancouver Rape Relief organization. When Nixon revealed herself as trans, the organization refused to allow her to enrol in counsellor training. This decision culminated in a British Columbia Supreme Court ruling and a case that remains ongoing (see Prasad 2005; Namaste 2005).[20] The case pivots on arguments about the authentic embodiment of femaleness (see Bindel 2004). As I have attempted to argue in this chapter, this return to sex as the arbiter of reality actually supports the two-sex model and a commitment to socially imagined sex differences that are no more fixed than gender is.

Emerging trans narratives challenge the opposition to sex reassignment. As explained above, modern psycho-medical discourses compel individuals to identify themselves as only one of two sexes and (corresponding) genders. Until recently, trans narratives have been scarce because trans survival has largely depended on the ability to disappear (i.e., not be identified as a trans person). But in the 1990s, a distinct set of trans narratives contested the view that shared experience defines gender. These analyses contend that if gender can be learned, then 'womanhood' is available to anyone with the capacity to learn (Denny 1998; Feinberg 1996; Lewins 1995; More and Whittle 1999; Prosser 1998; Rothblatt 1995; Sanger 2006; Stone 1991; Stryker 1994, 1995). Such narratives reflect a tension within trans communities between those who want to pass as genitally 'correct' women or men and an increasing number of trans people who either seek disruption of the sex/gender system or simply want to live in a world that does not discriminate against them.

Trans people agitating today against the two-sex and gender system are challenging their 'deviant' status within psychology in much the same way that homosexual people challenged their disease status during the 1980s. For example, Kris Feinberg (1996) refuses to legally conform hir sex to hir expression of gender, and s/he adopts the term 'hir' as a term to designate neither 'him' nor 'her'. Instead, s/he directs hir efforts towards questioning society's need to categorize by sex at all: for Feinberg, the requirement to pass is itself a product of oppression. Kris asks 'does the fact that everywhere I go everyone calls me "sir" make me a man? Does the fact that I have breasts and a cunt make me a woman?' (Feinberg 1996, 158). Bornstein remarks, 'I know I'm not a man—about that much I'm very clear, and I've come to the conclusion that I'm probably not a woman either, at least not according to a lot of people's rules on this sort of thing' (1994, 8). Bornstein argues that transsexual people cannot become men or women—not because they are 'inauthentic' as some believe but because trans people who refuse to identify themselves as 'female' or 'male' radically deconstruct sex and gender. Bornstein's autobiography highlights the fact that if trans people reveal anything at all, it is how messy the sex/gender binary really is.[21]

The problem with the 'authentically experiencing woman' argument is that despite the emphasis on sociality, it nevertheless adheres to the concept of sex as real. One of the founders of sociology, George Herbert Mead (1934), forcefully argued that the self cannot exist without society: the continuous interactive process among individuals establishes and maintains conceptions of self by reflecting back images of the self as object.[22] For Hansen, this is the 'genius of our individuality, for we are not born with individuality—we create it' (1976, 21). Consequently, it is immaterial whether trans people can or cannot 'know' that they are the 'opposite' sex or whether sex reassignment surgery constitutes an ethical resolution. As Goffman argues:

> Our concern . . . ought not to be in uncovering real, natural expressions, whatever they might be. One should not appeal to the doctrine of natural expression in an attempt to account for natural expression, for that . . . would conclude the analysis before it had begun (1976, 7).

Goffman (1976) notes that while gender identity does not exist in any essential way, the 'schedule' for its portrayal does, and it is often mistaken as 'essentially real'. So to the extent that trans people are able (or want) to 'pass' as 'real' women or men, gender is revealed to adhere to particular bodies in a haphazard manner. Trans people in effect render visible the invisible signs on which society relies to produce gender. These signs are pre-established performances that transsexuals, *like all other individuals*, are confronted with:

> The more closely the impostor's performance approximates to the real thing, the more intensely we may be threatened, for a competent performance by someone who proves to be an impostor may weaken in our minds the moral connection between legitimate authorization to play a part and the capacity to play it (Goffman 1971 [1959], 66).

Trans people wryly note that 'however strange a cross-dresser looks, a genetic woman can always be found who looks even stranger' (Taylor 1995, 6).

On the one hand, we seem particularly aware of the social aspect of knowing gender—Raymond's definition emphasizes women's identity based on *social interaction* with patriarchal structures. On the other hand, to reject trans women's claims to 'womanhood' is to claim to know gender, which cannot be done without recourse to biology—which is antithetic to the whole point of sociological arguments.[23]

Narrative is the major mechanism for constructing the trans person's phantasmatic 'feeling'. As Shilling points out, modern subjects are increasingly produced through embodied biography, 'a project which should be worked at and accomplished as part of an individual's self-identity' (1993, 5). Narrative restructuring is a constant process, usually beginning years *before* the trans person is constructed through medical technology, contrary to Hausman's claim that trans people are a medico-technical creation. This narration is an inherently interactive process (Gagné and Tewksbury 1998). What Hausman also fails to recognize is that narrative restructuring is a process common to *all* individuals. How else do girls learn that their vaginas place them within a particular relationship with patriarchy if not through social interaction and narrative integration?

Differentiating between 'authentic' and 'inauthentic' narratives is a moral exercise, and calling for a return to bodies and sex, as Hausman does, provides no more reassurance of authenticity than gender does. Moreover, Hausman invokes a literalizing (trans)/deliteralizing (gender) binary that reinscribes the sex/gender binary. The purpose of trans autobiography is to tell a different story and to make this difference processable. Therefore, the enterprise is ambivalent: 'in coming out and staking a claim to representation, the transsexual undoes the realness that is the conventional goal of this transition' (Prosser 1998, 11). While Hausman diverts the *literal* creation of sex into a culturo-technical creation, I suggest that the transparency of trans creations of sex and gender makes theirs perhaps the more honest representation.[24]

Sex dimorphism versus sex diversity

At the beginning of this chapter, I alluded to the idea that there is more than one way to interpret the title question. We have explored the ways in which assumptions about sex and gender work together to create and maintain our contemporary hierarchical gender structure. Much of this structure is based on the implicit assumption that nature neatly differentiates all living organisms into female and male categories, that these categories are mutually exclusive and stable, and that the division serves evolutionary purposes. In this final section, I offer a short foray into the wonderful diversity of living organisms that seriously calls into question this assumption.

Biology provides a wealth of evidence to confound static notions of sexual difference.[25] Human bodies, like those of other living organisms, are only 'sexed' from a particularly narrow perspective. The *vast* majority of cells in human bodies are intersex (and this category itself is only possible if we maintain a division between 'female' and 'male' chromosomes), with only egg and sperm cells counting as chromosomally dimorphic. *Most* of the reproduction that we undertake in our lifetimes has nothing to do with 'sex'. The cells in our bodies engage in constant, energetic reproduction in the form of *recombination* (cutting and patching of DNA strands), *merging* (fertilization of cells), *meiosis* (cell division by splitting the chromosome number in half—for instance in making sperm and eggs), and *mitosis* (cell division with maintenance of cell number). Nor does reproduction take place between discrete 'selves', as many cultural analyses would have it. Indeed, only by taking our skin as a definitive impenetrable boundary are we able to see our bodies as discrete selves.[26] Our human bodies are more accurately 'built from a mass of interacting selves . . . the self is not only corporeal but corporate' (Sagan 1992, 370). Our cells also provide asylum for a variety of bacteria, viruses, and countless genetic fragments. And none of this reproduction requires any bodily contact with another human being. Moreover, there is no linear relationship between sexual dimorphism and sexual reproduction. Male sea horses, pipe fish, and hares get pregnant. Many species are male and female simultaneously or sequentially. Many types of fish change sex back and forth depending on environmental conditions (see Rothblatt 1995).

Indeed, what I would call our bodily state of sexual *indifference* is founded on an entire evolutionary legacy. During most of our evolutionary heritage, our ancestors reproduced without sex. Currently, most of the organisms in four out of the five kingdoms do not require sex for reproduction. Imagine *The joy of sex* for plants, fungi, and bacteria. *Schizophyllum*, for instance, has more than 28,000 sexes. And sex among these promiscuous mushrooms is literally a 'touch and go' event, leading Laidman to conclude that for fungi there are 'so many genders, so little time . . .' (2000, 1–3). Thus sexual 'difference' might be culturally significant, but this term obscures the much more prevalent sex diversity among living organisms.

Questions to Consider

1. Before reading this chapter, did you know that infants born with intersex conditions in Canada are routinely sex-reassigned through hormone treatment and surgeries? If not, why in your opinion is it not commonly discussed in Canadian society?
2. Why do people think that trans people must negotiate gender in ways that from-birth women and men do not?
3. In what ways do sociologists argue that gender creates sex?
4. How does nature demonstrate sex diversity rather than sex dimorphism?
5. What would social interactions be like without gender or sex?

Notes

1. The priority accorded reproduction as the 'source' of sex differences has been argued elsewhere (see Delphy 1994; Hird and Abshoff 2000).
2. Indeed, the terms 'vagina', 'labia', 'uterus', and 'ovaries' were only created as products of the later 'two-sex' schema.
3. Societal response to intersexuality varied. Societies that depended most on rigid social boundaries were more likely to persecute intersexuals. Greece and Rome, for example, burned intersexual babies alive. During the seventeenth and eighteenth centuries, intersexuals could choose their 'gender' but were prosecuted if they attempted to change genders more than once (Feinberg 1996).

4. This was also true for transvestites. A woman's desire to approximate the male was considered 'healthy' and normal compared to the abomination against the natural order of male supremacy that the male desire to don women's clothing intimated (Bullough 1975).
5. Judicial hearings detail behaviours such as dress, posture, language, and role assumed during intercourse as important indicators of the individual's 'gender'.
6. Laqueur (1990) shares a poignant and reflexive story about watching his father, a pathologist in the 1930s, painstakingly examine bodily organs from autopsies. To demonstrate that the body does *not* express its 'truth' to be 'read', Laqueur admits finding in his father's study a paper entitled *Further studies of the influence of various hormones on the masculine uterus*. The story demonstrates that detailed dissection may still produce evidence of a male uterus when the dissector operates within a schema that maintains that male bodies have uteruses (for instance, the 'one-sex' model).
7. The following two sections are taken from Hird (2000).
8. Accounts differ as to the statistical frequency of intersexuality. The Intersex Society of North America (ISNA) states that one in every 2,000 infants is born with some form of intersexuality from approximately 14 different causes (Nataf 1998).
9. CAH is the only intersex condition that poses a potential real emergency risk in the newborn period. Some infants with a CAH condition do not make sufficient amounts of cortisone and/or do not regulate the level of salt (through hormones) in their bodies.
10. Money's management philosophy has been almost exclusively adopted, and the vast majority of published literature has been written or co-written by Money. Very few physicians seem prepared to contradict Money or provide alternative management theses; notable among the exceptions are Diamond (1982) and Diamond and Sigmundson (1997).
11. It is further testament to the variability of 'sex' that several factors can be used singly or in tandem to 'determine' an individual's 'sex: chromosomal sex, hormonal sex, gonadal sex, genital sex, and reproductive sex.
12. Despite the increased risk of stenosis or injury that accompanies early vaginal construction, some physicians 'prefer' to complete all surgical procedures before the child reaches 18 months of age (Perlmutter and Reitelman 1992).
13. Indeed, surgical teams consider that one of the worst mistakes they can make is to 'create an individual unable to engage in genital [i.e., heterosexual] sex' (Kessler 1990, 20).
14. Kessler quotes one interviewed endocrinologist as saying 'why do we do all these tests if in the end we're going to make the decision simply on the basis of the appearance of the genitalia?' (1990, 13).
15. It should be pointed out that David Reimer did not have an intersex condition.
16. Many intersexuals do not become aware of their condition until adolescence.
17. The term 'trans' is used as an umbrella term to include individuals who do not understand themselves to be the sex they were assigned at birth. It includes, for example, individuals whom society knows as 'transsexual'.
18. Physicians are more likely to endorse surgery for people with intersex conditions than for trans people, even when they are behaviourally indistinguishable (Green 1969).
19. Whittle (1998) points out that male-to-female transsexuals seek inclusion within the group (i.e., women) that patriarchy oppresses, leaving behind whatever benefits they derived from their male status.

20. In 1997 the Rape Relief organization obtained an exemption from the British Columbia Human Rights Code to maintain a women-only hiring policy. Nixon challenged this exemption through the courts and initially won her case. In 2000 the BC Supreme Court overturned the court ruling, and the case goes on.

21. For further disruptive transsexual narratives, see Ekins and King (1996) and More and Whittle (1999).

22. What might now be termed the 'performative' aspect of identities Mead emphasized as the continually renegotiated character of social action, which produces malleable identities and which allows for the possibility of contradiction and conflict.

23. Emerging trans analyses contest this *explicit* emphasis on sociality for its *implicit* reliance on biology. For instance, Prosser (1998) presents a compelling theory of the mechanisms through which trans people feel themselves to be the bodies of the 'opposite' sex. Interestingly, it is precisely the psychic investment in the materiality of the body that enables the trans person to imagine surgically constructed genitals as real. Prosser argues that in the same way that people who have lost limbs maintain the feeling of those limbs phantasmatically, trans people are able to recognize the post-surgical constructed body parts as the same parts that they 'felt' phantasmatically before surgery.

24. Hausman was pregnant during the writing of *Changing sex* and expressed her terror at the thought of having a child with an intersex condition. The desire to have a 'normal' child reveals much about Hausman's own normative positioning with regard to trans.

25. This section is taken from Hird (2004).

26. Lewis Thomas puts it more directly: from the point of view of the mitochrondria in our bodies (which occupy as much space proportionally in their 'world' as we do in ours), we 'could be taken for a very large, motile colony of respiring bacteria, operating a complex system of nuclei, microtubules, and neurons for the pleasure and sustenance of their families, and running, at the moment, a typewriter' (1974, 72).

Chapter 4

Why Be Queer?

Barry D. Adam

INTRODUCTION

Is the question 'why be queer?' yet another claim for tolerance or multiculturalism? Is it about me, a heterosexually identified person sitting back and deciding whether I will let them, the queer people, do their own thing? Or about me, a gay, bisexual, lesbian, or transgendered person pleading once again to be left alone to conduct my own life? Is it yet another affirmation of the individualist ethic that stands in for a morality of advanced capitalist societies like our own—I do my thing, you do your thing, we won't bother each other, and thus we realize society as we know it?

In this chapter, I would like to push against this doctrine, which has become almost a convention in Canadian society—and perhaps not so bad a convention given the alternatives that prescribe censorship, suppression, persecution, or worse. The argument I will advance is that queerness cannot so easily be assigned as a trait of 'other' people and that looking at the world through a queer optic tells us a lot about how that world is organized and affects everyone. In short, we are all implicated in the queering of some people and not others, and queer dynamics circle back to shape who we all think we are and the spaces we accord to ourselves and others for self-expression. Queerness is in some sense inescapable: it inhabits so-called alpha males (perhaps especially alpha males) as much as it does lesbians. Why be queer? It is not so much a question of being queer or not but a story of resisting, denying, and externalizing—or allowing and embracing—things queer and all of the implications that follow.

MINORITIZING, UNIVERSALIZING

So are homosexual people a minority, or is erotic and affectionate feeling for other men and women within all of us, whether a little or a lot? In this insoluble dilemma rests a large story about how people make the worlds they live in, divide it into basic categories, draw distinctions between self and other, and conflict over who gets to wrap themselves in the flag of the right and the good and who is exiled from this charmed circle (Sedgwick 1990). It is not difficult to see how all this works in societies like our own: there is a divide—on one side heterosexuals, on the other lesbians and gay men. But what interests both sociology and queer theory is: why do we think that? How did it get that way? Is it true?

On one hand, the answer to the latter question is clearly affirmative. Lesbian, gay, bisexual, and transgendered (LGBT) people have come to be identified as a people not unlike such familiar ethnicities as Italian-Canadians or African-Canadians (presuming that LGBT are allowed to play a part in the national imaginary at all). They are, in sum, a part of the whole yet separate. They have an identity marked out from the rest, a geography with neighbourhoods and venues of their own, cultural artefacts like festivals and magazines, and a history. And there are good socio-historical reasons why Western societies have arrived at this point. LGBT identities have been forged over centuries of change.

The shift away from agrarian production to wage labour in Western capitalist societies reorganized traditional kin relationships, diminished parental supervision of subsequent generations' choices in partners, and concentrated large numbers of people in urban environments (Adam 1996). These changes have been profound for everyone regardless of sexual orientation and have created the conditions for: greater faith in romance as a determinant of partner selection, enhanced ability to create households on one's own volition (rather than living with families of origin), and greater possibilities for meeting new people in the expanding cities. These changes were grounded in opportunities afforded by wage labour with its (limited) financial autonomy, at first mainly for men and subsequently for women as they too entered wage labour. In addition to these socio-economic preconditions in Western societies, overt persecution by Judeo-Christian authorities against 'sodomy' pressed those whose emotional lives were with people of their own sex into a camp of the sexually 'other' and invented, then sharpened, a boundary that reinforces that 'otherness'.

On the other hand, the answer to the question as to whether homosexual people are a distinct minority is clearly negative. The historical and anthropological record shows that the foregoing brief history of the West was not inevitable, but just one of several possibilities. For example, the anthropological record reveals that at least some indigenous societies on every inhabited continent include socially valued relationships with a homosexual aspect. These relationships fall into a few major patterns typically defined by life stage, gender, status, and/or kinship (Adam 1985; Greenberg 1988; Murray 2000). One major pattern, well-documented in the Americas and Polynesia, is the 'berdache', 'two spirit', or transgendered form in which gender fluidity, gender mixing, or gender migration appears to be possible for some men and a few women. In these societies, homosexual relations are part of a larger pattern in which men and women take up some or most of the social roles and symbols typical of the other gender and enter into marital relations with other people who have conventional gender attributes (Jacobs et al. 1997; Lang 1998). A second major pattern takes the form of hierarchical, military, age-graded, and mentor/acolyte relationships in which adult men who presume control over women also assume sexual rights over younger, subordinate males (Dover 1978; Herdt 1984; Adam 1985; Halperin 1990). Examples of this pattern have been documented in ancient Greece, medieval Japan, pre-colonial Africa, and Melanesia.

A third pattern, sometimes overlapping with the first two, orders homosexual relationships along the same kinship lines as heterosexuality. Thus if members of a particular clan are considered appropriate marital partners (and others are deemed inappropriate), both males and females of the appropriate clan may be considered attractive and acceptable partners. There are Australian and Melanesian cultures in which, for example, one's mother's brother was considered both an appropriate marital partner for girls and an appropriate mentor (including a sexual aspect) for boys (Adam 1985). Similarly, in some societies where the accumulation of bride price is the prerequisite to attracting a wife, occasionally women with wealth can avail themselves of this system to acquire wives (Amadiume 1980), and men can provide a corresponding gift to the families of youths whom they take into apprenticeship. These kin-governed bonds have been documented in some societies of Australia, Africa, and Amazonia. These major patterns do not exhaust the full range of cross-cultural homoerotic bonding, nor do they explain the gay and lesbian worlds of today. However, they do point to the fact that there is no unitary idea of homosexuality in different societies, no single role or attitude toward same-sex sexuality, and no predominant conception of social approval or disapproval.

Historical research shows that same-sex eroticism and affection tend to coalesce around four major themes in Western societies. David Halperin (2002) finds that male bonding is typically associated with or moulded on these territories of meaning: effeminacy, pederasty or 'active' sodomy, friendship or male love, and passivity or inversion. Martha Vicinus (1992) identifies the social scripts of the 'passing woman', the 'mannish woman', the 'libertine', and the 'romantic friend' as sites in which female bonding is most often found. All of this is to say that sex between men or between women has often not been the primary category of interest but rather a practice or trait that gained visibility or frequency as part of these social forms. Same-sex attraction and bonding, then, appears to arise more often in a few major patterns and social sites, entering into the lives of majorities at times or at times minorities of the inhabitants of a society. Conversely, homoeroticism may be shaped by or pressed into these patterns or driven underground according the precepts and prejudices of these societies.

The political and philosophical traditions of the West are rooted in a society deeply affirmative of homosexual relations of the mentor/acolyte model. Indeed, most of the heroes of ancient Greek mythology had male lovers; the founding of political democracy is attributed to the male couple Harmodias and Aristogeiton, who slew the tyrant Hyppias in 514 BCE (Halperin 1990; Foucault 1978). Socrates, in unexpurgated translations of *The symposium*, rhapsodizes about how the love of youths leads to the love of beauty and thus to the love of wisdom. Yet modern Western tradition has suppressed, denied, and appropriated this homoerotic heritage, consigning it to sin, sickness, or crime. The gradual shaping and consolidation of Christian doctrines into the orthodox canon law articulated by medieval theologians and the propagation and enforcement of these views by the Roman Catholic church from the twelfth to the fourteenth century and onwards replaced the heroic friendships valued by the ancients with the idea of the sodomite (Jordan 1997).

Like the traditions it suppressed, the concept of the sodomite cannot simply be equated with modern ideas of the homosexual. In ecclesiastical law, sodomy typically referred to a vague, sometimes comprehensive category of sexual practices that lacked pro-natalist objectives, including, for example, non-reproductive heterosexual acts and bestiality as well as homosexual practices. The consolidation of church power through the first millennium of the Christian era included the gradual eradication of indigenous European forms of sexual friendship (Boswell 1994). By the fifteenth and sixteenth centuries, sodomy became a charge pursued by the Inquisition, with varying degrees of rigour in different countries, along with its campaign to suppress Jews, witches, and other forms of religious nonconformity. In the sixteenth through the twentieth century, Christian orthodoxies imposed by military conquest on indigenous populations of the Americas, Africa, and Asia actively extinguished local forms of same-sex bonding as part of larger campaigns of cultural colonialism or forced these local forms underground. The conceptualization of homosexuality as a sinful, non-reproductive sexual act then became widely established as governments and empires acted in concert with established churches to enforce cultural and juridical dominion over much of the world's population in the Christian realm.

As nation-states emerged from empires in the eighteenth through the twentieth century, many of them organized their criminal codes out of the legacy of canon law, depending on the social ingredients that went into state formation and their relation to church control. Nation-states might be thought of as places where particular social groups defined by capital, race, language, religion, gender, and sexuality forge hegemony over a territory (Corrigan and Sayer 1985). These groups institutionalize their own cultures as national cultures, thereby generating a range of subordinated and minority groups who must fend for themselves in an alien world. With the rise of nation-states in the context of a Eurocentric, Christian, modern world system, the modern conception of homosexuality has emerged as a sexual act attributed to a class of people subject to social sanction and criminal penalty (Adam 1995; Stychin 1998). As the world economy mobilized masses of people in cities and as states devised more efficient systems of supervising, regulating, and policing their populations, homosexual men (and later women) began to fall into the criminal justice systems of Europe. From the early example of the fifteenth-century Venetian republic to eighteenth-century campaigns to catch and suppress organized sodomy (that is, the nascent gay world) in Britain, the Netherlands, and Switzerland, state agencies (and at least in Britain, societies for the reformation of morals as well) swept up hundreds of men and some women in its punitive nets. The legacy of this nexus of church and state-building has been the disciplining of same-sex eroticism, the categorization of its adherents as a people apart, and the invention of homosexuality as a juridical and medical category.

By the nineteenth century, gay and lesbian venues had been firmly established in the major cities of Europe and North America and became subject to occasional exposés by police, physicians, and moralists, who have bequeathed us often shocked descriptions of 'colonies of perverts'. In Western societies such as our own then, people with homoerotic interests and gender dissidents have been forged into peoples with LGBT identities— or perhaps better said, LGBT identities have arisen among those willing to stand up for the right to love and live with the person(s) of one's choice. Why be queer? It is less a question about a 'fact' than a defence of a larger world of choice, an aspiration to find a way to what feels right in relating to other people, and a discovery of innovative ways to connect erotically and emotionally.

In Canada, LGBT communities and movements have often sought to realize these aims by availing themselves of and working with the avenues afforded to citizens in a liberal democratic society. These avenues and rights have been not so much pre-ordained as struggled for, contested in court, and demanded of recalcitrant governments (Adam 1995; Kinsman 1996). In the 1950s and 1960s, when public debates centred on whether homosexuals were criminals or mentally ill, the struggle was to gain freedom from police harassment and psychiatry. Canada decriminalized homosexuality in 1969 (for two consenting adults in private), and psychiatry began to de-pathologize it, beginning in the early 1970s. In the last decades of the twentieth century, a long struggle in provincial legislatures, courts, and finally the federal government succeeded in including 'sexual orientation' in human rights law, a symbolic affirmation of the full citizenship rights of lesbian, gay, and bisexual people (but less clearly transgendered people, a struggle that continues). At the turn of the twenty-first century, relationship recognition, and marriage in particular, became the next frontier.

So are we not back to minority rights, some version of multiculturalism, or the concerns of a minority that by definition need not occupy the energy and attention of the majority? Sometimes it may seem so, but more often the implications are much more far-reaching.

DISCIPLINING GENDER AND AFFECTION

Homophobia (that is, anti-LGBT sentiment and practice) is scarcely a thing of the past. Indeed, it is alive and well in many places, most notably schools, conservative religious institutions, some arenas of government, and certain regions and populations. An obvious answer to 'why be queer?' might be: 'No way. I don't want to be derided, despised, even attacked'—which leads in turn to the question, why are so many resources put into keeping homophobia active? What are the many popes, presidents, preachers, mullahs, and schoolyard bullies gaining from the volley of hate that they actively lob in the direction of anyone they can label, whether they have any idea of their actual sexual orientation or not? Homophobia is more than prejudice that will simply wilt in the face of reason (Adam 1998). Consider this finding from a study of 10 to 14-year-old schoolboys:

> In many countries it is now commonplace for researchers and media commentators to voice particular concern about two features of masculinity: young men's worsening record of academic attainment in comparison with girls and their propensity for violence. . . . [V]arious studies have identified the

forms of masculinity that gain most respect as involving hierarchies based on toughness, threat of (or actual) violence, casualness about schoolwork, 'compulsory heterosexuality' and a concomitant homophobia. . . . As a result, boys and young men are forced to position themselves in relation to these issues, whether or not they wish actually to be violent or disengaged from schoolwork (Phoenix et al. 2003).

Homophobia is not just anti-LGBT activity then; it functions as a whip to keep everyone toeing a particular gender line. It operates particularly forcefully among men and boys, demanding a strict conformity that few can ever believe they have finally and comfortably attained. It works as a policing mechanism, both among males policing each other and as a vigilance over oneself. It is comprehensive and demanding, disciplining presentation of self, manners, and gestures. It prescribes the things in which one can legitimately take an interest, forcing other interests into the closet. If doing well in school becomes one of those supposedly insufficiently masculine things to do, then there are many boys convinced that they must sabotage their own potential on the altar of toughness. Of course, homophobia also regulates relationships among males, limiting warmth, affection, and mutual support. It even prescribes what one can wear, eat, drink, say, or dream of lest one fall vulnerable to the charge of being a 'sissy'. It is ubiquitous and relentless: the epithet 'that's so gay' has become one of the most widespread insults in Canadian schoolyards today despite the fact that it almost never refers to anything that is characteristic of gay worlds or sensibilities.

So is homophobia an essentially male dynamic? Traditionally, masculinity and femininity have not been simple mirror images of each other. Girls and women have usually been afforded more leeway in gender in that many accomplishments and activities associated with men can also be done by women without impugning one's integrity as female. Feminism as well has developed and consolidated a strong critique of the disadvantages of strict conformity to feminine gender requirements, defined them as a form of oppression, and pointed out how they have inordinately limited women's access to employment and opportunity. Nevertheless, women are far from immune to homophobia. Opponents of the women's movement were quick to try to paralyze it by charging that feminists were 'just a bunch of lesbians', and the movement did some soul-searching before deciding that it was the gender whip of homophobia that was the problem, not lesbians in the women's movement. Anti-lesbian ideologies and practices typically aim to thwart women from making their own choices and asserting their own independence (Rich 1989). Today, the heightened visibility of things gay and lesbian has amplified anti-lesbian homophobia in everyday life. As Human Rights Watch (2001) found in its survey of schools in the United States, girls also increasingly suffer the verbal and physical violence of homophobic bullying.

By now it should be evident that homophobia does not act alone but operates like and often together with a number of other 'isms' like sexism, racism, ableism, and prejudice based on social class. All of these practices share similar tactics through which people perceived to be vulnerable are picked out for special persecution. It is not surprising then to see that studies of prejudice find that those who rank highest in measures of homophobia are precisely the same people who are more likely to score highest for racism and sexism (MacDonald et al. 1973; Henley and Pincus 1978; Morin and Garfinkle 1978, 31; Adam 1978, 42–51; Larsen et al. 1983; Bierly 1985; Herek 1988; Britton 1990; Seltzer 1992).

The link between homophobia and sexism is strong. How can males revile all things feminine in themselves and other men without affecting their valuation of women as a whole? These 'othering' dynamics of homophobia can mesh with racism and able-ism in that schoolchildren of colour or different abledness can be particularly vulnerable to being labelled and minoritized. That neither Hamed Nastoh nor Azmi Jubran were gay in sexual orientation did not stop them from being gay-baited and gay-bashed throughout high school (Teeter 2005; Ramsay and Tremblay 2005). Nastoh committed suicide at the age of 14 in 2000. The response of the Surrey school board, responsible for the school that he attended, has been a refusal to permit any anti-homophobia curricula in Surrey schools. A ruling in Jubran's case by the British Columbia court of appeal in 2005 upheld the finding of a human rights tribunal that school boards cannot shirk their responsibility to make schools a safe place for students.

Schoolyards are just microcosms of larger social forces. Conservative religious organizations have frozen homophobia into religious doctrine and do not hesitate to avail themselves of human rights legislation guaranteeing religious freedom in order to promote homophobia at the same time that they actively seek to deny the same human rights protection to LGBT people. The Canadian same-sex marriage debate has drawn together the conservative and fundamentalist wings of a wide range of religions from fundamentalist Protestants to the Roman Catholic hierarchy, along with conservative Jews, Muslims, and Sikhs. At the same time, some adherents of all these faiths have organized to oppose conservative leaders because they understand all too well how the dynamics of 'othering' can and do hurt them as well and that the prerequisite for a peaceable society with social justice is an end to the politics of exclusion. At the United Nations, the recognition of basic human rights for LGBT people faces opposition from a powerful bloc composed of the United States (as successive Republican governments have remained captive to the Christian right), the Vatican, a set of Islamic states, and assorted dictatorships (Barris 2005). This same bloc stands in the way of the advancement of women in wresting control of their own reproductive potential from patriarchs and governments.

There are homophobia hot spots associated with governments as well. In the United States, the most notorious instance is the military with its active and official policy of exclusion (Scott and Stanley 1994). In Canada, it is censorship imposed by several layers of official regulation—from Canada Customs and Revenue regulations to obscenity law, bawdy house law, and provincial film classification—that falls heavily on the small cultural institutions of the LGBT community (Cossman et al. 1997; Weissman 2002). There are as well more subtle forms of homophobia—as when LGBT lives are closely policed and thrust into a 'closet' because everything LGBT people do is supposedly about 'sex' and therefore must be kept secret. Same-sex courtship, romance, partnership, home-building, mutual support, and communication through the arts are not always allowed the same public manifestation accorded to that of others but rather are often subject to warning labels and restrictions.

QUEER = RELEASE

So why be queer? By now it must seem as though there are rather a good many reasons not to be, but I want to argue that most of us have a great deal to gain by throwing off the ugly taskmaster of homophobia that dictates who we must be and dare to want to be.

Is there something about a queer viewpoint on the world that is interesting, insightful, and beneficial to all? If there is a 'gay sensibility', it is not shared by all LGBT people, but it may be appreciated by many who are not gay. If it does exist, it is not easy to define, since LGBT people have at least as many viewpoints and disagree with each other as much as anybody else. Even so, there is in the arts and literature of LGBT communities something of a tradition of critical awareness, irony, and 'camp' that understands the pomposity and dead weight of the moralists and bullies who take themselves too seriously and seem to have nothing better to do than try to run other people's lives. There is a long tradition of laughter that extends from gay bars to philosophical texts in response to a machismo that believes in itself, dogmatic righteousness, and gunslinger swagger. After a century, the plays of Oscar Wilde and Noel Coward still delight as they slyly send up the pretentiousness and absurd officiousness of social worlds trying to act the way they are 'supposed' to. Philosophers such as Wittgenstein, Barthes, and Foucault have stood out in their interrogation of the hidden assumptions and power dynamics of Western modernism. While their stance might not be linked to their homosexuality, one still might argue that their experiences gave them a vantage point on the world from which these underpinnings became more visible (Halperin 1995). Some of the most fundamental texts that puncture the ostensible 'naturalness' of gender also benefit from the queer optic (Rubin 1975; Butler 1990; Butler 1993b), as do some of the comical texts that deflate puffed-up gender defenders (Simpson 1994).

Why be queer? Or more precisely, why tolerate the tyranny of homophobia? One can only wonder at the deformation of male character caused by the taboo on all things 'feminine'. Gentleness, style, aesthetics, dance, even intellect fall under the searchlight of homophobia as it casts its chill over ever wider territory. The emotionally crippled male has become a virtual icon of women's literature and psychology as women try to cope with the 'stiff' consequence of male gender disciplining (Faludi 1999). At one time, Englishmen could kiss each other with impunity; then sometime around the sixteenth century, this act too began to fall under 'suspicion' (Bray 1982). Now, according to the New York Times, a lot of men dare not even sit next to each other in a theatre, eat together in a decent restaurant, or talk honestly with each other about their deepest concerns without triggering a fear of suspected same-sex intimacy (Lee 2005). Fortunately, there remains considerable cross-cultural variation in inter-male gestures of casual affection: men from Morocco to China can walk arm in arm or hold hands in public without fear of reproach. But will Western gender panic begin contaminating their relaxed approach to affection, or will we in the West begin to learn something from them?

Homophobia also places women on a gender tightrope when they dare to enter traditionally masculine realms. The high rate of expulsion of women from the US armed forces is a case in point: the image of women carrying out the demands of military service soon attracts the homophobic gaze, since the gender whip requires that military women act both as 'women' and as 'men' simultaneously (Scott and Stanley 1994). That raises the question as to whether increasing equality for women disrupts gender or stimulates a wave of gender policing (or both). As long as the entry of women into more and more male-identified fields makes the male pretence that men alone are capable of doing these jobs appear increasingly ridiculous, there is hope that gender discipline will collapse of its own absurdity. But at the same time, there are signs that the easy expression of intimacy among girls and women is falling under 'suspicion', pressing them toward homophobic male standards of coldness.

The truth is that there have never been firm boundaries dividing sexual orientations in the lived experiences of most people. Studies of sexuality repeatedly reveal considerable behavioural bisexuality, experimentation, fluidity, and change over the life course. Some of these ambiguities have been recognized in schools in the form of gay/straight alliances that challenge homophobia without requiring members to declare an identity allegiance. But we are still left with the question: why is so much energy put into labelling other people 'gay' and drawing the boundaries that enforce a dictatorship of gender conformity? Why be queer? Challenging homophobia has the potential to make everyone much more at peace with themselves—even lesbians and gay men who themselves are hardly immune to the demands of gender. Still, LGBT people are necessarily on the front lines of resistance to homophobia, often the pioneers who innovate new kinds of relationship (Weeks et al. 2001; Adam 2004; Adam 2006) and challenge the boundaries that reserve jobs for one gender or the other. A little more queerness in a lot more people might expand everyone's horizon of personal expression and opportunities.

Questions to Consider

1. What social and historical conditions led to the formation of people identified as gay, lesbian, bisexual, or transgendered?
2. What forms do same-sex bonds take in different societies around the world? What does this say about common notions of homosexuality?
3. Does homophobia affect nearly everyone regardless of sexual orientation?
4. Has the fear of things queer stunted the growth and expression of men and women?

Chapter 5

Is the Self Social?

Stephen Katz

INTRODUCTION

This chapter explores one of sociology's most foundational questions: is the self social? In doing so, I examine several major theoretical and methodological approaches to the relationship between Self and society used by sociologists to analyze the interdependency of inner lives and social worlds. These approaches include symbolic interactionism, micro-sociology, social psychology, and ethnomethodology, as well as more recent developments in the sociology of the emotions, identity and aging, and power. Most students of Canadian sociology are more familiar with the macro-theories of political economy, social inequality, institutional structures, and social movements than with literature on the social dimension of the Self, which focuses on identity formation, concepts of personhood, relations of intimacy, sociology of the body, self-reflexivity, and emotional styles. The overall aim of this literature, however, is to link the large-scale structural constraints, networks, and systems to the everyday contexts in which they are lived out and made meaningful. Thus we should think about everyday life as a bridge connecting the micro to the macro, made intelligible through a social imagination in the sense of the term proposed by C. Wright Mills and, as noted in the introduction, as that which 'enables us to grasp history and biography and the relations between the two within society' (Mills 2004 [1959], 3).

The idea of a social bridge is difficult to grasp because while one's biographical life is part of the ongoing historical processes of the wider society, it is experienced as intensely personal and deeply individual. For instance, glancing in a mirror produces more than a momentary reflection. The glance also brings to the pause at the mirror a self-consciousness of the expectations and opinions of other people. This is why the mirror is an ideal device for rehearsing, playing out, or 'making ourselves up' in preparation for the inevitable interactions we encounter in the outside world.

Food offers another example. It is a biological necessity, but we eat food at *meals*, which can be social events. When, where, and with whom we eat, who prepares the food, how we adapt to eating rules and appropriate manners (or lack of them), which expressions of pleasure or disdain are acceptable—these are all cultural conventions that determine our participation at meals. This chapter also considers many other situations that illustrate the permeability and fluidity of the boundaries that demarcate the personal from the public and manifest themselves in almost everything we do. Indeed, we become sociologists when we step back from the most ordinary aspects of collective existence—working, talking, hanging around, creating, playing—and observe their role in shaping our sense of competence, difference, and vulnerability and grounding our narratives of Self as coherent and common sense. However, the journey to the social Self starts with the body and the evolutionary experimentation that made us human.

BORN TO BE SOCIAL

Think about being born as a unique primate. Among primates, humans are born the most helpless, yet we live the longest and take the longest time to mature. Human fetal bodies have the longest gestation period (nine months in the uterus), our bones (especially skull) take the longest time to ossify, and our teeth are the latest to erupt. Compared to other primates, we are slow to walk, feed ourselves, and reach sexual maturity. Most important, our brains are very late in reaching their full size. The brains of rhesus monkeys reach 65 per cent of their final size by the time they are born and those of chimpanzees 40.5 per cent. Yet humans achieve only 23 per cent of final brain size at birth—less than a quarter of our final brain growth. Chimpanzee and gorilla brains reach 70 per cent of their full size in the first year of life; human brains do not reach 70 per cent of their full size until the third year of life (Gould 1977). Thus humans are considered the most youthful primate because their prolonged *neotenic* or *exterogestational* postnatal development ensures an extended retention of youthful mammalian features (such as a large brain relative to body size and playful curiosity).

In short, with so little of our development occurring by birth, we must develop the bulk of our brains and everything else *outside of the uterus*. This means that it is through *social* practices—learning, observing, interacting, speaking, symbolizing, fighting, dreaming—that we become human beings. We must learn to interact our way into life. So biology and society have conspired not only to create the very bodies that bear the signs of social development, evolutionary experimentation, and pre-adaptation to social existence but also to make it impossible *to be* a person outside of society. We can only gain a sense of Self through growing (up) in the company of others and embodying the richly meaningful social worlds we co-create for each other. This is where the work of sociologists who study the Self has been so important, as the following section makes clear.

THE SOCIOLOGY OF THE SELF AND SOCIAL INTERACTION

This section introduces four key thinkers who are considered the founders of the social dimension of the Self: Georg Simmel, George Herbert Mead, Erving Goffman, and Harold Garfinkel. While they are all delimited by their individual historical and intellectual contexts, their novel theoretical approaches to social interaction have been taken up and elaborated on by many others who strengthen the currency of these founders' ideas with new research and social questions.

Georg Simmel and the forms of modern life

Georg Simmel (1858–1918) was a German sociologist and keen observer of the vast changes wrought by the upheavals of modernity. He was one of the first social theorists to consider the inner, personal consequences of modern life and its special cultural features, such as the interpersonal relations of exchange established by the money economy (1990). Simmel also wrote about the most obvious events and ordinary places often neglected by sociologists. As David Frisby (1992) points out, in Simmel's mind society itself could be seen as a work of art. Simmel grew up in Berlin, a large metropolis with a population of two million by the beginning of the twentieth century. It was the central hub for migration from eastern Europe and later Russia, and its university, the University of Berlin, was a major international centre of learning and research. Simmel lived right in the busy central commercial district of Berlin until the age of 56 in 1914 when he was appointed chair of philosophy at Strasbourg University and had to leave the city, a move he regretted despite the fact that anti-Semitism had barred him from a professorial position in Berlin. Such biographical details are important because sociology is a discipline forged by the lived experiences of sociologists as well as by their intellectual accomplishments. For instance, Simmel's leadership in urban sociology and his writing of 'The metropolis and mental life' in 1903, along with other articles on Rome (1898), Florence (1906), and Venice (1907), was deeply influenced by his residence in vibrant and cosmopolitan Berlin. Like Max Weber, Simmel understood that concepts of individualism were bound up with the coldly efficient bureaucratic and impersonal economic processes of modernity, but Simmel introduced a very different idea about society based on a micro-sociological framework. He envisioned society as a dynamic complex of individual interaction, reciprocity, and activity, a series of concentric events rather than an objective set of conditions. In Simmel's words,

> The essence of aesthetic observation and interpretation lies in the fact that the typical is to be found in what is unique, the lawlike in what is fortuitous, the essence and significance of things in the superficial and transitory . . . To the adequately trained eye, the total beauty, the total meaning of the world as a whole radiates from every single point (1896, in Frisby 1992, 18).

We can already hear in this statement a bold new emphasis on individual participation and everyday life as the bases of society. In *On individuality and social forms* (1971), he delineates the cultural *forms* by which specific human activities and identities can be made meaningful. Just as we use a relatively stable set of grammatical rules to write or speak in order to make sense to each other, so too do we rely on a socially meaningful set of *forms* to act and create our social worlds. For example, taking turns would be a kind of social *form* because there are culture-bound rules for taking turns or standing in line that involve patience (up to a point), maintaining appropriate body distance, and conforming to behaviour that avoids going 'out of turn' or 'butting in front'. Without a theory of forms, research on observing human interaction provides only a stream of images without any understanding of them. However, theorizing forms without the support of human observation is just an abstract, empty exercise. Simmel understood that together, forms and observations make for an exciting and boundless opportunity for sociologists to see behind all that we take for granted as mundane and familiar.

In his many books and articles, Simmel advanced the notion of cultural forms to account for the special features of modernity: fashion, city life, art, love and lies, consumer identities, and the dilemmas of new personal relationships. In his review of Simmel's career, Johannson (2000) reminds us that the social Self is framed both by cultural forms and the struggles against them. This problem haunted Simmel, who pondered whether the Self could transcend cultural forms despite the reality that meaningful behaviour makes no sense without them (Simmel 1968 [1918]).

George Herbert Mead and symbolic interactionism

George Herbert Mead (1863–1931) was a philosopher and an American professor at the University of Chicago, a major centre for academic sociology in the late nineteenth and early twentieth centuries. He was a key figure in a school of thought that came to be known as symbolic interactionism (see Blumer 1969). Mead was influenced by philosophy (especially pragmatism), biology, physics, psychology, and thinkers such as William James, John Dewey, and Wilhelm Wundt. He encapsuled his main ideas about the Self in his book *Mind, self and society* (1934). What is fascinating about Mead's work is his dissection of the Self into its various interactive components that emerge through socialization. Mead proposed that children engage in a play stage of personal development during which they imitate parents and other authority figures, public celebrities, and super-heroes. They have 'imaginary' invisible friends, play at pretend worlds, and invent play language to fabricate stories. With maturity, people enter the game stage that requires interaction with a plurality of roles according to specific rules. Such roles are no longer acted out imaginatively as in the play stage but are restricted to the rules of 'the game'.

Mead's term for this plurality of roles is the 'generalized other', a loose collection of all other roles to which we must orient ourselves. It is from this sense of a generalized other that we also feel judged and monitored in our social interaction. That is why we often say that 'society thinks' or 'everybody knows'. As we mature from play to game stages, we also develop a socially conscious repertoire of rules for self-recognition. Here Mead's distinction between the 'I' and the 'me' as the subjective and objective parts of the Self is notable. The 'I' reflects on the self and makes decisions and plans. The 'me' is a repository of social rules and personal biography and therefore judges the plans made by the 'I' against experience, competence, and wisdom. For Mead, the 'I' is impulsive, subjective, uncertain, surprising, and creative, while the 'me' hears, watches, reflects, judges, and censors the impulsiveness of the 'I'. The 'I' and the 'me' are also engaged in what Mead called a constant and dynamic 'internal conversation' that animates social consciousness and situates the Self in the world.

While Mead's ideas may seem psychological, they are sociological to the extent that he was committed to demonstrating the symbolic nature of the Self. The meanings, definitions, and identities associated with the Self derive from the social contexts in which they are constructed, shared, communicated, and interpreted as significant. For Mead, the Self is a process, not an entity, moulded by individuals who both act and are acted upon. We need others to confirm and understand us because we define ourselves according to how others define us. This means that human attributes such as goodness, badness, selfishness, stupidity, sexiness, and intelligence are not necessarily fixed but are symbolically assigned. How do we know a child is acting badly? Mead would ask, under what conditions is the child defined as bad? What kinds of behaviour have been symbolically labelled as bad? How is the child's understanding of bad and good actions based on the parents' reactions? In social interaction, it is the constellations of meanings associated with gestures, language, and expressions that guide our taking account of each other and adjusting ourselves in the process. For example, on a train people individually and consciously enter, stand, sit, and depart, but they also collectively and unconsciously encounter, interpret, adapt, and symbolically communicate with great skill. In Meadian thought, as with Simmel's ideas, the focus is on the process of reciprocal social interaction that forms the basis of society. Self-identities are formed in such interactive contexts.

Erving Goffman and the interaction order

Canadian-born Erving Goffman (1922–82) was a pioneering sociologist who invented new ways of studying the Self as it pertains to the body, talk and conversation, deviance, and relations of power.[1] In his texts, Goffman's goal, as he explained in one of his last addresses, was 'to promote acceptance of this face-to-face domain as an analytically viable one—a domain which might be titled . . . the *interaction order* . . .—a domain whose preferred method of study is microanalysis' (1983, 2). Goffman carried out his study of the 'interaction order' by developing a specific *analytical vocabulary*, a model of *dramaturgy*, and a structural framework of *frame analysis*.

Goffman's *analytical vocabulary* or 'flair for taxonomy' (Burns 1992, 358) is evident in all his writings and exemplifies how the sociology of the Self necessitates its own terminology. A simple example is the situation in which a gathering of people becomes a social web of information because, as Goffman says, they are co-present and simultaneously giving and 'giving off' information. Members of the gathering provide information when they talk about directions to a restaurant or tell a personal story. They also 'give off' information through nuanced body language, vocal tones, use of repetition, facial gestures, and so on. Another example is what Goffman called impression management, the performances that we enact to present ourselves favourably to others and avoid social blunders (Goffman 1971 [1959]). Impression management also involves face-work—the mannerisms that we employ to stave off embarrassment or avoid offence and thus 'save face' (1967). Here the face functions as both the physical and symbolic face of the Self. As Cupach and Metts (1994) point out, sometimes we use preventive face-work strategies such as hedging, being overly polite, or appealing to suspended judgment. Sometimes we work to save the face of others and apologize for friends or family members in embarrassing predicaments. We even go as far as excusing the behaviour of our pets to save face, as is the case in Clinton Sanders's research on dogs (1990; 1993).

Dramaturgy is a theatrical model borrowed by Goffman to help him analyze the self-to-self interactions of social performances. Goffman took the metaphors of the theatre, with its 'roles', 'masks', 'actors', 'stages', and 'dramas', to show how we generate specific self-identities through our appearance, facial expressions, and manner. Our personal 'fronts' are like costumes that, again, we work to manage. While we perform and play 'on stage' there are also a variety of 'back stages'. Back stages are where we prepare, recuperate, adjust, and simply rest from our on-stage roles. Thus for sociologists, the back stage is as interesting as the front stage because the back stage is the social sphere where we take off our masks, reveal ourselves, and say and do what we really feel.

Goffman's third theoretical innovation was his structured framework or *frame analysis*, which he designed to show how similar concepts could be applied to different situations (1974). For example, 'taking turns' is a framed ritual that can apply equally to academic conferences, sports competitions, dinner party discussions, or family speeches at wedding ceremonies. Goffman's frames, similar to Simmel's forms, combine subjective participation and reflection in accordance with established principles of social organization. They can apply to ceremonies, contests, games of make-believe, pranks, hazing rituals, and so on, each with its own special code by which people understand the rules of participation. Often we come to realize that we are acting within frames only when a frame changes or is broken.

Think of a situation in which two children are playfully pushing each other and wrestling around. Suddenly one child's pushing becomes a little harder, and the code has changed from one of play fight to actual fight, from fake aggression to actual aggression. Hence the subjective experience for the pushed child also changes along with the shift in the other child's aggressive behaviour, while the frame changes from make-believe play to a possibly threatening contest. This is immediately known and felt because the consensus between the two children about the playful interaction in the frame is broken, as signified by possible utterances such as 'hey, this isn't fun anymore', 'hey, that really hurts, stop it!' or an appeal to witnesses with 'did you see that?' or 'help!' The frame might be repaired if the aggressive child backs off, apologizes, and offers to restore the play frame again.

Goffman's unique analytical language, theatrical model of dramaturgy, and structured frame analysis have been criticized for their overreliance on metaphorical reasoning (Nash and Calonico 1996). However, Goffman's contributions to post-war micro-sociology were considerable, and like Simmel, Mead, and the symbolic interactionists, Goffman opened a myriad of routes pointing to the everyday sociology of the Self.

Harold Garfinkel: The ethnomethodological structure of social worlds

Ethnomethodology is an original school of thought that tackles the construction of reality within social worlds of meaning. It was established by Harold Garfinkel

(1917) of the University of California. Garfinkel encapsulated his ideas in the text *Studies in ethnomethodology* (1967), and he along with other ethnomethodologists such as Harvey Sacks studied people's own 'ethno' or common sense methods of knowing and enacting the social rules around them. Garfinkel's first research concerned juries, which he noticed had different interactive, linguistic, and behavioural patterns in the courtroom compared to back stage in the jury deliberation room. Thus verdicts and decisions were never just legal interpretations of a case because they also involved practical ethno-interpretations of jurisprudence, evidence, and truth. Inspired by this research and strongly influenced by the phenomenological theories of Alfred Schutz, Garfinkel advanced the following key ideas about Self and social worlds: a) the meanings and experiences of social worlds are constructed through social interaction; b) social worlds provide their own common sense vocabularies to account for their existence, which participants use to understand their lives outside of the official, legal, or professional versions of such worlds; c) social worlds reveal their meanings, vocabularies, and rules when they are breached, violated, or upset. This last point is theoretically important because it gave Garfinkel and his students a way of experimenting with the violation of everyday routines. Garfinkel designed a project around the maintenance of 'trust' (1963) by sending graduate students into various ordinary situations and asking them not to abide by the expected rules. As he said, Garfinkel was after 'the nastiness of surprise' to expose the fragility of social worlds and the relational identities within them (see also Pollner 1967).

Although not exhaustive, Simmel, Goffman, Garfinkel, and subsequent approaches have expanded our understanding of how the Self is social. They have also indicated why sociologists should care about linking large-scale structural problems with micro-social relations, intimacies, identities, conversations, and the everyday dramas of individuals and groups. One area where researchers have advanced these links is the sociology of emotions, to which this chapter now turns.

THE SOCIOLOGY OF EMOTIONS

On the one hand, sociology has focused on the emotional conditions of modern society. Karl Marx wrote about 'alienation' as the personal consequence of the exploitative labour process in capitalist society. Max Weber recast the spiritual development of the Protestant 'ethic' as a self-disciplining regime essential to the entrepreneurial 'spirit' of capitalism. Weber also criticized the later private experience as a 'disenchantment of the world' that arose with modernity. Émile Durkheim emphasized that solidarity and sacredness were both objective social facts and subjective emotional states. Georg Simmel observed a series of emotional reactions to modern urban life, such as the blasé attitude of boredom and sensory overload (see also Kashima and Foddy 2002). On the other hand, the sociology of emotions has only emerged as a distinct sub-field since the 1980s, largely through the research of Arlie Russell Hochschild.[2]

The challenge facing Hochschild and other sociologists is how to apply critical methodological rigour to emotions that are felt as intimate and interior experiences. The language of emotions also makes it difficult to imagine their accessibility to sociological research when we are constantly told to 'go with', 'trust', and 'follow' our feelings as if they were the deepest, most natural, and most authentic part of ourselves. Lupton notes, 'As an outcome of the association that is commonly made between emotions and authentic selfhood, we often use our perceptions of the emotional self as rationales for explaining why we behave in certain ways' (1998, 91). However, emotions *are* sociological because they find meaning and expression through interactions, relationships, and exchanges between people in social contexts. For example, the contexts in which an emotion such as anger is expressed (to 'let it all out', to 'lose one's temper', to 'blow up', to 'cry out', etc.) are acceptable only when collective feeling/rules allow for them. If feelings are expressed at the wrong time, in the wrong place, or in the wrong way, we learn to react instantly with embarrassment, defensiveness, fear, protection, or upset. Certain spaces encourage and sustain specific emotional reactions, such as crying at movies or being 'sexy' in singles' bars. Disneyland counts on adults as well as children instantly feeling playful and silly once inside its gates. Shopping malls call out to us to be whimsical and spontaneous (to buy things, of course). Funerals evoke sentiments of sadness and loss. Fashion tells us to be 'cool' or 'hot'. Video games elicit states of excitation and loss of control. Talk shows capitalize on the performance of strong emotions emphasizing individual confession, suffering, and narratives of recovery. Courts of law expect dispassionately presented accounts.

Feelings also have histories, which again suggests their social nature. For instance, depression is one of the most publicized emotional problems today and attracts extensive psychological, biological, pharmacological, and behavioural research. Depression is also part of an everyday vocabulary and mixes easily with common sense talk about feelings of sadness, anxiety, stress, disappointment, and confusion. Rom Harré and Robert Finlay-Jones in 'Emotion talk across times' (1986) take a longer view of depression by looking at the 'obsolete' historical emotion called accidie. Since the beginning of early Roman Christianity, acedia (as it was initially called) was a term applied to the emotional state of being spiritually lost, weak, and miserable. Acedia could also lead to vice and sin. Its cause, especially for religious persons, lay in the lack of joy and conviction they felt when fulfilling spiritual tasks. Thus treatment for acedia required spiritual counselling and encouragement. When 'acedia' became 'accidie' in the Middle Ages, it grew as both a moral and an emotional problem.

However, in late medieval and Renaissance societies, melancholy emerged as a related emotional condition, the symptoms of which included sadness, laziness, forgetfulness, and gloominess, leading, in extreme cases, to suicide. Medicine at that time involved a diagnostic system based on balancing bodily fluids or humours: blood, phlegm, yellow bile, and black or blue bile. Each humour was aligned to a specific colour, season, and position of the stars and planets. An excess of yellow bile could create cholera (orange 'anger'). Too much phlegm could result in 'lethargy'. Melancholy was 'blue' and characteristic of night time, autumn, and chilliness. In 1586 when Robert Burton wrote *Anatomy of melan-*

choly, melancholy was known as a condition that could afflict everybody; indeed, it was seen as part of the human condition itself and gave the sufferer reflexive opportunities, as Burton says, "'to be more exact and curious in pondering the very moments of things'" (Burton in Harré and Finlay-Jones 1986, 224).

Melancholy was an aggregation of feelings appropriate to the personal dilemmas of early modern life in which sadness and confusion along with intellectual insight were thought to be the emotional counterpart of the enterprising spirit of the Renaissance as it broke with the religious bonds and certainties of the past. Today we do not suffer from the spiritual idleness and lethargy of accidie, or from the humoural imbalances and seasonal effects of melancholy. We do suffer from depression as a mood disturbance, however, and trace it to biological (neurological disorder, serotonin malfunction), psychological (experiences of isolation and abuse), and social (unemployment, poverty, marginalization) determinants. Thus clinical as well as cognitive therapies are prescribed. Yet accidie, melancholy, and depression have an intriguingly similar feeling base, which as historical research documents has woven its way through the experience of Self as some emotional states become obsolete and others take their place with new authority and legitimacy. If we approached other emotions in the same way—according to their supposed causes (spiritual, medical, psychological), places of emergence (the body, the mind, the soul, the brain), authority figures (the priest, the physician, the psychiatrist), and forms of expression and discourse—we might also discover the social conditions underlying our own emotional states and their connection to worlds that seem so different in time and space.

A sociologically relevant emotion linked to depression is self-esteem, which sociologist John P. Hewitt (1998) considers a 'myth' because we *believe* in self-esteem despite the scattered nature of the scientific research. Self-esteem has become an explanation system for who we are and why we succeed or fail. As an emotional meter ('high' or 'low' self-esteem), it is a powerful metaphor trumpeted alike by motivational speakers, industrial leaders, exercise and diet experts, education reformers, and self-help proponents who advocate assertiveness and recovery. Whereas self-esteem originally referred to the honourable recognition of a person's accomplishments earned over a lifetime, today it means a person 'feeling good' about himself or herself. If self-feelings have replaced self-accomplishments as the most important indicator of personal achievement today, Hewitt asks whether self-esteem is truly the master emotion it is claimed to be. Further, he questions whether self-esteem programs in schools do stimulate successful performance and if not whether it is realistic to expect such programs to resolve the educational problems of students that are likely due to social inequality, school underfunding, and issues of housing and employment. As Hewitt says, 'the chorus of voices in praise of self-esteem merely drowns out the voices of others who argue that it is the social system itself that produces and perpetuates inequality' (1998, 95).

WHAT IS LOVE?

It would be impossible in a discussion of the sociology of the Self and the emotions not to include *love*, our culture's most cherished yet elusive personal aspiration. Love is really a multi-faceted emotion, articulated by the central image of the human 'heart', by which we become attached to others, God(s), nature, pets, nations, children, and Self. Our popular culture and media float endless messages encouraging us to do 'anything for love', including dying for it. Of the many facets of love, it is romantic love that seems to loom so large in our lives as the purest form of emotional truth. However, as John Gillis claims (1988), the experience of love in Western societies has dramatically changed over the past four centuries. From the sixteenth to the eighteenth century, the body and its fluids, movements, and actions were seen as the seat of emotional expression and force. The body *was* emotional, and through it love was ritualized less as a kind of *drive* than as a public *script* to be acted out in the presence of others. The signs of romantic love, such as holding hands, kissing, and embracing, had weighty social meaning because they demonstrated a person's affections. Since love was a physical essence, magical charms, potions, certain foods and herbs, divining, and fortune-telling could affect it. If marriage followed the proper enactment of the script of love, then marriage too was a public project involving family arrangements. Thus the experiences and expressions of romantic love were far less gender-differentiated than they are today because they were not based simply on private intimacy. But the magic of love has certainly not disappeared, as advertisements for aftershaves, perfume, diamonds, pearls, and of course chocolate indicate with their extravagant promises of instant attraction and romance.

In the nineteenth and early twentieth centuries, love became an emotion associated with deep, pure feeling. The social conventions of the new middle class degraded bodily expressions of emotion as dangerous and vulgar and reduced physical love to sexuality. By the mid-nineteenth century, wedding convention dictated that women should be dressed in white and veiled to symbolize feminine purity. Not surprisingly, this was also the period when homosexuality and lesbianism were constructed as deviant and unnatural and non-Western peoples portrayed as promiscuous and uncivilized. Most important, discourses on love were imbued with scientific gender-specific theories of sexual difference, pathologies, 'needs', and 'drives'. For women, the enforced personal search for and expectation of love became the sentimentalized route to a new femininity characterized as 'soft', 'weak', 'vulnerable', and 'delicate' (Cancian 1986). Today the world of Harlequin novels, soap operas, and Valentine's Day and anniversary celebrations continue to remind us that women are supposedly so preoccupied with romance that they accept sexually passive roles. In her study comparing marketing images in the personal ads of women and men, Elizabeth Jagger (2001) shows that the descriptors for women focus on the body and ideals of caring and nurturing. Slim, fit, petite, attractive, along with warm, supportive, fun, and committed, are the kinds of terms used to define the romantic feminine image, with fewer references to career success or independent lifestyle than in the personal ads for men.

By claiming that emotions have unique histories, cultural contexts, and social meanings, sociologists are not denying the private life of feeling or the power of emotional experiences as life-shaping individual events (see Bendelow and Williams 1998). The emotional progression from dating to falling in love to marriage is akin to the human maturation process itself and part of the architecture of the modern soul. This is obvious in the cluster of troubling love-related emotions such as jealousy (see Clanton 1989). Indeed, there is often a discrepancy between what is expected of us and what we actually feel, as is the case in traditional weddings when emotional levels are pushed so high that they require careful management by the bride and groom (Hochschild 1998). Hence the value of the sociology of emotions is its capacity to map the structures that give emotional work its meaning and at the same time critique the social order in which emotions are hierarchically arranged. Even in our post-modern world where virtual and electronic technologies can make identities spurious, experimental, multiple, and fantastical and 'saturate' (Gergen 1991) or 'McDonaldize' (Ritzer 2002) the Self, emotions still constitute a realm of social meaning that ground the Self in reflexive action (see Hall 1995; Bargh et al. 2002). In the end, if we learn that we do not always feel what we are supposed to feel and seek to be otherwise, then perhaps this is not necessarily a bad thing but rather a sign of our critical agency to challenge our society's restrictive making of our inner selves.

SELF AND IDENTITY IN TIME

To expand our understanding of the social Self further, this section looks at the life course and social time. The progression from birth, babyhood, childhood, and adolescence to middle-age, old age, dying, and death seems to occur quite naturally, as if human maturation is simply a matter of identities, bodies, and ages developing in tandem. This is why developmental thinkers such as Sigmund Freud, Erik Erikson, and Jean Piaget theorized that individual growth was a succession of psychophysical stages of abilities, energies, hormones, and needs. However, sociologists also ask about the social construction of the life course. When does childhood begin and end? When are you supposed to be 'grown up'? What is a 'mid-life crisis'? These are social and historical questions about aging that emerge from the political making of the modern population (Hareven 1995; Settersten, Jr 2003). For example, childhood is a relatively recent category, which has been extended into increasingly later parts of the life course because of institutional changes in education, law, the family, and work and the consumerist marketing of children's products, buoyed by professional expertise about childhood (Steinberg and Kincheloe 1997; Driscoll 2002). Similarly, adolescence is a term invented in the early twentieth century with the publication of American psychologist G. Stanley Hall's influential text, *Adolescence: Its psychology, anthropology, sociology, sex, crime, religion and education* (1904). The title of this book readily suggests that adolescence was already a problematized category and source of cultural anxiety about juvenile deviancy, which still exists today in public discourses about 'risky' youth (Bennett 2001; Mitchell et al. 2004).

The *aging* Self is another important dilemma because we are unsure when old age begins and how to age successfully across the transitional boundaries marking work and retirement, parenthood and grandparenthood, and caregiving and care-receiving roles. For these reasons, as Karp and Yoels point out (2004), there is a tension between age norms and age meanings. Age norms structure the life course according to social practices and standards, which are often contradictory or double standards, particularly around gender. For instance, it is considered normal for older men to marry younger women but not the reverse, although on average women outlive men. Women are considered 'grown up' only when they display signs of being nurturing and sacrificial towards their husbands, children, and families, whereas male maturity is linked to work, career, and retirement. While age norms may dictate what is appropriate behaviour for each age, they also vary culturally and historically. Today, the greatest source of variation comes from consumerism, which, in its quest to keep a middle-class public mired in a losing battle against aging, has radically altered our age norms by obscuring traditional divisions between young and old. Marketing strategies also challenge conventional medical and political life course models to create new consumer age groups such as 'boomers', 'empty-nesters', 'pre-teens', and the 'young-old'. The age at which people go to work, get married, or have children also fluctuates according to ethnic, regional, and class differences.

Age is a multi-dimensional process because it involves a 'feeling age' as well as biological, psychological, social, and chronological ages. Feeling age is where aging identities and experiences of Self intersect. For example, women often remark on the fact that they are not 'looked at' and thus feel 'invisible' in middle age and later, especially after living through an earlier socialization process that emphasized the importance of physical attraction. British cultural sociologists Mike Featherstone and Mike Hepworth use the term 'mask of aging' to identify the growing gap between the experiences and the 'look' of aging (Featherstone and Hepworth 1991; Biggs 1997). Just as middle-aged and older people are encouraged to feel themselves as young, they are betrayed by their aging bodies and pressed to grow older without aging (Katz 2001). While body technologies and cosmetic treatments are making it easier to choose to 'look as young as you feel', they also illustrate the extent to which our culture is caught between unrealistic expectations to remain young and the realities of aging against which we must struggle in the future. In the past, aging identities were greatly affected by stereotypes of incapacity, decline, poverty, and dependency. Today, as Western societies face rapidly growing aging populations, there is a prevailing myth fanned by anti-welfare ideologues that aging populations will bankrupt the welfare state, overburden social and medical programs, and deprive younger generations of social security resources (see Gee and Gutman 2000). The effect of this scenario on older persons is pressure to conform to governmental health promotion agendas and heed the cosmetic, financial, recreational, exercise, and nutritional industries that promise healthy, active lifestyles (Katz and Marshall 2003). Where poverty, disease, despair, and decline exist, they are unfairly publicized as the result of individual failure.

Given the complex relationship between the stages of the life course and age norms, age meanings, and age feeling, the aging Self becomes a dialectical space of interaction between inner and outer conditions. In the words of philosopher Gilles Deleuze, the aging Self could be considered a type of *folding* (1993): a dynamic shaping and pleating of subjective worlds as they interact with the external imperatives for living in time. As such, life courses are the 'inside of the out-side' (Deleuze 1988, 97), both uniquely individual and biographical and collec-tively sustained by the cultural priorities around successful aging. In gerontology, research on life-course narratives supports this folding image by examining later life as a time of wisdom and perspective when self-consciousness is shaped through the art of articulating and sharing coherent stories about who we are and where we might be heading in the future (Gubrium and Holstein 1998; Kenyon et al. 2001).

OTHER SELVES, OTHERS WAYS TO BE

Thus far, this chapter has claimed the Self as social because of its construction through meaningful social interaction, collective emotional states, and aging identities. However, the horizontal plane of social interaction is crosscut by a ver-tical plane of power relations, often expressed as social norms and moral codes of conduct. Such norms and codes are largely responsible for sustaining dominant cultural notions about deviance and difference. Thus micro-sociological studies that tackle the social construction of these notions are crucial to our understand-ing of how the division of populations into 'normal' and 'abnormal' categories affects our everyday lives (see Beaman 2000). Of particular importance is how we see our 'selves' in relation to 'others'.

While crime is one obvious area in which critiques of deviance, social con-trol, and Self/Other constructs have been vital to sociology (see chapters 12, 13, and 14), health is another prominent area because deviance and sickness are so entwined, as are the institutional and legal responses to them. Peculiar to our contemporary era, however, is the fact that the major illnesses of developed soci-eties are no longer infectious epidemics or sanitation problems but neurological and personal spectra of disorders—particularly Alzheimer Disease (AD), atten-tion deficit disorder, autism, depression, and anxiety disorders. These problems have neither precise causes nor definite cures. They are not transmitted through infection or contact, and diagnostic testing is often vague and uncertain despite new genetic research. Pharmaceutical companies are investing heavily in the development of top-grossing sales of medications targeting these disorders because millions of individuals are now considered to be suffering from them. Hence we have an interesting situation whereby typically normalizing and med-icalizing forms of power run up against widespread disorders that are difficult to trace, codify, institutionalize, rehabilitate, cure, or generally 'treat'. At the same time, this situation can teach us a great deal about how the attributes of success-ful selves are socially ordered, with rationality, language, memory, and self-con-trol being the most prized. People judged as deficient in or lacking such attributes become problems. For example, autistic children used to be considered mentally retarded, and people with Alzheimer Disease have always been regarded as non-existent selves, bodies without minds. If we looked at autism and AD in other ways, however, what might they tell us about the nature of different selves? How might they provide insight into other ways of being human, beyond tradi-tional sociological models of deviance?

Since neurological scientists Leo Kamer and Hans Asperger first began researching autism in the 1940s as a disorder located in the brain, the image of autism has been that of a rogue brain bypassing the protective mantle of the Self and the mind. The research on autism shows that brain, mind, and Self have a unique relationship that produces the obsessive behaviours and intense vulnerability to environmental stimuli that we know to be autism's main features. In a collection of writings in his *An anthropologist on Mars* (1995), Oliver Sacks explores how neurological disorders such as autism provide new prospects as well as problems to those afflicted with it. Included in his book is the story of Temple Grandin, a professor of veterinary biology at Colorado State University in Denver. Grandin is internationally renowned for engineering new humane livestock facilities and slaughterhouses—and is also autistic. Her own writing (Grandin and Scariano 1986; Grandin 1995; Grandin and Johnson 2004) and speaking engagements have been tremendously helpful in bringing to public awareness the experience of being an autistic Self. While she has no problem communicating with cows, Grandin has many problems dealing with people, with whom she has learned to build a 'normal' presentation of Self to express the emotional cues and behavioural codes others expect of her. When Sacks visited one of Grandin's slaughterhouses, he saw how human creativity can derive from the fixations and obsessions with detail, patterns, and routines that are typically autistic. The poetics, imagination, and emotions of 'normal' selfhood may appear to be absent in autism, but understanding people like Temple Grandin reveals that autistic persons are greatly concerned with their place in the outside world and at the same time with forming a sense of Self as an expansive and compensatory resource to secure inner life in relation to that outside world.

As with autism, it is claimed that Alzheimer Disease is on the rise, and it has been called 'the disease of the century' (Robertson 1990). Many of us know people or have family members with AD and are aware of the tragic suffering that comes with the loss of their cognitive and physical abilities. In the later stages of AD, it is not unusual to wonder whether there is still a person 'there' at all—someone who still feels, laughs, cries, and experiences pain and joy. Like autism, AD is a recent medical category, discovered in 1907 by German medical researcher and neuropathologist Alois Alzheimer, who considered it a very rare form of pre-senile dementia. The prognosis was that if AD occurred as a pre-senile dementia between the ages of 40 and 60, it would inevitably be followed by full-blown senile dementia after the age of 60. In the 1960s and 1970s, AD was expanded to encompass other cognitive and behavioural problems, including senility itself. Today, AD is part of a disease movement, with millions of dollars invested in the promise of a cure or at least treatments aimed at reversal.

Outside of the medical research and disease etiology, what does AD tell us about the Self, especially as loss of Self, language, and memory appear to be its main characteristics? Tom Kitwood was a British social psychologist and dementia researcher who, along with others, pioneered radical 'person-centred' approaches to AD (Kitwood 1997). Their approach emphasizes that AD is not just a progressive brain disorder but a condition that can also be affected by individual social and psychological conditions. Individuals who suffer from dementia still retain something unique about their sense of Self, which can be expressed through the movements and gestures of their bodies (Kontos 2004). Selfhood may not be expressed in rational or comprehensible ways, but neither should it be dismissed. Just as Sacks discovered the creative potential of people suffering neurological challenges, gerontologist and dramatist Anne Basting organized story-telling workshops for people with AD in a project called Time Slips (2001; www.timeslips.org). After collecting 100 stories, she transformed them into a play that has been performed in several places to great acclaim. Basting's interest in these stories is not as partially remembered narratives or as data for reminiscence therapy but as stories with an artistry and spontaneity that does *not* rely on memory. Indeed, the Time Slips stories and plays are less about dementia than about the expression of Self. However, the coherence of Self in the stories is located relationally—between persons—not based on the individual. As Basting says,

> The stories are composites of the voices of all participants—the facilitators and the storytellers. The stories do not tell the narrative of one independent self, but of relational selves. They help us hear the experience of dementia without mistakenly falling back on a mythic construction of the independent self (Basting 2001, 89).

Basting's story-makers are freed from the binaries of having to be right or wrong, rational or nonsensical, independent or dependent. Unbound from the conventional logic that there is no Self without cognitive functionality and the means to express it rationally and cogently, the story-makers connect to life in new ways. As with autism's unmediated Self, the Alzheimer relational Self should lead us to suspect that there are other kinds of Selves out there, waiting to tell us even more about how thin the line is between Self and others and how narrowly and contingently constructed are the rules about what is normal and what is not. As Michel Foucault has stated, the process of subjectivization not only 'results in the constitution of the subject' but also in a subjectivity 'which is only one of the given possibilities of organizing a consciousness of self' (1989 [1984], 330).

CONCLUSION: FROM SHELBY TO THE WORLD

In W.O. Mitchell's novel *Roses are difficult here* (1990), a young sociologist from Ontario, Dr J.L. Melquist, decides to study a small Canadian prairie town fictionally called Shelby. Two townsmen, Matt and Clem, meet at the office of the local newspaper, the *Chinook*, to discuss the sociologist's arrival. Clem says, 'Just what is she doin' here in Shelby?' Matt replies, 'Looking us over'. Clem asks, 'What for?' and Matt explains, 'She's—ah—she's a sociologist.' Clem, more befuddled, asks, 'What the hell's that?' Matt, again trying to calm things, responds, 'Tell you the truth, Clem, I'm not too clear about that myself. Sociology is a—type of science— or, ah, study.' Clem continues, 'What of?' Matt gets more technical, saying, 'Humans. Functioning of human society—fundamental laws of human relationships.' Finally, Clem poses the most important question yet: 'Just what the hell has all that got to do with us?'

This chapter has attempted to answer Clem's questions and explore the 'laws of human relationships' as they are lived through the Self as a social process. Sociology is about more than making connections between those who study it and those who are studied; it is also about demonstrating that the individual and society are intrinsically woven together. Thus the inhabitants of Shelby come to learn through the reflexive prism of Melquist's sociology that their social world is not an isolated community but part of the continuing universal experiment of social, large-brained, neotenic primates that began at the dawn of humanity.

Questions to Consider

1. Is everyday experience a bridge between outer worlds and inner lives? Give specific examples to support your response.
2. With critical reference to the theorists presented, do you think the Self is socially created?
3. How can we say that emotions have social and historical meanings and forms of expression when they are felt as so deeply personal and intimate? In this sense, what is love?
4. Do dominant notions of the 'other' configure dominant notions of the Self? Does our knowledge of autism and Alzheimer Disease confirm or challenge your response?

Notes

1. Goffman wrote wonderfully creative books such as *The presentation of self in everyday life* (1971 [1959]); *Asylums: Essays on the social situation of mental patients and other inmates* (1961); *Stigma: Notes on the management of spoiled identity* (1963); *Interaction ritual: Essays on face-to-face behavior* (1966); *Relations in public: Microstudies of the public order* (1971); and *Forms of talk* (1981).
2. Hochschild's text *The managed heart: The commercialization of human feeling* (1983) was a seminal study of the exploitation of emotional labour in the workplace. She later examined the problematical consequences of the blurring of emotional life at work and at home in her book *The second shift: Working parents and the revolution at home* (1990; see also Hochschild 2003).

IMAGINING THE SOCIAL

Part 2 shifts the focus of our discussion from self-identity to more direct concerns around the concept of the 'social'. Recall that the 'social' refers to a subject terrain that emerges when we focus directly on collective relations in and of themselves—without reducing this terrain to individual or psychological matters. More specifically, the essays in this Part question what that social may be, offer suggestions on how to address it (as well as why it is important to do so), and examine the concept's contemporary relevance.

In the opening chapter, Annette Burfoot responds to the question 'what is social reality?' She immediately rejects visions of 'social reality' as something stable, fixed, or absolute. She argues instead that social reality is a dynamic, shifting set of cultural constructions. These constructions materialize only because of context-specific cultural meanings, and so the idea of social reality is best understood through an analysis of culture. Thus she focuses on cultural studies as 'a relatively recent approach in sociology that both enriches and exposes what we understand as social reality and how we define it'. To understand how culture produces social realities, Burfoot suggests that we tap into insights gained from the ways that the discipline of cultural studies has developed over time. She highlights its focus on 'culture', 'cultural products', and 'cultural production', which it approaches through various theoretical perspectives, including psychoanalysis, ideology ('the socio-political organization of ideas'), semiology ('the study of signs and symbols'), and discourse analysis ('the illumination of how meaning-as-power flows through our taken-for-granted parlance or way of speaking'). Each of these objects and approaches sheds a different light on how to understand and examine the cultural creation of social reality.

The following chapter by R.A. Sydie wades directly into a not unheard view that social theory is abstract, 'obtuse, difficult, and of dubious relevance to everyday life'. In responding to the question 'is social theory useful?' Sydie begins by noting that early social theorists (e.g., Martineau, Durkheim) formulated theories about the 'personal troubles' as well as the 'societies' of the time. They did so with the aim of developing harmonious and peaceful social formations. Their theories served this aim, not as irrelevant abstractions but rather as direct explanations of everyday practices designed to point the way toward better relations with others.

Yet we all theorize whenever we try to make sense of our practices. What distinguishes sociological from everyday theorizing, however, is its commitment to critique. Sociological theory is useful because it raises basic questions about the very foundations of everyday social relations, and it does so with the aim of undoing specified (unjust, unequal, tyrannical, etc.) conditions. Theorizing demands a self-questioning social theorist (e.g., a feminist theorist) who understands the precariousness of being simultaneously creator and creature of the social relations criticized. With this in mind, Sydie explores how various modern social theorists developed universal explanations of 'order and progress' when offering theories of modern society. She usefully indicates how current (post-modern) conditions have undermined modern social theory, including its emphasis on homogeneous, universalizing images of progress, knowledge, and society. This undermining has demanded new approaches to the concept of society (to address diversity, for example) and opened the way for new forms of social theorizing. However, Sydie is clear: 'The explanatory capacity of social theory is important in confronting the abstractions of power, and there is as much need for social theory today as there was in the nineteenth century.'

'Does the past matter in sociology?' is the interrogative lead of Rob Beamish's chapter. His formulation of C. Wright Mills's sociological imagination takes as a starting point the personal troubles that Canadian sprinter Ben Johnson faced by having his Olympic gold medal stripped away because of steroid use. Beamish then locates this event within the wider social history of the Olympic Games to reflect on the powerful social pressures that Johnson faced when deciding to take steroids. This historical approach to sociology demonstrates just how complex the issues surrounding performance-enhancing substances are at the level of world-class sport; it also challenges the simple condemnation of *individual* athletes. Specifically, this chapter makes clear that without a lucid historical sense of the development of the Games, many important social factors that led to Johnson's personal troubles would be overlooked. For example, Beamish's analysis shows how such issues as increasing commercialization and professionalization have significantly eroded Coubertin's founding 'amateur' sport aspirations for the Games. Further, the Nazis confirmed the political, symbolic, and propagandistic utility of the Games in 1936, a facet of the Games that continued to be developed and exploited throughout the Cold War. Such historical developments shed light on the kind of broader pressures imposed on athletes to perform. In this context we can better understand Johnson's decision to use a performance-enhancing substance. That is, his biography and troubles are located within a wider social history that generates demands on athletes quite at odds with the fraternal public image of the Olympic Games. And it is precisely because the past matters in sociology that we can provide a macroanalysis of such micro 'troubles'.

In Chapter 9, Nob Doran responds to the question 'what do official statistics tell us about ourselves?' He does so by narrating his own personal intellectual journey through various social theories dealing with the status of official statistics. The chapter expressly challenges the common sense view that official statistics provide an objective, impartial representation of different aspects of society.

It outlines two levels of critique directed at this view. On a micro level, Doran describes how ethnomethodological approaches in sociology alerted him to the subjective, everyday decisions that statistical researchers must inevitably make when creating statistics, especially the founding categories (e.g., suicides, homicides) to which purportedly impartial statistical methods are directed. Rather than leading sociologists to accept social statistics as impartial knowledge, this approach directs them to examine the everyday social relations that produce particular statistics. Doran argues that Dorothy Smith's feminist and Marxist-inspired formulations improve on this approach by explicitly focusing on how power creates official social statistics. On a macro level, he sees Foucault's claim that power and knowledge are inseparably connected as opening the way for sociologists to examine the types of power that create statistical knowledge. Doran then outlines various debates on the precise form of that power.

As Lois Harder makes clear in her chapter, despite a few people who reflect on social welfare's potential to survive, Canadians continue to demand publicly funded social programs and assess governments partly on their ability to provide effective social services. In effect, they have responded in the affirmative to the question 'is social welfare viable?' However, she argues, this endorsement does not capture several important changes to the very idea as well as the provision of social welfare. Harder outlines the unique history of social welfare in Canada, then turns to an influential attack on (Keynesian) social welfare precepts that emerged in the 1980s (especially in the area of social assistance), launched by people aligned with broadly based 'neo-liberal' frameworks. They did so from within a rapidly changing socio-economic context and alongside a protracted constitutional crisis. Despite internal differences, advocates of neo-liberal thinking sought to reduce the state's role in regulating markets, families, and communities and called for a thriving 'private sphere'. When directed to social welfare, this approach called for a system overhaul that emphasized private (consumer) 'choice' and 'responsibility'. Harder highlights how such thinking helped to bring about significant changes to social welfare, examining four policy examples: the National Child Benefit, employment insurance, social assistance, and health care. These examples show the extent to which social welfare is directly involved in shaping individual and social identities, 'integrating citizens into the prevailing mode of economic production', and legitimating particular forms of government. They indicate that the viability of any vision of social welfare (such as Keynesian or neo-liberal) is dependent on just how far it reinforces social relations between individuals, families, communities, markets, and the state.

The final chapter in Part 2, 'Who Governs Whom in Canada?', begins by recalling one of the book's recurring themes (see Chapters 1, 6, 9, 12, 13, 14, and 18): governance—or the ways in which people's thoughts and actions are part and parcel of the ways they are controlled and governed. The chapter recognizes that we are all governed by a complex interface of formal, informal, local, and general control techniques. These techniques include 'formal laws and rules, social conventions, guidelines, suggestions, timetables, family obligations, our expectations of ourselves, nature, and so on'. Much of the chapter is devoted to a careful examination of specific examples of governing in the Canadian context. For instance, Moore examines the case of Robert Latimer, convicted of murdering his 12-year-old daughter, who had a serious disability. She contrasts the formal law governing this action (first-degree murder) in the Criminal Code of Canada with the conflicting social conventions around morality—specifically, the right to die because of prolonged suffering versus the right to life independent of the quality of that life. Moore's examination demonstrates the limits of Durkheim's 'collective conscience' theory as a way of understanding how we are regulated. Through other examples, including witchcraft and sexual orientation, the chapter further elaborates and develops the sociology of governance.

Chapter 6

What Is Social Reality?

Annette Burfoot

INTRODUCTION

Since the inception of sociology, the question of what is real in the social world has both excited and hampered the study of society and the meaning of social relations. Consider the questions raised by early sociologists such as Émile Durkheim (1952 [1897]). He sought statistical ways of identifying, measuring, and predicting social 'realities' such as one's matrimonial state and its effect on suicide rates. Now compare this with the C. Wright Mills (1959) 'sociological imagination', which, as previously noted, sees a link between personal problems (like losing your job and feeling very depressed as a result) and social or more widespread issues (for example, an economic recession or socio-technical change). In both cases, the question of what constitutes social reality is fundamental.

For Durkheim, there appeared to be some relationship (a positive correlation) between men being married and lower suicide rates. Is it then a social fact that in order to be happy as a male in our society you need to be heterosexual and married? Today we challenge such assumptions as social facts. We also look at society from more varied perspectives, including perspectives that generate different social realities by asking different questions based on different assumptions. So the reality of higher than average suicide rates among young homosexual males may be presented more along the lines of Mills's sociological imagination as an individual anguish that results not from a failure to meet heterosexual norms but as a result of widespread homophobia. The facts have changed; social reality has shifted. And how has that happened?

This is where it is important to add culture to the mix because it gives us even more avenues to explore rather than to simply unearth new social facts. Instead, we question how social realities are themselves constructed. In other words, the study of culture in sociology has helped to sharpen the discipline by shifting the focus from a scientific model of exploration, reporting, and experimentation of social facts (as if they were fixed things) to the critical study of complex socio-cultural relations that generate social facts through dynamic and fluid processes. For example, in the documentary film *Paris is burning* (1990), 'houses' of young gay men in New York City compete at balls as they parade various carefully constructed looks (some as exaggerations of femininity, some as parodies of masculine culture). It was this culture that inspired the popular culture icon Madonna to write and perform her song 'Vogue' (1990), which in the song's video version also featured members of the House of Extravaganza, one of the groups of transsexuals from *Paris is burning*.

It was this culture that gave rise to the verb 'to vogue'—to carefully masquerade and exaggerate a certain look. Within this culture, sexuality is worn like a mask and sexuality's socio-cultural manufacture is revealed. Suicide among these young men is also featured in the film—but so is brutal gay-bashing leading to murder. The latter indicates continued social sanctions against what the young men perceive as normal sexual practice. Madonna's apolitical appropriation of this gay cultural practice, the delight and pride among the young men at the balls, their formation of a new community complete with transsexual 'mothers' who provide support and encouragement to otherwise socially ostracized young men and boys, the difficulty of living outside the norms of heterosexuality, and sexuality as masquerade are all lessons that can be learned from a cultural study of this film.

In this chapter we will examine cultural studies as a relatively recent approach in sociology that both enriches and exposes what we understand as social reality and how we define it. We will first examine cultural studies through the history of the study of culture since there have been important changes and fiery disputes as to what constitutes cultural studies itself. Several key arguments continue today, and rather than weaken the field, as some argue, we will see how they enrich it as well as the discipline of sociology. We will conclude with the state of cultural studies today with particular attention to what is happening here in Canada.

Back to the Future: Cultural Studies from the Sociology of Culture

It might seem logical to approach a history of cultural studies from 'the start', normally thought to be situated in the late nineteenth century when culture became the subject of philosophical and political debate in particular. However, we shall start with the most recent approaches and work our way back. This strategy will move us from the material with which we have the most experience to material that may be more difficult to grasp or locate in experience. It will also help to explain how we arrived at the current situation. What follows begins by looking at several important trends—namely, trends that engage concepts and issues of social marginalization in culture. We then move to the establishment of cultural studies as one of the first and most successful interdisciplinary studies in contemporary academia. This leads us to the early youth studies and popular culture studies in the UK that helped to establish the Centre for Cultural Studies at the University of Birmingham. We will examine how current cultural studies arose from both criticism of and approaches (theoretical and methodological) established by the Birmingham school. Current theories and methods serving cultural studies, such as discourse analysis, material culture, and visual culture (to name just a few) also emanate from well-established sub-disciplines, including many sociological ones.

A good deal of attention has been paid to the study of the culture generating and surrounding hip hop (George 1998; Potter 1995; Rose 1994). This music genre, perhaps more than any other, illustrates the problems of producing culture from the margins, a social location that is typically understood as the space furthest away from the site of political control (or the ideological centre). In the case of hip hop, poor urban black kids, initially from the streets of various New Jersey cities, began a form of musical ballad that combined chanting, singing, and lecturing in a street-like dialect familiar to their specific lifestyles and experiences. It also had a particular look that included oversized jeans intentionally worn provocatively low-slung and unhemmed, the material constantly dragged and torn, thus literally taking apart the then-current designer-jeans couture. The hip hop look also included status-seeking emblems such as chains, some golden, with diamante-encrusted logos, often taken from high-end luxury cars like the Mercedes. Lyrics spoke, and continue to do so today, directly to young black men about the oppression of blacks in the United States and often evoked a frustrated and militant response to this oppression. Consider the following lyrics from 'Breathe' (2004) by the hip hop artist Fabolous that is both a celebration of the artist having made it and a criticism of continued racial harassment:

> U niggas can't share my air
> Or walk around in the pair I wear
> And I'm getting better year by year
> Like they say Juan do
> Cops couldn't smell me if you
> Brought the canines through
>
> but I keep the glocks in the stashes
> cuz the cops wanna lock and harass us
> and they make it hard to BREATHE
> they has to react
> like havin a asthma attack
> when they see the plasma in back

Along with such lyrics, the look was meant to alienate parody and criticize a dominant white culture while advancing a raw new street-based black one. It was a cultural practice from the margins. Logos were taken by the artists and their fans, often in rampant shoplifting, from prestigious designers such as Hilfiger, Polo, DKNY, and Nike to feed the hip hop look. Designers realized the profit potential from their logos appearing in a cultural venue that was being picked up and mass-marketed as an exciting new sound and look to all of America and beyond, not just to black communities in the US northeast. Rappers who triggered the trend in the 1980s also started what Naomi Klein calls 'cool hunting' or logo appropriation (Klein 2000). For example, in 1986 the rap group Run-DMC featured their favourite brand in the song 'My Adidas' (rap is commonly understood as the cultural precursor of hip hop). Now consider what happens when, initially reluctant to sponsor the group since rap was then seen as culturally insignificant in the popular music world and politically problematic because of its militant message and blatant criticism of dominant culture, Adidas executives attend a Run-DMC concert:

> At a crucial moment, while the rap group was performing the song ['My Adidas'], one of the members yelled out, 'Okay, everybody in the house, rock your Adidas!'—and three thousand sneakers shot in the air. The Adidas executives couldn't reach for their checkbooks fast enough (Christopher Vaughn, quoted in Klein 2000, 74).

Pilfering from the apparent dominant culture in the form of logo appropriation in black music culture was then 'blown up' by hip hop during the late 1990s and the early years of the new millennium. But as Klein points out, the companies whose logos are 'hunted' and displayed in now highly popular hip hop videos and concerts enjoy a very profitable return in this newly defined youth market. Designers for companies such as Nike appropriate the appropriated look, reproduce it on a massive scale, and sell it back to the communities that created the look. Is this a successful cultural production from the margins, or is it cultural appropriation for profit?

In contrast, Rinaldo Walcott (2000), a Canadian academic concerned with black culture in Canada, raises another issue associated with racialization and music—namely, national identity. He examines the Canadian rapper Devon (Devon Martin) and his 1989 album *It's my nature* as an example of a common ground marked by racialization of blacks beyond national boundaries. Walcott describes this territory in terms of Devon's open criticism of the Los Angeles and Toronto police forces in his notorious and successful song 'Mr Metro' (written after he was stopped by Los Angeles police just for being near the scene of a crime). He reveals how blacks throughout North America are associated more with criminality and violence than with any national identity and in fact are denied the advantages of citizenship. In the same vein, Walcott also describes the relocation of rapper Maestro Fresh-Wes from Canada to the US as a worrying of the category Canadian. Walcott explains how the financially successful rapper released his first album from his new home, *Naaah, dis kid* can't *be from Canada* (1994), as a way of confirming his Canadian identity through the double negative. He describes how a national identity is denied blacks in Canada by dominant cultural practices that effectively marginalize most Canadian blacks as delinquents and potential criminals and denies them the privileges of non-blacks such as: no police harassment, no automatic policing of their neighbourhoods, free and unproblematic choice of residence.

To connect these cultural studies to questions of what constitutes Canadian social reality does not take much effort. Before the explosion and dissemination of black culture throughout mainstream North American society via rap and hip hop, either little attention was paid to black populations or it focused on purported criminality and deviance. In Kingston, Ontario, a police report based on the new and controversial practice of monitoring for potential racial profiling by police revealed that blacks living in the Kingston area (0.6 per cent of the city's population) were three times more likely to be stopped by police than whites and 'black male youths were targeted more than any other group in the city' (McMahon and Armstrong 2005).

Before publication of the report, this problem was unearthed through an internal investigation of the Kingston police force following allegations of racially motivated police checks and arrests of the youth Mark Wallen, who between the age of 16 and 19 twice had guns pulled on him by police officers without any charges laid (Armstrong 2004). One of these incidents, and the basis of Wallen's grievance, started with an anonymous tip to the police officers involved from a passer-by (white) who claimed that two black youths were ambling down the sidewalk looking into cars. Wallen testified at the grievance hearings that he and his friend were walking home from a basketball game when police stopped them on the street for questioning, a procedure that included one of the officers pulling out a revolver and training it on the two young men (Armstrong 2004). The officer responsible for pulling his gun on Wallen explained that the youth looked much older than his 18 years and indeed he thought that Wallen was in his 30s. This, along with his appraisal of Mark's overall attitude as aggressive, was offered as a defence of the officer's behaviour. Mark, in return, said he was frustrated at being stopped by police for no apparent reason and told his friend that he did not have to answer the officer's questions. In an earlier incident, Mark and his brother were stopped by police while driving their father's car—a Mercedes. They were pulled from the car and searched by police.

Hip hop highlights the normalization of this treatment of black young men by police. It also reveals the normalization process as a racialization that, for example, led to the need for the Kingston report. Whether or not one believes the report's findings and other claims of racially motivated police harassment, police profiling now has a place at the table. The issue becomes one to tackle and thus is culturally located in the social spectrum: it becomes a *sociological* issue. Note that cultural studies does not seek or claim a single approach to this particular issue. In fact, there is a great deal of debate about mainstream culture's appropriation of black culture and political resistance as hip hop. Questions arise such as: Has hip hop lost its critical edge and become a mass-produced copy of the genre with no political bite in which even white hip hop artists such as Eminem prosper? Has the culture of hip hop changed the social reality of inner city black youth, or has it cleverly packaged race-based dissent so that calls for material changes simply peter out? Has racialization in the US and Canada changed as a result? What about those who are also racialized as 'other' but do not fit the hip hop profile, such as young black women?

In both rap and hip hop, not only have women had a very difficult time in becoming recognized artists but the representation of femininity can be highly problematic, especially in terms of sexual objectification. Consider the following lines from the chorus of the song 'Ain't got nothing' by David Banner, listed as one of the top hip hop songs in May 2005:

Now we can take a walk to my truck (BUT I AINT GOT NUTTIN)
And I ain't tryin to say you're a duck (BUT I AIN'T GOT NUTTIN)
And I ain't tryin to say you're a ho (BUT I AIN'T GOT NUTTIN)

The lyrics become much more sexually explicit and continue along the theme of the 'brother doin' bad' who has no money but wants sexual contact with a black woman on demand. The tone is aggressive and the message is clear: why should he have to pay for sex, especially when he has been beaten down by a white-dominated society? It also implies that sexually appealing black women are sex workers. To those who watch music videos in general, it is no news that the images accompanying many hip hop songs include scene after scene of highly sexually objectified young black women (and occasionally white women) as props and the necessary signs of the black man having 'made it'. These women are trophies alongside collections of fast cars, golden chains, and diamante-encrusted logos. So for black women, hip hop may not be the cultural celebration and resistance to dominant culture that it can be for black men.

Cultural critic bell hooks, who has done much to advance speculations of gender and race in cultural studies, has a relevant approach to this apparent race/gender dilemma. In an essay titled 'Eating the other: Desire and resistance' (2001), hooks points to how dominant white culture is fascinated by others (usually referred to as the 'other' as a way of highlighting the process of domination). Using diverse cultural examples such as literature, film, and advertisements, hooks demonstrates how this fascination is based on a hidden and essentialist understanding of social reality according to whiteness or being white (this refers to the notion that biological factors such as racial difference determine social outcomes such as violence and sexual practices). She argues that it is usually the racialized 'other' that is accused of essentialism (including the oversexed black male) while whiteness remains relatively unexamined. She locates the relatively recent resurgence of 'black nationalism', which we can match both historically and culturally to the rise of rap and hip hop, within white cultural imperialism and white yearning to possess the 'other' by invading black life and appropriating and violating black culture. As a survival strategy, black nationalism surfaces most strongly when white cultural appropriation of black culture threatens to de-contextualize and thereby erase knowledge of the specific historical and social context of black experience from which cultural productions and distinct black styles emerge (2001, 431).

Nationalism here can be understood in the context of what Wolcott describes as black culture reduced to one of violence, criminality, and social marginalization. This also makes problematic the simple reading of hip hop culture as sexist. According to hooks, we need to examine the invisible role of dominant (white) attitudes towards gender, especially in the context of the now widely distributed and consumed culture of hip hop. Her examples include an overheard conversation between young white, upper middle-class male students at Yale University about having sex with as many young women from racially diverse (non-white) backgrounds as possible. She describes this as part of white culture's desire to consume the 'other' as difference. And by setting the table, so to speak, the 'other' is objectified and made exotic—or desirable and ready for consumption by the dominant culture. Applied to the example of hip hop and its treatment of femininity, we could argue that sexual explicitness is a response to this cultural construction by whites of what it means to be black. It is a masquerade of racial stereotyping.

Consider this interview following the release of the Kingston report on policing and racial profiling:

> At just 14, Jahbari Blackstock, who is black, said he's been stopped by police about 10 times in the last year, which he considered 'not that much'. Each time, police took down his name, and each time, he said he wasn't committing a crime and has no criminal record. The Queen Elizabeth Collegiate and Vocational School student said he was usually stopped walking to and from basketball practice. . . . He said he was questioned last week by an undercover police officer as he walked past a house where police were conducting an apparent drug bust. Blackstock was wearing a shirt with the words 'G-Unit', named for a popular hip-hop trio. He said the officer quizzed him about his clothing. 'He was like, "Are you the G-Unit?" and I was like, "No." He was just being stupid' (McMahon 2005).

Blackstock's experience with the Kingston police reveals a kind of 'play' with racialized types and the cultural masquerade. First, the black youth knowingly wears a shirt branding a hip hop group famous for its militant pro-black nationalist stance. The police respond to this signal of racialized defiance as potential trouble and stop the boy on the street for no other reason, thus reinforcing the position of blacks, especially young black men associated with hip hop culture, in the dominant culture. Blackstock knows that the police officer is testing the strength of that connection by asking in effect, 'How militant are you?' The line between the cultures is clearly drawn by Blackstock's use of the word 'stupid'. A black teenager calling a police officer stupid could mean big trouble for the youth, but here it is more a response to the officer trying to connect to Blackstock's world in a joking manner. But sociologically speaking, it is no joke to be stopped by police 10 times in one year for walking home from basketball practice (another culturally heavy symbol, racially speaking)—which is probably why youths like Blackstock wear shirts expressing militant attitudes toward racialized black life. And they do so effectively by parading the objectification of blacks and their culture.

Now consider the following lyrics listed as the number one hip hop song in May 2005 on an Internet site for hip hop lyrics. The song is '1, 2 step' by the female hip hop artist Ciara:

> This beat is outrageous, so contagious
> Make you crave it, jazz made it
> So retarded, top charted, ever since the day I started

Strut my stuff and yes I flaunt it
Goodies make the boys jump on it . . .

I shake it like jello, make the boys say hello . . .
Because I'm 5 foot 2, I wanna dance with you
And I am sophisticated fun, I eat filet minon [*sic*]
I'm nice and young. Best believe in number one

Besides being an exaltation of music and dancing and an acknowledgement of the jazz roots of hip hop (another popularized cultural form appropriated from blacks), the song also articulates a young black woman's enjoyment of her sexuality as it plays with the popularization of black culture. Just as she seems to acknowledge her fame as out of her control ('so retarded'), she knowingly flaunts her 'goodies' at the boys. She may not be able to control the sexual objectification of black women, but she can acknowledge and exploit her own objectification.

The Rise of Popular Culture from Youth Studies

Before race became complicated with gender within cultural studies, much attention was paid to the process of masquerade in terms of femininity (assumed to be white; see Doane 1982). And Madonna was its primary icon. As video became the dominant vehicle for delivering popular music in which the role of femininity was chiefly a highly objectified sexual backdrop, Madonna began to perform what was initially deemed outrageous. As an Italo-American raised as a Catholic, she sported huge crucifixes and made a video featuring a sexual rapport with Christ ('Like a prayer'). She emphasized her sexualized attributes to the point of not only of wearing her underwear as outerwear but also extending her bras into exaggerated cone shapes. Her videos and live performances became legend for breaking boundaries of moral decency (apparently masturbating on stage and including so-called deviant and relatively explicit sexual practices in videos such as 'Like a virgin', which was banned from television). The successful popularizer of cultural studies John Fiske (1989) argued that Madonna masqueraded femininity and by doing so offered resistance to cultural domination or hegemony. And each time Madonna challenged socio-cultural norms (a woman popularizing and arguably resisting the sexual objectification of feminine sexuality), young women and girls picked up on these signs of resistance and paraded them as well. This interaction between a popular cultural icon and fans (consumers of culture) also became the object of study. Like Blackstock wearing the G-Unit shirt, Madonna-wear became big business in terms of accessories and fashion.

As we saw in hip hop cultural production, this raised questions and debates about whether the cultural consumers were truly liberated or victims of the artful appropriation of marginal or resistant cultures by mainstream cultural producers. For example, jeans (once the uniform of labourers) were initially appropriated by young white men in the 1950s as a way of resisting the cultural norm for the ideal attire and look for young men: short hair and suits or at least flannel trousers and white shirts. The Hollywood star and martyr for disenfranchised youth of the time, James Dean, personified the look in *Rebel without a cause* (1955), a film based on a real-life case study of a 'juvenile delinquent' by Dr Robert Lindner. In the 1980s when jeans were appropriated by haute-couture designers, rebellious young consumers tore them, laced them with safety pins, and splashed them with acid. Then in the 1990s and early in the twenty-first century, at first young black men wore them many sizes too big and slung low, dragging and tearing the cuffs. Now young women wear them 'too small', exposing their midriffs and tearing them to reveal their buttocks. And so it seems the consumer/producer see-saw goes. Or does it? Has the consumer ever truly controlled the scene (now a scene where nothing is 'too' anything and money can be made on virtually any way of wearing jeans, as a 2004–5 advertising campaign of The Gap highlighted)?

These two issues—masquerading femininity and the role of consumption (especially of popular culture)—were critical to early cultural studies in the 1980s and 1990s. The work on masquerade was inspired by the feminist film critic Laura Mulvey, who exploded onto the scene with her article 'Visual pleasure and narrative cinema' in 1975. Here she argued that there was an intended 'gaze' or way in which the person viewing the film was constructed by the film itself. Using psychoanalytic theories, Mulvey also argued that this gaze is typically male or that culture is constructed around masculine desires. So when viewing a film in which women appear as sexually objectified, we can understand that this look is manufactured to satisfy a male audience. Mulvey's argument was not meant as a technique for distinguishing sexist films from the rest but for demonstrating that the dominant culture was constructed according to a male gaze. Or in other words, this male gaze was everywhere and fundamental to all mainstream culture. Mulvey's article, now considered a classic in cultural studies, has inspired a great deal of work in how cultural domination functions and in the exploration of modes of resistance such as the role of masquerade (recognizing the male gaze, turning it inside out, and parading it as such. See Doane 1982). It has also led to contemporary considerations of race and sexual orientation, such as those considered above, and complicates the concepts of the 'other' and cultural resistance.

The question of consumer-controlled culture has been present since the start of cultural studies. In the 1950s, British and American sociologists and anthropologists became interested in a new social subgroup—namely, youth (Brake 1980; Bernard 1961; Mannheim 1952). These were the post-war years (soon after the Second World War), and Western economies were on the rise, especially in the United States. Some argue that the inception of the study of youth culture was related to increased leisure time and a rise in numbers of young people, commonly assumed to be young white men with little to do but 'hang around' and cause trouble and concern for those from dominant social groups. Popular cultural representations can be found in the American films *West side story* (1961) and *Rebel without a cause*. The academic study of such groups as culture began in the United Kingdom where the dominant critical sociology was class analysis. Scholars such as Stuart Hall, a founder of the University of Birmingham's Centre for Cultural Studies in the late 1960s, applied principles from class critique (chiefly Marxism) to the study of youth culture and popular mediums of cultural expression, including television and advertising (Hall 1959; Hall and Whannel 1998 [1964]). At that time, Marxism was the chief critical theory in the UK. Fundamentally concerned with the social and political organization of labour and capital, culture within the Marxist arena of critical thought was seen as the logical, intellectual appendage of the ruling (capitalist) class. In other words, those who controlled capital (the stock of valuable accumulated goods designed to contribute to further production of goods) controlled cultural production. In the original social science of Marxism, culture did not figure prominently: it was class consciousness (being aware of how one was oppressed in their class position) that would lead to social change (revolution), not cultural control.

Consequently, Hall received a great deal of criticism from his colleagues for his arguments that culture could be a site of social change according to the principles of Marxism and that cultural change helps to get rid of class-based oppression. To make matters worse, Hall's analysis of youth culture and popular cultural forms questioned the very idea of class, how it was formed, and how class domination could be resisted. He argued that popular culture was 'one of the places where socialism might be constituted' (1981, 239). If we think back to the examples of hip hop and the masquerade of Madonna, we can apply what Hall argued. In his analysis of popular music of the 1950s and 1960s, Hall along with Paddy Whannel described 'teenage culture [as] a contradictory mixture of the authentic and the manufactured: it is an area of self-expression for the young and a lush grazing pasture for the commercial providers' (Hall and Whannel 1998 [1964], 63). We can see the same recognition of a marginal subculture in these cases (gay young men in New York City, black inner city youth, and young women) and the same tension at the site of culture between locally produced resistance and commercial appropriation and mass distribution. What is missing in Hall and Whannel's analysis of this particular youth culture are the complications created by considerations of gender, race, and sexual orientation. And this is what happened at the Birmingham Centre: feminists and other 'others' took the reworking of Marxist critical thought by Hall and his colleagues as an invitation to advance critical thinking through cultural studies.

THEORETICAL UNDERPINNINGS OF CULTURAL STUDIES: POST-STRUCTURALISM

By now you should be getting the picture of cultural studies as both a multi-disciplinary and an interdisciplinary enterprise that helps to create social reality. Besides Marxism and political economy, cultural studies also build on a host of other theories and criticisms directed at social change. The objects of study—culture and cultural products as well as cultural production (or the process of culture)—lend themselves well to psychoanalysis (particularly Freud's theory of the unconscious), ideology (the socio-political organization of ideas), semiology (the study of signs and symbols), and post-structuralist discourse analysis (the illumination of how meaning-as-power flows through our taken-for-granted parlance or way of speaking; see this book's introduction).

In order to understand how cultural studies developed existing theories of social change within post-structuralism, it helps to examine some principal components of Sigmund Freud's theory of the unconscious. Sigmund Freud (1856–1939), founder of psychoanalysis, was medically trained and specialized in nervous diseases. His great work, *The interpretation of dreams*, was published in 1900 and introduces his theory of the unconscious as a topography for understanding the psyche. Freud used dreams to enter into the patient's unconscious mind to determine anxieties and fears hidden and disguised there. He describes the manifest (obvious) content of the dream as that which the patient presents. The latent (hidden) content is the underlying issue (fear, anxiety, pain, etc.). To find the underlying issue for interpretation—to use dreaming to release the underlying issue such as great fear or anxiety—is 'dream work'. It is this type of work that relates to cultural studies, but instead of analyzing individual dreams, cultural studies scholars investigate the common imagination or popular cultural representations to find underlying or latent meaning. For example, Freud's theory of the unconscious places a great emphasis on sexual repression and fetishism. We cannot reveal our true (sexual) desires openly, so we find other avenues such as transferring the desire to another object (a fast car, for example). Because of the frustration of not being able to express the true desire, the object becomes a fetish or part of a ritualized expression.

Laura Mulvey used concepts of this psychoanalysis to develop her theory of the male gaze. She described how women's bodies on film screens were the sexual objects of heterosexual masculine desire. Again, not referring to a single case or working within the confines of mental illness, Mulvey applies Freud's concept of the unconscious to a common cultural practice—in other words, to all of society. Thus Freud's psychic categories and the creation of the unconscious are used to understand the operation of potent cultural images and often to dissect or find the underlying (latent) meaning in (manifest) images within a broader socio-cultural context. Dream work is used to understand how such images and symbols distort underlying *social* anxieties and fear: they become fetishized and ritualized in common cultural practice.

One of the ways in which Marxism is brought into cultural studies is through the concept of ideology. This is the term that Marx used to describe how class consciousness was obscured for the benefit of the ruling classes, and it can be related to the type of repression raised by Freud. Again, it was not Marx's chief goal to focus on ideology but on large-scale social and economic change. However, it was the ideology concept that was picked up in cultural studies, particularly the way it was reworked by people such as Louis Althusser, who argued that the personal and the political could not be treated separately (as did Marx). Althusser (1918–90) was a French communist philosopher and Marxist theoretician who extended Marx's theory of political/economic state structures to other areas of society and in an innovative way: ideologically (1971). Althusser distinguished what he called *state ideological apparatuses* (ISA) from repressive forms of state control (the threat of physical violence by an army, for example). He downplayed Marx's separation of society into public and private spheres and focused attention on how these spheres are maintained both as distinct from and as a part of the ISA. Ideology then involves the indirect control of social institutions and the definition of social institutions. Culturally, ideology can involve censorship as a means of control. Associated with the ruling or dominant class, ideology always represents the interests of that class over those of marginalized others. Here we can see how Althusser activates Freud's concepts of desire, repression, and representation at a socio-political level. And this is the way that Althusser's ideology was used in early cultural studies.

As Freud's dream work demonstrates (1966 [1916]), images are powerful vehicles of human desire. Although not directly related to Freud's psychoanalysis, a science of the study of signs and symbols—semiology—was developed shortly afterwards. Roland Barthes (1915–80), a French literary and cultural critic, originally worked as a semiotician, then, conflating high and low cultural forms, moved beyond semiotics. He is best known for analyzing popular images, including ads, and connecting them to politics as a cultural expression, particularly in the form of sign-based myth (1972). The semiology developed by Ferdinand de Saussure (1983 [1916]) provides a technique for reading beyond the obvious or manifest image to a deeper or embedded meaning (much like Freud's dream work). Basically, the equation reads as follows: signifier (the image presented) > (points to or signifies) signified (what the image represents) = the sign (embedded meaning). Applied to our earlier example of hip hop culture, the formula would produce: diamante Mercedes logo worn by young black male hip hop artists > success = Afro-Americans making it in a white-dominant culture.

However, Barthes moved beyond this approach to a second level of meaning in the social production of signs: myth. Here he refers to a broader and political context of the sign. Following his method with the above example: Afro-Americans making it in a white-dominant culture > initial black resistance to white dominant culture, which now embraces black culture in terms of production and consumption = the myth that North America is a racially tolerant society. We can see this myth at work in the interaction between the Kingston police officer and the young black man Jahbari Blackstock. The police officer refers to Blackstock's T-shirt sporting the hip hop group G-Unit as a recognized sign of potential trouble in the form of racially driven militant activity. However, the officer is not serious in his suspicion that Blackstock is the G-unit or guilty of the type of militant behaviour the group sings about as he walks home from basketball practice. And both Blackstock and the officer know that, as is illustrated by Blackstock claiming that the officer was 'just being stupid'. Yet the larger picture is that the young man, along with a disproportionate number of other young black men in Kingston, are regularly stopped by police and checked up on or policed. Thus the myth of a separate black nation is maintained, characterized by dominant culture as deviant and ready for violence, at the same time that police forces try to appear racially tolerant.

Finally, let us look at one of the more difficult concepts used widely in cultural studies: discourse. As employed by the French philosopher, historian, and social analyst Michel Foucault (1926–84), discourse is much more complicated than simply what is said. Like Althusser, Foucault argued for a relocation of power away from the large macro-sociological structures such as class referred to by previous sociologists and other social critics. Foucault claimed that power resides in multiple relations of force rather than in social institutions and structure or in any individual, groups of individuals, or characterization of individuals (1980a). This makes problematic any claims of cultural dominance by gender, race, or sexual orientation—which is not necessarily a bad thing. Foucault spent a good deal of time tracing the history of ways of knowing about certain things, including mental illness, sexuality, and criminality. He focused on the use of language in these studies (hence the use of the term discourse) and how not simply words but entire vocabularies and grammars (ways of putting things properly) guide power relations and the consequent treatment of people as normal or deviant. Thus the problem is not with racial or sexual difference but with the discursive production of race and sexuality, especially in terms of how difference is articulated.

This focus on the production of knowledge and discourse allows for much more fluid interpretations of power and emphasizes how meanings interrelate. For example, if we are to have a dominant culture, there must be one that is dominated. Thus white dominant culture and black resistance in the form of hip hop are necessary components of contemporary racial discourse. The power in this situation flows through this discourse rather than residing with either group or with individuals in either group. So until the issue of how and why we participate in racialized discourse is addressed, not much will change. And that seems true if we consider the long history of black popular culture and its relationship to white culture, particularly in North America. Jazz originated as an Afro-American cultural form that was appropriated, integrated, and adopted by white culture, ironically as a high art form. Similar lines can be traced in the history of rap and hip hop, with some jazz artists such as Miles Davis appearing in hip hop videos.

SOCIOLOGY OF CULTURE

Before cultural studies emerged as a discipline in academia and before post-structuralism, culture was the focus of much debate during the first half of the twentieth century, particularly in the context of its growing social role as a result of emergent means of mass production and the growth of a cultural industry. We can locate the origins of the study of popular culture in that period (as distinct from the earlier study of culture as a high art form and a necessary component of civilization and social progress, which we will examine next). Much of this debate took place in and around political economy and Marxism and addressed issues of cultural labour, cultural industrialization, and the role of capital production. One important strand in the debate came from the so-called Frankfurt School of social theory, with Theodor Adorno and Max Horkheimer (1979 [1947]) in particular worrying about culture and its ideological use by fascist and then capitalist interests.

Keep in mind the times in Europe, where these sociologists lived and first began to work: fascism was on the rise and was soon followed by a world war (see also Chapter 8). In that context, culture was used for the first time on a massive scale for political ends. In fascism, this technique is referred to as propaganda and functions as a method of stupefying the public through popular means to advance a political cause. According to Adorno, a similar argument could be made about the popular music of the time, which was disseminated through sheet music and the gramophone, then radio and cinema. Adorno not only pointed to the means of mass distribution but linked it to the cultural industries producing the music and their intentional design of this popular culture as populist—that is, designed to meet the base desires of the majority of the population, who were assumed to be uneducated in the ways of cultural appreciation. This school of thought is currently enjoying something of a renaissance when applied to critiques of globalization and the impact of major cultural industries such as Disney, especially on so-called Third World cultures.

In contrast, a contemporary of Adorno, Walter Benjamin, also focused on the technological shift in cultural production and dissemination and the concurrent rise in the social role of popular culture but saw political possibilities there. He did not adhere to the notion of the masses as cultural dupes—people who could be easily led by those who controlled popular cultural production. Although he was very critical of fascist propaganda and the aestheticization of politics (the emphasis on 'looking good' over political content), he also found a rich ground for study in terms of art, authenticity, and the populace in 'the age of mechanical reproduction' (1968). The Canadian professor of English, Marshall McLuhan—famous for the expression 'the medium is the message'—focused on the mass media, especially television (1994 [1964]). Somewhere between the positions of Adorno and Benjamin, McLuhan characterized various modes of mass communication for popular consumption as either 'hot' (books, radio, and film) or 'cool' (television) and thus indicated their respective socio-cultural value: hot media meant an interactive relationship between the product and the consumer, and cool media indicated a passive one.

When I teach a third-year undergraduate course in cultural studies, I often begin by asking the students what they characterize as culture. Despite all that I have described above, especially the growing importance of the role of popular culture as part of the social appreciation of culture in general, they often refer to things associated with what can be characterized as 'high brow' or 'high culture'. As an excellent contemporary presentation of what this means, I use examples from the television show 'Frasier'. This spin-off from another show, 'Cheers' (which celebrated working-class bar culture in Boston), focused on the private lives of two brothers, Frasier and Niles, both psychiatrists living a very upper-class lifestyle in Seattle. The brothers frequent the opera, the ballet, and classical music concerts. Both play classical piano and were educated at an Ivy League university (Harvard). They enjoy fine wines and frequently dine out at the best restaurants. They both live in high-class condominiums decorated with valuable antiques as well as fashionable modern furnishings and art. Thus their upper-class standing is heavily signed by evidence that they are 'cultured'. As well as a surprising contemporary popular definition of culture, this parody of high-brow culture would seem an appropriate characterization of the meaning of culture to those who were among the first to study it socially and critically: Mathew Arnold (1822–88) and F.R. Leavis (1895–1978).

Both Arnold and Leavis were educated in English literature at highly respected universities (Oxford and Cambridge respectively) and became well-known cultural critics. They were considered arbiters or judges of what was culturally valuable, which was informed by their education in classical English literature and modern equivalents. Arnold defined culture as 'sweetness and light', the 'creative power of genius', 'real thought', 'real beauty', and 'the best that has been thought and said about the world' (1999 [1875]). He analyzed cultural appreciation, including appreciation of popular culture, in terms of three classes: the aristocracy (whom he called 'barbarians'), the emergent middle class ('philistines'), and the working class (the 'populace'). None of these classes, he said, were capable of discerning what to Arnold was real culture; this had to be done for them by people who were educated properly (although he did not hold out much hope for the populace as cultural consumers, describing their particular culture as one based on beer-drinking and brawling). Arnold also believed that culture and cultural critics played an important role in sustaining and advancing social progress: without them we would be simply barbarians, philistines, and a brawling mass. This, he argued, required a stable social state (remember that the times in which he was writing were filled with social change: political uprisings in parts of Europe, the industrial revolution, massive migrations from the countryside to cities, waves of immigration into and from the UK, and class unrest).

Leavis, one of modern English literature's most famous critics, also pointed to changing times as a threat to what he understood as culture in terms of 'the consciousness of the race' (1999 [1930]). He identified a social crisis spawned by mass production and standardization of writing by the press and talked about the 'surrender' of intellect to base emotions in the rising new industry of cinema. And he characterized much of cultural production in the early twentieth century as a levelling down to the common denominator. 'This century [twentieth] is in a cultural trough,' he claimed, 'and the situation is likely to get worse before better' (1999 [1930], 19). This limited and elitist view of culture and its social role was radically challenged by subsequent critics and scholars of culture, particularly in how mass and popular culture were reconstituted as significant to social progress.

There are some who argue that cultural studies today has become too focused on popular culture. Others still automatically characterize popular culture and its mass distribution as sociologically and culturally insignificant. There is still great hesitation today, for example, in allowing cultural studies programs and courses in universities and colleges, since it is assumed that studies of, say, rap and hip hop could not possibly be worthy of serious academic attention. On the other hand, we see interesting developments in cultural studies, such as the application of post-colonialism, technoscience, and a new and expanded appreciation of visual culture.

In the year 2000, the Third International Conference in Cultural Studies, 'Culture at the Crossroads', was held at the University of Birmingham in the UK, attracting more than 1,000 participants from around the world. Both the title of the conference and its location are significant to the current state of cultural studies. Although the title refers to 'culture' being at a crossroads, it could also be read as referring to cultural studies itself. After a very successful run as one of the most widely recognized sites of cultural studies, the Birmingham Centre closed in 2002. The closure was due in part to the decentralization and dissemination of such studies to various academic sites throughout the UK and the rest of the world. For example, in 2003 Italian scholars published a special edition of the journal *Quarderni di estetics & ermeneutica* called *Cultural studies, estica, scienze umane*, and one goal of the millennium conference in Birmingham was to extend cultural studies debates to countries beyond northern Europe, North America, and Australia. The centre's closure was also in part due to the politics of academia, especially in the northwestern part of the world where it is turning increasingly to education on demand—with dominant, usually economic interests at the centre of the demand. Communication and information technology courses and departments are on the increase, as are biological (especially medical) and biotechnical subjects. At the same time, classical academic studies (Greek, Latin, English literature, and philosophy) along with other courses and programs such as cultural studies—all considered extraneous to the new socio-economic role of the university—are increasingly viewed as adjunct to or are dropped entirely from the academic program (Fox 2002).

Interestingly, and in contradiction to this scenario, students—undergraduate and graduate—remain interested in cultural studies, and as newly invested clients of the higher education industry, they can effectively call for courses and programs either directly or indirectly associated with the discipline.[1]

As we have seen, cultural studies is fundamentally interdisciplinary and critical, which makes it difficult for universities to accommodate the ways in which it is organized. Consider the following comments about cultural studies taken from John Hartley's *A short history of cultural studies* (2003, 1–2):

- Some say that it is too political. Others that it is not political enough.
- It has no method. It has no subject of study. It has no discipline. Or—it is too institutionalised academically.
- It belongs in low-prestige teaching colleges, not high-end research universities. Or—it can only be practiced by researchers who already know about the politics of knowledge in an established discipline.
- It's undergraduate consciousness-raising. Or—it's the name given to the latest enthusiasm of senior writers in half a dozen different fields.
- It is too English. Or—it is too American.
- Too academic; not activist enough. Or—too activist; not scholarly enough.
- It celebrates when it should criticize. Or—it criticizes when it should undertake policy research for external clients.

If this were not so true, it would be funny.

Despite the difficulties in finding an academic home, cultural studies does continue, and two relatively new sub-fields in or near cultural studies are worthy of mention here: visual culture and technoculture (also referred to as techno-science). The former refers to the shift from written text as the central focus in studies of culture, especially classical studies (remember that Arnold and Leavis, both literary critics, argued that it was in literary culture that the best of society was to be found). The visual culture approach works instead on the assumption that we have become (again, since mass literacy is a relatively new phenomenon) an image-based society. Everything from signage in international airports to medical imaging is analyzed, again within typically critical and sociologically progressive theoretical contexts. For example, I am interested in anatomical modelling and imaging that dates back to eighteenth-century Europe as an entry into an analysis of modern medicine, the body, and gender formation (Burfoot 2005).

This research and visual culture also engage with the work of those associated with technoculture, such as Donna Haraway's famous figure of a cyborg as marker of the discursive nature of science and technology (1985). Technoculture arose out of at least two other streams, one of which engaged with the new technologies and social spaces associated with virtual reality and cyberspace. The other was the growing interest in the social and cultural studies of science and technology in general. Throughout both streams run theoretical discussions and interesting applications. Subjectivity is problematicized by and sometimes collapsed with technology. 'Technoculture' or 'technoscience' become loaded terms in the sense that they point to discursivity in an area (science and technology) once held as given and somewhat sacred. Just as we uncovered the multiple meanings of racialization in hip hop cultural production, so there are now debates as to what constitutes being human in discussions of 'Alife', or artificial life (Kember 2003), and 'posthumanism'. (Hayles 1999). Objects of study include computer gaming, internet dating, biotechnology, and genetic engineering *as* culture.

At this point you may have a better idea of what cultural studies is than what culture is. This is intended. After more than 100 years of studying the concept, there is simply no nice pat definition of culture available. We have seen how approaches to culture have varied from laments for a passing golden era of high art to a complex celebration and critique of everyday life and its cultural manifestations. Very important sociological issues have been raised throughout this period, and many continue to be raised today, including: how culture is produced and who or what controls that production; how we talk about culture—as images, as signs and myth, as ideology, as discourse; how we mediate or understand our world through culture and our places in it in terms of who we are and who we are allowed to be; and how things such as the social expectation of heterosexuality can be challenged and changed culturally. Such issues also implicitly address the question 'what is social reality?' because what we take to be reality in social contexts is directly contingent on cultural relations. For example, how do you walk home from basketball practice in Kingston, Ontario, as a young black man wearing a G-Unit T-shirt and avoid getting stopped by the police?

Questions to Consider ────────────────────────────────

1. Why is the following finding not necessarily a social fact: according to suicide rates, in order to be happy and less likely to commit suicide, young men need to be in a heterosexual relationship and married?
2. How can marginal cultural production of popular music, especially rap and hip hop, become cultural production?
3. How does gender discrimination figure in marginal cultural productions such as rap and hip hop?
4. How do aspects of culture function in the exchange between the Kingston police officer and the young black man Jahbari Blackstock?
5. Can you find an example of a cultural production that is produced by and remains under the control of its consumers?

Notes ────────────────────────────────

1. This may be why McMaster University recently started a program in globalization and cultural studies and why Queen's University is now in the process of applying for a graduate program in cultural studies at the request of the School of Graduate Studies. Other Canadian cultural studies programs include the undergraduate and graduate degrees offered at Trent University (Department of Cultural Studies), Simon Fraser's School of Communications, the University of Alberta's Modern Languages and Cultural Studies, Concordia's Communication Studies, and Communications Studies at McGill University. Many other programs adopt courses or rely on the literature associated with cultural studies, such as the McLuhan Program in Culture and Technology at the University of Toronto and the Joint Graduate Program in Communication and Culture offered by York and Ryerson universities. And many faculty and other scholars associate with cultural studies in one way or another while not necessarily being tied to any such program.

Chapter 7

Is Social Theory Useful?

R.A. Sydie

INTRODUCTION

Students facing the prospect of encountering theory may react with fear and loathing in large part because anything that carries the label 'theory' is assumed to be obtuse, difficult, and of dubious relevance to everyday life. This perspective is ironic given that the 'founding fathers and mothers' of sociology regarded their theoretical expositions primarily as useful and important contributions to the conduct of everyday social life. As Harriet Martineau remarked in 1869 (vol. 2, 335), 'the science of Human Nature . . . is yet in its infancy' but social theory as the 'science or the knowledge of fact inducing the discovery of laws' was the 'eternal basis of wisdom, and therefore of human morality and peace'.

Consequently, while some theoretical expositions may be described as 'language-challenged' and difficult to understand, social theory did aspire to be useful for the harmonious conduct of life in society. One of the major sociological theorists, Émile Durkheim, maintained that the sociological study of society should be combined with the intention of 'improving it' and that he would 'esteem our research not worth the labour of [a] single hour if its interest were merely speculative' (1984 [1893], xxvi). For the classical social theorists such as Durkheim and Martineau, the focus was on the everyday social problems of modernity ushered in by the European Enlightenment and the manner by which these problems could be alleviated or overcome. In contrast then to the common observation that X may be the case 'in theory' but 'in practice' Y is more likely, these sociological theorists maintained that the theoretical X was an essential explanatory part of the practical Y.

WHAT DO THEORISTS DO?

Theory is the 'act of viewing, contemplating, considerating' and it usually involves some imaginative interpretation of what is referred to by theorists as 'data'— which for social theorists is the raw material of everyday life. As Bauman (1990, 8) claims, the 'central question' for sociological theory is 'in what sense does it matter that in whatever they do or may do people are dependent on other people; in what sense does it matter that they live always (and cannot but live) in the company of, in communication with, in exchange with, in competition with, in coop-

eration with other human beings?' Sociological theory is therefore 'first and foremost a *way of thinking* about the human world' (Bauman 1990, 8; emphasis in the
original).

Now, we all make sense of our everyday lives in a theoretical manner and
make decisions about our conduct and responses to our world based on our theoretical suppositions, especially if the usual tenor of that world is disturbed. For
example, in the late 1960s Western women began to question the assumption that
their natural destiny in life was to be wives and mothers. Betty Friedan's book, *The
feminine mystique*, pointed to the sense of malaise women, especially educated
middle-class women, felt about the social pressure to realize their 'femininity'
solely in their roles as mothers and housewives. She called this 'the problem that
has no name' because women did not articulate their personal troubles, feeling
instead that there must be something wrong with them, especially when the suburban American woman was the 'envy, it was said, of women all over the world'
(Friedan 1963, 13). This problem with no name that produced a sense of personal
failure eventually became, through informal discussions, a collective issue that
coalesced into a mass movement for women's liberation. Second-wave feminism's
slogan, 'the personal is political', was a powerful way of describing the collective
sense of oppression that the no-name problem represented. While it quickly
became apparent that these early feminist organizations were dominated by the
concerns of white, middle-class, Western women, nevertheless the everyday issues
of housework and child care, often thought of as trivial private concerns, or the
more serious issues of gendered wage inequities, rape, prostitution, and women's
health, could no longer be ignored as strictly personal issues that each woman
dealt with by herself.[1]

Feminists theorized women's position and relationships in society in collective terms and in doing so generated a radical rethinking of how power operates,
how it structures gender relations, and what constitutes the political. This theoretical examination of gender relations also had real, practical effects; indeed, the
central focus of any feminist work was to connect the everyday experiences of
women to the relations of ruling—that is, the 'social relations and organization'
that pervade women's worlds but are 'invisible in it' (Smith 1992, 91).

Theory, then, is useful in making sense of our everyday lives. But if theorizing is something that all of us do, then what special claims can the sociologist or
any other specialist advance with respect to theory? What sets social theory apart
from our everyday sense-making? In what way can it be useful in explaining the
puzzle of social life? In the case of the women's movement, for many years women
had expressed discontent with what were deemed personal troubles that they
encountered in their lives, and they came up with a variety of explanations as to
causes. However, these explanations, which may have been accurate as to causes,
did not produce a *critique*. That is, women may have *criticized* the various situations, but the social theorist does not rest with finding fault or venting frustration but tries to examine the troubles in relation to the whole social context or
culture. Critique is both a reflection on the social and an attempt to go beyond
mundane criticisms to ask 'why' and 'what is the evidence'—both for the social

behaviour and for any of the proffered explanations. To refer to a guiding theory of this text, the 'sociological imagination' of the theorist translates 'personal troubles into public issues, and public issues into the terms of their human meaning for a variety of individuals' (Mills 1959, 187).

In the explanatory and interpretive role played by the theorist in making sense of the social world, the role and the use of social theory is not a seamless endeavour. First of all, the theorist is part of the very social realm that is to be explained, and the concepts and ideas that form the basis of the theories are also drawn from the same social world. Consequently, theorists must be self-reflexive—that is, aware of the contingencies of the vantage point from which they begin their reflections. It is the vantage point that must be kept in mind when looking at the work of the classical theorists. The narratives they produced were coloured by their location in Western, largely European or North American societies. Consequently, they did not doubt that they were witnessing social progress toward modernity in contrast to what they perceived as traditional or primitive societies in other parts of the world. The ethnographic and anthropological reports that proliferated during the nineteenth century, facilitated by the various colonial and imperial extensions of Western powers, seemed to provide 'evidence' for the belief that the West was modern and the 'rest' was backward. As a result, the early theorists believed that their analyses would contribute to social progress not only for their own societies but eventually for all other societies, which could be brought into modernity under the benevolent guidance of Western 'experts'.

For the classical theorists, a new world was possible, and the sociologist as the expert in the nature of the social could help to usher in this new, more harmonious world. For example, without necessarily agreeing with the specifics of Marx's predictions for the future society and how it might be achieved, the classical sociologists did generally endorse his notion that 'The philosophers have only *interpreted* the world, in various ways; the point is to *change* it' (1947, 199).

While the optimism of the classical sociologists about the production of a new social world has been considerably modified in current theoretical work, sociology nonetheless remains committed to addressing the pressing social issues of the time in the hope of alleviating the various troubles that affect individuals in their every day/every night lives (Smith 1978). It is *how* those pressing troubles can be understood theoretically as public issues that is subject to dispute. The nature of the contentions can be summarized as a question: is the social world that the theorist confronts today still modern or is it post-modern? This is an important question because the answers will guide how the social theorist might identify and address significant social issues and problems.

MODERN SOCIAL THEORY

Two intentions were the godparents of sociology. The new discipline was supposed to make the fact of society accessible to rational understanding by means of testable assumptions and theories, and to help the individual toward freedom and self-fulfillment (Dahrendorf 1973, 58).

One of the 'truths' that most of the classical social theorists adhered to was a faith in the value of a scientific approach to the problems of the modern world. Henri de Saint-Simon (1814, 136) maintained that the 'Golden Age of the human race is not behind us but before us; it lies in the perfection of the social order.' It was the clear, scientific eye of the social theorist that would provide the direction for the perfection of that social order. This assumption was predicated on the belief that there was a 'real truth' to be discovered that would provide irrefutable grounds for any political action and that social subjects, as rational individuals, had the right to emancipation or liberation. But the achievement of harmonious social order required an understanding of the nature of society apart from individual members. The collective nature of the social was addressed using the concepts of community, social class, social solidarity, power, and authority. And all of these concepts related to the way that theorists addressed the public issues preventing the achievement of the 'Golden Age'. These issues were capitalism, industrialization, urbanization, secularization, bureaucratization, excessive individualism, and alienation.

The specific solutions offered by the classical theorists to these central issues varied, but they were framed by the confidence that the application of science to the examination of the social, in the same manner that it was applied to the natural world, would provide definitive answers as to how the progress and happiness of human beings could be achieved. The theorist would produce 'objective' and hence irrefutable knowledge about the social world. For example, Comte believed that society—or at least European societies and most certainly France—was poised on the cusp of the positivist, scientific stage and that under the social theorist's scientifically based directions, the improvement of society was imminent. By discovering the invariant laws governing the social, the theorist could determine what *is*, what *will be*, and what *should be* and 'put an end to the revolutionary crisis which is tormenting the civilized nations of the world' (Comte 1975, 37). As Comte stated, the theological or metaphysical abstractions and fantasies by which theorists had explained the social world in the past could now be rejected. The real nature of society would be revealed and humanity freed to pursue order and progress through positivist sociological science.

Durkheim was also insistent on the priority of the social over the individual and the pre-eminence of science in attending to the pathologies of modern life. For Durkheim, society was a real entity, a reality sui generis, and 'it is on this principle . . . that all sociology has been built. This science, indeed, could be brought into existence only with the realization that social phenomena, although immaterial, are nevertheless real things, the proper objects of scientific study' (Durkheim 1895, lvii). The social theorist was the expert in deciphering the 'real' nature of this entity—society.

As noted in the previous chapter, Durkheim offered proof of the scientific validity and usefulness of social theory in his study of suicide. He suggested that suicide was a sociological as well as a psychological phenomenon. That is, in contrast to reliance on 'personal', subjective, or psychological explanations for suicides, objective knowledge of the nature, types, and rates of the 'public issue' of suicide could be discovered that could provide for social regulation of this pathology. It was the nature and degree of social solidarity in a society that provided the key to the reasons for and prevalence of suicides. In other words, Durkheim theorized a 'collective inclination' to suicide that 'varies inversely with the degree of integration of the social groups of which the individual forms a part' (1951 [1897], 209). Consequently, the social theorist who diagnosed the nature of social solidarity could suggest solutions to the pathology. Durkheim used a variety of statistics to identify four types of suicide—anomic, fatalistic, egoistic, and altruistic suicides.

These four theoretical types remain a fruitful source for the examination of suicides today.[2] Egoistic and anomic suicides are seen to be particularly prevalent in modern industrial societies. The 'excessive individualism' of modern society produces a 'weakening of the social fabric' so that the individual is left without any community or group support and will be prone in times of trouble and stress to egoistic suicide. Regarding anomic suicide, the breakdown of the moral community under modernity means that passions and desires are not socially controlled so that, for example, economic success becomes an end in itself rather than a means to an end. When this goal is thwarted, the individual is left with no support. Thus it was not surprising to Durkheim that the industrial and commercial sector and the liberal professions showed particularly high suicide rates because these occupations and professions are subject to less stringent social and moral controls (Durkheim 1951 [1897], 257). It would seem that this remains an issue, as the example of Japan illustrates. Currently, Japan has one of the highest suicide rates in the world, and after the economic downturn of the 1990s the rate increased by 60 per cent. Rates are highest among middle-aged and elderly men with financial problems (*Globe and Mail* 2005a). The high rate of Native Canadian suicides may also be related to the anomie generated by the breakdown of traditional cultural practices and beliefs and the consequent lack of restraint that the collectivity or society as the 'moral power superior to the individual' can produce (Durkheim 1951 [1897], 249).

The egoism and anomie detected by Durkheim have an affinity with the concept of alienation developed by Marx. For Marx, modern capitalist industrial society was an alienating place because of the divorce of human beings from their natural state as productive workers. While alienation is not confined to capitalist industrial societies, it does take a particular form in such societies: namely, individuals are alienated from their work, the product of their work, their humanity (or 'species-being'), and other people. In modern capitalist society, work is no longer a pleasure or a calling for most people but simply the way by which they can provide for what is pleasurable and interesting to them—their leisure time. The popularity of 'TGIF' is an example of what Marx was talking about. We put in our time at work, where we conform to the various expectations of the job, only in anticipation of the weekend's freedom from work when we can 'really be ourselves'. Life begins when work ends, and work 'has no meaning . . . but as earnings, which bring [the worker] to the table, to the public house, into bed' (Marx 1849, quoted in McClellan 1971, 143).

The product of work is also estranged from the worker: what they make does not belong to them, and in most cases workers must purchase the products they have had a part in producing. Increasingly today, the end product of work in advanced capitalism is ephemeral—memos, emails, text messages, teleconferences, meetings, and consultations. This 'work' does not immediately produce tangible physical products, and its effects on the lives of others are not simply local but can have a global reach. For example, the person you contact when you have trouble with your computer here in Canada may well be sitting in India. The alienation from others is even more evident in the possibilities that cyberspace offers for abstract connections that can dispense with any concern for the 'real' person; indeed, disembodiment and often concealment of identity is the 'nature' (that is, really the 'artifice') of the cyber-subject.

The alienating nature of modern social life is inevitable, given the demands of a capitalist, industrial social structure. Rationalization and objectivity are key to the success of capitalist modernity, which offers greater freedom to individuals at the same time that it constrains and regiments individuals. Capitalism enables the endless 'pursuit of wealth, stripped of its religious and ethical meaning' but in turn produces 'specialists without spirit, sensualists without heart' (Weber 1904–5, 182). The rational treatment of both people and things eliminates 'respect, kindness and delicacies of feeling' and if the individual who is 'interested solely in money' is 'reproached with callousness and brutality', s/he is unable to understand this because s/he is acting with 'logical consistency and pure impartiality' and not with any 'bad intentions' (Simmel 1900, 434). For example, Peter Pocklington's selling of Wayne Gretzky—despite widespread objections from the Edmonton community—was entirely consistent with the rational expectations of capitalist profitability, which exempted him from any need to take note of personal needs or values or the sentiments of the community about the loss of the hockey star.

One of the ironies of classical social theorists' analyses of modernity is that the attempt to provide a 'science' of society that would correct the problems and miseries of modern society was often instrumental in producing more sophisticated alienating social structures and conditions. The pursuit of good order and progress matched the political needs of the modern state, which operates through and is legitimized by the application of rational legal rules (Weber 1947). Bureaucracy is the structure that provides the efficient and effective means of ensuring the objective, collective application of these rational legal rules. It is bureaucracy that ensures that any idiosyncratic needs and desires of individuals are controlled and regimented in the interest of social order. The modern state is about 'red tape', 'about setting the rules, defining patterns and maintaining them, administration, management, surveillance and supervision. It is about anticipating and preventing all deviance from the norm and all breaching of the rules', and the social theorist was the expert who could provide reliable information as to how to prevent 'everything haphazard, erratic, unanticipated and accidental' from occurring (Bauman 2000, 76). This is not to say that sociologists deliberately set out to preserve or augment the powers of the modern state, but those who insisted on the *scientific* status of the sociological enterprise saw their task as offering *objective knowledge* to society at large but especially to policy-makers and politicians. However, it was not theorists but politicians who were responsible for the translation of this knowledge into social practices. That is, it was not the task of the social theorist as *scientist* to *evaluate* the nature and consequences of the knowledge they produced or to necessarily recommend actions.

The ethical dangers of the 'pure science' position was not without critics. C. Wright Mills, in the mid-twentieth century, pointed to the 'abstracted view that hides' the 'humanity' of those affected by bureaucratic decision-making. This view leads to the frightening 'lack of moral sensibility raised to a higher and technically more adequate level among the brisk generals and gentle scientists who are now rationally—and absurdly—planning the weapons and strategy of the third world war' (Mills 1963, 238). Mills pointed out that 'These actions are not necessarily sadistic; they are merely businesslike; they are not emotional at all; they are efficient, rational, technically clean-cut. They are inhuman acts because they are impersonal' (238). Again, there are present-day parallels. For example, Mills would not have been astonished, although he would probably have been outraged, by the abuse of military prisoners in Iraq, the rape and sexual coercion of refugees by United Nations officers, or the increasing reliance on technologies that enable the depersonalization of the enemy as merely a blip on a screen, which in turn can result in 'unfortunate' friendly-fire accidents.

A rationalized, bureaucratic modern society is a technologically efficient instrument for dealing with the complexities of capitalism, industrialization, and urbanization. The ideal modern subject is a disciplined subject who follows orders, and any qualms about the orders and the required actions are suspended or silenced (a convenient template for genocide or any other modern atrocities visited on various peoples). The social theorist has contributed to the contours of rationalized, bureaucratized modern society by providing concepts and managerial techniques that are useful to policy-makers and politicians. This complicity with modern institutions of power and authority was not overtly duplicitous; rather, it was often done with the best of motives as, for example, in the sociological research connected with welfare state provisions. A welfare state requires information about its population if interventions in the lives of people are to be effective and efficient. Sociology has been adept at providing demographic statistical portraits of, as well as field research findings on, various populations to assist policy-makers. These abstract classifications and surveys of collectives, sorted by such categories as age, sex, class, and race, provide the 'objective' basis for management of a welfare state. The problem is (as anyone who has confronted any welfare state bureaucracy often discovers) that the statistical category to which the bureaucracy assigns them does not seem to fit the realities of their lives and their specific needs. So although most social theorists have been alert to the dangers of co-option by undemocratic, authoritarian regimes or institutions, their own expertise in respect to the first of Dahrendorf's intentions (to make the fact of society accessible to rational understanding) can produce problems with respect to the second intention of advancing the freedom and self-fulfillment of the individual.

The nature of the theoretical enterprise—the analysis of social reality in clear, objective terms that make the 'fact of society' accessible—can therefore contribute to what Weber described as the 'iron cage' of the rationalized, impersonal, bureaucratic world in which rationality can easily become irrationality in even the most mundane contexts of everyday life. For example, when you have to listen to automated phone messages asking you to press a series of numbers, you may feel frustrated when no single option quite matches the problem you want addressed. This is made worse when there is no 'person' you can reach at the other end of the telephone exchange. This frustration occurs even though the procedure was designed to deal rationally and efficiently with customer inquiries.

The minor irritations of voice mail and the more major frustrations of welfare state bureaucracies are representative of social engineering that contradicts the second, emancipatory intention of the sociological enterprise—'to help the individual toward freedom and self-fulfillment'. Mills's point about science remains pertinent: 'Science . . . is not a technological Second Coming.' That its 'techniques and its rationality . . . are given a central place in a society does not mean that men [sic] live reasonably and without myth, fraud, and superstition' (Mills 1963, 238).

Classical social theorists produced useful analyses of the nature of modernity, but as a *science* of society, the reviews and results have been mixed. Similarly, modernity in its various concrete manifestations and its ideological promises has become suspect. The issues identified by social theorists as characteristic of modernity—capitalism, industrialization, bureaucratization, urbanization, excessive individualism, alienation, and secularization—remain problematic, although the way they are manifested has changed. For example, extremes of wealth and poverty have increased as capitalism extends its reach globally, seemingly indifferent to any coherent control or regulation, certainly not by national governments. Industrialization is equally a global phenomenon but one that has sidelined the former industrial powerhouses of the West. In addition, the corporations based on new technologies that move into many communities to replace the heavy industrial plants do not halt the decline of those communities because their head offices are usually located far away from the old urban industrial centres.

The hegemony of 'pure' science is also challenged by various problems with its results—for example, the seeming revolving door of new drugs hailed as panaceas for various debilitating illnesses, only to be rather quickly revealed as producing unsuspected, often deadly side-effects; or the environmental transformations and degradations that can produce catastrophic consequences; or the revelations of 'cooked' results by top scientists. The individualism and alienation that was of central concern to the classical theorists of modernity remain, exaggerated by the simulated, wired world we inhabit. The racial and gender inequities that a few of the classical social theorists recognized also remain critical, unresolved issues. Finally, the secularization that was regarded as an inevitable result of modernity has not materialized in quite the manner foreseen by many theorists. On the contrary, in the most powerful capitalist liberal democracy, the

United States, religion remains a critical component in all dimensions of social and political life. In addition, the fundamentalism that affects all religious denominations has become a decisive and divisive factor in global politics.

It is not surprising therefore that there is considerable skepticism today about the promise of modernity to usher in a Golden Age of order and progress. Certainly, Dahrendorf's second intention—the contribution of social theory to universal freedom and self-fulfillment—remains elusive. Seidman (1991, 132) maintains that currently, 'Theory discussions have little bearing on major social conflicts and political struggles or on important public debates over current social affairs.' Nonetheless, the explanatory capacity of social theory remains important in the face of the abstractions of social power and the forces that 'seem' inevitable, intractable, and beyond individual capacities for change.

For some theorists, modernity is finished: we are now post-modern. Interestingly, C. Wright Mills, discussed above as an early critic of modernity, stated in the mid-twentieth century, 'We are at the ending of what is called the Modern Age', which is being 'succeeded by a post-modern period' (1963, 236). But what is post-modernity? Can it represent a more positive future for all individuals? And what is the use of social theory if we are post-modern?

HAVE WE BECOME POST-MODERN?

> ... it is probable that now and for the foreseeable future we, as philosophers, as much as we may be concerned by politics (and inevitably we are so concerned), are no longer in a position to say publicly: 'Here is what you must do'.
> ... This is not to say that there are no longer any intellectuals, but that today's intellectuals, philosophers in so far as they are concerned by politics and by questions of community, are no longer able to take up obvious and pellucid positions; they cannot speak in the name of an 'unquestionable' universality (Lyotard 1988, 301).

The confident assertion that knowledge, especially scientific knowledge, can act as a progressive force for the freedom and emancipation of humanity by revealing the 'truth' about social and political reality has, according to post-modern theorists, been shown to be a delusion. In fact, truth claims need to be examined with suspicion because they are claims to power (Foucault 1977b). For example, among the problems with the modernist picture were the gendered and racist assumptions that remained unexamined in the account of the classical theorists. A case in point was Comte's belief that women were not fitted for intellectual pursuits 'either from an intrinsic weakness of her reason or from her more lively moral and physical sensibility, which are hostile to scientific abstraction and concentration' (1853, 505). Indeed, 'sociology' proved that 'the equality of the sexes ... is incompatible with all social existence' (1975, 269). Patriarchal power was thus affirmed as inevitable and immutable.

Comte's views on gender relations were reflected in the work of many of the other classical theorists, and this is not surprising because they were part of a particular discursive regime that endorsed this view as an appropriate and meaning-ful way of understanding gender relations. As Foucault (1991, 79) put it, 'men govern (themselves and others) by the production of truth', and the production of truth is 'not the production of true utterances, but the establishment of domains in which the practice of true and false can be made at once ordered and pertinent.' And the 'truth' of gender was natural difference that in turn endorsed patriarchal power relations (see Chapter 4). It is this contingency of knowledge that is central to the 'post' of post-modernity. Plurality, diversity, difference, complexity, and contingency replace the confident universalizing theories—the 'grand narra-tives'—of the classical theorists about the nature of social life.

These characteristics of post-modernity have critical implications for the continued relevance of social theory. If theory has to abandon its generalizing, universalizing ambitions (Featherstone 1988), what remains? How can the theo-rist claim any authority to speak about the social when any such reflections are regarded, for example, as simply variants on language games or culturally specific notions, none of which can claim any privileged status? More troubling is the issue that although the idea that Western intellectuals have the authority to speak *of* or more arrogantly *for* the 'other' has been rejected, can we be sure that current notions of post-modernity are not another variant on this old theme? That is, can the peasant farmer in Latin America or the exploited garment worker in south Asia understand their social world as a post-modern space in which individuality, lifestyle choices, and playful consumption are the order of the day? Is this con-ceptualization of a post-modern social world another Eurocentric universalizing theoretical stance?

Whatever the answers to these questions, it is clear that it cannot be business-as-usual for social theory (Bauman 1992, 54). The most critical point that makes business-as-usual improbable is that social theorists can no longer claim a central place for 'society' as the basic, fundamental theoretical concept. The classical con-cept of 'society' was always tacitly tied to the idea of the nation-state, despite recognition that nation-states are not themselves closed entities. Although it was recognized theoretically that nation-states were 'porous', most theorists continued to confound society/nation-state as the framework for analysis, and the primary models were Western democratic states. It was the use of 'society' in this manner that enabled social theorists 'to speak of social laws of regularities, of the *norma-tive regulation* of social reality, of *trends* and *developmental* sequences' (Bauman 1992, 60; emphasis in the original). It was this conflation that made social theory 'useful' to nation-states, especially Western nation-states, in controlling 'less developed' or 'less advanced' sectors of their own societies or other 'uncivilized' societies.

The social engineering work of social theorists is no longer as useful or ne-cessary because political life is clearly revealed as unrestrained by the boundaries of specific societies/nation-states. Global social order is the work of, for example, transnational corporations, NGOs such as the World Bank, and international con-sortiums and agencies. Furthermore, nation-states (at least Western states) no longer need to employ the coercive disciplinary practices of modernity to ensure order and legitimacy. Social order and citizen compliance can be secured more easily by 'seduction' (Baudrillard 1983a). Advanced capitalist societies are now more focused on consumption than on production as the motor of economic growth. Workers no longer need to be controlled directly with coercive measures. Control can be exercised through the persuasion to consume. This spills over into political practices that are increasingly reliant on impression management and image manipulation. Seduced by consumer culture, bombarded with infomercials and slick advertising, and subjected to the constant creation of new 'needs' in the interest of transforming the self in new and desirable ways, citizens have great difficulty articulating their personal troubles as public issues.

Seduction, however, is always limited, if only because there are multiple systems of power that compete for the affections of citizens. Furthermore, people are not robotic dupes. For example, the 'crisis' of voter apathy, or more descriptively voter cynicism, is partly explained by people's realization that elections do little to alter fundamental problems with party politics and the mundane, practical problems of everyday life (Habermas 1975). This is a 'crisis' largely in the view of political elites whose legitimacy is rendered questionable when it rests on poor voter response, but it can have the paradoxical effect of forcing political attention to some pressing issues as a means of regaining voter confidence.

While self-enclosed notions of 'society' are now difficult to sustain and global forces tend to endorse a fatalistic approach to generating solutions to local or even national public issues, social change is not always a top-down process. Furthermore, most of us identify ourselves as Canadian citizens living in the nation-state of Canada, and the continued proliferation of grassroots pressure groups indicates that the solitary post-modern individual is not always '[l]ost in the crowd', feeling 'unimportant, lonely and disposable' but can come to understand personal troubles as public issues (Bauman 1990, 68). The forces that seem to be overwhelming, constraining, and even inevitable can yield to citizen pressure. For example, in Canada the adoption of pay equity policies and the decriminalization of abortion were a result of sustained lobbying from various women's movement groups.

The troubles for modern citizens generated by capitalism, industrialism, secularization, bureaucratization, and so on remain troubling, the difference today being that the specific ways in which they trouble our possibly post-modern, everyday lives have changed because global social contexts are unstable, complex places that require new, innovative approaches to such troubles that cannot be undertaken solely within the purview of the single nation-state. For example, environmental decisions made on the other side of the world can have profound consequences for Canadian society and our environment. Indeed, on a global scale, the recent Millennium Ecosystem Assessment report stated that the human imprint has put such a 'strain on the natural functions of the Earth that the ability of the planet's ecosystem to sustain future generations can no longer be taken for granted' (*Globe and Mail* 2005b). The Kyoto agreement is clearly not going to be sufficient to halt or reverse this global environmental issue. Nonetheless, the 'trouble' we experience with the effects of environmental degradation remains a public issue for our own society and our own local communities (however they are conceived). As a result, we still need social theory to help make sense of the abstractions of social power and the various 'forces' that appear so constraining. We need to understand the 'extralocal determinants' of our experiences that do not 'lie within the scope of everyday practices', and it is the discovery of these determinants that is the 'sociologist's special business' (Smith 1987, 161).

DOES THEORY STILL HAVE ANY USE?

> In my own limited view, . . . we are not 'post' modern yet, although it is arguably the case that the fundamental contradictions at the heart of modernity are more exposed and much is up for grabs in the way we conceive the possibilities for knowledge, for freedom, and for subject-hood in the wake of this exposure (Gordon 1997, 12).

The classical theoretical narratives of modernity no longer hold up, but the 'post' of post-modernity does not necessarily mean a radical rupture or break with the social and political issues addressed by those narratives. If post-modernity is understood as 'after' rather than 'anti' modernity, this 'clears the ground for new political and social strategies which embrace difference, pluralism and the incommensurability of culture and values' (Turner 1990, 12). In addition, it is important to remember that for a vast number of global citizens, the distinction between the modern and the post-modern is only likely to make sense in their everyday lives in relation to policies and practices that affect their personal well-being. This is an important point that should guide the theorist, especially if s/he is to play a useful and critical role as a public intellectual able to diagnose *and* critique the conditions and relations of our time and reveal the ways in which personal troubles are public issues. The political role of the social theorist of modernity/post-modernity is a reflexive, interpretative role that claims the 'right to expose the conceit and arrogance, the unwarranted claims to exclusivity of other's interpretations, but without substituting itself in their place' on the understanding that choices made about 'how to go on' in this world are not 'given', waiting to be revealed, but something that has to be worked for (Bauman 1992, 214). Agger (1991, 185) suggests that the theorist needs to 'engage (and enrage) the public'; as a result, the theorist will never win a popularity contest among those who claim power and privilege. But in the complex, risky, global social world we all inhabit, the 'global vocation of the social theorist is . . . to be *positively*—as opposed to negatively and nostalgically—analytical and *critical*' (Roland Robertson 1990, 57).

The explanatory capacity of social theory is important in confronting the abstractions of power, and there is as much need for social theory today as there was in the nineteenth century. The meaning of Dahrendorf's first intention—making the fact of society accessible to rational understanding—may have been reformulated to encompass the ways in which 'society' is problematized. At the same time, the healthy scepticism about science needs to be tempered by recognition that scientific theory and practice is currently under siege by religious zealotry which can hinder the pursuit of the second intention—helping individuals to realize freedom and self-fulfillment. This latter intention remains the critical, ethical, and useful basis for the social theorist and social theory.

Questions to Consider

1. How do concepts of community, social solidarity, and social class remain important in explaining social issues in the twenty-first century?
2. Can the Internet produce a global community?
3. What issues for global security are raised by Western consumer culture?
4. How do media reports of non-Western conflict encourage the perception of 'otherness' among the participants?
5. Examine how social locations affect the judgments made about terrorist troubles and help to perpetuate social problems.

Notes

1 The class and race-based issues were quickly identified by feminists as something that required theoretical *and* pragmatic actions. They remain, however, significant issues in the feminist pursuit of improvement in all women's lives.
2 For example, Brym and Hamlin (2004) have recently conducted research on the high suicide rates of the Brazilian Guarani-Kaoiwa, using Durkheim's work as a basis for their investigations.

Chapter 8

Does the Past Matter in Sociology?

Rob Beamish

No one can take that [gold medal] away from me! (Ben Johnson, 24 September 1988)

INTRODUCTION

At the 1988 Olympic Games in Seoul, South Korea, Ben Johnson took just 48 strides in under 9.8 seconds to become the world's fastest human, the gold-medal champion in the Games' premier event, the pride of Canadians, and the potential recipient of millions of dollars in endorsement revenue. Within three days, Johnson was stripped of his medal, condemned as a cheater, vilified by many Canadians, and faced an uncertain financial future (see CBC 2005). Does any of that matter now? Why did Johnson use steroids? Has the world of Olympic sport changed in the intervening period? These are questions that many sociologists find interesting and important; they also demonstrate how much the past matters to good sociological analysis.

In this chapter, I will begin with the question: what social pressures led to Johnson's use of steroids? The full answer to that question provides a good, comprehensive background for considering questions about the relevance of change over time. In answering such questions, this chapter will demonstrate the extreme complexity surrounding the use of performance-enhancing substances in world-class sport and why condemning individual athletes is more problematic than most recognize. Most important, the chapter will indicate why the past is always of critical importance to sociological analysis. It will explore how a historically informed sociology leads to insights one would otherwise miss.

THE PRINCIPLES BEHIND THE REVIVAL OF THE OLYMPIC GAMES

Between 1500 and 1900, the key countries in western Europe were completely transformed. Britain, France, and to a lesser extent Germany changed from societies that were led and dominated by kings, queens, and a feudal aristocracy to societies in which business owners held the bulk of economic and political power. The consolidation of capitalism led to new and very different ways of thinking about the world, conducting one's affairs, and carrying on everyday activities. But not everyone thought well of the changes.

French aristocrat Baron Pierre de Coubertin was deeply troubled by what he regarded as a catastrophic spiritual and moral decline in Europe. At the close of the nineteenth century, Coubertin initiated a far-reaching, innovative educational program that he hoped would end the growing materialism of industrial capitalism and return Europe in general and France in particular to its 'traditional values'. Education in the late nineteenth century, Coubertin argued,

> has made the present generation stray into the impasse of excessive specialization, where they will find nothing but obscurity and disunity. They believe they are very powerful because they have great appetites, and they believe they are very wise because they have a great deal of scientific data. In reality, they are poorly prepared for the troubles ahead. Intelligence is smothered by knowledge, critical minds are debased by an overwhelming mass of facts, and adolescents are trained into the mentality of the anthill, surrounded by the artificial and the accepted, with categories and statistics, a fetish for numbers, an unhealthy search for detail and the exception (2000, 559).

Coubertin thought that the solution to Europe's decline lay in a combination of the ideals of ancient Greece and the 'muscular Christian' philosophies of England's Canon Kingsley and the Reverend Thomas Arnold (Coubertin 2000, 294–5). The ancient Greeks had believed that humans were comprised of mind, body, and character. Character—Coubertin's chief concern—was not formed solely by the mind but also by the body. As a result, sport played a fundamental role in the spiritual vitality of the ancients. These beliefs paralleled the muscular Christians' use of traditional English games to build character and moral virtue in young boys and men. Coubertin was convinced that sport, appropriately structured, could play a pivotal role in revitalizing moral and spiritual fibre (532, 308).

The revival of the ancient Olympic Games, Coubertin insisted, would instil 'a marvellous solidification of the human machine'. The Games would create 'a delicate balance of mind and body, the joy of a fresher and more intense life, the harmony of the faculties, a calm and happy strength' (534, 536). Resting on a strong philosophical foundation and displaying the same pomp, ceremony, and spectacle as the ancient Games, the modern Olympics would build character, spirit, and strong moral fibre among European youth (536–7, 543).

The image of sport that motivated Coubertin was genuinely inspiring. 'The athlete,' he wrote, 'enjoys his effort'[1]:

> He likes the constraint that he imposes on his muscles and nerves, through which he comes close to victory even if he does not manage to achieve it. This enjoyment remains internal, egotistical in a way. Imagine if it were to expand outward, becoming intertwined with the joy of nature and the flights of art. Picture it radiant with sunlight, exalted by music, framed in the architecture of porticoes. It was thus that the glittering dream of ancient Olympism was

born on the banks of the Alphaeus, the vision of which dominated ancient society for so many centuries (2000, 552).

Coubertin's Games would immerse European youth in a sacred event that would renew the spiritual vitality of the participants' souls. The Olympics would involve 'a religious feeling' whereby athletes would embrace 'the spirit of chivalry' (654, 588). Two elements were vital: beauty and reverence:

> If the modern Games are to exercise the influence I desire for them they must in their turn show beauty and inspire reverence—a beauty and a reverence infinitely surpassing anything hitherto realized in the most important athletic contests of our day. The grandeur and dignity of processions and attitudes, the impressive splendor of ceremonies, the concurrence of all the arts, popular emotion and generous sentiment, must all in some sort collaborate together (545).

The Olympic spirit was far removed from sport tainted by commercialism and the overly competitive zeal that already characterized athletic competitions in late nineteenth-century Europe. Prize money, trophies, and records were for the 'fair grounds and common athletic stadiums'. Coubertin's innovative educational project would welcome only those who sought to cultivate the spirit of Olympism. 'Fair or temple': Coubertin argued that 'sportsmen must make their choice; they cannot expect to frequent both one and the other'. An athlete who bathed in the sacred rituals of the Games would become infused with the traditional values of ancient Greece and be ready to lead Europe out of the crass materialism of the capitalist world. Conducted properly, the Olympic experience would create the 'transposition from the muscular to the moral sphere, the basis of athletic education' (593).

Coubertin believed that all this was possible because the Games would forge 'an *aristocracy*, an *elite*' that would 'also be a *knighthood*'—'"brothers-in-arms", brave energetic men united by a bond that is stronger than that of mere camaraderie, which is powerful enough in itself'. Chivalry would be the Games' code of conduct in which 'the idea of competition, of effort opposing effort for the love of effort itself, of courteous yet violent struggle, is superimposed on the notion of mutual assistance' (581). Coubertin's Games would bring chivalrous brothers-in-arms together in the cauldron of competition so that they could emerge as strong, morally sound leaders for Europe (see Beamish and Ritchie 2004).

COUBERTIN AND THE AMATEUR ATHLETE

In view of his goals, it was not likely that professional athletes could fulfill Coubertin's objectives, although there was no principled reason to exclude them from the Games—a professional athlete could, in theory at least, leave pro sport and embrace the Games and the spirit of Olympism. Nevertheless, the members of the first International Olympic Committee (IOC) decided that the best way to attain Coubertin's lofty objectives was to restrict the Games to the social stratum that was most suitable for the leadership roles Coubertin had in mind—the upper class. As a result, the IOC restricted the Games to amateur athletes, which meant Olympic competition was really only open to aristocrats and people of substantial means. It was this group of young men with their broad life experiences, the IOC argued, who would genuinely benefit from Coubertin's project.

It is important to point out that it was the IOC and not Coubertin himself that insisted on the amateur restriction. For Coubertin, it was more than a matter of choosing people with the correct social aspirations. His vision was more subtle and profound than simply restricting the Games to amateur athletes; his ideal, rooted in the traditions of classical Greece and nineteenth-century England, was based on the view that 'the "real" ruler-gentleman was a qualitatively distinct form of humanity', and this was the type of person that Coubertin wanted to expose to the athletic/religious experience of the Games (Moore 1966, 488). Playing without pay was of little consequence compared to the deep spiritual commitment and experience that Coubertin wanted from the Games' participants. For Coubertin:

> sport was a religion with its church, dogmas, service . . . but above all a religious feeling, and it seemed childish to me to make all this depend on whether an athlete had received a five franc coin as automatically to consider the parish verger an unbeliever because he receives a salary for looking after the church (2000, 654).

Honour rather than amateurism was the chief criterion Coubertin wanted to use to determine who could take part in and benefit from the Olympic experience. 'We must establish the tradition that each competitor shall in his bearing and conduct as a man of honor and a gentleman endeavor to prove in what respect he holds the Games and what an honor he feels to participate in them,' Coubertin wrote. To ensure the Games' integrity and confirm that each athlete was genuinely committed to their intended spirit, Coubertin wanted to revive the 'ceremony of the oath' from the ancient Olympics (546).

Unable to sway the IOC's belief that amateurism should determine who could participate in the Games, Coubertin grudgingly acquiesced to the restriction even though it was actually far less limiting than he wanted—'amateur' was simply a category of status, whereas honour was a commitment to specific values, goals, and objectives. In addition, honour was central to the chivalric code and the traditional values of Europe that he sought to re-establish.

IMMEDIATE CHALLENGES TO COUBERTIN'S PROJECT

If the modern Olympic Games were designed to reverse the slide of Europe into the moral abyss of industrial capitalism and its crude materialist philosophy, Coubertin discovered very quickly that the actual possibilities open to them were limited by the market economy and the network of social institutions associated with it. To launch his project, Coubertin and the IOC had to draw on the support of commercial interests and capitalist entrepreneurs. Thus, for example, it was only due to the financial largesse of wealthy businessman George Averoff that the ancient stadium in Athens was renovated in time for the first modern Olympiad (Guttmann 2002, 15–16). More important, rather than combating the crass materialism of capitalist society, the IOC had to hold the Paris, St Louis, and London Games (1900, 1904, and 1908 respectively) in conjunction with world's fairs, which celebrated technology, science, industrial capitalism, and modern culture—the very forces that Coubertin blamed for the demise of Europe's spiritual values.

Undoubtedly, the greatest concession that Coubertin and the IOC had to make was an agreement with Coca Cola (and other sponsors), which negotiated an exclusive-rights package for the Amsterdam Games. The 1996 Games in Atlanta were not the first 'Coke Games', and Coca Cola uses its history of involvement as part of its Olympic advertising in the nostalgia-oriented markets of contemporary North America—'associated with the Games since 1928'. In the same way that the citizens of ancient Troy took the Greek gift horse inside their city's walls, only to discover that it contained the invading forces that would capture the city, the Amsterdam agreements welcomed into the Games the crass commercial forces that Coubertin had wanted to repel. Sponsorship at those Olympiads set the dangerous precedent of tying the Games to commercial interests rather than fighting against them. The decision converted Coubertin's sacred project into a profane billboard celebrating modern commerce.

Three further divisive forces that have plagued the Olympics were also present from the outset—nationalism, professional athletes, and the 'cult of victory'. In preparation for the inaugural 1896 Games, Russian, British, German, American, and French officials all resisted the IOC's amateur restriction. Wanting to use the Olympics to demonstrate national strength in international competition, each of these countries wanted to use the best athletes available. Happy to pay lip service to Coubertin's ideals, the leaders of Europe were really interested in the quest for victory, the symbolic value of winning on the world stage, and the pursuit of national interests rather than international harmony.

The disjuncture between Coubertin's principles and the real world of international sport, even at the turn of the twentieth century, was also evident in the conflict between the IOC and the Fédération Internationale de Football Association (FIFA). Soccer was Europe's premier sport, but it was absent from the initial Games because the best players in the world were all professional and thus ineligible. When the IOC tried to include soccer in the 1928 Games, only 17 teams could meet the eligibility requirements. FIFA suggested that the IOC should relax its rules and either let professionals play or allow amateurs to receive financial compensation for the work time they would lose while at the Games. The staunchly amateur International Association of Athletics Federation (IAAF) pressured the IOC to reject FIFA's proposal, and soccer was excluded from the 1932 Olympics. Recognizing the value of an international spectacle, FIFA established the World Cup in 1930—the direct antithesis of the Games. The World Cup involved the best players in the world in a tournament where the only thing that mattered was winning. The World Cup was overtly commercial and fostered national rivalries rather than reducing or eliminating them. Thus the Olympics had a direct competitor that celebrated all the features of industrial capitalist society that the Games condemned.

By 1936 compromise was possible. The IOC wanted soccer, and FIFA no longer worried about the quality of the players participating in the Olympics since the world's best players were featured at the World Cup. The amateur players at the Games represented soccer's best developing talent and served as publicity for FIFA's main event (see Senn 1999, 9–11, 45–6). From the IOC's perspective, the stand against FIFA was a victory because the world's most popular sport entered the Games on the IOC's own terms. Even in the face of tremendous pressure from FIFA, the media, and various world leaders, the principle of amateurism had been maintained.

THE NAZI OLYMPICS

After 10 Olympiads, additional social forces were pushing the Games further away from Coubertin's ideal and toward an overall ethos that would lead to the events in Seoul. Of all the forces that sociologists would focus on to understand Johnson's victory—and subsequent disgrace—national interest and international politics are among the most important. This is not surprising in view of Coubertin's original objective, but it was not until the 1936 Games in Nazi Germany that the full symbolic power and political importance of the Olympics was completely demonstrated.

In the aftermath of the First World War, the rest of Europe was slow to welcome Germany back into the international fold. As the new German Republic established itself, European leaders gradually warmed to greater German participation in western European affairs. The IOC's decision in 1929 to grant Germany the 1936 Games was an important gesture that demonstrated the reintegration of Germany into the European mainstream.

Unfortunately, even though the IOC gave the Games to a liberal democratic regime, political events in Germany shifted drastically, and Adolf Hitler became German chancellor in 1933. The IOC considered withdrawing the Games, but there was no other host to take them over. Hitler and the Nazis were ambivalent about the Olympics and considered declining the opportunity, but Joseph Goebbels, head of the Ministry of Public Enlightenment and Propaganda, recognized that there might be a unique opportunity to use the Promethean symbolic power of the Games to project specific images of Nazi Germany domestically and internationally (see Teichler 1975).

The Games were not an isolated project for Goebbels's ministry; they were just one part of an ongoing, multi-faceted program of political propaganda. Prior to the Berlin Games, the Nazis had routinely exploited the newly emerging technologies of mass communication to spread their propaganda domestically. Hitler's speeches to vast rallies relied on state-of-the-art public address systems and were broadcast on radio and shown in movie theatres across the nation. To ensure that their message reached the homes of every German, the Nazis supplied radios set to the Nazi's transmission frequency to every family that wanted one.

The Nazis' trademark propaganda events combined dramatic music and the tightly choreographed movements of hundreds of performers inside imposing neo-classical-styled stadiums before thousands of spectator/participants. Drawing some of their inspiration from Hollywood's large-scale productions, the Nazis orchestrated powerful, emotion-laden Gesamtkunstwerke (total works of art)—music, choreography, drama, and neo-classical architecture were blended into captivating, exhilarating, and emotionally draining experiences (Clark 1997; Speer 1969).

The 1934 Nazi party congress in Nuremberg gave Hitler and the Nazis the opportunity to develop ceremonies that would best convey the Nazi message. World-renowned filmmaker Leni Riefenstahl—the most innovative and experimental of her time—produced films of the party congress and the 1936 Games. The similarities between the two events and Riefenstahl's films *Triumph of the will* and *Olympia* show how calculated the Nazis were about the exploitation of the Games for their own political purposes (see Sontag 1980).

In both events and even more in the carefully cropped and painstakingly constructed film 'documentaries' of them, the power and order of Nazi Germany was conveyed through the movement of hundreds of people into huge geometric formations that symbolized the transformation of a formless mass into a disciplined, united force. Hitler's entrance through the wide aisles of the assembled throng and his climb to an elevated podium represented his emergence from the people and ascendance from the rank and file to Germany's top position—Führer of the German Volk. At both events, Hitler is shown as a man of the people and the personification of their will. Riefenstahl edited both films so that the viewers' attention is continually shifted from the massed ranks or spectators to the Führer, to the enormous swastika banners in the stadiums. One cannot miss the intended message—'ein Volk, ein Führer, ein Reich' (one racially pure people, one leader, one empire).

Both films suggest that they are documentaries simply following the natural flow of events, but they are carefully constructed narratives that present well-crafted images and messages to viewers. And the climaxes of the two events were identical. The closing ceremonies of the 1936 Games replicated Albert Speer's 'cathedral of light' at Nuremberg: he placed powerful anti-aircraft spotlights around the perimeter of the stadiums at Nuremberg and Berlin, sending powerful beams of light deep into the night sky. 'At first the columns of light were straight up,' Mandell (1971, 277) wrote about the Games' closing ceremonies, 'but then the infinitely distant tops of the shafts gradually converged to enclose the darkened stadium in a temple composed entirely of glowing spirit' (see also Speer 1969, 96–7). The spectacular effect was a moving conclusion to the Games and *Olympia*, symbolizing the majesty of the Olympics as well as the imperial stature of Nazi Germany.

The Nazis introduced two further innovations to the 1936 Games that further served their political and propaganda goals. One was the torch relay—not invented for the Atlanta Games but originating in 1936. The relay, which carried strong echoes for every German of the victorious torchlight parade through the

Brandenburg Gate past the Chancellery when Hitler took power on 30 January 1933, symbolically linked ancient Greece—the racially homogeneous apogee of ancient civilization—with the Third Reich to which the torch was now passed.

Second, Nazi ideology celebrated and glorified youth, strength, struggle, and conquest. It emphasized genetic and racial endowment in the natural, Darwinian struggle for the survival of the fittest. Coubertin's Games already celebrated nature, power, and struggle; all the Nazis had to do was carefully weave into the Olympic aesthetic the ideology of racial supremacy so that their message could be seen and understood. While some people have argued that Jesse Owens's four gold medals undermined Hitler's political objectives, the reality is that the Führer's message was clear to sympathetic or undecided German viewers as they saw the host nation top all other countries with 33 gold, 26 silver, and 30 bronze medals (the US won 24, 20, and 12). Germans knew that they were once again among the most powerful and successful nations of the world. Interestingly, of all the Games he saw, Coubertin stated that the Berlin Olympics were the closest to his idea of the sacred Olympic festival/spectacle (Teichler 1982).

OLYMPIC PRINCIPLES AND THE REALITY OF COLD WAR SPORT

Suspended during the Second World War, the Games returned in 1948 in a modest format. But the next Games were far from low-key. Although Canada, Britain, France, and the United States had been allied with the Soviet Union in the fight against Germany, tensions between the capitalist West and the communist Soviet Union arose immediately after the war. The 1952 Helsinki Games was the first occasion that the world's two new superpowers, now on opposite sides of the emerging cold war, would confront each other in the international arena.

The US already had a long history of victory at the Games. Drawing on scholarship athletes who trained and developed within well-funded college programs, the US had a significant advantage over other countries sending athletes to the Games. In contrast, during its brief history the USSR had intentionally stayed outside the Olympic movement and supported the less competitive Workers' Sport Movement—a rival to Coubertin's project.

However, in the post-war era Joseph Stalin, secretary general of the Communist party of the Soviet Union, made it his primary objective to surpass the capitalist nations of the world in every realm of social life, including sport (Riordan 1977, 161–2). To that end, the USSR initiated a nationally coordinated development program for Olympic sports. The program included an infrastructure of high-quality facilities, professional coaches, scientific training programs, and physiological, bio-mechanical, and psychological research in the pursuit of improved athletic performance, as well as a financial incentive program for successful athletes (Riordan 1977, 162–4; Senn 1999, 85). By the late 1940s, Stalin was ready to compete directly with the West and sought formal admission to the Olympic movement. The IOC for its part was willing to admit the Soviets so that the movement would be truly international.

The Helsinki Games represented an international media event of enormous magnitude. The Soviets shocked the world by jumping out to an early lead in the unofficial medal and point standings and remained there until the final day of competition when the Americans finally edged them out for first place overall. The drama of the Games and the attention they drew around the world demonstrated once again the tremendous political significance they held.

Attracting little attention at the time, the USSR's performance in weightlifting had a far-reaching impact on the Olympic movement—an outcome that led directly to Seoul. Watching the Soviets win three gold, three silver, and one bronze medal, US weightlifting coach Bob Hoffman told the Associated Press that the Soviets were 'taking the hormone stuff to increase their strength' (Todd 1987, 93). During the 1954 world weightlifting championships, Hoffman and American team physician John Ziegler declared that, in their minds at least, the Soviets were using testosterone to enhance the muscle-building capacity of their weightlifters.

Ziegler returned to the US with one objective in mind—to level the playing field for American weightlifters. With the assistance of Ciba Pharmaceutical Company, he developed the synthetic steroid methandieone (or Dianabol), which he gave to weightlifters at the York Barbell Club in Pennsylvania (Goldman 1984, 94; Ryan 1976, 516–17). 'The news of anabolic steroids spread through the athletic community like wildfire,' Ziegler associate Bob Goldman (1984, 94) noted, 'and soon drugs and stories of drugs became the chief topic of conversation at training camps and the subject of articles in all of the sports magazines'. By the early 1960s, steroid use was widespread among athletes in any of the strength events—weightlifting, shot put, discus, hammer throw, etc. (Yesalis and Bahrke 2002, 53). While the use of steroids is important to note, of greater consequence is the approach to sport their use indicated. After the Helsinki Games, the cold, calculated, scientifically assisted pursuit of victory and national honour emerged as the key force guiding the serious competitors and nations at the Olympic Games. They would be increasingly dominated by 'instrumental reason'—a term that describes situations in which reason alone is used to determine the best, most efficient means to a particular end without regard to the broader context of action and decision-making.

Even though sports leaders would ultimately view steroids as the most evil of the numerous performance-enhancing substances, it was cyclist Knud Jensen's death, allegedly due to a nicotinyl alcohol and amphetamine mixture—designed to enhance endurance—at the 1960 Summer Games that led the IOC to try to limit and regulate the emergent instrumental rationality in world-class sport. Yet the shadow of a scientifically based, politically inspired, all-out quest for victory loomed ominously over the movement.

While a crucial factor in the events that led to Ben Johnson's world record and Olympic gold performance in 1988, politically motivated instrumental rationality was associated with two additional social pressures that complemented the investment nations made in the Games. The first was an increasingly professionalized approach to world-class, high-performance sport, and the second was the growing interest that various media and sporting goods manufacturers had in the Olympic Games. For instance, the USSR/US confrontation in Helsinki made the perfect story line for television—still in its infancy as a mass entertainment medium—because for the first time, spectators around the world could experience the drama as it happened. Merchandisers saw the Games attracting increasingly larger audiences that could be targeted for sales. When the Games proved themselves as a successful television spectacle, the networks were willing to pay the IOC millions of dollars for exclusive broadcast rights. The networks then sold advertising time to merchants wanting to reach the highly coveted audience of males between 18 and 35 years of age. But political drama alone was not enough: American (or at least Western) athletes had to win, and world records had to fall. Those results would only occur if Western athletes trained as rigorously as the Soviets, who were supported by a well-funded state system of scientifically based athlete development. Western athletes needed financial support and a scientific infrastructure. Under-the-table performance fees quickly emerged for the very best world-class, high-performance athletes in the highest-profile sports, and Olympic athletes began to train for more extended periods of the year until by the 1970s, world-class sport had become a virtually full-time commitment.

All of these forces together continued to feed off each other, setting in motion a spiral that extended its reach with each Olympiad or televised world championship. Amateurism became a burning question, especially since many in the IOC felt that the Games had to move with the times. Yet despite resistance, IOC president Avery Brundage realized a 20-year-old dream in 1962 when the IOC incorporated Rule 26, the amateurism code, into the Olympic Charter.[2]

Even though Brundage had succeeded in enshrining amateurism in the charter, he also knew that the increasing use of performance-enhancing substances on both sides of the Iron Curtain still left instrumental rationality untouched. Victory-at-any-cost had to be controlled; the Olympics 'must' be drug-free. As a result, the IOC established a medical committee to study drug use in sport and recommend how the IOC could protect the integrity and purity of the Games.

Within two years, the committee recommended to the IOC that it had to take a public stand against drug use, enforce that position with drug testing, and make eligibility dependent on athletes signing a pledge confirming they did not use performance-enhancing substances (Todd and Todd 2001, 67). Over the next three years, the medical committee determined which specific performance-enhancing substances and practices it would not accept and developed the first banned list, leaving all substances and practices not on the banned list as legitimate. The IOC added Rule 28 to the Olympic Charter, stating that 'the use of substances or techniques in any form or quantity alien or unnatural to the body with the exclusive aim of obtaining an artificial or unfair increase of performance in competition' was forbidden.

Rule 28 demonstrated two important points about the trajectory the Games were following. First, the use of performance-enhancing substances was clearly antithetical to the spirit Coubertin had intended for the Games. He wanted them to be morally uplifting as athletes competed in 'the spirit of chivalry'—'"brothers-in-arms", brave energetic men united by a bond that is stronger than that of mere camaraderie'. Instead, the Games centred on winning, which meant that athletes increasingly used every means possible to win gold. Rule 28 was designed to curtail at least some of those means to enhancing performance. Second, Rule 28 was aimed at the growth of scientifically assisted performance-enhancement in general. The cult of victory and the instrumental rationality of sport science were two sides of the same coin, and neither had any place in Coubertin's original vision of the Games. The IOC hoped that it could find a bureaucratic solution—the introduction of rules—to stop the trajectory of the Games towards the unrestricted, scientifically assisted pursuit of the linear record. Unfortunately for the IOC, the US and the USSR were not the only nations intensively focused on demonstrating national strength through the international sport spectacle.

COLD WAR SPORT: EAST GERMAN VERSUS WEST GERMAN

At the end of the Second World War, Germany was divided into four sectors, each occupied by one of the allied victors—Britain, France, the US, and the USSR. The Soviet sector was in the eastern half of Germany and became the German Democratic Republic (GDR) under the political leadership of Walter Ulbricht, the first general secretary of the Central Committee of the Socialist Unity party (Sozialistische Einheitspartei Deutschlands). Like Stalin, Ulbricht recognized that sport provided an excellent vehicle for building national pride in the new socialist society. Just four years after the end of the war, and before the GDR was admitted into the Olympic movement, Ulbricht took the first steps toward building what became the world's most powerful centralized sport system.

Ulbricht began by establishing the State Committee for Physical Culture and Sport (Staatlichen Komitees für Körperkultur und Sport, or STAKO) and gave it a clear mandate to mobilize all the resources needed for the development of a world-class sport system (Spitzer, Teichler, and Reinartz 1998, 38–43).[3]

STAKO's approach to sport was simple: find the best means to the only end that mattered—gold medals. 'In the most important sports,' the STAKO mandate directed, 'top athletes should be concentrated in facilities where the requirements for the systematic improvement of performance are present or can be created.' Specific sports like track and field, swimming, gymnastics, boxing, cycling, wrestling, rowing, soccer, volleyball, basketball, and handball were singled out for particular emphasis. Each of these sports was on the Olympic program, and most of them were individual sports in which a single outstanding athlete could win multiple medals in contrast to team sports like hockey in which 22 athletes can win only one medal for the nation. Following the Soviet example, the GDR opened children's and youth sport schools (Kinder- und Jugendsportschulen), which implemented a carefully designed developmental progression for child athletes as they moved from primary or junior elementary schools to middle and senior elementary schools (Röder 2002). STAKO ranked athletes to increase their motivation to excel and determined the level of coaching they would receive and the competitions they could enter. A 'master of sport' category provided role models to increase the profile of sport and draw young children into the system.

In the immediate post-war period, the GDR and the Federal Republic of Germany (FRG)—or West Germany—were excluded from the Games. In 1952, along with admitting the USSR to the movement, the IOC also recognized the FRG's National Olympic Committee (NOC). Since the IOC would only recognize one NOC per country, the GDR remained excluded from the Games. However, under pressure from the USSR and other NOCs from East Bloc countries, the IOC relented and recognized an East German NOC, although it would permit only one German team to enter the Games.[4]

Official recognition led to a revitalization of the East German system. In 1957 Ulbricht replaced STAKO with the German Gymnastics and Sport Federation (Deutscher Turn- und Sportbund), headed by Manfred Ewald. Under Ewald, who held the post until just before the fall of the Berlin Wall in 1989, the GDR began to extend its system so that it would soon rival the Soviets for world supremacy in high-performance sport (Gilbert 1980; Hoberman 1984, 201–7).

In the initial years, the FRG dominated the combined German Olympic team because of its superior industrial and financial strength, larger population base, and well-supported voluntary, club-based sport system. By the early 1960s, however, as world-class sport became more intensely competitive, training obligations increased, and athletes had to make an increasingly full-time commitment to sport, the FRG's German Sport Federation (Deutscher Sportbund, or DSB) recognized that significant changes were needed for the FRG to stay competitive. The DSB sought out partnerships between corporations and high-performance athletes so that West German athletes could build long-term careers while still concentrating on their high-performance sport commitments (Lehnertz 1979, 50).

Two decisions in the mid-1960s had monumental impact on the FRG and GDR in particular and the world of high-performance sport more generally. The first was to allow both Germanys to send their own teams to the 1968 and all future Olympic Games. Now the GDR could compete head-to-head with its Western rival while also demonstrating its strength in comparison to the world's two leading sporting nations—the US and the USSR.

Second, in 1965 the IOC granted the 1972 Games to Munich, West Germany. The GDR immediately recognized the opportunity this represented. 'Olympic history,' GDR sports leaders gloated,

> has struck hard at the enemy of sport, the enemy of our Republic, and our socialist system. The anti-sport powers of the Federal Republic of Germany must now, in their own land, organize and prepare for the first fully sovereign Olympic team from the German Democratic Republic. They are the ones who, for the first time at the Olympic Summer Games, must raise the flag of the GDR, and rehearse and play our national anthem (Society for the Promotion of the Olympic Idea 1972, 16).

To maximize their chances of victory, Ewald immediately focused on the improvement of 'supplementary materials' (unterstützende Mittel)—performance-enhancing drugs. Using 'supplementary materials' was not new: since at least 1966 male athletes in the GDR had taken steroids made in the state-owned pharmaceutical firm VEB Jenapharm. Ewald's approach was new because it drew on extensive, high-level, classified laboratory research funded by the state so that the GDR could have the most scientifically advanced program of steroid use (see Franke and Berendonk 1997). While not the sole reason and likely not the primary one behind the GDR's success—the financial investment, number of full-time coaches, attention to detail, and extensive recruitment of athletes were all superior to those of other nations—the tight community of world-class, high-performance athletes on both sides of the Iron Curtain knew about the widespread use of banned substances in the GDR. If they were to keep things fair and equal, some athletes, coaches, and sports leaders faced some difficult decisions.

The prospect of embarrassment on its own soil spurred the West German DSB to significantly revitalize its high-performance sport system and it began with its first-ever high-performance sport plan. The plan drew heavily from the East German model, which was not only the FRG's chief concern but had also demonstrated how much success a well-funded, rationalized sport system could generate. The new plan recommended the hiring of national team coaches and the creation of high-performance training centres (Stützpunkte). The Stützpunkte would allow athletes to remain and train at home throughout most of the year, and at designated times they could be brought together to train with other provincial or national team athletes under the guidance of the FRG's best coaches (see Giesler 1980). Within a decade, there were over 180 Stützpunkte for national-level athletes.

Like the East Germans, the DSB established a sport and athlete ranking system, promoted long-term planning within its national sports organizations, and sought improvements to the pedagogical, medical, and psychological development of athletes. Similarly, programs of early talent identification were introduced, 35 elite sport schools were established, and after the FRG placed behind the GDR at the 1968 Games, the DSB introduced sport boarding schools to maximize talent development (Lehnertz 1979, 37–52; Bette 1984, 25–8).

There were two outcomes from these developments in East and West Germany. First, the East German system, which was modelled to a large extent on the Soviet high-performance sport system, became the blueprint for the West German system, which in turn became the model for the high-performance sport system in Canada when it was granted the 1976 Games. Not only did Ben Johnson begin his career within the nationally coordinated Canadian high-performance sport system but it became the model for the Australian and ultimately the American high-performance sport systems (Beamish 1993; Beamish and Borowy 1989; Green and Oakley 2001). Granting the Games to Munich and allowing the two Germanys to compete directly with each other led to the accelerated development of centralized high-performance sport systems that sought national aggrandizement through Olympic gold-medal performances above all else.

Second, nationalist political ambition was intensified as the main driving force behind the developing high-performance sport systems on both sides of the East/West divide. State-controlled funds were poured into centralized sport systems that concentrated on gold-medal production. The world of high-performance sport became increasingly professionalized, requiring a greater commitment from athletes, coaches, and administrators, and training and athlete preparation was dominated more and more by scientific instrumental rationality.

THE REST OF THE ROAD TO SEOUL

Enshrining the amateurism regulation in the Olympic Charter in 1964 did nothing to alter the trajectory toward the increased professionalization of the Games' athletes (see Killanin 1976). In terms of training, Olympic athletes increasingly had to commit to a full-time undertaking. Thus, for example, training time for track athletes doubled between 1950 and the late 1960s. Workloads increased in various ways—increases in the total amount of training; increased intensity in each session; more work compressed into shorter time frames; increased duration of work in training intervals; and/or reduced recovery time between intervals (Pfetsch et al. 1975, 40–52). Between 1960 and 1968, Soviet swimmers' training distances jumped from 594.7 km to 1,064 km per month, with the portion dedicated to high-tempo work rising from 18.0 to 57.4 per cent of a workout. For Soviet women, the distances rose from 482.4 km to 1,045 km, and high-tempo work moved from 18.5 per cent to 59.0 per cent of a workout (Lehnertz 1979, 12–13). In addition, exercise physiologists believed that if athletes trained close to exhaustion during practices there would be a rebound during the recovery phase to an even higher level of energy. Recovery from these extensively increased workloads was seen in the late 1960s and early 1970s as key to athletes rising to the top rungs of world-class sport.

In view of these changes in athlete training, a joint IOC/NOC commission reviewed the amateurism question in 1969 and 1970. The commission recommended that the IOC adopt an 'eligibility code'. A staunch supporter of amateurism, Brundage conceded on the name change but maintained as restrictive a code as ever. The new Rule 26 in the Olympic Charter—the eligibility code—excluded most if not all of the funding strategies that Western and East Bloc countries were using. 'Individuals subsidized by governments, educational institutions, or business concerns because of their athletic ability are not amateurs', the Rule began:

> Business and industrial concerns sometimes employ athletes for their advertising value. The athletes are given paid employment with little work to do and are free to practise and compete at all times. For national aggrandizement, governments occasionally adopt the same methods and give athletes positions in the army, on the police force, or in a government office. They also operate training camps for extended periods. Some colleges and universities offer outstanding athletes scholarships and inducements of various kinds. Recipients of these special favours, which are granted only because of athletic ability, are not eligible to compete in the Olympic Games (cited in Killanin 1976, 152).

Despite the new rule, top world-class athletes continued to receive state subsidies in the East or under-the-table fees in the West. Long before Nike took the world stage, brothers Adolf (Adi) and Rudolf (Rudi) Dassler competed against one another as owners of the rival Adidas and Puma shoe manufacturers, while a host of German and French ski manufacturers used the Winter Games to market their products to the world (Killanin 1976, 151; Senn 1999, 136). According to Brundage, downhill skiers were 'more brazen than the other athletes in their sub-version of Olympic rules' (cited in Barney, Wenn, and Martyn 2002, 105), and it was Austrian skiing sensation Karl Schranz who created the crisis that led to the end of amateurism. In a media interview inside the Olympic Village during the 1972 Sapporo Winter Games, Schranz said that he made $40,000 to $50,000 annually from appearance fees and endorsements. The IOC's Eligibility Commission had to disqualify him from the Games.

The IOC now had to either enforce the eligibility code by excluding the top athletes in the world—athletes who ensured large television audiences and revenues for the IOC—or revise Rule 26. The IOC decided to bring Rule 26 in line with the reality of world-class high-performance sport as it had developed to that point. After 1974, Rule 26 stated,

> [t]o be eligible for participation in the Olympic Games, a competitor must observe and abide by the Rules of the IOC and in addition the rules of his or her IF [International Federation] as approved by the IOC, even if the federation's rules are more strict than those of the IOC [and] not have received any financial rewards or material benefit in connection with his or her sports participation, except as permitted in the bye-laws to this Rule (cited in Killanin 1976, 143; see also International Olympic Committee 1989, 18, 43–4).

The new rule led to two significant changes in the Olympic Games. First, under the charter's by-laws, athletes could receive money and material benefits for their athletic performances. The revision not only made it absolutely clear what type of athletes could compete at the Games, those athletes were the direct antithesis of the type Coubertin had wanted in the Olympics. The fundamental reason for reviving the ancient Olympic Games was overturned; the Games would no longer focus on 'chivalrous athletic effort', 'intertwined with the joy of nature and the flights of art'. The sacred aspects of athletic competition—'radiant with sunlight, exalted by music, [and] framed in the architecture of porticoes'—was gone from the IOC's agenda. From 1974 onward, the Games centred on the best eligible athletes competing for Olympic gold, financial rewards, and national prestige. The Olympic Games had become an overtly commercial enterprise that was concerned about generating profits rather than future world leaders.

Second, the IFs now controlled which athletes could compete at the Games. Since IFs set the eligibility criteria annually (not just quadrennially) and had strong commercial incentives to ensure that the best athletes in the world took part in their world championships, the restrictions on fully professionalized, world-class, high-performance athletes were removed for all intents and purposes.

Although the IOC was willing to open the Games to increasingly professionalized athletes, it was still concerned about the use of performance-enhancing substances. In 1967 the IOC drafted its first list of banned substances—ranging from cocaine, pep pills, and vasodilators to alcohol, opiates, and hashish—and indicated that it would test athletes (Todd and Todd 2001, 68). It is important to note that steroids had entered the Games in 1952. Fifteen years later, they were banned even though the IOC could not test for them until 1973 and did not test for them until 1976. In that 24-year interval, for political and commercial reasons having nothing to do with steroids, the Games had shifted to the all-out pursuit of gold-medal performances and the shattering of world records. The ban rested on weak—often corrupted—moral authority and was widely disregarded (Todd 1987, 97; Todd and Todd 2001, 70–3). Even though steroid use in the West is not documented as extensively as it is in East Germany, abundant evidence demonstrates the widespread use of performance-enhancing substances by the late 1960s. Connolly (1989), Francis (1990), Dubin (1990), Franke and Berendonk (1997, 1264), and Todd and Todd (2001) all indicate that steroid use was prevalent if not pervasive among numerous athletes in the West (see also Beamish and Ritchie 2004). Decathlete Tom Waddell's estimate that more than a third of all the male athletes attending the pre-Olympic training camp at Lake Tahoe in 1968 were using steroids is typical of that period (Todd and Todd 2001, 69; see also Yesalis and Bahrke 2002, 53–4). There was no compelling reason for their use to decline over the next 20 to 30 years. On the contrary, the increasing financial rewards accruing to gold-medal winners made the use of an ever-growing array of performance-enhancing practices more prevalent than ever.

CONCLUSION

Is history important for a sociological understanding of Ben Johnson's performance in Seoul? Definitely. First, history puts the race into a more complete and informative context. Johnson's decision to take steroids occurred within a system that was very different from what it claimed to be in public. Although Coubertin's lofty goals excluded the use of performance-enhancing substances—victory was of marginal importance—the Games developed differently. Indeed, by 1974 the IOC had formally removed the restriction on amateurism and jettisoned Coubertin's primary principle (Beamish and Ritchie 2004).

The political importance of the Games was a decisive factor leading to Johnson's victory in Seoul. The Nazis demonstrated the propaganda value of the Games in 1936, and from the first 'superpower' confrontation in 1952, the US, USSR, GDR, and other nations used athletic performances in world-class high-performance sport to demonstrate their national power and vitality.

An historically informed study of the Games reveals that steroids and other performance-enhancing substances have a long history in Olympic competition, and their importance grew after 1952. The decision to hold the 1972 Games in Munich further accelerated their use. With the opportunity to upstage and embarrass the FRG on its own soil, the GDR developed an extensive state-funded program involving 'supplementary materials'. Johnson benefited indirectly from that program, but more important, the GDR's politically motivated, instrumentally rational approach to Olympic sport set the context within which the Seoul Games were conducted.

Studying the past also demonstrates that for almost 25 years after the first use of steroids, the Olympic Games were essentially an open competition. Despite a questionable moral ban on their use, the IOC did not test for performance-enhancing substances until 1976, and testing procedures and protocols were highly suspect throughout the remaining decades of the twentieth century (see Yesalis and Bahrke 2002; Hoberman 2001; Voy 1991). Rather than undermining the Games, athletic performances that continually pushed back the limits of human performance enriched the IOC, advanced national political agendas, and turned the Olympics into a multi-million-dollar media spectacular, produced by professionalized, high-performance athletes. Elaborate, extensive, well-funded high-performance sport systems in the advanced industrial nations of the world combined with multinational commercial interests to construct a spectacle in which performance-enhancing substances are really one factor that has negligible influence on the direction and outcome of the Games even though they are demonized as the villains undermining Coubertin's lofty goals.

For the sociologist, all of these points are relevant for a careful assessment of Johnson's 1988 performance. On the basis of this analysis, Johnson's decision takes on a different light: moral condemnation is more difficult to justify. Johnson and other athletes in Seoul competed in the midst of powerful historical forces that induced many of them to place a gold-medal performance above all else. Some (or many) took chances—risked using substances for which they might get caught—to keep the competitive conditions fair, to win Olympic gold, to enhance their nations' prestige, and perhaps to gain substantial financial rewards. After they had dedicated years of their lives to that one competition, not trying to make the competitive conditions equal would have been the irrational, deviant decision.

Has anything changed substantially since 1988? Olympic sport remains a fully professionalized and commercialized undertaking. Athletes still pursue performance maximization with single-minded determination. Olympic victory is even more dependent today on the scientifically assisted pursuit of the outer limits of human performance. Ironically perhaps, the performance demands at the world-class level today are so extreme that ergogenic aids have become central to the regular practices of athletes in numerous sports. As a result, even though the World Anti-Doping Agency pursues 'the drug cheats' with increasing fanfare, it is undermined daily as the politically motivated instrumental rationality that entered the Games in the mid-twentieth century is woven ever more completely into the lives of world-class high-performance athletes (Brown 2001; Hoberman 2001; Yesalis and Bahrke 2002).

Questions to Consider

1. In your view, are Baron Pierre de Coubertin's original goals in re-establishing the Olympic Games in 1896 still evident today?
2. How did high-performance sport—or Olympic sport—change during the twentieth century? What is the particular significance of the 1936 Games and the introduction of Rule 26 in the Olympic Charter?

3. Has the nature of high-performance sport been changed by social forces? Explain.
4. Did Ben Johnson cheat? How would you defend your answer to that question?
5. Does the past matter in sociology? Are there other events in Canadian social life that you can identify in which understanding social change over a period of time makes what seems to be a straightforward issue—Ben Johnson cheated—into one that is much more complex? As Ben Johnson's coach Charlie Francis said, 'It *is* a level playing field; it's just not the one that most people think.'

Notes

1. A man of his times, Coubertin assumed athletes to be men.
2. Rule 26 stated: 'An amateur is one who participates and always has participated in sport without material gain. To qualify as an amateur, it is necessary to comply with the following conditions: (a) Have a normal occupation destined to ensure his [*sic*] present and future livelihood; (b) Never have received any payment for taking part in any sports competitions; (c) Comply with the rules of the International Federation concerned; (d) Comply with the official interpretations of this regulation (see Killanin 1976, 150).
3. 'There must be closer cooperation among the Free German Youth, the trade unions, the sport associations, and the People's Education Ministry,' the mandate read, 'so that there is a broad mobilization of youth and activities and that at least a million citizens of the German Democratic Republic take part in these activities creating an impressive testament to the defense of the German Democratic Republic' (Spitzer, Teichler, and Reinartz 1998, 40).
4. At the 1956 Olympic Winter Games in Cortina d'Empezzo, the East Germans provided 18 team members to 58 for the West Germans; in the 1956 Summer Games the ratio was 37:138. Combined German teams took part in two ensuing Olympiads—1960 and 1964 (German Sport Association 2003, 10).

What Do Official Statistics Tell Us about Ourselves?

Nob Doran

INTRODUCTION: EARLY EXPERIENCES WITH 'OFFICIAL STATISTICS'

My recollections of my first term in the 'honours, social science' undergraduate program at the University of York, England, are strongly marked by the sociology seminars I attended as supplements to the weekly lectures given to the whole first-year cohort. The first seminar topic was entitled 'In what ways do sociological explanations differ from common sense ones—indeed do they?' And it was here that I was first introduced to a world of scholarship completely different from anything I had ever experienced before. Whereas the formal lectures often took for granted the 'factual' nature of 'official statistics', these seminars exposed me to an alternative approach that documented how these 'official statistics' and the type of sociology that used them (I later found out that it was called positivist sociology, signifying that it was a form of social science modelled on insights from the natural sciences) were integrally based on the mundane 'common sense' assumptions that *tacitly* informed their compilation.

More important, this academic insight seemed to fit with what I already knew about the 'official statistics' process. Growing up on a Luton[1] council estate[2] and frequently hearing of encounters between acquaintances and police officers, as well as having had one or two of them myself (over issues like cycling without a light or cycling the wrong way down a one-way street), I was aware that it was common knowledge that 'official statistics' relating to crime and delinquency were compiled from the everyday practices of police officers. They decided to apprehend some people formally while dealing with others informally. And from sociology seminars such as these (which seemed to better explain my experiential world than the emphasis on the factual nature of 'official statistics' that I was receiving in the formal lectures), I went on to discover other related critiques of official statistics. Although I did not know it at the time, these critiques had first emerged in the 1960s and early 1970s. By the time I entered university, they were not uncommon. Moreover, the points they were making helped to change the way that sociology understood itself and also changed the way that I understood myself. So let us take a look at some of the studies that intrigued me in those early days of my intellectual and scholarly formation.

MICRO-CRITIQUES OF 'OFFICIAL STATISTICS': GARFINKEL'S LEGACY

My first seminar reading (Douglas 1970) had already alerted me to this alternative intellectual route. But I went on to discover other insightful analyses from similarly trained scholars. Douglas himself had written a book (1967) on the problems involved with the official statistics on suicide, but it was from Atkinson's work (1971; 1982) in this area that I probably learned the most.[3]

Drawing on his own empirical research, Atkinson proceeded to demonstrate the mundane, taken-for-granted, common sense knowledge that competent coroners use on a daily basis in order to make their decisions about how an unexpected death should be recorded. According to Atkinson, suicide is 'essentially a socially rather than a naturally defined form of behavior' (1971, 168). Thus researchers need to examine how social definitions are produced in everyday social life. When Atkinson examined the coroners' practices, he discovered that interpretive decisions resembled certain predicaments that judges face in courts of law when weighing evidence (1971, 174). That is, competent coroners use an array of informal common sense methods to help them come to a verdict regarding unexpected deaths.

For example, coroners will weigh considerations such as the following: the presence or absence of a suicide note (suicide notes are commonly understood as being good indicators of a suicide), the mode of death (certain ways of dying, such as hanging, are commonly understood as indicative of suicide, while others are routinely treated as probably not indicative, such as road deaths), the location and circumstances of death (an overdose taken in the middle of the woods, for example, is more likely to be understood as suggesting a suicide than an overdose in bed), and the life history and mental condition of the victim (coroners routinely assume that certain biographies are indicative of suicide).[4] But—and this was the crucial point—there is no mathematical formula for precisely determining how these different clues should be put together to unambiguously determine that an unexpected death was in fact a suicide. Both the layperson's reasoning about suicide and the coroner's reasoning employ similar informal methods. Each weighs and sifts through evidence before coming to a decision *for all practical purposes*, based on the information available.

Other early and influential studies that examined the ways in which 'official statistics' were produced included Cicourel on fertility (1967; 1973), Garfinkel on suicide (1967), Sudnow on deaths (1967), Cicourel on juvenile delinquency (1968), and Cicourel and Kitsuse on educational decision-making (1963). Other studies examined the mundane methods used to produce other socially relevant but not necessarily 'official' statistics. For example, MacKay's (1974) work examined the everyday methods used by teachers to produce supposedly objective scores for children's reading abilities from the standardized tests they administer. Garfinkel's (1967) work included an examination of the mundane common sense methods that went into the production of quantitative studies of psychiatric admissions (see Sharrock and Anderson 1986, 44–7, for an interesting Canadian example).

Although different in their substantive areas of investigation, most of these studies shared a common theoretical perspective. They pointed out a radically new direction for empirical social research. In contrast to the conventional sociology of that time, this school of 'ethnomethodology', as its founder Garfinkel named it,[5] prioritized quite different concerns. As has already been shown, it posited that official statistics could not simply be accepted as 'social facts' to be utilized for positivistic analysis. Rather, these statistics were 'practical accomplishments' (Garfinkel 1967) produced by the routine yet often tacit and taken-for-granted methods employed by their compilers.[6] And it was this concern with 'sense-making' that became central in the ethnomethodological perspective.

In fact, the ethnomethodologists invited other sociologists to study this process of sense-making and to make it a central feature of their analyses. And in order to prioritize the study of people's sense-making activities, older sociological conventions had to be radically altered. Garfinkel, for example, argued that it was no longer tenable to treat the 'social actor' as a 'judgmental dope'. Rather, s/he must be treated as a 'practical, rule-using analyst'. In other words, the dominant sociology of that time had tended to see the individual as acting in accordance with a certain 'normative' system (internalized through the socialization process and providing him/her with a set of 'norms' to *choose* to follow).[7] In contrast, the ethnomethodologists drew attention to the interpretive rather than the normative basis of social life. For them, we all are social actors living in an eminently practical world where rules act more like signposts.[8] As laypeople, we are constantly analyzing and interpreting our surroundings in order to make sense of what is going on around us while simultaneously acting in that social world.

From this engagement with the ethnomethodological approach, I learned some early and very valuable lessons—not just that 'official statistics' are compiled from the mundane, common sense assumptions about how our social world routinely works (which are then tacitly put into practice by, say, coroners) but a number of foundational theoretical lessons as well. Perhaps most important, I learned that the social world can only be known from within (Turner 1974, 204–5) and that the sociological researcher cannot escape using his/her own 'cultural competence' in order to make sense of his/her everyday world. Just as native speakers of English (or any other language) make sense of each other because they are constantly using a socially shared language (yet this is simply taken for granted by everyone involved), sociologists could also benefit from seeing social life as being structured like a language. And this view had consequences for future research. Just as linguists might study language systematically to show the underlying linguistic patterns taken for granted by native speakers, and just as anthropologists might study a foreign culture to display the meaningful pattern that culture has for its own members, the ethnomethodologists proposed to carry out somewhat similar analyses in the study of the mundane social world that we all routinely share.

Yet despite the force of these early ethnomethodological arguments, I nevertheless felt that the approach still lacked any explicit discussion of features that seemed quite integral to everyday life. Questions of power and conflict were everyday features of my life and the social world in which I lived; yet ethno-methodologists rarely paid attention to these key aspects of social life. Fortunately, in my early intellectual formation I did find some writers who took these questions of power in the everyday world quite seriously. And I learned the most from a feminist scholar—Dorothy Smith.[9]

EVERYDAY POWER RELATIONS WITHIN 'OFFICIAL STATISTICS': LEARNING FROM FEMINIST SCHOLARSHIP

I was first formally exposed to the work of Dorothy Smith in my second or third year as an undergraduate. I was introduced to an analysis (Smith 1978) in which she built on her existing ethnomethodological skills to display the 'common sense practices' by which a group of friends routinely came to recognize that another friend of theirs, K, was becoming mentally ill.[10] However, Smith's intent in that pioneering paper was not just to document these common sense practices but also to argue that they worked as mechanisms for excluding someone (1978, 50–2) and as strategies for freezing someone out of a relationship (1978, 25). And as I was soon to find out, this concern with how people get excluded became a central theme in much of Smith's subsequent work. In fact, much of the rest of her career is devoted to the analysis of exactly how women have been (Smith 1987) and still are excluded from what she often calls the 'ruling relations' (1999, 73–95).

But it was not long after this first encounter with Smith's work that I discovered her own powerful critiques of statistics. They were not only insightful but promised an understanding significantly different from the analyses developed by the ethnomethodologists. What she especially wanted to draw attention to was the transformative power of certain official discourses on everyday experience such that people's (especially women's) subjective experiences, their lived 'actuality' (1974b, 261) as she soon began calling it, get excluded, marginalized, or discarded. And official discourses, such as statistical ones, play a significant part in this process.

Smith's early work in this area isolated three related targets for analysis: first, the statistics routinely produced by (certain) sociologists in their empirical research; second, the official statistics routinely used but not necessarily produced by sociologists in their research; and third, the prevailing official statistics concerning the relationship between women and mental illness. She deals with the first two issues in her groundbreaking article, 'The ideological practices of sociology' (1974a), and the third in an article published a year later. In this early work, it is apparent that she had learned much from ethnomethodology but now wanted to move in a more critical direction. And for this she looks to Marx for help. That is, she combines the ethnomethodological insistence that people's taken-for-granted, common sense worlds constitute a paramount reality[11] (all other realities, such as social scientific ones, are parasitic on it) with Marx's concept of 'ideology'. This allows her to claim that social sciences like sociology are concretely engaged in ideological work. Let us examine her claim more closely.

For Smith, social science and ideology should be opposing terms: we need to be able to differentiate them. And just as Marx in his day was able to examine the science of economics and show its ideological nature, Smith subjected sociology[12] to similar scrutiny. For Marx, this necessitated critically analyzing concepts that nineteenth-century economics took for granted: the division of labour, exchange, competition, and so on. Specifically, he examined the historical and institutional structures that produced such concepts. So whereas economics viewed its concepts as 'natural'—as being outside of any history or institutional structure—Marx insisted on relocating them in their specific social and historical contexts. For Smith a century or more later, if we want to get beyond ideological knowledge we have to pursue analysis through the concepts of the social sciences to their other side—to the 'practical activity of actual living individuals' (Smith 1974a, 42). It is only through such a process that we are able to pass from ideology to knowledge.

But whereas this (1974a) article pointed out the ideological nature of the statistics produced by sociologists themselves, another article a year later (1975, reprinted 1990a) focused on the ideological nature of 'official statistics' (at least those of mental illness). Here Smith elaborates the exact nature of her critique of 'official statistics' on mental illness but also clarifies an explicit feminist focus on women's shared experiences and culture. Moreover, her feminist approach is distinctly influenced by her ethnomethodological training. As she points out in the article, whereas other feminist scholars had critiqued the official (US) statistics on mental illness primarily in terms of their accuracy, Smith wants to do something quite different.[13] Building on her prior work on ideology, she wants to show how the statistics are worked up in the first place so as to produce a certain 'reality' of mental illness, a reality that is taken for granted by professionals but that has been compiled by the transformation of the actual lived experience of women.

Specifically, she says that we cannot divorce mental illness from the practices of psychiatry that produce it. And building on her earlier claim that 'the actualities of living people become a resource to be made over into the image of the concept' (1974a, 51), she shows how something similar is at work in the social production of 'social facts' such as mental illness. For example, a psychiatric diagnosis of depression that focuses on a 'withdrawal of interest . . . a slowing of mental and physical activity' may act as a set of instructions for a physician to select out of the actual everyday experiences of someone only those particulars that can match this abstract description. In this process, according to Smith, the psychiatric grid is 'specifically inattentive to the actual matrices of the experiences of those who are diagnosed' (1990a, 129). Thus Smith gives us this account written by a working-class woman experiencing the 1930s Depression years:

> This constant struggle with poverty this last four years has made me feel very nervy and irritable and this affects my children. I fear that I have not the patience that good health generally brings. When I am especially worried about anything I feel as if I have been engaged in some terrific physical struggle and go utterly limp and for some time am unable to move or even think coherently. This effect of mental strain expressed in physical results seems most curious and I am at a loss to properly explain it to a doctor (quoted in Smith 1990a, 128).

Smith goes on to say that this account and this woman's life could quite easily be converted into a case of 'depression'.[14] Yet the woman herself makes no mention of mental illness. Instead, as Smith points out, 'she speaks of arduous work, commitment to sustaining children, exhaustion, perhaps of fear and anxiety, of an unbearable load that is daily borne. She shows us strength rather than illness' (1990a, 129). Yet this 'lived actuality' is discarded in the psychiatric working up of the case. And this point is of crucial importance because, as Smith discovered when she talked to other women who had been labelled mentally ill, 'the threat of invalidation or discounting recurs again and again in experiential accounts' (133). In other words, the problem with statistics on women's mental illness is not so much their accuracy but rather their power to invalidate or discount the experiences of the women who have been so labelled.

In many ways, Smith's work not only advanced the original insights of the ethnomethodologists with regard to our understanding of social statistics (official and otherwise) but her concern with how the everyday is infused with issues of power, control, and authority suggested an important redirection of those original critiques. Nevertheless, I was not totally satisfied with Smith's own theorizing on this subject. Although I had been impressed with her redirection of the ethnomethodological insights, I found her utilization of a relatively straightforward Marxism rather difficult to digest. Specifically, Smith has always preferred to use Marx's own work rather than that of later Marxist scholars in developing her feminist theory, yet for me it was unclear to what extent Marx's own descriptions of working-class exploitation could still be productively used a century or so after his death.

I had been brought up in a working-class home, with my father working in manual jobs all his life, including 23 years in a car factory (I lasted three weeks there). Yet I was also a product of the British welfare state (which among other things introduced the possibility of a university education to students like myself), so the classic texts of Marx that I was formally taught at the University of York seemed almost as foreign to my lived experience as the introduction to the positivist sociology that I had also experienced there. Moreover, the lack of reception that my burgeoning ethnomethodological interests met from most of the lecturers at York alerted me to the everyday power relations inherent within academia. So it might not be too surprising to hear that I left York feeling a certain degree of frustration with the academic enterprise. Unfortunately, my struggles at the micro level were also being matched by macro-level developments. That is, I graduated into the aftermath of a socio-economic and political crisis, the severity and global effect of which only became clearer over time. Yet its effects on my life and employment prospects were immediate and dire. With the thoroughgoing implementation of 'Thatcherism' underway, I escaped to Canada to improve my employment prospects by taking an MA and waited for things to improve. Thus my life experiences meant that I could not have the easy attraction to classic Marxist texts (like *The German ideology*) that Smith had, despite the appeal of much of her micro-work. So I had to search further afield for some other way of figuring out not only my original welfare state/working-class upbringing but also the rapidly changing macro-social world that was now pushing me in completely unexpected directions.

MACRO-CRITIQUES OF 'OFFICIAL STATISTICS': FOUCAULT'S LEGACY

Having quickly completed an MA and finding that the situation in England had not improved, I decided rather equivocally to persevere and obtain a doctorate in sociology despite my earlier reservations about the discipline. But as a foreign student with no money, I was totally dependent on being awarded funding for graduate studies. As a consequence, I unfortunately ended up in a doctoral program primarily committed to traditional sociological theories (e.g., the structural functionalist model criticized earlier) and traditional positivist research methods (e.g., the use of statistical analysis where possible). Not surprisingly, I found it hard to reconcile this type of sociology with the insights that I had found so compelling in my undergraduate formation. Fortunately, I met one or two professors familiar with this alternative approach, and through one of them I was introduced to the work of the French philosopher Michel Foucault. And as a result, my hitherto largely indigestible doctoral diet started to become much more appetizing.

Crucially for me, Foucault's willingness to examine rather than just accept 'social scientific knowledge' seemed to complement rather than contradict my earlier ethnomethodological formation. His emerging focus on questions of both power and knowledge, not just knowledge alone, seemed immensely attractive. The ethnomethodologists and feminists had taught me so much already about the ways in which power and knowledge actually operate at the micro levels of social life. Yet Foucault's work held the promise of extending those insights to the macro level as well. Further, he offered a new theory that positioned power and knowledge not as distinguishable but as inextricably connected concepts—hence his designation 'power/knowledge'.

Although he had begun his career by exploring the foundations of human sciences like psychiatry, pathological anatomy, economics, philology, and biology, by the time I was introduced to his thinking he had already started explicitly exploring the relationship between knowledge and power. That is, he was now claiming that an integral connection existed between the workings of modern forms of power and the knowledge produced by various social sciences. And in order to make this relationship visible, he argued that it was necessary to excavate the common roots of this power/knowledge relationship. He called this type of research work 'genealogical'. Thus his classic genealogy, *Discipline and punish* (1977b) argued that if we want to fully understand the modern positivist science of 'criminology', we need to understand its historical origins. Specifically, Foucault shows that twentieth-century criminology posited the 'cause' of crime in some pathology of the (typically working-class) delinquent. However, this 'knowledge' did not originate from the groundbreaking writings of a few intellectuals such as Lombroso (1911) (as criminology's self-understanding might have it). Rather, it emerged out of a practical early nineteenth-century political concern to contain a supposedly dangerous and insurrectionary working class. The introduction of the prison along the lines of Jeremy Bentham's panopticon model not only 'disci-plined' working-class individuals into becoming 'docile bodies', it also acted as a laboratory within which 'knowledge' could be compiled about the criminal.[15] Finally, and perhaps most importantly for me at that time, Foucault argued that this power/knowledge had the ability to subjugate other lay and competing understandings (of crime in this instance). As a result, this new science of crimin-ology was able to become treated as factual knowledge because by the late nine-teenth century it had been able to discount and marginalize the alternative 'political' explanation of crime (put forward by workers' newspapers), which posited the exploitative organization of society, not the individual, as the cause of criminal activity (1977b, 287).[16]

OFFICIAL STATISTICS AS TECHNOLOGIES FOR GOVERNING POPULATIONS: LEARNING ABOUT BIO-POLITICS

Foucault's first genealogical analysis highlighted the role that one institution and one modern social science played in the workings of power/knowledge.[17] How-ever, it said little about the way that other sciences, especially those more explic-itly concerned with statistics and numbers, might operate. Fortunately, Foucault quickly turned his attention in this direction. Thus his next book (1980a) explicit-ly introduces readers to the notions of anatamo-politics and bio-politics (1980a, 139). He articulated these notions as the two poles of power/knowledge, one that concentrates on the examination of the individual body (criminology, for exam-ple, could now be seen in terms of the notion of anatamo-politics) and the other, bio-politics, that focuses on the gathering of knowledge of the 'social body'. But both have their origins in concerns with power, not in impartial science.

That is, their emergence 'since the classical age[18] in the west' (1980a, 136) radically altered the way power operates. From a traditional power focused on sovereignty, rights, laws, etc., the ultimate weapon of which was the sovereign's ability to take life, a different form of power emerged, one focused on the con-trol and management of life rather than on the ability to cause death. Moreover, this power no longer divided the world up between the friends of the sovereign (who obey 'his' law) and his enemies (who transgress 'his' law); instead, it 'effects distributions around the norm' (144). In other words, the social body is to be 'known' in order that it can be better controlled, regulated, and so on. Thus for Foucault, the emergence of sciences like demography are crucial to understand-ing bio-politics (140).

But for me, it was Hacking, one of the first to use Foucault's theorizing in an empirical fashion, whose work (1982) shed the most light on the specific rela-tionship between bio-politics[19] and statistics. What intrigued me the most about Hacking's work was not just his early application of this Foucauldian concept but rather his suggestion concerning what he called the 'subversive' effect of enumer-ating—that counting needs 'categories' in which to place people. For example, he points out that the naturalness with which people understand society as being divided into social classes comes from the mundane work of state bureaucrats in the early nineteenth century who radically transformed the ways in which people were classified—because in order to 'count' people, these bureaucrats first needed to devise 'easily countable classifications into which everybody had to fall—and thenceforth did' (1982, 280). In other words, for Hacking, the taken-for-granted way in which Marx and others saw their social world as being divided up naturally into classes might have something to with the mundane workings of state bureaucracies hungry to count and not just with the development of capitalist relations of production.

Yet Hacking is equally attentive to more overt questions of power. That is, he also points out that an 'avalanche of printed numbers' occurred in the early nineteenth century—between the 1820s and the 1840s, to be precise. And these dates are important because this was a period of revolution in Europe (Hacking points out that the timing of this avalanche coincides nicely with the two French revolutions of 1830 and 1848). This avalanche represents what he calls 'an overt political response by the state', an attempt to obtain 'information about and control of the moral tenor of the population' and, perhaps as important, to ensure the 'preservation of the established state' (1982, 281). And even though the overt revolutionary threat did disappear, the categories remained and eventually became 'natural' ways in which people came to understand society.

Armed with theoretical tools such as these, I attempted to use them in my own fledgling research career. Specifically, I chose to carry out a genealogical study of one specific feature of the welfare state—workers' compensation. I would do this with the analytical tools supplied to a large extent by Foucault. Specifically, I attempted to analyze how certain sciences (including statistical sciences) of the individual body and the social body[20] that had emerged during the crucial two-decade period that Hacking had identified (1820–40) not only created new 'subversive' categories of understanding[21] but eventually created an entirely new rational scientific discourse organized around a new legal and linguistic category of 'no-fault liability'. This new (medico-legal) discourse was not only successful in replacing an older common law system based on the apportionment of blame: it also successfully subjugated workers' own understandings of their embodied health and how it should be treated. Perhaps because of my earlier familiarity with and sensitivity to the micro-sociological approaches discussed above, I also came to the realization that this new discourse of workers' compensation tended to render nonsensical the voices of workers like Pete Youschuk (Doran 1986, 11–20) whose embodied experience did not fit the categories provided by the discourse. For example, when I first met Pete, he was almost totally disabled from working as a coal miner most of his life. Yet when he said things like 'you just give me back my health' (1986, 15), it made me realize that the workers' compensation system was incapable of understanding such a demand. Instead, all it could do was provide compensation after his health had been destroyed.

Unfortunately, while I was carrying out this research it also became clearer to me on a personal level that the crisis I had escaped in England by coming to Canada was not simply confined to Europe. By the time I graduated in 1986, the economic situation in much of Canada had worsened considerably. Observers have seen it in a variety of ways in retrospect, depending on their political and/or intellectual backgrounds, but all have agreed that some form of transformation was taking place and that the movement was in general terms away from the promotion of the welfare state model of society and toward some type of (revamped) liberal model. In fact, the subject matter of my dissertation—workers' compensation—was also beginning to go through these dramatic changes just as I was finishing off that project.

However, for people living through it at the time, things did not look so clear. Nevertheless, I was certainly transformed in this process. I was thrust out on the sessional teaching circuit, not only having to obtain annual work visas rather than student visas but also with the realization that the economic climate was worsening abruptly around me. Moreover, I was once again subjected to official 'counts'. This time, it was at the level of the Canadian state. While teaching as a sessional instructor, I would systematically make applications for permanent-resident status in Canada. However, my early applications were routinely refused on the grounds that I could not reach the 70-point tally needed to qualify. Officially, Canada had little need for sociologists. Yet they did have a need for criminologists. Consequently, I was now encouraged to reinvent my 'self' as a person capable of teaching criminology courses. And through this informal process, I eventually obtained my 70 points, my permanent-resident status, and a full-time position at a primarily undergraduate institution with teaching responsibilities largely in the area of criminology (even though I had never taken a course in that field).

While teaching myself how to give courses on crime, deviance, etc., to large undergraduate audiences, I not only continued trying to figure things out with regard to my own personal life but also continued to try to figure out certain unresolved issues that had emanated from my earlier research. This necessitated my having to clarify certain features of that work. For example, whereas I had explicitly used Foucault's genealogical method to study the roots of workers' compensation, I now needed to clarify the fact that I had in practice combined this approach with an earlier, ethnomethodologically informed theoretical position: that the social world could only be known from within. That is, like the ethnomethodological and feminist scholars discussed above, I had begun my analysis from the paramount reality of the everyday world (although unlike Smith's experience, mine was a world organized around class as much as gender). But once I had clarified this point to myself, I realized that what I had been trying to articulate was more than just 'subjugation' (Foucault 1980b) or 'mediation' (Doran 1986). Rather, the notion of 'codification' (Doran 1994b; 1996) seemed to better express the specific nature of the disqualification of workers' voices that I had uncovered. This was because it drew attention to the fact that an existing embodied culture was 'transformed' by these sciences but was then given back to these same workers as an 'official discourse' in which they should understand themselves.[22] And crucially, much of that codifying work was done by statistical sciences that operated on and transformed a prior shared, embodied culture, thus rendering it nonsensical. For example, whereas young workers in the 1830s had simply demanded that their health be protected, within a decade statistics had been compiled suggesting that accidents (rather than health) were the major

problem within factories (Doran 1996). A few decades later, statistics were showing that accidents were unavoidable, despite workers' vehement protests to the
contrary (Doran 1986). The end result was that by the end of the century, a new
'official' discourse (organized around the notion of no-fault insurance) had been
constructed, and this was then given back to workers as the preferred way in
which they should understand their own bodies (Doran 1994b).

This self-clarification at the micro level was accompanied by related attempts
at clarification at the macro level. Here the major issue that kept preoccupying me
was the apparent societal mutation that seemed to have transformed me, the
workers' compensation system that I had carefully examined, and perhaps entire
welfare state societies themselves. Further, I was trying to resolve this issue in part
by examining certain new forms of statistics that seemed to be emerging alongside this mutation (Doran 1994a; 1999) but also by consulting those writers who
shared my ongoing worries about the relevance of the traditional Marxist
explanatory framework yet who still wanted to keep the analysis of class a central
focus. And although Baudrillard (1983b) was somewhat helpful with his thesis on
the 'death of the social' (as he called the ending of the welfare state era), it was only
when I discovered Donzelot's mature (1988; 1984) work that I started to get some
real clarity on this mutation that had transformed the welfare state in the late
twentieth century—and also on the prior mutation that had introduced the welfare state (Doran 2004). But as most of Donzelot's work was only available in the
original French, it took me a considerable time to master it. And in the meantime,
other Foucauldian scholars had started to analyze these same transformations
from a distinctly different perspective. Nevertheless, these 'governmentality'
scholars had some illuminating insights regarding 'official statistics'.

OFFICIAL STATISTICS AS TECHNOLOGIES FOR GOVERNING 'FREEDOM': LEARNING FROM THE GOVERNMENTALITY SCHOLARS

At first, I simply assumed that these governmentality writings were continuations
of Foucault's earlier concerns with power/knowledge. However, I came to realize
that a significantly different theoretical trajectory was being suggested. And
although there now exist a number of lucid introductions to the governmentality
perspective, Rose's work (1999) merits some attention for several reasons. First, he
pays explicit attention to the mutations in the forms that governmentality takes
over time, such as the specific mutation from the 'social' to 'advanced liberalism',
which caught me and many others in its throes, and second, he specifically focuses
on the constitutive role that 'numbers' have played and continue to play in the
governance of Western societies.

The earliest governmentality scholars (Burchell et al. 1991) had noticed that
Foucault in his later lectures became preoccupied with what is called 'the art of
governing' and especially with its liberal formulations since the late eighteenth
century. Picking up on his earlier work on bio-politics, Foucault was now suggesting that the 'discovery of population' in the late eighteenth century constituted a decisive turning point for the emergence of specifically liberal forms of

governing because governing for the first time became conceptualized in terms of 'the people' rather than the 'sovereign'. In other words, this bio-political reformulation of society being comprised of a 'population of individuals' had profound consequences for any subsequent conjoining of knowledge and power. And it is Rose in particular who develops this thesis so as to highlight its connection to the freedom of those individuals. For him, 'the importance of liberalism is not that it first recognized, defined or defended freedom as a right of all citizens. Rather its significance is that for the first time the arts of government were systematically linked to the practice of freedom' (Rose 1999, 68). In contrast to many contemporary social sciences that simply assume that our societies are based on freedom or that this supposed freedom is in fact a sham,[23] Rose's approach seeks to understand, via genealogical analysis, how 'societies of freedom' (whether they be organized around 'freedom of the market' or 'freedom from want' or 'freedom to choose', etc.) and 'free individuals' (who are 'free' from hunger or 'free' to work or to consume or to self-actualize, etc.) get fabricated in the first place (see Chapter 1). So let us first take a moment to acquaint ourselves with a few of the central features of Rose's Foucault-inspired approach.

Traditionally, the analysis of liberal societies has preoccupied political scientists as they routinely concern themselves with the overt forms of politics and law prominent there. But Foucault's writings have taught scholars to go beyond traditional analyses of topics such as rights, law, democracy, constitutions, etc., and to examine the forms of 'knowledge' typically associated with these forms of power. For example, Rose points out that (liberal) governing is always accomplished through rationalities; that is, governing always takes place within a general context of meaning that gives it its sense. And for Rose, these rationalities constitute the 'framework of truth' surrounding any actual politics. Further, the tacit, taken-for-granted discursive work that establishes the different 'regimes of truth' that have constituted liberal governing can be empirically studied. In fact, the specific regimes 'of liberalism, of welfare, of neo-liberalism' (Rose 1999, 28) all get subjected to exactly this type of analysis in his text. Similarly, according to Rose, governing always has to operate through some form of intelligibility, and the preferred forms within liberal governing are 'scientific languages' or 'veridical discourses' (1999, 9) rather than, say, other discursive forms like religion. Thus Rose might draw our attention to the emergence of 'scientific' dichotomies such as 'normality/pathology' and 'functional/dysfunctional' to point out how these and similar terms are used to help govern society. In addition, the governmentality perspective is very concerned with 'space', especially the establishment of 'governable zones'. For example, certain abstract spaces that we have come to take for granted (such as the economy or the nation) have had to be historically constructed as 'realities' (i.e., as spaces in which certain activities but not others could and should legitimately take place). And whereas Foucault had illustrated this claim with his discussion of how the economy as a space outside of government intervention had been invented through the writing of texts like Adam Smith's *Wealth of nations* (1976 [1776]), Rose pays attention to how other equally 'irreal' spaces became constructed (e.g., the 'social') or are in the process of being constructed (e.g., the 'globalized economy', the 'community') as discursive 'realities' within which we have to think and live.

But governmentality is not just concerned with the creation/invention of spaces to govern; it is also concerned with constructing human 'subjects' to govern. And these subjects have also changed over the past few centuries. For example, in the early nineteenth century, subjects had to be made 'free' to pursue their individual economic needs, while by the end of that century, subjects had to be made 'social' so that they could understand themselves as part of a social state. More recently, subjects are now being encouraged to become autonomous and concerned with their own 'selves'. In fact, they are now encouraged to govern themselves in ways that they produce themselves as consumers and entrepreneurs. And certain governmental technologies are used to help produce subjects in these various ways. Whereas the prison and the schoolroom were two of the technologies that emerged in the regime of liberalism for producing human subjectivity, Rose argues that in Western societies today, 'consumer discourses' and 'therapeutic discourses' have emerged as the more relevant technologies to assist us in the construction of our advanced-liberal forms of 'self'. Thus today we are constantly being encouraged through discourses like advertising to create our own lifestyles while often being simultaneously encouraged to explore and fulfill ourselves with the aid of the varied scientific discourses emanating from the 'caring professions' and others.

Although I was initially surprised at some of the directions in which he was taking Foucault's work, Rose's empirical attention to the details of the English-speaking cultures in which I had lived for most of my life certainly attracted me to his particular application of Foucault's work. And perhaps more important for me, whereas Foucault had died before he could fully articulate his theorizing on governmentality, Rose has used Foucault's rather cryptic comments on the subject to produce not only a powerful theoretical adaptation of the original power/knowledge thesis but one that seeks to explain that 'mutation' that escaped Foucault: namely, the movement from the 'social' to 'advanced liberalism'. For me personally, this was useful because it helped me to understand the transformation that I had experienced, one in which the discursive space of what constituted 'social reality' had seemed to mutate, while at the same time individual notions of the self were also being called upon to become objects of personal transformation. In other words, I not only lived through a social transformation that saw the social reality of the welfare state become something quite different—a new world of advanced liberalism—but I was also encouraged to reinvent my own embodied self as part of the process. That is, I had to create a new 'self' for myself—as someone with pedagogic expertise in criminology, not just sociology.

Within Rose's adaptation of Foucault's theorizing, statistics play a rather crucial role. In fact, whereas Foucault's own comments on statistics remain scattered,[24] Rose's work singles out 'numbers' for sustained analysis. Moreover, he deliberately seeks to rethink prior Foucauldian understandings of statistics in the process. So in contrast to Hacking's interpretation of statistics as 'state-istics' used to 'control and subordinate individuals and populations' (Rose 1999, 215), Rose wants to link them to the art of governing 'free' societies. Specifically, he suggests that strategic links have been made between statistics and democratic forms of governance such that numbers have been integral features of democratic governance since the late eighteenth century. And although he acknowledges that this government strategy is harder to detect if one examines the European evidence as Hacking did, a genealogical analysis of statistics in the US would reveal that it not only emerged there but has flourished there. So let us take a brief look at a couple of the ways in which 'numbers' helped in this development.

Most obviously connected with the creation of the space of democracy was the linking together of the original US constitution with the 'counting' of the people. And whereas political scientists, constitutionalists, and so on have traditionally tended to overlook the role of the census in the constitution, Rose sees this as a good example of the insights that a governmentality perspective can provide. That is, from its inception US democracy is configured by calculation. Because the composition of the lower House would be based on the population of each state, regular counts of the country's population would help to ensure the viability of this notion of democracy. But within this newly constituted democratic space, 'political subjects' were to be constructed with a delicate regard for calculation. Thus at the start slaves were to be counted as three-fifths of a free person for the purposes of democratic representation, while a century or so later, when census returns indicated that the country might be 'overrun by hordes of "degraded" immigrants' (222), it resulted in the legislative introduction of immigration quotas. Finally, in the twentieth century, new 'official statistics' were created in response to the Great Depression such that an irreal space was created in which governing could be done for 'social' purposes, not just for the economic purposes that had dominated prior statistical thinking.

But 'numbers' were not used just for the fabrication of these constituent spaces of US democracy: they were also used in the fabrication of the American individual. Rose points out that from its early days, the US encouraged the fabrication of individual subjects who were numerate in their everyday lives since this would allow them to take an active part in the commercial workings of the republic. Consequently, decimalization and the teaching of arithmetic were prioritized by US governments in the nineteenth century. It was believed that decimalization would allow 'the whole mass of people . . . to compute for themselves whatever they should have occasion to buy, to sell or measure' (Thomas Jefferson 1790, quoted in Rose 1999, 225), while 'educators looked to mathematics as the ideal way to prepare a republican citizen' (Cline Cohen 1982, quoted in Rose 1999, 226). Underlying these movements, according to Rose, was a belief that free and democratic subjects should not be guided by 'feeling, passions and tumults' (225) but by a sense of detached calculation.

OFFICIAL STATISTICS AS TECHNOLOGIES OF THE CAPITALIST STATE: LEARNING FROM THE STATE FORMATION SCHOLARS

Although I learned a lot from the governmentality viewpoint, I was still left a little uneasy with the analysis. Most important perhaps, Rose's rethinking of the bio-political research of scholars like Hacking (that had so influenced me in my earlier scholarly formation) has meant that the governmentality approach now seems to have lost much of its critical edge, especially with regard to the understanding of 'numbers' that Rose now provides.

Fortunately, there has been a recent response to this governmentality perspective that has attempted to restore a more critical edge to our understanding of statistics. Curtis (1995; 2001) in particular has attempted to reintroduce concerns with issues such as 'domination' by utilizing governmentality work on statistics alongside certain insights culled from Marxist-inspired work on 'state formation'. Whereas traditional Marxist scholarship had also analyzed liberal societies, its typical focus was not in showing that 'liberal societies' and 'free individuals' were the socio-historical constructions that Rose suggests. Instead, this critical scholarship wanted to demystify the ideological nature of such societies and their individuals by uncovering the exploitative relations of capitalism that lay behind these apparent freedoms. And although the state formation school still understands itself as Marxist in origin, it wants to provide a much more subtle explanation of social life, and especially the state, than did the traditional Marxist analyses. In their ambitious (1985) text, Corrigan and Sayer attempted to provide an account of the state that avoided what they identified as one of the major inadequacies of previous Marxist explanations: a tendency to focus too much on the coercive and exploitative nature of the state under capitalism.[25] In contrast, Corrigan and Sayer point to the state's central role in producing consensus. Thus for them, the making of cultural meaning is a central task of the state: states 'define in great detail, acceptable forms and images of social activity and individual and collective identity . . . for instance, the distinction between "political" and "industrial" strikes (or much more generally, between "public" and "private" life) becomes second nature within our culture' (1985, 3–4). According to them, it is this power of the state to help produce what gets taken for granted within our culture that needs analysis. They call this process 'moral regulation'. It is 'a project of normalizing, rendering natural, taken for granted, in a word "obvious" what are in fact ontological and epistemological premises of a particular and historical form of social order' (1985, 4). But what is crucial here is that the state still acts as the 'collective misrepresentation of capitalist societies' (1985, 8).

Empirically, according to Corrigan and Sayer, this 'making of a culture' is an extremely long historical process, and in the specific culture that they study—that of England—they show that the process of imposing meaning has taken many centuries.[26] Furthermore, it is no easy task because it is a process by which 'state agencies attempt to give unitary and unifying expression to what are in reality multifaceted and differential historical experiences of groups within society, denying them their particularity' (1985, 4). Corrigan and Sayer argue that in order to successfully accomplish the task of simultaneously creating unity while denying particularity, state formation must move in two different directions:

> On the one hand, state formation is a totalizing project, representing people as members of a particular community—an 'illusory community', as Marx

described it. This community is epitomized as the nation, which claims people's primary identification and loyalty . . . On the other hand, as Foucault has observed, state formation equally (and no less powerfully) individualizes people in quite definite and specific ways. We are registered within the state community as citizens, voters, taxpayers, ratepayers, jurors, parents, consumers, homeowners—individuals (1985, 4–5).

It is by building on this pioneering work that Curtis aimed to document state formation in the Canadian context of the mid-nineteenth century.

Specifically, Curtis (2001) wanted to focus on the role of the state as a cultural leader through the 'fashioning of imaginaries' (37)—that is, through the articulation and promotion of 'constructed or imagined visions of social life' (24). In other words, it is this concern with the 'totalizing' practices of the state and how it works to produce the (Canadian) 'nation' as an 'illusory community' that really animates Curtis's work. Yet he also wanted to show the very important contribution that Foucault's theorizing on 'population' could make to this project. Thus whereas Corrigan and Sayer had briefly identified the 'statistical idea' as one of the mechanisms by which the nineteenth-century English state had worked to (consensually) govern the working classes, Curtis combined their brief discussion with Foucault's much richer theorization on the topic. That is, Curtis sees the Foucauldian contribution as allowing him to display more precisely those individualizing and totalizing features of modern state power that come from the routine operations of censuses. So let us briefly illustrate some aspects of these processes at work.

With regard to the 'individualizing' features that population counts produce, Curtis focused on the disciplinary features of censuses. For example, with the changes introduced in the 1852 Canadian census, it became possible for 'individuals', not just households, to become the objects of 'disciplinary practices' such as the ones Foucault had first identified in *Discipline and punish*. Foucault had shown how the architectural design of the new 'panoptic' prison was not only able to 'individualize' prisoners but was also able to produce them as 'docile bodies'. In a somewhat similar fashion, with the 1852 introduction of the 'nominal census', individuals could now 'become the objects of projects that seek to change their conduct by effecting their bodily forces, by tying them to physical space or social categories, by colonizing their wills' (Curtis 2001, 41). In other words, the state could now 'know' individuals and attempt to shape their conduct in ways that had been impossible before (Curtis 2001). And as a result, subsequent census work sought to 'reassign human beings to what are considered their 'normal places' (2001, 311)—but places where, it must always be remembered, the sense of 'normal' was in fact a state creation. So, for example, new directions for the 1860 census introduced by the deputy minister Joseph-Charles Taché sought to assign individuals to the place where they were 'legally domiciled' rather than the place where they were physically located on the day of the census (2001, 271–3). But Curtis was well aware that there might be specific political consequences of such a seemingly straightforward administrative decision. He wrote, 'given that representation in the House of Commons was to be determined by the census's returns of population and that Quebec was particularly subject to rural outmigration, it must have been obvious to Taché that the *de jure* principle was likely to increase the number of seats accorded to Quebec in general and to rural districts within that province in particular' (2001, 272). Nevertheless, this decision stabilized individuals within one 'normal place' and ended many of the earlier problems regarding how best to count the floating population.

With regard to the state's 'totalizing' tendency, according to Curtis this is a process through which 'individuals may be grouped together into categories within which their health, understandings, morals, and desires become the objects of particular governmental projects' (2001, 41). And whereas Curtis's research tends to underplay the effects that the Canadian census has on 'individual subjects', he certainly cannot be criticized for the amount of time he devotes to demonstrating the competing totalizations that were produced from these census counts in the mid-nineteenth century, the struggles that emerged over them, and the subsequent successful implementation of one particular 'totalizing' and 'coherent imaginary' (24). Equally important, this successful imaginary was able to assert itself as an authoritative and legitimate representation of social relations under the capitalism of that time. Let me explain briefly.

The Act of Union of Upper and Lower Canada in 1840 was quickly followed by a Census Act that sought to impose the prior Upper Canadian census model onto all of Canada. Yet for the residents of Canada East (what is now Quebec), the entire census project was something of an imposition. With no parallel history of census-taking, with no compatible local government infrastructure, with the continuing existence of feudal local government relations, and with an ongoing popular resistance to censuses in general, the first census attempts yielded poor results in Canada East—so poor that the 1847 census was not taken and the central government was forced into reacting to the problem by creating a Board of Registration and Statistics. And although the subsequent 1848 census was also very imperfectly taken, state officials nonetheless used the data to produce an imaginary of the Canadian colony as being well on its way to assimilating the French, in line with the proposals of the 1939 Durham Report that had been put forward for the future development of Canada. However, such a totalizing picture was quickly challenged. That is, although the statistical report was originally written to shed light on an issue between a colony and its mother country, it was quickly reinterpreted within the Canadian Parliament as an issue of democracy. French leaders like Louis-Joseph Papineau drew on alternative numbers (from information given by local curés and from the relatively well-developed system of vital statistics in Canada East), which suggested such a significant population in Canada East that 'representation by population' should immediately follow. The struggle over which totalizing imaginary of the Canadian population would become dominant and what exact form it would take had now begun.

Whereas the results of the censuses in the 1840s had been used to construct an imaginary that addressed itself to imperial concerns, censuses in the 1850s were marked by the state's attempts to create a somewhat different totalizing statistical picture of Canada. This was most evident in the creation of a Board of Agriculture, an entity that strongly 'shaped Canadian statistical practice by tying it to concerns with agricultural development' (Curtis 2001, 142). Just as important, this new vision of Canada as having a primarily agricultural future (and definitely not an industrial one) was also coupled with a vision of Canada as welcoming (English-speaking) immigrant farmers. According to Curtis, the result of the establishment of the Board of Agriculture was that the 'leading, but not the sole, project of government guiding the imaginary of population, came to be an advertising project' (2001, 141). In other words, the board became heavily involved in producing statistical information that helped to promote the colony as a favoured place for (primarily British) immigration.

Yet the decade of the 1850s was also marked by an intensification of the debate over representation by population. Although results from the 1852 census had been so unfavourable to the French that they quickly silenced their previous demands for representation by population, they were still able to construct a plausible alternative imaginary out of them, one that focused on the fecundity of the French race and its ability to resist assimilation. But even though Canada East's politicians had abandoned their call for representation by population, many in Canada West, spurred on by what they understood as favourable immigration trends in their section of the colony, were becoming more and more vocal about 'rep by pop' because it would now favour Canada West, not Canada East. Perhaps not surprisingly in such a volatile, politically charged atmosphere, the results of the next (1861) census were also hotly debated. Yet eventually out of this controversy a new imaginary did emerge, and it tried to forge yet another vision of the Canadian population. Crucially, state officials no longer attempted to construct a vision that would draw on statistics to promote and advertise the agricultural fortunes awaiting British immigrants. Instead, the statistical vision included a powerful commemoration and celebration of the history of a people—the French in North America.

With the reorganization of the state's statistical arm in 1864, not only did it become 'rationally bureaucratic' (Curtis 2001, 237) but the new deputy minister, Taché, also redirected its focus. On the one hand, he made future census-taking more systematic and impartial, but he also translated certain aspects of his own personal vision of French-Canadian society (as primarily pastoral, fecund, and agricultural) into a coherent imaginary, one that was discursively created as a result of several of the statistical projects he established. For example, he obtained public funds to carry out a genealogy of the French-Canadian population, yet it was quite selective in its compilation and construction. As Curtis notes, 'It fuelled an imaginary in which a handful of French men and their loyal spouses, sheltered under the Cross of the Lord, and slaking their thirst in the Fountain of the Wisdom of the Church, pursued their historic mission of civilizing North America' (2001, 251).

Other work done by people associated with Taché furthered this construction. For example, doubt was raised about the accuracy of previous census results for Canada East, and employees in the department subsequently set about 'correcting and reconstructing' (254) the prior census returns. Yet despite the selectivity of these practices, because census-taking itself had been made systematic, the department's work succeeded in becoming authoritative. This was demonstrated right after the first census carried out under Taché's guidance. The city of Montreal disputed the results for Montreal produced by the state and did a recount. Yet the recount could not dislodge the new view of the state census as an authoritative, accurate representation of the country. In other words, the 1871 Montreal 'check census' is now largely forgotten. In contrast, the state's vision of the 'Canadian' nation became more and more prominent throughout the next century.

To conclude, Curtis's detailed examination of this 30-year period nicely shows the struggles that took place around the ways in which population could and would be represented within the Canadian state. Moreover, he shows how central state officials were eventually able to create an acceptable and coherent imaginary out of this conflict. The imaginary became so authoritative and stable that the census was no longer the subject of fierce political debate but instead achieved a sense of legitimacy and accuracy. Yet according to Curtis, we must never forget that this outcome represents a form of domination because the imaginary can assert its own favoured understanding of population only at the expense of other competing imaginaries.

Towards the end of his book, Curtis gives us one revealing indication of just how such domination might operate at the level of the everyday. He suggests that the establishment of this totalizing understanding can be imposed at the level of individual subjectivity as well. Curtis points out that as a result of all the mundane work carried out by state officials for more than a century and a quarter, it was impossible for individuals in Canada to 'know' themselves 'officially' as Canadian. That is, they could not declare themselves officially as of 'Canadian' origin on the census form. Instead, they had to understand themselves in other standard census terms (Irish, Scottish, French, Italian, etc.): they could not understand themselves as simply 'Canadian'.

CONCLUSION: BECOMING 'EDUCATED' ABOUT 'OFFICIAL STATISTICS'

Foucault's work on power/knowledge has allowed us to rethink in novel ways how we might conceive of 'official statistics' at a macro level. Moreover, as we have seen, Rose and Curtis have taken these insights about bio-politics and numbers in two rather different directions. Nevertheless, both approaches have given us new insights into the relationships between statistics, society, and the individual. Rose's attention focused for the most part on the constitutive role that statistics have played in the historical construction of liberal societies (such as the space of democracy in the US) and of 'free' individuals (such as the American 'calculating' citizen). In other words, the governmental technology of statistics was an integral component of how US society, and its citizens, were to be invented and fabricated. Curtis also focused on the constitutive role that statistics played in the historical formation of what would become the 'official' understanding of Canadian society. However, his main concern was with showing not only the conflict and struggle that created this selective vision of Canada but also that the vision was an 'illusory community' because the real, historical particularities of its component communities had to become submerged in order to form that artificial unity.

Undoubtedly then, both theoretical perspectives provide us with some very significant insights into the governmental technology of 'official statistics'. And our general sociological understanding of how society works is greatly enhanced by such analyses. But just as the ethnomethodological and feminist analyses of statistics illuminated puzzling aspects of my (and many others') social world when I was an academic neophyte, the governmentality and state formation approaches are now helping me to figure out some of the equally puzzling aspects of the tremendous social changes that I personally experienced, and was caught up in, since that infancy. To give one example, Rose's insights that official statistics were used in the US as a technology for governing the influx of immigrant populations helped to illuminate one aspect of my own biography and my struggles to obtain landed-immigrant status in this country.

To conclude, this chapter has been concerned with displaying the importance of a critical awareness of 'official statistics'. But I have not been content with simply suggesting that these statistics may be inaccurate in some way or another (as the ethnomethodologists implied). Rather, I have also tried to show what these statistics do. For some feminists, they tended to disqualify (women's) voices; in my own work, I have shown how certain statistics helped to 'codify' emerging cultural voices (specifically those of young workers at the particular point in time when the factory system was becoming widespread). We have also seen that for other (governmentality) scholars, 'official statistics' are intimately bound up with the socio-historical construction of discursive spaces (e.g., American democracy) and of individuals themselves (e.g., 'calculating' citizens). Meanwhile, others (in the state formation school) understand official statistics as mechanisms for helping the state to create a dominant imaginary—even if that discursive creation is illusory.

Finally, what has also been implied throughout this chapter is that anyone's (including your own) receptivity to scholarly material does not just depend on its persuasive ability or on the claimed accuracy of its analysis; it also depends on the situated embodiedness of you, the reader. Although sociologists have been rather slow in recognizing this fact, it is now being realized that how we as readers 'decode' any text depends on the personal experiences that we bring with us to the reading experience. In other words, your understanding of your own age, class, gender, ethnicity, etc., will affect how you decode any text. But what is equally important for you as students to realize (especially as you are now in the very process of becoming 'educated' about your 'self' and your social world) is that we invent and create our 'educated selves' through this process as well. What I have tried to do in this chapter is to make that process more explicit by attempting to show how I decoded the texts that I encountered in my education and what I learned (about myself and my societies) in the process.

Questions to Consider ————————————————————————————————

1. What does it mean to think of a suicide statistic as a 'verdict' rather than a 'social fact'?
2. When Smith looked at the statistics on mental illness in women, her focus was not on their 'accuracy or otherwise'. What was her focus?
3. Through his historical analysis, Hacking shows us the connection between the two words 'state' and 'statistics'. What is this connection?
4. Curtis suggests that there is a close connection between the emergence of a particular conceptualization of 'Canada' and the practice of taking censuses. Suggest one or two reasons why he sees this as a form of politics.

Notes ——

1. When I was small, Luton was a large industrial town that had been extensively surveyed by sociologists interested in examining the changing fortunes of the industrial working class (Goldthorpe et al. 1968a; 1968b; 1969). Today there is little industry left, yet Luton is still being surveyed. Recently, it came top of the list of 'crap towns' in the UK (Jordison and Kieran 2004).
2. Although I know of no easy cultural equivalent to the 'council estate' in Canada, I have heard terms like HLM (habitation à loyer modéré) used in French culture and 'the projects' used in US culture to describe superficially similar phenomena.
3. In part, this may have had something to do with the fact that Atkinson's work on the 'interpretive foundations' of suicide seemed to me at that time to suggest a serious problem for the positivist approach within sociology, especially in the format pioneered by the academic founder of sociology, Emile Durkheim.
4. As one of Atkinson's coroners (1971, 181) stated with regard to a suspect's life history: 'broken home, escape to the services, nervous breakdown, switching from one job to another, no family ties—what could be clearer?'
5. In part because he wanted to stress the similarity between this type of research program and studies like ethnobotany or ethnomedicine. Just as the latter were concerned with examining lay (ethno-) understandings of botany or medicine, ethnomethodology was concerned with examining the lay understandings of the social world that people ordinarily use in their everyday activities. That is, it was concerned with showing the 'lay-methods' that people use to make sense of social life (Garfinkel 1974). For a contemporary discussion of the name and its utility, see Francis and Hester 2004, 198–214.
6. This concern with studying different aspects of social life as 'practical accomplishments' can be succinctly demonstrated through an example. Garfinkel encouraged his students to go home and act like a lodger or a boarder in their own homes for an hour or so. What this experiment vividly demonstrated was the usually tacit work that goes into the 'practical accomplishment' of routine family life. When the students slightly adjusted their routine methods (behaving politely, talking formally to their parents), they produced a quite different understanding of family life. Frequently, the routine orderliness of family life was temporarily but seriously threatened as parents desperately tried to 'make sense' of what was going on.
7. This normative approach was heavily influenced by the structural-functionalist socio-

logical perspective developed by Talcott Parsons (1902–79). From this perspective, one might see norms as being routinely installed in children so as to give them the energy and directions for acting in socially appropriate ways in the future. More formally stated, these norms act as 'potent energizers motivating lines of effort and striving, on the one hand, and as bases for selecting and integrating courses of action, on the other' (Gouldner 1970, 191).

8. Wittgenstein, a philosopher who has had a tremendous influence on many sociologists and ethnomethodologists, drew attention to this understanding of rules. Signposts may suggest a route forward, but they do not compel us to follow this route. For example, you may choose instead to take a more scenic route, or you may choose to follow a different route, perhaps one that is less congested at that time of day. See Wittgenstein (1953, 80) for more details.

9. Of course I also learned a tremendous amount from other feminist scholars throughout my entire intellectual formation, especially writers whose critiques targeted the power relations inherent in the world of social sciences (e.g., Smart 1976, 1989; Harding 1986; Haraway 1988; McRobbie 1980; Hartsock 1987). Yet Smith's ethnomethodological attention to the specific, empirical ways in which power gets constituted has not only remained a constant source of inspiration but provides a specificity sometimes lacking in other critiques.

10. In this powerful analysis, Smith systematically documents how a story written by one of the friends, Angela, to show how K became recognized as mentally ill uses a number of 'common sense' methods to produce itself as a 'plausible' account of someone becoming mentally ill, an account that any competent reader would tend to agree with after an initial reading.

11. A good discussion of this progression can be found in Smith 1987, 69–78. Here she makes clear her debt to the pioneering work of Schutz on these issues. See Schutz (1962) for further discussion.

12. What she means by sociology here remains rather imprecise, unfortunately. However, from the context she seems to be focusing on one of the contemporary positivist versions that had emerged at that time in response to perceived problems with both the structural-functionalist and Marxist interpretations of social life.

13. That is, although she begins by showing the problems involved in 'reading' statistics as some type of representation of reality, she really wants to show that 'reading' them in this way, even by feminist scholars, may be missing something more fundamental. Thus she cites several feminist scholars who examined the statistics on women and mental illness and proposed to explain the high rates either in terms of women's oppression (1990a, 109) or in terms of women's roles in modern industrial societies tending to produce higher rates of mental illness than among men (112). Yet in both cases these arguments are based on the examination of statistics that show higher rates of mental illness for women. Now, although Smith does point out that the Canadian numbers do not seem to support the types of conclusions that the American feminists Chesler, Grove, and Tudor make (and she gives some reasonable suggestions as to why the numbers might be counted differently by different analysts and in two different countries), her real aim is to move beyond this conventional paradigm, which simply wants to frame the issue in terms of the accuracy (or otherwise) of the statistics. Instead, she wants to focus

on the social organization of these statistics.

14. In another article (1990b), she shows the mundane techniques by which this social process is carried out.

15. In other words, because this kind of prison had a certain architectural design in which prisoners were housed individually in cells under constant 'panoptic' surveillance, they could be both disciplined and observed very easily. Consequently, the prison allowed for this mutual production of power/knowledge—in the form of 'disciplined' individuals and 'scientific' knowledge of the delinquent.

16. This is why genealogical analysis is so necessary for Foucault, because 'only the historical contents allow us rediscover the ruptural effects of conflict and struggle that the order imposed by functionalist or systematizing thought is designed to mask' (1980b, 82).

17. However, it must be stressed that Foucault finishes by suggesting that this 'disciplinary power' was proliferating and expanding throughout the twentieth century so that by the time Foucault wrote the book, he believed that we were inhabiting a 'carceral network' (1977b, 301). That is, more and more institutions were starting to use these panoptic features, with the ensuing result that 'docile bodies', not just the ones produced in the prison, were being created in numerous other locales as well: the school, the hospital, etc. Simultaneously, these locales were also able to produce 'scientific knowledge' of their populations, such as educational pedagogy and medicine.

18. The 'classical age', meaning the 'episteme' running approximately from the mid-seventeenth century to the French Revolution at the end of the eighteenth century, has frequently been the object of Foucault's attention. Significant portions of many of his earlier works—e.g., *Madness and civilization* (1977a), *The birth of the clinic* (1975a), *The order of things* (1973), *Discipline and punish* (1977b)—were devoted to the examination of this period.

19. Bio-power and bio-politics seem to be terms that Foucault used at this time more or less interchangeably.

20. What Foucault would understand as exemplars of anatamo-politics and bio-politics.

21. For example, although 'black spit' was a typical mining community phrase to describe a common illness in the early nineteenth century, in order to count 'occupational deaths' for official purposes, the secretary of the General Registrar's office in Britain, William Farr, encouraged the use of a medical 'nosology', which had the effect of eliminating such lay terms. See Doran 1986, 391–416.

22. It has only been relatively recently that I have been able to start situating this notion of 'codification' within the existing critical, social scientific literature. For details, see Doran (forthcoming).

23. Within modern sociology, schools like the structural-functionalist and the symbolic interactionist tend to gravitate around the first of these poles; on the other hand, the Marxist school and its variants tend to see this freedom as largely illusory.

24. Or they are in the process of being translated. For example, the Collège de France lectures for 1977–8 and 1978–9 are scheduled for publication in 2006 and 2007. Nevertheless, Burchell et al. (1991) may be usefully consulted as it brings together some of Foucault's own writings on this subject (87–105) as well as discussion by others (181–97, 164–5, 123–4).

25. This is a tendency that started with Marx himself. He had understood the state as primarily a committee of the bourgeoisie passing laws in the interest of capitalism (and he himself had had few critical remarks about 'official statistics'—in fact, he is well known for using them in his own analyses). And although Lenin also tended to focus on the coercive elements of the state, later Marxist theorists have in fact attempted to produce much more subtle theorizations. Thus Althusser focused on the state as the privileged site for ideology to be produced, while Poulantzas argued that the state is relatively autonomous from capitalism. That is, while working to ensure the 'long-term survival' of the capitalist system, the state may often pass laws that work against the direct interests of capital. But perhaps it was Gramsci who inspired Corrigan and Sayer the most, for he often formulates the state as being the cultural leader that is constantly engaged in the activity of establishing and maintaining 'consensus'. For a good overview of Marxist understandings of the state, appropriate for those with little background in the field, Carnoy (1984) is still quite useful.

26. They are unapologetic in their acceptance that they are giving a 'history from above' (1985, 12–13) that shows how different elites in English history worked to fashion and impose such cultural world views.

Chapter 10

Is Social Welfare Viable?

Lois Harder

INTRODUCTION

The question of social welfare's survival emerged during a specific political moment when longstanding assumptions about the relationship between citizen and state were being challenged. People concerned with growing government debts and declining economic competitiveness asserted that overly generous welfare states created a passive, dependent citizenry with a weak work ethic. People concerned with democratic citizenship argued that social services were not meeting user needs or desires, and worse, that social programs reinforced rather than ameliorated inequalities. Moreover, these concerns were being expressed in a context of globalizing economies, transformations in labour markets, and changing family formations—a context that undermined the basic assumptions on which the Keynesian (or post-Second World War) social welfare structure had been built.

When the debate surrounding social welfare's viability (and hence survival) was at its most intense (the 1980s and early 1990s in Canada), the crux of the controversy centred on the adjective 'social'. Several chapters have so far addressed this term, but with regard to the debate over social welfare's survival, the 'social' was understood to mean welfare that was publicly provided or state-provided. At stake here is whether and the degree to which citizens' well-being ought to be a concern for the state. In fact in Canada, only a few voices advocated absolving the state of any responsibility for citizen well-being. Most of the discussion focused on the purposes and means of providing welfare and the correct proportions of the welfare mix—that is, what the optimum division of responsibility should be among the state, market, community, family, and individual in providing for people's needs. In effect then, Canadians have decided that social welfare is viable and should survive. We continue to demand publicly provided social programs, assess the quality of our governments at least partly in terms of the services they provide, and expect that legislation and state action will reflect and enforce the (contested) social norms that shape our interactions. But the mere claim that welfare is viable obscures some profound changes in social welfare provision. It is these changes and the shifting political and social context in which they emerged that will be the focus of this chapter.

Before we consider how and why social welfare was transformed, we need to understand what is meant by our central term. I want to do this initially by describing what social welfare involves rather than defining its purposes, since, as we shall see, the issue of defining social welfare's intent was central to the various positions in the debate over its survival/transformation. Included under the umbrella of social welfare is a range of familiar social programs that fall into three major categories: education (primary, secondary, and post-secondary), health (hospital care and doctor visits), and income supports (old age and disability pensions, unemployment insurance, and social assistance). Indeed, we are familiar with social welfare in a variety of guises—for example, student loans, minimum wage laws, child care subsidies, and parental leave programs.

Social welfare is delivered through two key modes, and our eligibility for social programs is assessed on varying criteria. With regard to modes, some social welfare programs are delivered as *direct services*. For example, children attend primary and secondary school; sick or injured people go to clinics and hospitals. Other programs are provided *indirectly*—that is, through the tax system. The Child Care Expense Deduction and registered retirement savings plans operate on this basis. Rather than governments setting up a program or a bricks and mortar institution, recipients are reimbursed or credited for having purchased a service in the marketplace. Indirectly provided social programs may reduce the tax owed by eligible citizens or provide funds to people who meet relevant criteria. A low income, for example, entitles people to the Goods and Services Tax Credit, paid quarterly, and low-income families with children receive the Canada Child Tax Benefit every month.

As these examples suggest, public institutions do not deliver many social programs. Instead, private providers, such as doctors, non-profit organizations, and even for-profit businesses work in a contractual relationship with state agencies in order to offer services to entitled citizens. This situation has characterized Canadian social welfare since its inception, but it has become a particularly heated site of contention at the moment when the longevity of purely public services is arguably in jeopardy. Proponents of public/private partnerships argue that such arrangements increase citizen (consumer) choice, enhance the flexibility of service provision, and reduce costs to taxpayers. In contrast, skeptics question whether it is appropriate that public monies should fund for-profit businesses, whether non-profit organizations can sustain their commitment to service provision over the long term, and whether contracted enterprises are sufficiently accountable to elected representatives and to voters.

Our eligibility for social welfare is also determined on a variety of bases, generally categorized as *universal*, *contributory*, and *means-tested*. Access to health care in Canada, for example, is considered a universal entitlement available to all Canadian citizens and permanent residents regardless of one's income. Employment Insurance (EI) and the Canada/Quebec Pension Plan (CPP/QPP) are contributory social programs in that all workers and employers pay a portion of their earnings into these schemes. As we will see, however, a series of conditions surrounding EI eligibility has made it more difficult to access benefits. Finally, means-tested programs are provided to people who can demonstrate that they lack sufficient economic resources to meet their basic needs. The programs for people with low incomes mentioned above are examples, but perhaps the most notorious means-tested program is social assistance or what is commonly understood as 'welfare'. Indeed, social assistance was a key site of policy reform in most Canadian provinces, where administrations drew extensively from US welfare reform initiatives that monopolized much of that country's political debate in the mid-1990s. Nonetheless, it would be a mistake to focus solely on social assistance in this discussion of social welfare's survival and transformation, since arguments concerning the state's role in providing for citizen well-being have taken place in a number of policy areas.

THE KEYNESIAN WELFARE STATE

When the debate over the fate and shape of social welfare was raging, much of the discussion focused around purposes and effects. Although state-provided social services have existed in some form since the nineteenth century in Canada, the high-water mark of social welfare came with the programs developed in the years following the Second World War. These programs, responding as they did both to the anticipated consequences of post-war military demobilization and to the pre-war economic depression, focused on protecting people from a variety of social, economic, and political risks. John Maynard Keynes, the architect of post-war economic management in industrialized countries, argued that the Great Depression resulted from inadequate demand in the market. In order to correct this problem, he argued, national governments needed to ensure that in times of economic downturn, people would still have enough money to purchase goods, thus sustaining individuals and families and keeping economies functioning. Keynesian welfare policies thus included unemployment insurance, family allowances, and old age pensions. Governments were to finance this intervention by increasing taxes in times of economic growth and by deficit spending in times of economic slow-down.

Keynes's influence on the policies of Western governments stemmed from the usefulness of his analysis and prescriptions in meeting a number of political purposes, although the debate over what these purposes were precisely remains ongoing. Broadly, scholars have advanced three rationales for the implementation of Keynesian social welfare programs. The first was that the development of social programs would counteract the growing power of workers in the political arena. The second was a belief that a relatively generous social welfare state would dampen the appeal of socialist alternatives to capitalist economies—an appeal that had gained adherents during the economic crisis of the 1930s. The third rationale was the argument that social programs would benefit businesses because they would help to create a healthy, well-educated population and thus reduce the causes of labour unrest.

However, the story of social welfare's development in Canada only partially fits within these rationales. In particular, the extent to which working-class mobilization propelled the adoption of Keynesian social policies in Canada was not as great as it was in some other industrial countries. Canada's industrial (manufacturing) workforce was/is relatively small and geographically concentrated in Ontario and Quebec. And while there were some very significant labour struggles and successes throughout the Depression and the war years, often framed in the language of socialism, these successes did not translate into support for a political party with a viable chance at gaining federal power (though there have been several provincial New Democratic Party governments) or in a significant 'worker' identity within Canada's social structure. Instead, Canadians have tended to identify themselves in terms of region and/or language. Indeed, as the details of specific social programs reveal, the federal government's application of Keynesian principles was as much about overcoming regional disparities and creating a common national identity as it was about addressing the demands of an insurgent working class (Jenson 1989). For example, the imposition of national standards in the Medical Care Act (1966), revised as the Canada Health Act (CHA) in 1984 and still in effect, and the Canada Assistance Plan (CAP) (1966–95) required provinces to adhere to certain principles in order to receive federal funding. These principles would ensure that regardless of where people resided within the country, they would be able to rely on a similar level of service.

The application of Keynesian strategies in Canada was also limited by two of its central assumptions: first, that they would be applied within the context of a relatively closed national economy, and second, that they would be applied by a strong central government. Canada, with its reliance on resource exports as its primary economic engine, was and continues to be an open economy. This means that foreign markets determine how much of what Canadian goods are desired. In comparison to the governments of other industrialized countries, the Canadian government, even in the days before NAFTA and contemporary globalization, thus had a relatively limited capacity to shape the conditions of production or to use national policy to heat up or cool down levels of demand in order to mediate fluctuations in the economy.

The second difficulty in applying Keynesian prescriptions was the degree of decentralization in Canada's federal system of government and particularly the fact that constitutional jurisdiction over one of the most important tools for implementing Keynesian prescriptions—social policy—lies within the purview of the provinces. This is not to say that the federal government has no role in social policy, as we have already seen with regard to the imposition of national standards. In fact, the federal government secured a constitutional amendment in order to take over responsibility for unemployment insurance and pensions, and it makes regular use of the tax system to provide indirect social programs. Ottawa has also regularly used its spending power as an incentive to encourage provinces to adopt particular programs and operational principles. Nonetheless, provincial agreement is a prerequisite for federal social policy initiatives. Given the range in ideology and fiscal capacity among provincial administrations and the long-standing tensions between the federal and provincial governments, there is no guarantee that any one pan-Canadian social policy agenda will be implemented.

The tension surrounding jurisdictional control over social policy points to one of the key rationales for social welfare's survival: the role of social programs in demonstrating to voters that their governments are actually doing something for them. Citizens want to be able to see what their tax dollars are buying them, and social programs fill this role. Moreover, in providing for the well-being of citizens, governments are engaged in articulating a sense of common identity, a sense of 'we-ness' that builds solidarity among citizens and can help to shore up support for a particular provincial (or federal) administration. The capacity of social programs to perform this role is powerfully demonstrated in Quebec where a succession of provincial leaders, whether federalist or separatist, have staunchly defended that province's constitutional autonomy in this domain. They insist that social programs are integral to the articulation and protection of Quebec's distinctiveness within Canada. And while Quebec may have a specific cultural rationale for its jurisdictional attachment to social policy that is less apparent in other provinces, provincial governments outside of Quebec also understand the political rewards and risks associated with social welfare provision.

However, the uncomfortable fit between the Canadian economic and political contexts and Keynesian prescriptions for a more secure and prosperous capitalism did not extend to Keynesian assumptions surrounding a supportive family form. Moreover, when the debate surrounding the viability of post-war social welfare was ignited, the heteronormative nuclear family form with a sole, male breadwinner was the one feature of the Keynesian policy lexicon that conservative critics continued to embrace. Because the institution of the family is presumed to be natural and necessary to the reproduction of the human species (see Chapter 4), the fact that its form and function are products of state policy and social custom is not always obvious. Indeed, the degree to which 'the family' is taken for granted is readily apparent in the plethora of welfare state scholarship that omits the family from analysis. Nonetheless, Keynesian policy does provide clear evidence of a governmental effort to implement a particular family form. For example, women's participation in the labour market had been actively encouraged during the war years when the call to arms drained industrial and agricultural workforces of their male employees. After the war, in an effort to free up industrial jobs for returning veterans, new tax measures were implemented that severely penalized families in which both spouses had incomes (Prentice et al. 1988). As well, employers were allowed to refuse to hire married women, and women did not have the right to demand the same wage as men when they performed the same work. Divorces were difficult to obtain; women could not establish bank accounts or acquire credit without their husbands' permission; and sexual assault laws did not recognize rape within the context of marriage as a crime. These policies (and others), in combination with a general societal sentiment that women's rightful place was at home tending to the domestic needs of their families, reinforced a male-breadwinner, nuclear model of the family.

THE CRISIS OF THE WELFARE STATE

The Keynesian model of social welfare was always subject to debate and contestation, but its viability did not seriously come under challenge until the 1980s. The reforming sentiment that had propelled Margaret Thatcher into power in the

United Kingdom and Ronald Reagan to the US White House also spilled over into Canada, where Brian Mulroney's Progressive Conservative government was elected in 1984. By this time, a series of economic and social changes had begun to undermine the foundations on which Keynesian social welfare had rested. Globalization challenged the viability of protecting national economies, while pressures to reduce government spending and to increase citizens' involvement in their own governance increased the appeal of decentralization. Further, the political urgency of shielding people from social risk had diminished as memories of the Depression and the Second World War grew hazy and the triumph of capitalist economies over their communist alternatives became ever more certain. Instead, the pressing issues of the day were what to do about government deficits, stagnating economies, rising unemployment and inflation, and (depending on one's political bent) moral decay.

The crisis of the Keynesian welfare state was common among industrialized countries, but in Canada this breakdown in the post-war social architecture gained added momentum because it coincided with a constitutional crisis. Although many concerns regarding the governance of the Canadian federation were broached during the period of constitutional negotiation (1968–95), Quebec's place within Canada was the primary source of contention. In addressing Quebec's demands for greater autonomy, Canada's federal government pursued two approaches. The first, advocated by Prime Minister Pierre Trudeau, was to undermine Quebec's claims to a collective distinctiveness by invoking the appeal of liberal individualism through his promotion of the Charter of Rights and Freedoms. The second, advanced by Prime Minister Brian Mulroney, was to respect Quebec's claims to autonomy but do so by extending the same level of autonomy to each of the provinces.[1] While Trudeau and Mulroney vehemently disagreed over the means to address Quebec nationalism, these diverging means—individualization and decentralization—stood against the pan-Canadian collectivism and centralizing impulses of the post-war era and would become central techniques in resolving the crisis of the welfare state.

With regard to social welfare, Anglo-American governments and their supporters focused on the expense and the consequences of social programs. This focus would prove to hold for both the conservative governments that instigated the initial wave of welfare reform in the 1980s and their more centrist successors in the 1990s and into the twenty-first century.[2] Whereas social welfare was originally envisioned as a means to offset social risks, detractors argued that it had engendered grave misuses of programs, undermined people's willingness to work, and created a dependent citizenry. People who worked in social service bureaucracies (sites of employment that had been central to increasing the number of women in the paid workforce) were accused of 'empire-building', advancing their own careers rather than attending to the needs of service recipients or containing costs to taxpayers. As well, a number of societal shifts and legislative reforms spurred on by feminists as well as by anti-racism and anti-poverty advocates sparked a policy backlash. Initiatives such as pay equity (equal pay for work of equal value) and employment equity laws (which sought to improve the representation of women, disabled people, visible minorities, and Aboriginal peoples in large government and corporate workplaces) were resisted or withdrawn on the grounds that their implementation was too expensive and (erroneously) that they valued quota fulfillment more than merit.[3]

Transformations in the family that had occurred as a result of women's increased participation in paid work and liberalized divorce laws—a transformation that was driven in equal part by feminism and economic necessity as a result of the decreased ability of a single income to support a family—were also identified as symptoms of welfare state crisis. Anti-poverty advocates assessed the consequences in terms of the 'feminization of poverty'—a situation in which increasing numbers of women found themselves among the ranks of the poor and increasing numbers of men found their wages declining and their conditions of employment more precarious just as women in the paid labour force did (Armstrong 1996). These concerns were often drowned out by conservatives who blamed women for abandoning their responsibilities to their families, an abandonment that was seen to be facilitated by social programs that enabled women to seek the support of the state rather than that of their husbands and families.

However, the most vicious rebuttal of Keynesian social welfare was reserved for the terrain of social assistance. Citing an upward trend in the number of benefit claimants, a number that did not diminish substantially during the economic recovery of the late 1980s, and borrowing from the anti-welfare rhetoric of the United States, Canadian governments implemented a series of measures to reduce benefits, tighten eligibility criteria, and detect fraud. Governments measured the success of their reforms in terms of caseload reductions—the number of people removed from the welfare rolls—but invested little energy in determining what became of people who, already in dire financial straits, could no longer count on public assistance. Moreover, in a context in which deficit reduction was, at least in some jurisdictions, the top governing priority, how those caseloads were reduced hardly mattered. The Alberta government's (short-lived) policy of giving social assistance recipients bus tickets to British Columbia, for example, was indicative of this lack of concern (Peck 2001, 218).

AFTER THE WELFARE STATE

Although vigorously resisted, the resolution of the 'crisis of the welfare state' was ultimately determined to lie in the neo-liberal strategies of privatization, marketization, decentralization, individualization, and familialization. The idea was to reduce the role of the state in the private sphere—the market, the community, and the home—and, where necessary, to resituate responsibility for public services to the level of government that would be most responsive to the needs of specific communities. Neo-liberals argued that a reinvigoration of the private sphere in all of its dimensions would create a 'virtuous circle'. Less regulation of markets and increased emphasis on the provision of social services through the market rather than through the state would encourage greater responsiveness to people's needs. Competition would keep costs low while encouraging innovation. A revitalized market would generate jobs, resulting in less need for social programs (although it was also important to reduce the generosity of income support programs so as to ensure that workers would be available and willing to work, thus driving down wages through competition in the labour market). Fewer social programs would reduce the costs of governing, thereby contributing to more robust national accounts, reduced taxes, and an enhanced climate for investment. People would be required to live by their wits, thus further stimulating innovation and competitiveness and encouraging the most talented and hard-working people to reach their potential rather than being held back by cumbersome and stifling state regulation and demotivating levels of taxation.

The growing popularity of this set of ideas formed the context in which the question of social welfare's survival was raised. But with the exception of a few extreme voices, Canadian neo-liberals did not advocate the total dismantling of the welfare state.[4] Instead, they argued for a reconfiguration of social programs and a reconceptualization of the relationship between citizen and state. The concern for security—for some certainty of help in times of need—was replaced by a focus on choice and responsibility. Neo-liberals (and indeed progressive reformers) asserted that people should be free to select services that best suited their needs and to pursue interests that would contribute to self-development. The possibility of making poor choices was a necessary corollary to this freedom, but such misfortune did not justify cushioning people against the inherent risks, according to this rationality. Rather, neo-liberals believed that the possibility of negative consequences would inspire people to take their decisions with greater care. Similarly, the emphasis on the 'social' in social welfare was also rethought. Whereas Keynesian social programs had rested on a notion of collective responsibility for individual well-being and had attempted to forge a national identity through a common entitlement to social benefits, neo-liberal reformers expressed some suspicion of the state having a role in articulating bonds of identification. They argued instead that ties of obligation and mutual recognition were stronger when they were formed through the conscious decisions of individuals acting within communities (Putnam 2000).

In the context of increased market and community provision, the benefits of citizen (i.e., consumer) choice received considerably more emphasis than the *responsibility* of providers to ensure adequate standards and reliable service. However, when neo-liberal reformers turned their gaze on the family and its role in assuming formerly state-provided services, responsibility emphatically trumped choice. Feminist critics of neo-liberalism have been particularly attentive to this development (Lewis 2001; Jenson and Sineau 2001). They observed the degree to which reduced hospital and long-term care budgets have translated into an increased reliance on the labour of family members. Work that had been performed by trained medical professionals became the task of a wife, mother, or daughter, whether or not she had the skill, time, or desire to assume these caring tasks. This assumption effectively fell back on 'traditional' as well as Keynesian ideas about the gendered division of labour despite the fact that wage rates and social policies no longer supported the male-breadwinner family model.

While it is certainly true that the availability of unpaid, caring work has been presumed in neo-liberal efforts to privatize public services, it is less clear that this presumption has necessarily reinforced the heteronormative nuclear family. In Canada at least, both federal and provincial legislative initiatives have moved to recognize the increasing plurality of family forms. Recognition of common-law relationships among both opposite and same-sex couples and same-sex marriage is indicative of this impulse. But while this recognition has stemmed in part from active demands for acknowledgement of the legitimacy of these relationships, recognition also enables the state to impose obligations on a wider array of relationships. For example, Canada's federal government requires that if you live with someone for a year in a conjugal relationship, you must include your partner's income on your tax return. The combination of incomes is then used to determine your eligibility for a variety of benefits. Often this income pooling will result in the termination of one's entitlement (Lahey 2000, 2). The state's expectation is that the partners combine their resources to care for each other, thus eliminating the need for state assistance. This expectation applies regardless of whether or not people actually organize their finances in this way (Lister 2004, 56–7). From the perspective of Canadian governments, what matters is family function, particularly in providing care, rather than family form. The fact that this responsibility still falls disproportionately on women can thus be seen as a 'choice' within the families themselves rather than the express purpose of public policy.

THE NEW SOCIAL WELFARE: SOME POLICY EXAMPLES

Persuading voters that a neo-liberal reconfiguration of Canada's social policy regime was worthy of their support required a careful plan of attack. While it was true that many people were displeased with elements of the Keynesian welfare state, they did not necessarily see the resolution to their concerns lying in greater reliance on the private sphere. Moreover, the neo-liberal reform effort also had to proceed carefully around programs that had most successfully articulated a collective Canadian identity. For example, the idea that ill health can befall anyone regardless of their life choices and that a robust public health care system is the most important defining feature of the Canadian identity (true in both Quebec and the rest of Canada) suggests that the old notions of collective identity and mutual obligation remain resilient in the face of neo-liberal alternatives (Brodie 2002, 169). Still, the neo-liberal marketing plan has had some notable successes. Canadians have generally accepted the characterization of post-war social programs—particularly income support programs—as passive, overly generous hand-outs that provide too soft a cushion. Canadians have been persuaded by proposals for the creation of an active citizenry, providing a springboard into the job market and a hand-up in times of need. The language of activity, encouragement, and expectations feeds into a sense that citizens need to become more responsible for their own well-being rather than blaming 'the system' for their troubles.

This altered sensibility regarding the message and purpose of social welfare has subsequently been expressed in social policy reform. Neo-liberal social programs have generally been less generous, with stricter eligibility criteria and a stronger requirement for people to account for their actions than was true for the social programs of the post-war era. These differences can be seen in changes to policy form. Neo-liberal reformers discounted the value of creating a sense of citizenship entitlement through the provision of universal programs, arguing instead that universal programs were overly inclusive. In the case of family allowance, for example, neo-liberals asserted that providing a monthly cheque to a wealthy banker's wife was a waste of public resources. Instead, it would be better to target benefits to people who really needed them. In this spirit, the federal government abolished the family allowance in 1993, replacing it with the income-tested National Child Benefit (NCB).

National Child Benefit

In many ways, the NCB is the consummate articulation of neo-liberal social welfare in Canada. Although framed in terms of an initiative to reduce child poverty, the program's design suggests that the primary focus of the benefit is to top up the earnings of low-income families, thus making low-waged work more tolerable and increasing the appeal of paid work over social assistance. The program has two parts, the Canada Child Tax Benefit and the National Child Benefit Supplement, and they are provided by the federal government through a monthly cheque to families with children under 18 with income below a certain threshold. From the perspective of the federal government, it does not matter whether your income comes from paid work or from provincial social assistance/welfare programs: if your family's net income as reported on your tax return falls below $22,615 and you have children, you are entitled to the full benefit (Canada 2004). In fact, however, this apparent focus on the well-being of children regardless of their parents' source of income is disingenuous. The program is designed to enable provincial and territorial governments to use the National Child Benefit Supplement portion of the payment as an incentive to encourage families on social assistance to find work and to reward low-income families in the paid workforce for their initiative. This incentive is provided by the expectation that provinces and territories will replace the portion of their social assistance payments allocated to children with the federal money. In turn, the provinces and territories are expected to put the money they are no longer spending on poor children towards developing programs for low-income families that will help them to maintain their participation in the workforce and provide benefits that might have only been available to them when receiving social assistance. Because the provinces can decide what these programs will be, they can tailor them to address their specific political and labour market priorities.

The National Child Benefit represents a more sober response to social welfare reform than a simple slash and burn, 'people should pull themselves up by their own bootstraps' approach. Instead, as Alexandra Dobrowolsky observes, it indicates a shift towards social investment. Investment, of course, focuses on future gains—hence, the NCB's ostensible concern for the well-being of children (Dobrowolsky 2004, 181). As well, the labelling of the program as child-centred helps to build political and public support by appealing to a widespread view that children are not responsible for the circumstances of their parents. Nonetheless, the state's interest in securing the well-being of children is achieved only indirectly. As the federal government observes, the purpose of the NCB is to encourage 'attachment to the workforce resulting in fewer families having to rely on social assistance—by ensuring that families will always be better off as a result of finding work' (Canada, in Battle 1999, 1233).

Announced in 1998, the NCB subsequently underwent developments that demonstrate the persistent tension between the economic logic of targeting benefits and the political logic of legitimating governments through the provision of social programs. The shift from universal to targeted programs was especially popular when Canadian governments were pursuing deficit reduction. Once governments attained budget surpluses, however, some of the enthusiasm for this approach began to decline. This shift in focus was manifested in a growing concern with the federal government's failure to acknowledge the costs incurred by families in raising children and with the obvious role of future generations in ensuring the future prosperity of the country (Lefebvre and Merrigan 2003, 18). Thus, the government has extended the NCB's reach such that at least a portion of the benefit now reaches 80 per cent of Canadian children (Boychuk 2001, 136).

Employment insurance

Changes to the unemployment insurance program (UI) also demonstrate a reformed sensibility with regard to citizens and social risk. When the UI program was at its most generous, stories abounded about workers who would leave their jobs after working for the number of weeks required to claim benefits and were later found enjoying the slopes at Rocky Mountain ski resorts. In the face of these alleged abuses and in a desire to increase workers' attachment to the labour force, UI was overhauled and renamed *employment insurance* (EI) in 1996. Eligibility for benefits became more stringent, measured by the number of hours rather than weeks worked. People could claim benefits only if they had been laid off, the percentage of earnings received decreased from 60 per cent to 55 per cent, and the period during which they could claim benefits fell from 50 to 45 weeks (Prince 1999, 181). One result of these changes has been a reduction in the number of workers eligible for EI dropping from 83 per cent of unemployed Canadians in 1989 (Prince 1999) to 38 per cent in 2002 (CLC 2003). Moreover, while EI eligibility criteria have become more stringent, all workers and employers are still required to contribute to the EI fund.

Social assistance

Neo-liberal reforms have also extended to means-tested programs. Social assistance came under particularly vicious attack because of its (unfounded) reputation as a program that supports laziness and irresponsibility. In several provinces, people who survived the first wave of caseload reductions subsequently found themselves facing a more or less strict expectation that they should work for their benefits. As one of its conditions for provincial eligibility, the Canada Assistance Plan had included a prohibition against the implementation of work for benefit or 'workfare' policies. In 1995, however, the federal Liberal government abolished CAP and replaced it with a new funding mechanism, the Canada Health and Social Transfer (CHST). This new policy eliminated CAP's national standards with the exception of prohibiting provinces from imposing a minimum residency requirement. It was in this new context that many Canadian provinces decided to experiment with workfare schemes.[5] Social assistance recipients also saw their benefits reduced, a reform justified on the grounds of increasing the attractiveness of paid work. Finally, some governments enhanced their powers to investigate welfare fraud, including the development of a welfare fraud hotline in Ontario. Through this mechanism, people were encouraged to police the behaviour of their assistance-receiving neighbours and report their suspicions to the state (Little and Morrison 1999).

While social assistance recipients thus found their lives subject to an intensified level of scrutiny and miserliness, the alternative of engaging in paid work offered few improvements. With the increased competitiveness of labour markets, a single wage has ceased to be adequate to support a family for all but the most well-paid professionals and entrepreneurs. Even in families with two earners, the combined income may not be sufficient to support a family. These circumstances have forced governments to acknowledge the existence of a new social category: the working poor. The NCB and its associated provincial programs, discussed above, play an important role in addressing this growing phenomenon and the political risks it poses for the neo-liberal project.

Health care

Unlike the transformed understanding of the citizen/state relation that has marked reform efforts in other social policy areas, the public and universal character of Canada's health care system continues to enjoy both strong public support and, at least rhetorically, political commitment. The indiscriminate character of disease and accidents and an awareness of the costs of a private health care system have sustained this high level of popularity. Nonetheless, a sense of crisis has emerged (Boychuk 2004, 236; Deber 2003, 20). Pitched battles in the federal/provincial arena over funding, in combination with Canadians' everyday experiences of long waiting periods for elective surgeries and the declining availability of family practitioners, have intensified the urgent need for reform. As well, new and expensive diagnostic techniques, surgical procedures, and medications are claimed to exact an increasing toll on the capacity of the public system to finance health care. A number of studies have been undertaken both federally and provincially to examine possible responses to these challenges, but so far, public resistance and government stalemates have prevented the adoption of far-reaching, system-wide reform. Instead, changes are being made incrementally and below the radar screen of public debate. Moreover, these changes often involve greater privatization, both through an increased expectation that families will take responsibility for recovering patients and fund drugs and procedures that are not covered by provincial health insurance programs and by permitting medical entrepreneurs to provide a growing array of services outside of the public system.

The fact that Canadians take so much pride in their public health care system and in the sense of collective responsibility that it is believed to convey belies the complexity of its structure. Hospital care and physician visits are universally covered under a single-payer system, the single payer being the provincial medical insurance program that is funded by both provincial and federal monies and governed by the principles of the Canada Health Act (Maioni 2003, 52).[6] Pharmaceuticals, dental and extended care, as well as medical services that are not covered by provincial insurance schemes, lie within the purview of the private sphere—either employer-provided insurance benefits or one's personal resources. Physicians are private businesspeople who bill their province of operation for the services they provide to patients. Indeed, as Raisa Deber observes, the degree of private provision is sufficiently extensive to classify Canada's health care system among the *least* publicly financed among industrialized countries (2003, 22). In some ways then, it might be argued that the Canadian health care system, with its mixture of public and private elements, has manifested elements of a neo-liberal structure since its inception. Recent pressures and reforms can thus be seen as intensifying the private dimensions of the system.

A unique feature of the health care debate in Canada is the degree to which the normative or moral issues surrounding public provision (collective responsibility) versus private provision (profit, personal responsibility) are regularly overshadowed by federal/provincial turf wars. Again, this fractiousness has its roots in the division of powers, in provincial aspirations for greater autonomy, and—especially—in the neo-liberal, decentralizing impulse that has resulted in a substantial federal withdrawal from the medicare field, particularly with regard to its level of financial contributions. Beginning in the mid-1980s and intensifying with the CHST, the federal government has implemented changes to health care funding, pushing more of the responsibility for financing onto the provinces (Deber 2003, 22). And while public expenditures on health care have not increased as a percentage of gross domestic product (GDP) and have actually fallen on a per capita basis over the past decade, the provincial share of health care funding has increased substantially (Boychuk 2004, 20). For many provinces, health care now constitutes the largest expenditure item in their annual budgets (Premiers' Council 2004). The provinces' fiscal crisis in health care has not, however, resulted in responsiveness to new federal health care initiatives. Antonia Maioni observes that the more cost-burdened the provinces are, the more territorial they become (2003, 52). From the provincial perspective, previous levels of federal funding must be restored before any new initiatives can be contemplated (Premiers' Council on Canadian Health Awareness 2004). Since this course of action provides little enhanced visibility for the federal government, the situation has become a stalemate. Public frustration with both levels of government has increased, contributing to some undermining of confidence in the system (Boychuk 2004, 20–1; Deber 2003, 22).

Medical advances and the dynamics of Canadian federalism are the primary motivators for health care reform, but increasingly we also see an emphasis on personal responsibility for one's health beginning to figure in the debate. Discussions of obesity in the general population and particularly among children, the risks of smoking and exposure to second-hand smoke, the impact of fast food on people's health, and the ways in which contemporary lifestyles have made us more sedentary all include an injunction to improve our personal behaviour. In policy terms, this injunction can be seen in proposals to give tax credits to people with gym memberships, to increase the cost of cigarettes and unhealthy food, and to develop personal health accounts that penalize people whose health costs exceed a set limit and reward those who live within or below that limit (e.g., Alberta 2001, 41–3). In part, these developments reflect the realization that efforts to promote wellness represent a more effective use of resources than treating illness. Yet the growing emphasis on individual responsibility could obscure the extent to which ill health is a generalized risk that can afflict anyone, regardless of their 'lifestyle choices'.

It would be both romantic and naive to assess the ongoing presence of federal and provincial governments in the health care field as attributable solely to strong levels of popular support for their presence: indeed, neo-liberal governance has a proven track record in selling fiscal restraint and in weakening citizens' allegiance to public programs. In addition, it is important to recognize the very real cost savings that result from a public system. In the game of attracting light-footed global investment, state-provided health care gives Canada a competitive edge in that it dramatically reduces payroll costs for employers and promotes administrative efficiency in the health care system (Charest 2003, 55). Moreover, as far as the provinces are concerned, it makes sense to retain a single-payer system in order to avoid a situation in which private insurers skim off the lowest risks, leaving the provinces to foot the bill for uninsurable citizens (Deber 2003, 24).

CONCLUSION

In this discussion of social welfare, I have argued that the question of its ongoing viability is a product of a particular historical moment in which the fiscal crisis of the state became the focus of public policy. However tempting the elimination of public responsibility for personal well-being might have been to some neo-liberal ideologues, a full-scale public withdrawal from the care of citizens was never really in the cards. The role of social policy in legitimating governments, in integrating citizens into the prevailing mode of economic production, and even in articulating a national identity has made social welfare a key instrument of governance.

These general claims about the significance of social welfare should not, however, blind us to the very significant differences in the way that social welfare is conceived and the dynamism in its purposes. The Keynesian social welfare system, as we have seen, established social programs that buttressed the specific workings of Canada's post-war economy, reinforcing the single-breadwinner, two-parent nuclear family with its gendered division of labour and building a sense of national identity. However, as political struggles were undertaken and economic structures shifted, this arrangement began to weaken, creating a crisis and subsequently a new neo-liberal attempt to articulate the relationships among citizens (as individuals and in families), the market, and the state. Under neo-liberal social welfare prescriptions, a globalized (or in the Canadian context, North-American-ized) economy is supported by active labour market policies, including a more competitive labour market, enhanced choices for service provision, and increased personal responsibility for forming and maintaining the ties that bind—whether these be at the level of family, the community, or the nation. What these changes demonstrate is that the viability of any specific social welfare order, whether envisioned by post-war Keynesians or contemporary neo-liberals, rests on whether it establishes a mutually reinforcing and supportive relationship among the individual/family, the market, and the state. It seems to me that some attempt to articulate a more or less coherent framework for these relationships will continue to be a feature of governance for the foreseeable future.

Signs of stress are already appearing in the neo-liberal social welfare regime. Concerns about the adequacy of private service provision, the inability of low-wage work to provide an adequate income, the inattention to work/family balance, and the consequences of budget reductions on public services are matters of growing public concern. How these concerns will be addressed is, again, an open question. Perhaps we will soon find ourselves asking, though this time in a new context, whether neo-liberal social welfare is itself viable and can survive.

Questions to Consider

1. What was the social and political context in which the question of social welfare's survival emerged?
2. How has Canadian social policy changed from the Keynesian welfare state to the neo-liberal era?
3. The chapter argues that during the Keynesian welfare state period, social policy was important in articulating a Canadian national identity. Is this still true? Why/why not?
4. The chapter notes that neo-liberal reforms to social welfare have included both individualization and familialization. Is this a contradiction? How do we account for the existence of both of these tendencies?
5. Why were social assistance programs singled out as the area of social policy most in need of reform?

Notes

1. Mulroney's efforts, articulated in the Meech Lake and Charlottetown accords, would fail to gain constitutional status, but the tenets of the agreements, at least with regard to Quebec, have been largely adopted.
2. The US returned to a right-wing Republican administration in 2000.
3. For a discussion of the federal government's unwillingness to abide by the terms of its own pay equity laws, see Fudge (2002, especially 115–24). Regarding employment equity, see Bakan and Kobayashi (2000). Employment equity laws in Canada required employers to hire job candidates from the four identified groups when there was no demonstrable difference between the equity candidate and the person from the non-

targeted group. Quotas were not part of this system, although it was expected that the representation of women, members of visible minorities, disabled people, and Aboriginal peoples would increase.

4. The terminology gets a bit complicated here. 'Neo-liberal' refers to a person or policy that advocates private over public provision. The term invokes the idea of 'liberal' in its original eighteenth-century form, which promoted the individual over the collective and the institution of rights as a means of protecting individuals from the incursions of the state. Both Conservative and Liberal governments in Canada have been characterized as 'neo-liberal' since the 1980s. The term 'neo-conservative' adds further complexity to the mix. Neo-conservatives are distinguished from neo-liberals at the level of morality. Whereas neo-conservatives and neo-liberals generally agree on issues surrounding the freeing up of markets from state control, they part company when it comes to the state's role in legislating morality. Neo-conservatives, for example, tend to support restrictions on abortion, advocate for the prohibition of same-sex marriage, and uphold traditional notions of the nuclear family, preferably with a stay-at-home mother. To the extent that neo-liberals weigh in on these debates, they generally tend to advance the opposing position.

5. There have been many concerns raised by researchers concerning the efficacy of workfare. The quality of employment, the provision of child care and transportation, and the multiple barriers to employment that some social assistance recipients face have all contributed to the very uneven success of workfare schemes. Moreover, in order for these initiatives to really meet their objectives, social assistance programs may consume substantially more resources than they did in their more 'passive' guise.

6. These principles include comprehensiveness, affordability, accessibility, portability, and public administration.

Chapter 11

Who Governs Whom in Canada?

Dawn Moore

INTRODUCTION: AM I GOVERNED?

Of course you are! Think about the start of a typical student's day. She wakes up, brushes her teeth, showers and dresses, listens to the radio to catch the weather forecast, checks what time she has to be at class today and when her assignment is due, remembers it's her mum's birthday on the weekend and jots down a note to call her, goes for breakfast in the dining hall and grabs a coffee (she slept past the allotted 'breakfast time'), waves to the desk clerk, and rushes out the door to get to her lab.

Each and every step along the way in this woman's morning she is being governed. She wakes up in a bed, not on the street or in the hallway. Both the law and social convention tell us that people should sleep in specially designated areas that are not public spaces. She conforms to more social conventions as well as rules of hygiene when she brushes her teeth and puts on clothes. We have an expectation in our society that students will not show up to class in their underwear or pyjamas. The weather dictates what clothes we wear. If it is winter this woman is not likely to want to put on a sundress, and if it is summer chances are we will not see her tugging on her parka as she heads out the door. She has a class schedule that she is meant to follow (more or less) and that dictates how she spends at least some of her time. The conventions of our families also dictate our actions. This woman knows that she is meant to respond to her mother's birthday with a phone call. If she forgets, her mother might be hurt or angry. The rules of her residence say that after 9:30 a.m. students only get beverages in the dining hall, not food. The desk clerk who waves back at her also serves a security or surveillance function. It is the clerk's job to make sure that only people who are supposed to come into the residence do get in. The clerk will stop a student from bringing a large hairy dog or a very drunk, loud guest up to his or her residence room.

We are governed all the time in many different kinds of ways. We are governed by formal laws and rules, social conventions, guidelines, suggestions, timetables, family obligations, our expectations of ourselves, nature, and so on. The sociology of governance is interested in all of these different ways in which our behaviours are shaped, guided, and dictated. Looking at the world from the point of view of governance allows us to ask some interesting questions, including: Who gets to govern? Who is governed? How does governance work? What if I do not want to be governed this way?

This chapter offers you different ways to think about these questions against the backdrop of Canadian society. Let us start with the term governance.

WHAT IS GOVERNANCE?

Typically, when we think of governing we think about the government. The picture in our heads might be Parliament Hill or the House of Commons. Governments at the federal, provincial, and municipal levels are all part of governance. That is because they are responsible for doing things like making laws, developing school curricula, and creating social policies. All of these things affect us in more or less direct ways. Traffic laws govern how fast we can drive on the highway. Education laws govern how old we have to be before we can drop out of school. Social policies govern who qualifies for welfare benefits (see Chapter 10). But as our example of a typical undergraduate morning illustrates, the kind of governing that the government does is not the only kind of governing that happens in Canada. We are governed by all kinds of other things. Governance, simply put, is a way of getting others or yourself to behave a certain way, do certain things, and not do other things.

WHO GOVERNS WHOM IN CANADA?

If governance has such a broad meaning, then who gets to actually do the governing? And who actually gets governed? In the broadest sense, the answer to both questions is everybody. None of us is solely a governor or a governed person. A prime minister governs our country. But the prime minister is also one of the governed. He or she must conform to rules of order in the House of Commons—for example, can speak only when the Speaker of the House gives permission. In the 2005 Gomery Inquiry, two former prime ministers were summoned to give testimony under oath. If a prime minister breaks a law, he or she can be charged with a criminal act.

Even those who seem most powerless and controlled in our society still participate in governing both themselves and others. Take the example of a four-year-old spending the day at home with her caregiver. That caregiver spends a good deal of time governing the four-year-old. The caregiver tells the child what she can and cannot do, that she must put on a coat, that she will be eating carrots with her lunch. But the four-year-old also governs. She is learning to govern herself by controlling her urge to hit her little brother. She also governs the caregiver. If the child gets sick, the caregiver will have to respond by taking the child to the hospital. If the child draws a lovely picture of a flower, the caregiver responds with praise.

We know, however, that some people and organizations have more power to govern than others. That is, we know that there are some people and organizations within Canadian society who tend to be the ones who engage in governance and others who are the ones who get governed. In a prison, we know there are guards and prisoners. In schools, there are teachers and students. But if everyone participates in governing, how can we explain situations in which there is such a power imbalance? One way to start to unpack the question of who governs whom is to try on different ways of seeing relationships of governance. Within the sociology of governance, there are a number of different lenses we can take up in order to try and understand these relationships.

WHAT ARE THE DIFFERENT WAYS WE CAN THINK ABOUT GOVERNANCE?

The collective conscience and forms of solidarity

Émile Durkheim, as noted in the book's introduction and elsewhere, was one of the first Western thinkers to argue that society exists independent of nature and is influenced and shaped by uniquely social forces. For Durkheim, the question 'who governs whom' was not as important as the question, 'what governs whom'. The 'what' for Durkheim was morality. Durkheim argued that societies have what he called a collective conscience—the shared morality or the set of values that everyone holds in common. The whole point of governing in a society, according to Durkheim, was to reaffirm and protect the collective conscience. For example, a society has a shared value that murder is wrong. When a murder happens, it offends that value and threatens the collective conscience—as though the murderer is saying 'I don't care about the shared values of this society—I am challenging them.' At this point, according to Durkheim, governance kicks in. The society responds to the murder because murder is wrong according to the collective conscience. The murder serves a function because it allows the whole society to get together and reaffirm its collective belief that killing other people is not OK. In punishing the murderer, the society can act out this belief.

The mechanics of this kind of governance and the nature of the collective conscience depends on the kind of society you are looking at. In his seminal work, *The division of labour in society*, Durkheim (1984 [1893]) mapped out two types of societies—mechanical and organic. The differences between these two kinds of societies come from their different economic structures. Durkheim wrote that a mechanical society is more 'primitive' in that labour is not specialized. These societies are imagined as small, hunter/gatherer kinds of societies in which there are a relatively few tasks that need doing and everyone does them. The mechanical society, according to Durkheim, not only has a primitive economic structure but also has a less developed collective conscience. Durkheim argued that the moralities of these kinds of societies tend to be extreme and strictly guarded. Mechanical societies have a high degree of solidarity because of their size and the strictness of their moral codes. In order to maintain solidarity within these societies, Durkheim argued, it is necessary to establish a relatively repressive form of governance that also includes fairly harsh penalties for offences to the collective conscience.

If the mechanical society is marked by its low-level division of labour, strict moral codes, and harsh consequences, the organic society is, in Durkheim's framework, more complex both in terms of its economic structures and its moral codes. Organic societies are marked by a diversified division of labour that relies on specialization and expertise. In an organic society, people have trained skills; there are professions and trades. It differs from a mechanical society in which everyone does more or less the same work. The result of this more complicated economic structure is a society with a less strictly defined collective conscience. Because these societies are bigger and more diverse, there are fewer shared morals. In a mechanical society, you might find rules governing everything from how women should wear their hair to the sleeping arrangements of a family. In an organic society, there are fewer rules. When someone breaks a rule in an organic society, the punishments tend to be less severe although still necessary in order to reaffirm the collective conscience. Durkheim held Western societies as the model for organic societies. In Western democracies, we formally regulate a wide range of behaviours through law. The Canadian Criminal Code, for example, has 15 different categories of offences, each of which designates a number of specific behaviours as punishable.

The case of Robert Latimer serves as a good example of how we can use Durkheim's idea of social solidarity in order to understand responses to Criminal Code infractions in Canada. Latimer was a farmer in Wilkie, Saskatchewan, whose daughter Tracy was born with severe cerebral palsy. Tracy could not communicate verbally, although she could laugh, cry, and make facial expressions. She was entirely dependent on others to keep her alive. She suffered multiple daily seizures, could not eat solid food, and, doctors felt, was in considerable pain every day. Tracy had undergone a number of major surgeries and was scheduled for more. Doctors expected that her mental capacity would never reach beyond that of a three-month-old. In 1993 when Tracy was 12 years old, Latimer killed her by asphyxiation. He placed her in the cab of his truck, attached a hose to the exhaust pipe, and ran the hose into the sealed cab. He turned the truck's engine on and sat outside, watching his daughter die.

When he was charged with Tracy's murder, Latimer defended his action by saying that efforts to keep Tracy alive amounted to cruel and unusual punishment since they only prolonged her suffering, stalling an inevitable death. He told the court that he felt his action was the most humane, totally justifiable, and defendable under the circumstances. Latimer argued he did not commit murder but rather had killed his daughter as an act of kindness and love.

The Latimer case was debated across Canada. While advocates for the disabled argued that Latimer should be punished to the full extent of the law (under Canadian law this would constitute a charge of first-degree murder), it appeared that the majority of Canadians felt that sentencing Latimer to life imprisonment would be too harsh a punishment given the circumstances and intent of the crime. Latimer was charged by police with first-degree murder but convicted at trial of second-degree murder. In a move never seen before in Canadian law, the presiding judge in Latimer's murder trial allowed an exemption in Latimer's sentence. Canadian law stipulates that those convicted of second-degree murder must serve 10 years in prison at the very least before they can apply for parole. When Latimer was sentenced, the judge stipulated that Latimer could apply for parole after serving only one year in prison.

Many Canadians saw the original sentence as a triumphant move forward in Canadian law. Supporters of Latimer and advocates of the right to die felt that Latimer's actions were morally different from those normally responded to with a second-degree murder conviction. Latimer had acted out of love, not anger, hatred, or greed. Giving Latimer a considerably lighter sentence reflected that moral difference. On the other side, however, advocates for both disabled and religious organizations argued that Latimer's original sentence undermined the dignity of disabled people and made the killing of a disabled person no more serious under Canadian law than stealing a car. Latimer's sentence was appealed. On appeal, the original sentence was overturned and the mandatory minimum sentence for second-degree murder instated. Latimer appealed this decision to the Supreme Court of Canada (SCC)—the highest court in the land. In 2001 the SCC upheld Latimer's conviction for murder and subsequent life sentence without eligibility for parole for 10 years.

How does the notion of social solidarity and functionalism help us to understand the case of Robert Latimer? In looking at this case, Durkheim would tell us that it has a certain functionality. The question of whether or not someone has the right to take another person's life in order to end suffering is an extremely moral one. Latimer's actions give society a chance to revisit the moral questions that arise out of such a situation. Does mercy killing merit the same punishment as killing based on revenge? Does mercy killing merit any punishment at all? Does one person have the right to decide when another person's life should end? In opening up both the public and legal debate on these questions, Latimer's case allowed Canadian society to re-evaluate its stance. In the end, the courts, in what many would argue was the best reflection of public opinion at the time, offered a softened response to Latimer that suggested that his crime was not as heinous as some but still maintained that what he did was wrong both morally and legally. So the case of *R. v. Latimer* was a chance for Canadian society to reaffirm its collective conscience around the notion of mercy killing.

Of course, this is not what actually happened in the Latimer decision. There never was and never will be a collective voice of Canadians who feel the same way about the Latimer case. The press coverage over the eight years it took for the case to wind its way through the courts shows a country divided on the issue, with citizens arguing all sides of the debate. The fact that there was not a collective and single voice of Canadians responding to the Latimer case illustrates a common criticism of Durkheim's ideas: it is difficult to imagine an organic society in which a collective conscience might exist. Given the diverse nature of the organic society that Durkheim described, it is inevitable that large numbers of people will disagree with each other on moral issues. Canadian law is full of examples of this. Canadians have differing opinions on abortion, the decriminalization of marijuana, the death penalty, the use of fetal stem cells, and so on. While it is true that when these morally loaded cases arise they do give Canadians a chance to revisit the issues and engage in public debate as well as raise the potential for law reform, the results of the debates are not likely to reflect any sort of collective conscience.

Let us turn to another way of thinking about governance in order to determine whose will gets reflected in attempts to make and change law.

Hegemony and ideological domination

Another way to examine how governance happens in Canada is to look at how different groups are governed. There are many different ways by which we can define different groups in Canadian societies. Groups might be defined on the basis of age, ethnicity, sexual orientation, and so on. In terms of governance, many social scientists are interested in how the question of social class organizes people into groups that are then governed differently.

The idea that people are governed on the basis of their social class is most famously attributed to Karl Marx, who argued that the economic structure of a society dictates who gets to be in control in that society and who does not. Marx was writing about society just after the Industrial Revolution. The Industrial Revolution changed the economic structures of society considerably, setting up a wide gap between workers (a group Marx called the proletariat) and owners of the means of production (the bourgeoisie). The division between these two groups became one of the hallmarks of capitalist society. The fact that the proletariat did not own the means of production (i.e., the factories or tools of the trade) meant that they were less powerful than the bourgeoisie. Not only did the proletariat not have money but they also lacked access to the power that Marx argued accompanied ownership of the means of production. He maintained that the nature of capitalism meant that society would always be governed unfairly, with the bourgeoisie at the top in control and the proletariat at the bottom with little power. His solution was to get rid of the capitalist economy and introduce a collective economy in which there were no class differences—everyone would own and work in the means of production. This thinking became the basis for the economic structures of some communist movements such as the communist revolutions in Central and South America in the 1970s, not to mention the USSR and China.

While Marx's ideas continue to have considerable influence on how people think about issues of governance and power, many social thinkers who came after Marx felt that his sole focus on economic structure was overly simple and did not accurately reflect the complicated structures of governance in capitalist societies. One theorist who took Marx's ideas and embellished them in an attempt to reflect these more complicated issues was Antonio Gramsci.

Gramsci was an Italian journalist, activist, prisoner, writer, and philosopher who was extremely concerned about social inequality. He did most of his writing in the form of journals he kept while imprisoned during the 1920s and 1930s for his political actions and writings. Gramsci's biggest concern was what he called ideological domination or ways of thinking and governing that kept some people on top to the disadvantage of everyone else. According to Gramsci, capitalist European and North American societies were governed by pervasive ideologies or ways of thinking that came from and benefited the ruling class. This ideological domination served to make sure that one group of people and their way of governing stayed in power. Gramsci defines hegemony as:

the 'spontaneous' consent given by the great mass of the population to the general direction imposed on social life by the dominant fundamental group (i.e. the ruling class) (1971, 12).

In other words, hegemony happens when a mass of people who are subordinate (in Marx's words, the proletariat, but we can call them the underclass) agree to be governed in a certain way, a way that is dictated by and usually directly benefits the ruling class (or the bourgeoisie). How does this work? Why would a group of people give their 'spontaneous' consent to be governed in a way that is not of their choosing and that benefits their rulers without really benefiting them?

There are two different ways by which this can happen. First, they can be coerced into it. As noted above, there are many examples of societies governed through brute force and oppressive laws. One of the strongest historical examples we have of this kind of coercive ideological domination is the outlawing and persecution of witchcraft. In the Middle Ages throughout Europe (and indeed in most of the world) most health care was provided by women who drew on specific spiritual traditions as well as traditional knowledge passed down from generation to generation. In the British Isles, these women came from the spiritual tradition of the Celts—a pagan form of worship. The women in each community who engaged in healing practices were known as witches. These women were midwives and healers, highly respected in their communities and regularly sought out to tend to both ailing people and animals. Because of their importance to the health of their communities, these women were also powerful.

The elevated status of women as healers began to change during the sixteenth and seventeenth centuries. In this period, the so-called 'witch craze' emerged, resulting in the imprisonment, torture, and death of millions of women. In a relatively short period of time, these women went from being revered, respected, and vital members of their communities to being condemned as evil, sinful, heretical witches who needed to be eliminated. A number of different reasons have been given for this notable switch in thinking about the position of these women in society, but for the most part there is agreement among scholars interested in the witch craze that society turned on these women because of a combination of religious and cultural factors.

Christianity had gained virtually universal sway in Europe, and the most popular understandings of Christianity during that time were very particular about the place of women. Women were not meant to hold positions of power in a society. Their practices of curing the sick and easing the pains of childbirth were often considered heretical interventions against God's will. God had 'ordained' that a woman's place was very much in the home, and her station was always understood to be below that of man. That led to the belief that women who dared to practise healing arts were acting against God. It was from this kind of thinking that links were seen between witchcraft and devil worship, for example.

Over time, modern medicine and the scientific model of healing that still pervades our society today began to emerge. Many of the premises of modern medicine directly disavowed the practices that women healers had engaged in for centuries. Modern medicine did not see a connection between spirituality and physical ailments, nor did the emerging doctors believe in the use of the herbs and other 'potions' that the witches used. Importantly, modern medicine was also almost entirely male-dominated.

The laws changed considerably over this period to accommodate these developments: it became illegal to practise medicine without a licence, illegal to practise 'witchcraft' or 'devil worship', and illegal for women to own property. During the height of the witch craze, some jurisdictions made it illegal for women to live alone or gather together without a man present. In Britain the crime of 'bewitching an individual to death' was punishable by execution, while a second conviction for engaging in 'any act of sorcery' also resulted in a death sentence. One of the favoured ways to 'prove' that a woman had engaged in sorcery or witchcraft was to have her confess, and torture was the typical means by which confessions were extracted. There are numerous accounts of the use of all manner of torture devices, including thumb screws, the 'iron maiden', hot pokers, water torture, and the bed of nails. The usual practice was to apply three degrees of torture to the accused woman, each degree worse than the one preceding. Not surprisingly, given the barbarity of the tortures, very few women were able to withstand the third degree (it is, incidentally, from this practice that we get the phrase 'the third degree'). By the end of the eighteenth century, virtually no one practised traditional healing arts because the fear of prosecution was so great. If a woman did practise healing arts, she ran the risk of being turned in by her neighbours, friends, enemies, or family, so pervasive was the thinking that witches were evil and needed to die.

The witch craze is an example of an extremely successful campaign of ideological domination through coercive means. Through the use of torture and execution (all of which were routinely carried out in public squares so as to make an example of the condemned person), women were rendered totally subordinate throughout the Western world. The witch craze worked to implement the dominant ideology of patriarchy, which holds that men are entitled to enjoy powerful positions in society and women are inherently meant to hold less powerful positions.

Ideological domination does not always occur through such coercive and brutal means. There are many subtle ways by which people can be governed such that they give their consent. In Canada, laws work to maintain the dominance of the ruling class: for example, Canadian law allows for the accumulation of wealth, and there are no laws about having too much. There are also no laws in Canada against not having enough money—it is not illegal to be poor in Canada—but many people would like the undesirable activities that some poor people engage in, such as begging and squeegeeing, to be outlawed. The government of Ontario, for example, decided to do something about these undesirable behaviours by enacting the Safe Streets Act in 2000. The legislation made it illegal for anyone to panhandle or engage in any kind of squeegeeing. People who broke these laws were given tickets and faced possible incarceration if they could not pay the fine. While the legislation clearly targeted a disadvantaged group of people (largely the urban homeless), few citizens of Ontario opposed it. In their book on the subject, Hermer and Mosher (2002) argue that the public quickly came to accept the legislation despite its obvious inequality because they were led to believe that people engaged in such activities were threats to public safety. Indeed, the title of the legislation confirms that it was meant to respond to concerns about public safety. Hermer and Mosher suggest, however, that the legislation had very little to do with public safety. Instead, they argue, it was meant to maintain a certain aesthetic of order in urban spaces by removing unsightly people from city streets. While the Safe Streets Act theoretically applies to wealthy and poor people alike, it stands to reason that those who are less financially well-off are more likely to be affected by such laws. Poor people can be criminally charged for engaging in an activity dictated by the economic structures of society (capitalism rests on the availability of a mass of unemployed people). In a sense then, it becomes a crime to be poor.

Discipline and normalization

As noted in Chapters 1 and 9, the practice of governing individuals and populations is not always as overt as those described above. The French intellectual Michel Foucault noted that governance often comes in extremely subtle forms. He mapped out different techniques by which people were not coerced into behaving a certain way but rather were trained or disciplined to so do. In one of his works, Foucault (1977b) gave an account of two forms of punishment carried out on offenders. One was a rather gruesome account of torture and execution, detailing the application of pincers and boiling water followed by the drawing and quartering of a man in eighteenth-century France. The second was an account of a daily schedule from a prison dated less than 100 years later. The notable difference between the two accounts is the move from very brutal punishments and forms of social control such as torture and execution to very regimented forms of punishment and social control as exhibited by the prison schedule. Foucault argues that the rise of the use of prison as the primary means of punishment (a trend we still see today) is indicative of a broader trend that favours *disciplinary* forms of governance over coercive ones.

For Foucault, discipline is governance on a subtle and ubiquitous scale. To be governed by discipline means to be governed thoroughly on a very micro level. Foucault suggested that military training was the ideal example of this kind of governance. As in prison, the strict regime of the military training camp means that a person's every action is tightly regulated. Mealtimes, bedtimes, rest times, training times, means of travel (marching in step), conversation (addressing superior officers by correct rank title), and even hygiene and dress are all regulated through military training. The idea is to create a perfectly trained soldier who will behave in exactly the same way as every other soldier without having to be forced to do so.

There are three characteristics of this kind of power. First, discipline involves *hierarchical observation*, which means that someone (or something) is watching. In the military, we see hierarchical observation in the form of commanding officers who watch over their trainees' every move, ready to correct an error in uniform or failure to complete a task in the proper sequence. Prisons have hierarchical surveillance in the form both of officers watching over prisoners directly as they go about their days (and nights) and also through the architectural design of the prison. One of the most popular designs for prisons, particularly when governments first started to build them in the eighteenth century, was borrowed from Jeremy Bentham. He called his model for a prison the *panopticon*. Canada's oldest prison, the Kingston Penitentiary in Kingston, Ontario, is designed on exactly this model.

The panopticon looks like a wagon wheel with a central hub and 'spokes' in the form of cell ranges coming out from the middle. The central hub is also known as the guards' tower, designed so that guards can see down each of the cell ranges and control the locking and unlocking of all doors (including cell doors) without ever having to leave the central hub. In addition, the hub is designed so that it is impossible for prisoners to know whether or not a guard is watching them. The term panopticon literally means 'see everywhere'. While guards can see out, prisoners can not see into the hub. The panopticon is still used as a basic design for prisons because it allows for constant surveillance of prisoners by very few staff. Because prisoners never know for sure whether or not they are being watched, the expectation is that they will behave themselves simply because the possibility of being watched by someone in authority always exists.

Our urban spaces contain various versions of the panopticon that we encounter every day. Technology has brought us surveillance cameras, which have become standard features of the decor in banks, shopping malls, and government buildings. More and more urban centres in high-crime areas are also equipped with surveillance cameras as a way of curbing criminal activities. The idea behind the use of these cameras is exactly the same as that of the panopticon. People are more likely to behave themselves if they think they are being watched, regardless of whether or not the cameras are actually recording anything or if anyone will actually view the surveillance tapes. This kind of watching is an extremely passive and subtle form of governance. No one is actually doing anything to anyone, but people still monitor their behaviours as if someone were watching them.

The second characteristic of discipline is that it *operates through the use of norms*. A norm is a generally accepted idea of how a person ought to be. In Western society, we have the norm of a good daughter as reflected in the behaviour of the university student described at the start of this chapter. A good daughter loves her parents, calls them on their birthdays, fulfils their expectations, gives them grandchildren, and so on. We can most easily identify norms in our society when we talk about faults. So if a woman fails to call her mother on her birthday, we might see this as a fault because she falls short of the norm of a good daughter. Canadian society is filled with norms of good behaviour and the identification of faulty or bad behaviour. For example, it may not be a crime to pick your nose every time you sit down to have coffee with your friends, but it certainly offends a certain norm of good behaviour. To pick your nose in front of others indicates that you are rude and offensive. We also disrupt norms when we transgress other social norms, such as turning on our friends, failing to be respectful of those older than we are, or failing to acknowledge the authority of those above us in the social hierarchy. For example, even though there is no explicit reason why physicians should always be addressed as Dr Suchandsuch, it is a norm with which most of us comply, even if they address *us* by our given names.

The importance of the norm as a tool of governing is made very clear by Foucault in his analysis of norms and madness. In another well-known text, *Madness and civilization* (1977a), he suggests that many of our ideas about insane behaviour come out of scrutiny of behaviours that can just as easily be understood as deviating from a particular norm. Until 1973, homosexuality was considered a form of mental illness: its symptoms and treatment were detailed in the *Diagnostic and statistical manual*—the handbook of psychiatry. People revealed as homosexual could be institutionalized as a way of 'healing' them (see Chapter 4). At the beginning of the 1970s, the Ontario legislature was deeply involved in attempting to 'cure' the homosexuality of prison inmates because it saw same-sex relationships within prison as indicators of an individual's higher chance of reoffending or committing additional 'deviant' acts.

Most people now accept that there is nothing sick about or wrong with people who are attracted to members of the same sex. The designation of homosexuality as a psychiatric illness was much more about the fact that people who engaged in homosexual activities went against the norm of heterosexuality deeply ingrained in our society. People eventually started to challenge the idea that homosexuality was an illness by showing that homosexuality is common and that people engaged in same-sex relationships are as 'normal' as anyone else in society. Canadian law is now moving more and more towards embracing same-sex relationships as part of the norm of Canadian society. In the case of *Vriend v. Alberta*, the Supreme Court of Canada declared that discrimination on the basis of sexual orientation was a human rights violation and that all citizens are entitled to protection from such discrimination. In the cases of *M. v. H.* as well as *Egan and Nesbitt v. Canada*, the SCC recognized that same-sex couples were entitled to benefits similar to those of opposite-sex couples (such as Canada Pension Plan survivors' benefits) and also liable to the same obligations (such as spousal support and equal division of a shared home on dissolution of a relationship). The most recent SCC decision concerning the normalization of homosexual relationships in Canada was the Same Sex Marriage Reference in which the Court said it was illegal to exclude same-sex couples from the existing definition of marriage.

The third aspect of a disciplinary regime is that *the consequences for failing to adhere to expected or prescribed behaviours are also varied and subtle*. Those caught through panoptic surveillance transgressing prison rules of conduct by, for example, passing something to another prisoner may have privileges such as seeing visitors or receiving mail taken away. Students caught skipping school and therefore failing to adhere to a set schedule might be given a detention or have their parents called in to meet with the principal. If you are rude to your friends, engage in offensive behaviour, or gossip behind other people's backs, you might find yourself ostracized, gossiped about in turn, or made fun of. The point is that the consequences of failing to comply with the governance structure in a disciplinary regime are not punitive in the sense that the criminal law is punitive. Instead, these consequences come in the form of what Hunt and Wickham (1994, 21) describe as 'micro-penalties and rewards'. Thus being a good friend has its benefits: one enjoys a degree of popularity and is protected from gossip and ridicule. Prisoners who conform to all behavioural codes often find themselves living under less restrictive conditions, with more privileges and less surveillance. Students with good attendance records might receive rewards and accolades from their teachers.

Who Has the Right to Govern?

Governance can take place in all manner of relationships and can be understood from a wide variety of perspectives. But how does it actually happen in Canada? What does the law tell us about who gets to govern whom and how these relationships are meant to work?

On the broadest scale, governance in Canada is divided among different forms of government. With some overlap among jurisdictions, the federal government, for example, is in charge of a wide range of areas, including international relations, income and excise tax, the Criminal Code, national defence, the environment, treaties with the First Nations, fisheries, air travel, immigration, and employment. The provinces are meant to deal primarily with education, highways, health care, social services, liquor law and distribution, casinos, utilities, and drivers' licences. Municipal governments are in charge of local by-laws, licensing pets, parking laws, city streets, property taxes, fire and ambulance services (and, in some cases, police), and some social services.

Canada also has forms of indigenous governance. The Constitution Act of 1982 recognizes Aboriginal rights as outlined in the various treaties struck during colonization. This acknowledgement also includes the right of Aboriginal communities to govern themselves. Notions of self-government are becoming more and more central to the ways in which the Canadian government deals with First Nations peoples. In large part, the increased move toward self-government is a bid by the Canadian government to rectify the wrongs done to Aboriginal peoples throughout colonization and in its aftermath. The involvement of European governments in Aboriginal affairs has historically been disastrous for Aboriginal peoples, resulting in the loss of life, health, safety, culture, land, autonomy, and children. Aboriginal communities work towards self-governance because they want to be able to dictate their own affairs and shape their communities independent of the Canadian government, and models of self-governance vary from community to community. Communities that have adopted a self-governance model do not exist outside of Canadian law: they are still governed by legislation like the Criminal Code and the Child Protection Act. The administration of these laws, however, and the establishment of other forms of law and governance often fall to the local government. Band councils, for example, can be responsible for a wide range of governing practices, including issuing licences, policing communities, the enforcement of Aboriginal laws and the running of Aboriginal courts, health care, education, family matters (such as adoption, marriage, divorce, and child protection), hunting and fishing regulations, housing, social services, and resource management. In many cases, Aboriginal communities will work in conjunction with non-Aboriginal governing bodies in order to fully administer all the different forms of governance within the framework of limited resourcing. Aboriginal communities that have established their own policing systems, for example, may have one or two officers who do the day-to-day work of policing (dealing with traffic violations, responding to small-scale crimes, crime prevention work, and public education). However, if a major crime such as a murder occurs, these small police services often simply lack the resources to deal with the crime adequately. A small local police service does not have forensic experts on staff or a scene-of-crime mobile lab necessary to support a large-scale police investigation. In these situations, the local band council will often seek the assistance of a larger police service such as the RCMP, which may come into the community for a specified period of time to assist with the investigation.

In Canada then, the formal right to govern is assigned through legislation to various levels and forms of governments. That is a good deal of power given to a small number of people. How do we make sure that our governments do what they are supposed to do? How do we make sure that they do not abuse their powers?

How Do We Control the Right to Govern?

The democratic structure of Canadian governance is one way by which we put limits on state powers. Our federal government is made up of three different branches, which are meant to keep each other in check. The executive branch consists of the prime minister and cabinet. These are the people who are directly responsible for drafting the laws and policies used to govern the country. Most of the decisions made by the executive branch have to be approved by the legislative branch of government. Parliament is the federal legislative branch, comprising the House of Commons and the Senate. The House is comprised of all the elected members of Parliament from across the country, while senators are appointed by the prime minister. Legislators debate and vote on pieces of legislation and are expected to reflect the will of the public. Finally, we have the judicial branch, and in Canada the highest level is the Supreme Court. The Court's duty is to hear cases pertaining to all areas of Canadian law and render final decisions on those cases. It has the power to uphold, strike down, or otherwise direct amendments to laws.

The Charter of Rights and Freedoms

The Supreme Court often hears cases in which a citizen claims that a certain law or practice of government is unfair. In order to make such a claim, the citizen (or group of citizens) often appeals to the highest law in the land—the Charter of Rights and Freedoms. The Charter was enacted in 1982 along with the new constitution, and it is the supreme law of the country. This means that all other laws must conform to the principles set out in the Charter, and many scholars see it as the ultimate check on governance in Canada. The Charter only applies to matters between the citizenry and the state, which means that issues of private law such as a dispute between two businesses over a contract are not governed by the Charter. It can only govern the laws and actions of a Canadian government.

The Charter sets out seven general areas of freedoms for all Canadian citizens, guaranteeing freedom of thought, conscience, religion, association, the press, expression, and assembly. It also outlines the rights of Canadians, such as the right to vote, to move about the country, to be taught in French or English, and to life, liberty, and security of person as well as rights upon arrest, rights to equality, rights to have the government function in both official languages, and the right to be protected from discrimination. Many of the legal disputes that reach the Supreme Court concern disputes around these rights.

The case of *R. v. Keegstra*, for example, involved a dispute around the guarantee of freedom of expression under section 2b of the Charter. James Keegstra, a high school teacher in a small town in rural Alberta, was also anti-Semitic and a Holocaust denier. Keegstra taught his students that Jews invented the Holocaust in order to gain sympathy. He argued that Jews are morally corrupt and untrustworthy and expected his students to regurgitate these views in tests and exams. Keegstra was charged and convicted under a section of the Criminal Code prohibiting the 'willful promotion of hatred against an identifiable group', and his case went all the way to the Supreme Court. Keegstra defended his actions by saying that the Charter of Rights and Freedoms guaranteed him freedom of expression. He claimed that because the Charter was the highest law in the land, it trumped the Criminal Code proscription of hate crimes. Essentially, Keegstra argued that he had a fundamental right to freedom of expression, which could not be overridden by the Criminal Code. Keegstra lost his case at the Supreme Court—but only by a vote of one.

The judges who voted against Keegstra reasoned that there was another provision in the Charter that allowed for the removal of any right or freedom guaranteed under the Charter if the removal of that right or freedom can be 'demonstrably justified in a free and democratic society'. This phrase comes from section 1 of the Charter, the intent being to leave room for the government's ability to create laws that do things like limit freedoms or treat people unequally. In order to enact those laws, the government must prove that limiting a right or a freedom is in the best interest of the public and the nation. We have many laws that limit our rights and freedoms in this way. The Criminal Code sets out penalties for people who break the law, penalties that include removing basic freedoms such as the freedom of movement and of association. Prisoners incarcerated in provincial prisons also lose the right to vote.

The case of Terry Parker is an interesting example of how the Charter works to protect some rights and protect the law's revocation of other rights. Terry Parker was an epileptic who suffered serious grand mal seizures on a regular basis. While he had tried all manner of treatments for his epilepsy, the only thing that seemed to control his seizures without debilitating side effects was marijuana. Parker smoked marijuana on a daily basis to alleviate his condition. He was arrested for possession and cultivation of marijuana, charged, and convicted. Parker argued his case to the SCC on the grounds that the Criminal Code provision that makes marijuana illegal violated his rights as guaranteed under the Charter. He argued that the law not only made it illegal for him to obtain the only substance known to improve his health but also meant that he could be incarcerated for trying to maintain his health. Parker argued that the laws against marijuana violated his rights to 'life, liberty and security of the person' as set out under section 7 of the Charter and his protection under section 12 of the Charter against 'cruel and unusual punishment'. The SCC found in favour of Parker. They reasoned that marijuana could be helpful to some people with certain medical conditions and thus the total ban on marijuana was not in accordance with the principles of fundamental justice set out in section 1. That is, the Court said that the government's laws concerning marijuana were not reasonable limits on rights and freedoms, nor did the reasons given by the government to maintain a total ban on marijuana justify the denial of sick people's access to the drug.

The result of the Parker decision was that the law on marijuana was deemed unconstitutional by the Supreme Court. When this happens, the government must either rewrite or eliminate the law. The Canadian government opted to rewrite the laws on marijuana, creating an exemption for those with a proven medical need to use the substance. Marijuana use is still illegal in Canada except for those who apply for and are granted exemptions under the Medical Marijuana Access Regulations. The regulations stipulate that people suffering long-term chronic illness, such as epilepsy or fibromyalgia, and the terminally ill might be eligible to receive an exemption. The exemption means that such persons cannot be arrested for growing or possessing marijuana. It also means that they can purchase marijuana from a licensed grower (there are only a few in Canada) who also has an exemption under the law. In order to aid in distribution, the Canadian government established its own marijuana grow operation in an abandoned mine shaft in Flin Flon, Manitoba. Activists and medicinal marijuana users claim that the marijuana produced in Flin Flon is substandard, chemically tainted, and difficult to obtain.

WHAT IF YOU DON'T WANT TO BE GOVERNED IN A SPECIFIC WAY?

Despite what Durkheim would have us believe, there are many laws and practices of governance in Canada that people simply do not agree with or do not conform to. Our governing structures and practices, both formal and informal, are constantly changing and being re-evaluated. The history of governance in Canada is replete with instances of people working to resist governing structures and change them.

One of the most famous examples is the case of *Muir Edwards et al v. Canada (A.G.)*, also known as the Persons Case because the decision finally rendered declared that women are 'persons' under Canadian law. The case was brought forward in the late 1920s by five women (known as the Famous Five): Henrietta Muir Edwards, Irene Parlby, Nellie McClung, Louise McKinney, and Emily Murphy. The women had gone to court in Canada to find out whether or not women could become members of the Canadian Senate. The law concerning appointment to the Senate stated that senators had to be 'persons', and the question these women posed to the court was whether or not women constituted persons. All levels of the courts in Canada concluded that women were not in fact persons. However, the women persisted in appealing these decisions until the case ended up in the British House of Lords (during this time Canada still had significantly strong ties to the UK, which meant that the highest court in the UK, the House of Lords, had the final say in Canadian legal disputes). The decision written by Lord Sankey found in favour of the women, arguing that women were indeed persons under Canadian law and as such could become senators. The case was a landmark for women's rights in Canada since it was the first time in Canadian history that women had gained this kind of legal recognition.

Of course, there are many other examples of people resisting and working to change laws and governing structures, although not all are as successful as the Famous Five. The debate around therapeutic abortions in Canada is one such example of contestation and resistance around Canadian law. Illegal until 1969, abortion was decriminalized that year but only if a hospital therapeutic abortion committee approved the procedure for 'medically necessary' reasons in each case. However, many doctors bypassed the regulations and performed abortions, and one of them was Dr Henry Morgentaler. Dr Morgentaler became the most vocal advocate for women's unrestricted access to abortion across Canada. He opened an abortion clinic in Montreal in 1973 and continued to operate there for 15 years in defiance of the law requiring hospital committee approval for abortions, despite raids on his clinic, death threats, and his arrest on two occasions. In his three separate trials in Quebec, juries simply refused to convict him. Then, following his arrest after opening clinics in Winnipeg and Toronto, Morgentaler took his case to the Supreme Court, which voted in 1988 to strike down all Canadian laws concerning abortion. Despite the Court's decision, conservative politicians and anti-abortion groups such as the Campaign Life Coalition continue to lobby Parliament for reinstatement of laws banning abortion. The campaign to stop abortions in Canada is a militant one. Beyond demonstrations outside abortion clinics, three Canadian doctors who performed abortions were shot at, and Morgentaler's Toronto clinic was bombed in the early 1990s. Anti-abortion protesters routinely picket abortion clinics and hospitals, sometimes trying to physically prevent women from entering the buildings. To date, these efforts have not resulted in the reinstatement of anti-abortion laws in Canada.

CONCLUSION

There is no easy answer to the question of who governs whom in Canada. Governance takes place on all kinds of levels with respect to many aspects of our lives. We are governed by laws, norms, and social expectations, and we participate in governing both ourselves and others. When we think about different ways of understanding the relations of governance, it is clear that there are a number of different perspectives we could adopt. We could understand governance through the lens of morality as Durkheim suggested. Alternatively, we could see it as a product of social inequality and domination as Gramsci did.

And Foucault asks us to look at governance through the lens of discipline or 'micro' governing strategies.

Canada has a complicated formal system of governing that is largely informed by the Charter of Rights and Freedoms. As the most important law in the country, the Charter is used to challenge other laws and governmental practices—but it does not provide ultimate protection: the Keegstra case shows us that our Charter rights can be lawfully violated in the name of the public good. Finally, there are ways that people can and do resist and change laws, as exemplified by the Persons case and the case of Dr Henry Morgentaler.

Questions to Consider

1. Does governing only happen from the top down? Can you think of examples in which people's actions influence the ways in which we are governed?
2. Can you think of any legal issues on which Canadians agree? If so, how do you know that everyone agrees?
3. What kinds of ideological domination affect your life? Is the university a place of ideological domination?
4. What do Hunt and Wickham mean by 'micro-penalties and rewards'? Can you think of any other examples?
5. Is there ever an instance in which it is justifiable to take away someone's rights? What criteria should be used in making that decision?

PART 3

CRITICAL IMAGINATIONS AND CANADA

The final part of the book turns to critical engagements, often using theoretical concepts and substantive issues raised in the first two parts. It considers how subjects and social milieus interact in complex ways in specific areas of Canadian society. At times these interactions are enabling and at other times disabling. And because the chapters are driven by sociological imaginations, each one asks questions concerned with critically understanding and engaging an aspect of what it is to live in Canada right now. In so doing, the chapters critically theorize the character of Canadian society itself.

Chapter 12, 'Is There Justice for Young People?', raises questions that are likely to resonate with many young people in Canada. Bryan Hogeveen extends his examination of governance to a group that the Canadian government historically helped to define as 'youth'. In order to respond to the question, he focuses attention on different visions of 'justice'. This allows him to make a clearer argument about the areas where youth justice in Canada is lacking. Hogeveen notes that current public (for instance, the media) portrayals of today's youth often associate young people with criminality and irresponsibility. These (mis)perceptions are reflected in changing approaches to youth justice. Paradoxically, however, such public perceptions continue to influence policy even though youth crime rates are declining steadily. Hogeveen provides several examples of the ways in which Canadian youth are specifically governed through discourses of criminality and risk, indicating thereby a new regime for regulating 'youth' that, for him, is far from just.

The next chapter tackles the question 'should policing be privatized?' and again invokes the concept of governance, this time with respect to policing in Canada. Curtis Clarke notes that Canadian policing is already, and has been for some time, privatized to a greater or lesser degree. Clarke attributes the steady privatization of policing to 'public service rationalization' fuelled by a neo-liberal ideology concerned with economizing state services (see also Chapter 10). Policing provides a useful site in which to examine the complex relationships between the state, ideology, and its citizens. For instance, through notions of the 'responsible citizen', neo-liberal discourses provoke a particular form of civic coordination. This civic coordination relies both on the policing (governance) of individuals by each other as well as on larger disparate private policing agencies invested in 'individual liberty and protection'.

Chapter 14, 'Do Women's Bodies Matter in Prison?', takes up some of the arguments presented in chapters 2 and 3 of this book. Sylvie Frigon provides a microanalysis of women within the Canadian penal system. Whereas the previous chapters in this section touch on the penal system, this chapter considers imprisonment in a sustained fashion. Specifically, Frigon argues that women's prisons are a dramatic illustration of how individuals (minds and bodies) are governed through a range of complex 'technologies of domination' and 'techniques of the self'. For instance, the daily rituals that women in Canadian prisons have to perform and their inclusion and exclusion within particular behavioural frames (when to wake up, what to eat, how family visits are structured, and so on) give us a sense of how prisons govern women through their bodies. But prisons also govern in a much less obvious, though no less effective, way. They incite women prisoners to identify themselves in specific ways (such as bad mothers, burdens on society, victims, and so on).

In Chapter 15, Patricia Monture considers the question of indigenous sovereignty. Her discussion raises a very important and ongoing debate that strikes at the heart of Canadian society: the place of multiculturalism and diversity. More specifically, she argues that the notion of multiculturalism generally lauded by Canadians often obscures the unique situation of indigenous peoples as the original settlers of geographic North America. Indeed, because indigenous knowledge generally stands outside of the dominant structures and institutions in Canada (derived from British and French colonialism), it occupies an 'outsider' position. As such, it is restricted to commenting on (through, for instance, rights claims) the limitations of these structures rather than constructing knowledges in their own right. Moreover, Monture raises the very important and related point that a discussion of 'indigenous' knowledge itself denies the diversity of these knowledges (based on tribal affiliation, age, gender, rurality, history, and so on). In the process, it further contributes to the 'othering' of indigenous peoples by homogenizing their experiences of living within Canada. Monture ends the chapter by asking what an indigenous sociology might resemble—one that takes on board the serious limitations of accounts of the indigenous within mainstream sociology.

On a related theme, Chapter 16 ('What is Sovereignty in Quebec?') enlists an analysis of a macro-governance. Rather than rehashing longstanding ideological arguments 'for' or 'against' Quebec sovereignty, Philippe Couton offers a distinctly sociological approach that reflects on the underlying assumptions necessary to sustain these positions. One such assumption is that the natural condition for any given society is independence. Couton forcefully argues that nation-states are not homogenous entities able to adequately 'speak for' the diverse populations that they claim to embody. Another assumption that Couton criticizes is that societies 'naturally evolve' to claim independent power. He argues that 'although there might be an evolutionary component to sovereignty...the way the issue is handled at the political level continues to matter a great deal'—as evinced, for instance, by events surrounding the adoption of Canada's Charter of Rights and

Freedoms. The chapter concludes by considering the viability of 'post-sovereignty' forms of government that do not rely on the precondition of homogeneity inherent in the modern nation-state.

Chapter 17 offers a sociological analysis of the Maritime region's economy. Specifically, Jennifer Jarman addresses whether or not a provincially and regionally encouraged call centre industry will revitalize the economy of Maritime societies. She does so by first outlining the region's historical reliance on a natural resource-based economy and its strategic position for trade in eighteenth and nineteenth-century world markets. Since then, the region has undergone many changes, and she argues that 'Now it faces major problems as its economies try to reinvent themselves after the decline of a number of major industries.' With this background in mind, the chapter analyzes a new call centre industry that is providing employment to many people in the region. On the basis of her field research, Jarman examines the contours of that industry in context. Analysis of this new development is complex. Despite several perceived problems with the industry—that it is transient, has an image problem (e.g., disturbing phone calls, 'sweatshop' labour), and involves close employee surveillance, and so on—she notes that it does provide entry-level jobs at the lower end of the service economy. Moreover, she argues that 'The advantage of "lower middle jobs" is that there are a lot of people with "lower middle" levels of education and experience in the region.' The industry has thus provided significant levels of employment, but Jarman also cautions that 'It is highly unlikely that one industry can change the features of a regional economy dramatically.' Thus she argues that the growth of the industry is important for Maritime societies, but its sustained social impact should not be overestimated.

Like the chapters on indigenous and Quebec sovereignty, the final chapter of the book ('How Do Migrants Become Canadian Citizens?') examines a fundamental aspect of the 'character' of Canadian society. Canada has always relied on immigration to populate the country and provide economic labour that fuels the economy, builds social ties, and indeed forms the nation itself. And yet, many years after Confederation (which itself was preceded by many years of 'informal' immigration), Canada is still struggling to come to terms with the implications of embracing the diversity of its peoples. Randy Lippert reviews immigration to Canada as a history mired in racial and ethnic prejudice and discrimination. He further problematizes the distinction between 'migrants', 'refugees', and 'immigrants', pointing out that these distinctions are a product of the governance of the movement of people. The chapter ends by considering the specific ways in which Canada transforms certain individuals, under particular circumstances, from migrants to citizens as part of a wider practice of governing 'responsible citizens' who will, among other things, sanction the very policies of immigration that they themselves were subject to. Since multiculturalism is one of *the* defining features of Canadian society, the chapter serves as an appropriate conclusion to a text concerned with fundamental aspects of 'being Canadian'.

Chapter 12

Is There Justice for Young People?

Bryan Hogeveen

INTRODUCTION

A recent article in the *Peterborough Examiner* proclaimed, 'Youth "justice" a joke'. A mother had been compelled to write to the paper after a group of 'teenagers' verbally accosted her 12-year-old daughter. While the mother assured readers that she had taught her daughter 'to be polite, mannerly and to respect other people', she contended that the Youth Criminal Justice Act (YCJA)—Canada's legislation governing offenders between the ages of 12 and 17—was making her job exceedingly difficult (O'Brien 2004). Parents, it seemed, were afforded no assistance from the Act. While this mother was certain that she could call upon the law to deliver *justice* for her daughter, the police informed her otherwise. If the YCJA provided no recourse for injured parties, where were parents (and their daughters) to turn for redress? An article with a similar refrain entitled 'Youth justice?' appeared in the *Halifax Daily News*. The reporter suggested that youth typically 'mock the system' and scoffed at a sentence of nine months' probation and 30 hours of community service for a young person convicted of tying a cord around a cat's neck and dragging it into the woods with the intention of killing it (Aikenhead 2004).

Embedded in these newspaper stories is a discursive construction of today's generation of youth as somehow more criminal, disrespectful, and precocious than youth in times past. For example, the second author stated, 'kids from previous generations didn't think they could get away with murder, so they didn't try.' Intrinsic to this statement is the ubiquitous assumption that somewhere in time (often when the writer was young) lies a golden era when juvenile deviance was hardly a problem. Our past, then, was a simpler time when youth respected elders, were silent, and obeyed their parents. Such an understanding of contemporary young people belies the absolute condition whereby youth have *always* discontented and troubled adults. In 469 BCE Socrates lamented, 'the children now love luxury. They have bad manners, contempt for authority, they show disrespect for adults and love to talk rather than work or exercise. They contradict their parents, chatter in front of company, gobble down their food at the table and intimidate their teachers.' This statement could just as easily have been typed on a computer as scribbled on parchment.

Troublingly, this conception of young people as predatory criminals and of the law as offering little recourse remains pervasive in an era of steadily *declining* youth crime rates. Focusing attention exclusively on adolescent patterns of offending masks such *in*justices confronting youth as inequality, silencing, and oppression. Admittedly, youth do commit crimes. However, they are at the same time highly overrepresented in rates of victimization and poverty, a fact often concealed in the preoccupation with patterns of criminality and efforts to strengthen juvenile justice legislation. Moreover, a particularly disturbing consequence of Canada's 'vengeance as justice' paradigm is the gross overrepresentation of Aboriginal youth in centers of detention. As a group, Native adolescents are among the most disadvantaged in Canadian society; they are also the most punished. While Native youth are the most disparaged, homeless, poor, and drug-addicted youth as well as 'squeegee kids' are other targets deemed suitable for public vengeance. Justice, it seems, is something done to young people, not something to which they are entitled. A different rendering of *justice* for youth would view them as requiring protection in the form of systems and a populace that respects their heritage, age, condition of life, and situation. To date, however, Canada falls well short of this ideal. Perhaps the 'joke' about youth justice is not the system that holds that name, but the way that disadvantaged and subjugated youth are treated.

Is there justice for youth? This chapter confronts the experiences of many youth—most often from the most disadvantaged backgrounds—and reaches the conclusion that there is little in the way of justice for them. First, I explore differing conceptions of justice in a section that underscores the (dis)connection between rights and justice. Next, I highlight three particularly lamentable instances of *in*justice experienced by young persons—child poverty, racism confronting Aboriginal youth, and the dislocation of girls under law. The final section examines the silencing of young people in Western society and urges us to listen to youthful voices.

WHAT IS JUSTICE?

We live in an era in which war, prison overcrowding, genocide, ethnic cleansing, and vigilantism are often justified in the name of justice. But what, exactly, *is* justice? Canadians employ the term as if its meaning were self-evident. Scholars trying to explore the meaning of justice find arriving at an adequate definition fraught with difficulty. While academics have done well in exploring how the question 'what is justice' is debated, they have yet to arrive at a definitive answer (Hudson 2003). Contemporary *theoretical* conceptions proceed from principles of *distribution* derived from philosophical and legal perspectives. Classical justice theorists such as John Stuart Mill, David Hume, and Immanuel Kant and more contemporary philosophers such as John Rawls offer normative principles intended to guide the allocation of society's limited resources (wealth, opportunity, income, etc.). These distributive theories of justice embrace everything from how situations facing the poor and downtrodden are handled to how society regulates violations of its criminal code. David Miller (1999, 1) offers the following succinct and powerful definition of this theoretical tradition: it involves 'how the good and bad things in life should be distributed among the members of a human society'. However rational this definition may seem, it is abstract, divorced from real life problems, structural disparities, and institutional discrimination (Young 1990). As such, resources are distributed such that the most affluent benefit while the poor and visibly different spiral into desolation and misery.

A significant part of the difficulty in answering the question 'what is justice?' centres on the fundamental ambiguity in the word itself. For example, it can refer to the bureaucratic structure for administering the legal process. Canada boasts a federal Department of *Justice*, which embodies and reflects this convention. It can be used in law and legislation to imply the impartiality of the system (e.g., the Youth Criminal *Justice* Act). Moreover, *justice* suggests a connection with law and order campaigns in which victims declare that they are owed retribution for pain suffered. In this context, *justice* being done means an ethic of punishment that delivers obvious signs of unpleasantness to offenders. This kind of justice can also reflect the public's desire to amend law, often in relation to existing but flawed legislation that seemingly promotes *in*justice. Until 2003 when the YCJA became law, Canadian youth were governed under the Young Offenders Act (YOA). Throughout the period leading up to legislative change, the YOA was consistently hailed as inequitable because it was seen as debasing the victims of juvenile deviance. Newspaper headlines suggested that federal young offender legislation was to blame for victimization and that tougher legislation would prevent the harm done to the injured (Hogeveen 2005).

For many, justice has been intimately connected with inalienable and omnipresent rights enshrined under legislation. For example, the Charter of Rights and Freedoms (Canada 1982) guarantees Canadian citizens and permanent residents: a) freedom of conscience and religion; b) freedom of thought, belief, and expression; c) freedom of association; d) the right to vote; and e) the right to life, liberty, and security of the person. Nevertheless, until very recently youth did not enjoy access to these guarantees in the same way that adults did. Under law and in society, children were traditionally not afforded dignity or respect, but were instead treated as chattel belonging to their father. The movement toward assigning rights to children, according to Katherine Covell and Brian Howe (2001), went through three fundamental stages. It passed from a laissez-faire philosophy in which children were considered parental property, to a humanitarian and sentimental rationale of children as a separate class of partially formed individuals, to the current discourse of children as people entitled to individual rights.

A turning point in rights allocation for youth occurred on 20 November 1989 when the United Nations Convention on the Rights of the Child was unanimously adopted. A convention is an expression not only of a moral stand but 'also of a legal agreement and international obligation' (Covell and Howe 2001, 20). In 1991 Canada ratified the convention, which comprises 41 articles divided into two broad categories:

1. civil and political rights, which include the right to self-determination and protection from arbitrary arrest;
2. economic, social, and cultural rights, which include the right to health care and education and freedom of religion.

According to Hammarberg (1990), human rights and protections set out by the convention can usefully be divided into three broad groups, often referred to as the three Ps: provision, protection, and participation. Rights of *provision* imply that youth must be afforded basic welfare, which includes the right to survival and development, education, and to be cared for by parents. Articles under the *protection* rubric ensure that children are sheltered from abuse, economic exploitation, discrimination, and neglect. Youth are also accorded the right to *participation*, which involves freedom of speech, freedom of religion, and the right of expression (Denov 2004).

Despite Canada's agreement to abide by the convention's conditions, substantial gaps remain between the state's promise and the real world. One of the greatest concerns for youth advocates is the general lack of awareness about the convention and the rights youth are guaranteed therein. According to Doob and Cesaroni (2004), youth have little understanding of what exactly rights are. Barry Feld (2000) suggests that young people typically see rights as something they are allowed to do and conditional on other conduct. Thus they do not understand the consequences of waiving their right to silence, for example, when a police officer warns them against self-incrimination. A study of high school students by Peterson-Badali and Abramovich (1992) found that very few youth could identify the most basic legal principles, such as the youth court's age jurisdiction (12–17). Moreover, when asked with whom their lawyer could share privileged information, many young people were certain that their legal representative was obliged to inform their parents and the judge what they revealed in confidence. To what extent are rights meaningful if young people are unaware of their implications and how they are exercised?

Equating rights with justice is spurious—at best. Rights conventions are of little utility when their intricacies are not widely known, understood, or distributed. They tend to float above relationships among individuals and provide little guidance on the ethical responsibility of one person to another. Rights discourses provide very little direction to those addressing inequality and subjugation in an *un*just society. Recall that rights and social goods are not equally distributed throughout the Canadian population. People on the margins are grossly overrepresented in poverty and incarceration rates. Is this a just state of affairs? If working-class and minority youth have become the foremost clients of state services that deliver pain and experience higher rates of poverty, it is *not* as a result of some innate propensity toward crime and unemployment. Rather, it is because they are trapped at the intersection of three transformations distinct to the neo-liberal organization of society that have targeted the visibly different and the socially marginal: economic globalization, dismantling the social welfare net, and intensifying penal strategies have all contributed to greater inequality and unequal distribution of scarce societal resources in favour of the affluent (Wacquant 2001). During the late 1990s, to paraphrase the title of Jeffrey Reiman's (1979) seminal work, the rich were getting richer while the poor were receiving prison. If justice is to ensure equal distribution of resources and goods to societal members, it would appear that Canada is moving in a most peculiar direction, especially as the situation pertains to young people.

JUSTICE AND THE POOR?

Child poverty continues to rise despite a booming economy and federal and provincial coffers bursting at the seams. In the current neo-liberal ethos, the gulf between the rich and the poor continues to widen. Statistics gathered by the federal government's Canadian Council on Social Development illustrate this growing divide most clearly. Between 1984 and 1999, the average net worth of the country's poorest families dropped by 51 per cent while for the wealthiest it increased by 42.7 per cent. Moreover, the number of familial units that paid more than 50 per cent of their gross income on rent rose by 43 per cent between 1990 and 1995 (Lee and Engler 2000). Burgeoning poverty rates are not the product of economic backwardness, recession, or decline. They are, however, conditioned by mushrooming inequality experienced in a context of widespread economic evolution and opulence. Perhaps the most puzzling element of the new marginality is that it is growing in an era characterized by a robust economy and sturdy growth that has benefited privileged members of Western society (Wacquant 1999). Although on the surface these two phenomena seem contradictory, they are in fact linked. Indeed, the shift to a new knowledge-based and global economy translates into a polarized workforce in which increased employment opportunities for the highly educated and technically trained abound while millions of unskilled labour jobs are lost to overseas production sites and automation (Ley 1996; Lévesque 2002; Enloe 1990). Although the country's economy continues to hum along, fewer are profiting from it. The further the neo-liberal economy proceeds, the more invasive and widespread poverty will become. The result is greater numbers of families looking to the state for assistance, which puzzlingly seems unwilling to offer *real* help.

The social welfare net that caught and propped up the downtrodden throughout most of the twentieth century has been seriously eroded as the neo-liberal economy continues to gain pace. Indeed, between 1986 and 1996, as measured in constant dollars, Alberta welfare benefits for a single individual deemed employable were slashed by 42.5 per cent while single parents with a child saw their benefits eroded by 23.6 per cent (Canadian Council on Social Development 2004). While poverty rates continue to climb, the net traditionally in place to soften the impact has been stripped away. Even the benefits available to ameliorate the conditions of the most vulnerable—Canada's children—are currently being clawed back by the state. For example, the National Child Benefit provides families with annual incomes of less than $22,615 with $126 per month for the first child and decreasing amounts for subsequent children. However, under a scheme initiated by the federal government, only working families are now allowed to keep the money while those most in need—individuals on social assistance and disability pensions—are denied support payments altogether (Della-Mattia 2004). Compare this with the $45 million per year that the Alberta government doles out to subsidize the local horse-racing industry. A growing group of destitute individuals, who require the greatest assistance, are having to scrounge for the crumbs that remain after services that the government deems more important (such as horse-racing) get their cut.

Tragically, youth are the hardest hit. According to the Canadian Council on Social Development, children between the ages of 15 and 24 had the highest poverty rate in Alberta. The council's 2003 report, *Campaign 2000: Report card on child poverty in Canada* (Canadian Council on Social Development 2003a), provided convincing evidence that despite seven years of economic prosperity, over a million children in this country continue to live in poverty. These figures establish that more children are poor than in 1989 when Parliament unanimously pledged to eradicate child poverty by the year 2000. Poverty, however, is not an equal opportunity oppressor. *Campaign 2000* presented evidence that 42 per cent of immigrant children lived in destitution compared with 17.4 per cent of non-immigrants of the same age. Moreover, 41 per cent of Aboriginal youth living off reserves were counted among the most impoverished (Canadian Council on Social Development 2003b).

Despite growing numbers and increasing need, provincial funding has not kept pace. To manage the excesses of and fallout from the current economic climate, state officials have not extended social welfare assistance to needy parents but resorted to pruning child welfare budgets and cutting jobs. The Children's Aid Society (CAS) of Halifax, for example, was forced in 2002 to cut a million dollars from its budget over a mere six months (Mills 2002). Funding cuts of this magnitude have serious and often severe implications because child welfare workers become overextended and managers feel pressure to reduce spending. In this desperate environment, youth in need have routinely been denied essential helping services such as treatment sessions and educational programs. For example, after the provincial government cut $1.1 million in funding, the British Columbia Ministry of Children and Family Development axed school meal programs, early academic intervention, and school-based support workers for inner city schools (Douglas 2002). Older youth have also seen essential and relatively inexpensive programs relegated to the dustbin of the neo-liberal state. While seemingly innocuous, bus passes allow the poor to cross the urban landscape to attend school or hold jobs. Without this resource, youth often lose their jobs and/or are expelled from school for non-attendance. Moreover, throughout the late 1990s many youth were incarcerated for breaching conditions attached to probation orders. For the most part, they were considered in contempt of court for failing to comply with a court order, typically their failure to fulfill community service hours. A typical scenario might involve a young person sentenced to 20 hours of community work as restitution for a minor infraction. All too often, young people who appear before Canada's courts are impoverished, which curtails the mere act of traveling across town to fulfill their community service obligation. Taking the young person's non-compliance as a sign of disrespect and contempt for authority, the youth court judge counterintuitively sentences the recalcitrant youth to additional hours of community service. The cycle continues until the frustrated judge surrenders and orders the offender incarcerated. This all too common and tragic occurrence could easily be prevented *if* resources were used intelligently.

Heavy caseloads and an overburdened child welfare system have forced child welfare workers to prioritize. Tragic outcomes emerge when cases of abuse are ignored in favour of more 'pressing' matters. Randal Dooley, for example, died of a brain injury after incessant beatings from his father and stepmother that left him with welts all over his body and more than a dozen broken bones. Randal's teacher brought the case to a Children's Aid Society worker who had little time to get involved and instead referred the teacher to the police. Jordan Heikamp starved to death at five weeks despite his teenaged mother's frequent encounters with social workers and nurses at a Toronto women's shelter. Children in need are slipping through the cracks as CAS workers must don blinkers in the face of increasing caseloads and paltry budgets.

In such an overburdened system, children are being placed in foster homes that meet only minimal standards. Bob Rechner, child advocate for Alberta, stated that 'when funding for foster homes and resources are tight, it's not surprising standards may not be strictly adhered to. There are many great foster homes in this province. Unfortunately, there are some retained as foster homes that probably shouldn't be, but there aren't alternatives' (Johnsrude 1999). The solution to this problem offered by Manitoba's Child and Family Services is particularly deplorable. Confronted by a lack of adequate foster homes and inadequate funding, child welfare officials rented a floor in a hotel to house youth awaiting placement. They were supervised by a single, hardly qualified staff member who entertained his/her charges with television. For some youth, this was their home for more than a year! The most vulnerable children in Canadian society are being short-changed, denied essential services as a result of shrunken social welfare spending. It should come as no surprise when many of these youth become inmates of Canadian penitentiaries.

While Canadians favoured tax breaks for corporations and the richest segments of society, they campaigned at the same time for increased rates of incarceration for young people—the most costly (both economically and socially) mode of penality. This situation is particularly troubling when we consider that a great number of young people are incarcerated for relatively *minor* forms of deviance. Indeed, a great number of inmates were sentenced to prison for such 'heinous' breaches of public order as failure to comply with court orders and property-related crimes. Perhaps as a result of the public's appetite for punishment, Canada's rate of incarceration for young people exceeds that of the all Western nations—including the United States (Hogeveen 2005). While Canadians could in the past point to greater tolerance toward the recalcitrant on their part than their American counterparts, these statistics suggest that 'we' are more like 'them' than many would like to believe.

More troubling still is that individuals warehoused in Canada's centres of detention are almost exclusively from the most marginal classes. Instead of distributing welfare benefits to the poor and suppressed, Canadians have placed this class under the authority of the criminal justice system. While social welfare schemes were shrinking, programs that coercively targeted the poor were expanding. Consider, if you will, the amount of relief that could be administered for the resources devoted to incarcerating excessive numbers of young people. Reflect on how much tuition could be paid with the $50,000 to $100,000 required to detain one young person for a year. Indeed, set against the backdrop of the type of crimes for which these youth are being detained, this expenditure seems extreme. Throughout the 1990s, when the tendency to lock up juvenile offenders was at its peak, so too was the erosion of welfare. One could interpret this as an indication that the only institutions and social programs Canadians were willing to support were those that delivered the most obvious signs of pain to the destitute and marginal.

In effect, centres of detention have become the social service to which the poor and oppressed have the readiest access. With the rising cost of post-secondary education and toughening criteria for welfare eligibility, the criminal justice system is the state service most available to the subjugated and marginalized. It seems that we have embarked on a path toward managing poverty and inequality through the carceral complex. No longer is the system asked only to deter crime but also to regulate the lower segments of the social order and to defend against the discardable, derelict, and superfluous (Wacquant 1999). Social welfare deterioration and the development of a penality of pain for those deemed undeserving converge to create a new form of governance aimed at controlling the downtrodden and destitute. The 'invisible hand' of the casual labour market finds its institutional counterpart in the 'iron fist' of the state, which is deployed to regulate the chaos created by the widespread social insecurity characteristic of neo-liberalism (Bourdieu 1998; Wacquant 2001). More than any other group, Aboriginal youth have felt the sting of the state's penal governance of poverty and marginality.

JUSTICE AND INDIGENOUS YOUTH?

Throughout history, Aboriginal peoples have been subjected to intrusive and invasive modes of state-level control aimed at reform, assimilation, and subjugation (Anderson 1999; Hogeveen 1999; see also Chapter 15). Wherever the Euro-Canadian state encountered indigenous people, the Native land was quickly vacated to make way for white settlement and capitalist expansion. Among the tools of colonialism employed to regulate and shore up the Anglo vision of the country's founders were the North-West Mounted Police (forerunner of the RCMP), law, reserves, a pass system, children's forced adoption by white families, and residential schooling. With the closure of residential schools and with many indigenous peoples now living off reserves, institutions of detention are now on the front lines when it comes to controlling the indigenous 'other'. Penal practices are applied to Aboriginal people with special diligence and severity. Ceaselessly denied entry into Euro-Canadian institutional life, increasing numbers of Native youth have been pushed through the state's justice process to the point that it is now, I think, possible to talk about the criminalization of indigenousness.

Government reports and investigations have consistently pointed to a gross overrepresentation of Native adolescents at the most punitive end of the system (Royal Commission on Aboriginal Peoples 1993; 1996). Peter Carrington and Jennifer Schulenberg (2004) suggest that indigenous adolescents are 20 per cent more likely to be charged when apprehended than non-Aboriginal youth. Moreover, Aboriginal youth are more likely to be denied bail, to spend more time in pre-trial detention, and to be charged with multiple offences (often for administrative violations) and are less likely to have legal representation in court proceedings (Roberts and Melchers 2003; Statistics Canada 2000). While Aboriginal youth accounted for 5 per cent of the total youth population in 1999, they occupied 24 per cent of the beds in Canadian detention centres. More tragic is the situation confronting indigenous youth in Canada's prairie provinces. In Saskatchewan and Manitoba, three-quarters (75 per cent for Manitoba and 74 per cent for Saskatchewan) of youth sentenced to custody were identified as Aboriginal while less than 10 per cent of Manitoba's youth population is Native (Statistics Canada 2000). No group has been more touched by Canada's appetite for youth incarceration than the First Nations. A Canadian Bar Association report suitably titled *Locking up Natives in Canada* provided evidence that a 16-year-old Aboriginal male had a 70 per cent chance of serving at least one prison stint before turning 25. The report continues, 'prison has become for young Native men, the promise of a just society which high school and college represents for the rest of us' (Jackson 1989, 216). Situated in the context of the historical assimilationist and destructionist policies of the Canadian state, centres of detention are the 'contemporary equivalent of what the Indian residential school represented for their parents' (216). Resorting to the imprisonment system to govern the indigenous 'other' shores up the Euro-Canadian social order and ensures in a punitive manner that this group remains separate and unequal.

Buttressing this systematic subjugation of those considered alien to the national body is the coincident dismantling of welfare programs during a period of intensified poverty among indigenous peoples—especially children. Not only are Aboriginal people highly overrepresented among the street population, they are more likely to be living in urban poverty and inhabiting living quarters deemed overcrowded than the general Canadian population (Canadian Council on Social Development 2003b). According to Aboriginal activist Cindy Blackstock (2003), Canada's indigenous peoples would rank 78th on the United Nations' Human Development Index (HDI)—which measures poverty, literacy, education, and life expectancy. Canada itself consistently ranks first. The HDI, developed by Pakistani economist Mahbub ul Haq, has become the standard means of measuring overall well-being, and especially child welfare, through three basic categories:

- *long and healthy life* as indicated by life expectancy at birth;
- *knowledge* as measured by adult literacy rate; and
- *standard of living* as derived from gross domestic product per capita.

When compared to people in the rest of the world, Canadians are well situated. But hidden among facts and figures is a long silent, oppressed, and subjugated population. Colonialism, it seems, is not an embarrassing period in the long-forgotten Canadian past. Instead it continues to rear its ugly head.

Given that the Aboriginal population is much younger than the Canadian average, the predicament facing the nation-state promises to shape the future of this country in very dramatic ways. A 2003 report by the Canadian Council on Social Development stated that the median age for Aboriginals was 24.7 compared to 37.7 for non-Aboriginals. Moreover, children 14 and under made up 33 per cent of the Aboriginal population compared to just 19 per cent for non-indigenous peoples. However, this growing group of young Aboriginals is more likely to live in poverty. More than half of all Aboriginal children were considered poor while only 23.4 per cent of all Canadian children suffered under this unfortunate condition (Canadian Council on Social Development 2003b).

This section has offered a glimpse into the brand of justice that the Canadian state considers First Nations groups deserve. Colonialism has produced a situation in which indigenous youth are subjected to racism and inequality at almost every turn. They are poor, hungry, excluded, and criminalized. Instead of responding to these disgraceful outcomes through social welfare, the carceral/punitive continuum has been mobilized to regulate its worst aspects. The upsizing of the state's penal sector, along with the downsizing of its social welfare institutions, has constituted a carceral complex directed toward surveilling, training, and neutralizing recalcitrant Aboriginal youth who exist outside Euro-Canadian mores.

JUSTICE FOR GIRLS?

Youth, especially the poorest and most marginalized, face pervasive discrimination, silencing, and victimization. While young people are often presented in media and popular discourse as particularly troubling, they are at the same time troubled (Tanner 1996). The latter part of this equation receives far less scrutiny than the former but is no less problematic. According to data gathered by Statistics Canada, those most likely to receive the sharp end of 'justice' are at the same time the most vulnerable to crime as well as social and economic subordination and are thus most in need of protection. Highlights of the *General social survey* suggest that youth are highly overrepresented as victims of crime. In 1999 youth aged 12 to 17 constituted 8 per cent of the population but were victims in 16 per cent of violent offences. The same study revealed that girls were overrepresented as victims of violent crime, especially sexual deviance (Statistics Canada 2001a).

Throughout history, the youth justice system has tended to neglect girls both as victims and as offenders. This is not surprising given that young girls have been highly underrepresented in crime statistics. Early criminologists and youth justice officials used this underrepresentation to bolster the view that wayward girls must somehow be defective. Discourses around female deviance embedded in traditional and positivist criminology illustrate this tendency. The founding *fathers* of criminology, such as Cesare Beccaria in 1778, Charles Hooton in 1939, and Otto Pollak in 1950, portrayed female offenders as a defective lot, the product of inferior breeding as well as biological and anatomical inferiority (Snider 2004). By the turn of the nineteenth century, offenders were considered mentally weak, but following the logic set out above, female 'deviants' were 'more terrible than any man' in that they were 'less intelligent, more passive, more deficient in moral sense, but stronger in sexual instincts' (Snider 2004, 232). Flowing out of this discourse were 'capricious and arbitrary status' offences—a category of offences that applies solely to youth, which if committed by an adult would not result in arrest (i.e., drinking, incorrigibility, truancy, and curfew violations)—that aimed to control female sexuality by incarcerating those who flouted norms of 'emphasized femininity', which stressed the importance of piety, domesticity, and above all monogamous heterosexual marriage.

Juvenile court officials cast a wide net over what they deemed 'sexuality'. Girls did not have to be caught in the act to be admonished by state actors. Franca Iacovetta (1999) charged that parents often brought their girls to the attention of police on the basis of neighbourhood gossip. Indeed, the mere suggestion of sexual activity could initiate state proceedings against young girls. Throughout the late nineteenth and early twentieth century, girls were routinely incarcerated for such aberrant conduct as holding hands or being out after dark in the wrong part of town in the company of a boy. Although girls drew the attention of juvenile court officials for their wayward sexuality, boys were detained for reasons not directly linked to violations of the normative sexual order. Instead, they were arrested for defying elite standards of appropriate conduct for working-class males by refusing to work, rejecting school, disobeying the law, and disrespecting their parents' requests for appropriate conduct.

Court records reveal the sexual double standard. Lauren P., who arrived in Canada from Ireland during the 1910s, was sent to live in an industrial school for the 'heinous crime' of flirting with boys at gasoline stations, staying out late, and going to movies—'often with rouge and lipstick' (Hogeveen 2002). Similarly, Amanda T., a 15-year-old girl whose father was killed during World War I, was brought before the court when her foster parents feared she had been sexually active. Their suspicions were raised when their foster daughter had become 'impudent of late' with a tendency to become 'foxy and cunning'. A physical examination conducted by the juvenile court revealed no evidence of venereal disease, but the state of her hymen betrayed the fact that she 'had been immoral'. The juvenile court found her guilty of vagrancy and she was sent to a home for girls (Hogeveen 2002). Boys suffered no such intrusion into their lives or invasion of their bodies. Indeed, on a very revealing occasion a young boy, fearful he had impregnated his girlfriend, timidly asked his probation officer for advice. The officer promptly ordered the impudent youth to be tested for venereal disease and do his *manly* duty toward his girlfriend. A similar confession would have landed a female youth in an industrial school for an indefinite period.

Not only was girls' sexuality policed through juvenile court and industrial school intervention, race relations were also governed through state-sponsored intrusion. A familiar refrain from white Anglo-Celtic elites who dominated social, economic, and political life during the early twentieth century was that 'the nation' was in danger of decline (Valverde 1991). In the eyes of many, 'nation' was a generic term that referred to those of Anglo descent while racialized 'others' were viewed with increasing suspicion. By the 1910s a widely accepted racial hierarchy was firmly established in Canada. This ordering was not solely structured by skin colour but also by degrees of whiteness. The mostly British upper middle-class professionals who spearheaded eugenics campaigns—promoting forms of social control aimed at improving the racial qualities of future generations (Garland 1985, 142)—constituted themselves and 'the nation' in opposition to immigrants from other cultures. Anglo-Celtic elites, bolstered by eugenics discourse, created a purportedly common sense racial logic that associated whiteness with the 'clean and the good, the pure and the pleasing' (Jackson 2000; Roediger 1991; Morrison 1992). It followed then that 'white' girls found associating with boys considered 'other' required training and reformation for the good of 'the nation'.

Such was the case in 1939 when Velma Demerson's father, with police in tow, stormed into the kitchen she shared with her Chinese lover as the pair was finishing breakfast. The officers arrested her under the 1897 Female Refugees Act, which allowed for the indefinite detention of girls between 15 and 35 suspected of drunkenness, promiscuity, and pregnancy outside of monogamous union. Velma was 18, pregnant, and in love. Pregnancy before marriage was one thing: that her boyfriend was not 'white' was quite another and a source of embarrassment to her father. Velma was sent to Belmont House—a female house of refuge—for being promiscuous, for being illegitimately pregnant, and for consorting with a Chinese man. There she spent six weeks working in the laundry before being transferred to the Mercer Reformatory. For her 'crimes' she was detained in a seven-by-four-foot cell with bars on the door to prevent her escape to wreak havoc on an unsuspecting public. Demerson gave birth to her son inside the institution with neither her mother, her father, nor her partner at her side. Soon after his birth, her son was whisked away. Women like Velma wallowed away and suffered tremendously within institutional walls without having committed any crime. In recent years, Demerson has sued and demanded an apology for her suffering from the Canadian government. She has received the latter but still awaits financial compensation for her torment.

*In*justices experienced by girls continue under contemporary youth justice regimes, in part because they remain 'too few to count' within the youth justice system (Adelberg and Currie 1987). Despite some modest increase in numbers, female young offenders constitute one fifth of all cases appearing in youth court. Their infrequent appearance before magistrates and in centres of detention helps to explain why relatively few youth justice resources are set aside for female offenders—it does not, however, excuse it. This condition is felt throughout the youth justice process as more and more female youth are subjected to institutional arrangements, risk assessment, and programming designed by men on the basis of boys' experience. Given that theoretical foundations have been developed out of male experience, females are excluded as subjects of knowledge and authorized knowers. The implications are profound. Existing theories of crime and deviance predict the greatest deviance by the most marginalized, alienated, and devalued by society. However, this condition applies to women much more than it does to men. Yet despite being devalued and alienated, girls do not commit crime at anywhere near the rate of boys (Reitsma-Street 1999). Thus it would be very useful if theoretical interpretations of juvenile criminality and the programming that flows from it reflected girls' experience. However, that has not been the case.

The dearth of resources devoted to female programming and lack of attention to girls' experience have further implications. For instance, while Alberta operates and maintains support for numerous open custody beds (institutions that are not locked) for male youth, only four are set aside for females. This situation is particularly egregious: incarcerated girls sentenced to open custody are not cascaded down to house arrest but relegated to locked units when open custody beds are unavailable.

Once they are inside, the abuses that girls experienced in the outside world sometimes continue rather than abating. A survey of youth in custody in British Columbia by the McCreary Centre (2001) found that almost a third of inmates disagreed with the statement 'staff are respectful and fair' and had experienced discrimination or harassment by staff. Moreover, girls in a study conducted by the advocacy group Justice for Girls reported feeling uncomfortable with frequent pat-downs by male staff (Dean 2004). Others revealed experiences that ranged from subtle to more overt forms of sexual harassment (Dean 2004, 51). Clearly, girls' encounters with the young offender system, both historically and today, serve to further their marginalization and foster additional injustices.

Voices of Youth?

The foregoing conditions have been produced by adult-conceived and implemented policy and practice. But if they are to be ameliorated, who should undertake the task? Who, we may ask, knows better what it is like to be young than those who occupy that generational position? The problem, however, is that youth are silenced. They are the subjects of adult-inspired intrusions, not their authors. In Western society, in fact throughout the global social field, adult views structure action and shape societal infrastructure while youthful voices remain silenced and frequently nullified. When the input of youth is solicited—which is hardly customary—it is often as an afterthought or as an aside. While the 'otherness' of young people renders them unique, it is often used to justify their exclusion as decision-makers in institutional arrangements that fundamentally affect their lives. Western discourse constitutes children as partially formed, in need of training and maturity—but most significant, inferior to adults.

Institutional arrangements that dot the Canadian landscape function to censor youth and fix them in a subordinate position. No one has to state overtly that youthful voices are less intelligent, barely cogent, and inferior to adults; it is simply understood. Indeed, pervasive discourses such as 'children should be seen and not heard' function to entrench the view that youth are somehow less than and 'other' to adults. However, this discourse is anchored in much more tacit albeit powerful ways. The fact that youth are not given the right to vote until they reach their eighteenth birthday speaks volumes about their silence (Mathews 2001). Moreover, when we consider the terms 'teacher', 'politician', and 'judge', we automatically assume that it is adults about whom we are speaking. But do youth have nothing of value to contribute to these important domains? Hardly. They find themselves on the outside, invited to participate only when something is being imposed on them—without, of course, any choice on their part. This order of things does not need to be taught in schools: it just is. Nevertheless, it is patently obvious through a cursory glance at the institutional hierarchy. Put simply, adults occupy all positions of influence.

This condition exists because of the way that fundamental resources are distributed throughout the social order. Those with the influence to speak and be heard derive their legitimacy from the field in which they exert their dominance. They are the spokespersons of the dominant order and work to ensure the continued existence of the status quo. In Western society, age is currency, and those who have accumulated the most experience as measured by years—only to a certain point, of course—inherit the symbolic power that accrues with it. Indeed, given that all individuals—young and old alike—inhabit the same social sphere, the right of the mature to power is recognized by all, especially by those who want one day to succeed them. Thus because the subjected and the elite inhabit the same social sphere in which the discourse of age dominance is pervasive, it remains largely unchallenged. This condition just *is*. Indeed, the institutional order functions above all to (re)produce the necessary social belief in the legitimacy of the existing order. Or, in the words of Toril Moi (1991, 1023), 'to make us believe that our rulers are ruling us by virtue of their qualifications and achievements'.

According to social theorist Pierre Bourdieu, every established social order necessarily makes its own arbitrariness seem a natural condition (Bourdieu 1977, 164). In Canadian society, where traditional hierarchies based on age remain relatively stable, our order of things appears self-evident, innate, and ordinary. Or to put it succinctly, in Canadian society the great majority are fully aware of their social positions and conduct themselves accordingly. In this order there remains little room for youth to manoeuvre into a more agreeable position. It would seem that the normative social order is fated to be replicated generation after generation. Those who benefit from the established order prefer not to unsettle the status quo. It is only the subordinated who have an interest in pushing back societal limits in order to expose the capriciousness of the presupposed order. Therefore, youth are left the task of unsettling the traditional norms that silence them.

In Edmonton, Alberta, a group of enterprising youth despondent over their silence has challenged contemporary orthodoxy by establishing and administering the world's only 'youth for youth' restorative justice program. A well-established definition of restorative justice suggests that it is an alternative criminal justice process whereby 'parties with a stake in a particular offence come together to resolve collectively how to deal with the aftermath of the offence and its implications for the future' (Marshall 1996, 37). In opposition to traditional youth justice processes in which adults predominate, the Youth Restorative Action Project (YRAP) was created, designed, and implemented and is currently administered by youth. It is made up entirely of young people—between 14 and 21, ranging from honours students to ex-offenders and recovering drug addicts—who consult with offenders to decide on appropriate sanctions within the frame of restorative justice. Adults are accorded no decision-making power and are almost entirely excluded from proceedings except in rare instances when they are called upon to provide clarification on technical points of law. YRAP paves the way for new discursive potentials and novel understandings that recognize the injustices and exclusions contained within established youth justice practice.

Unfortunately, YRAP is the exception rather than the rule. Youth continue to be silenced and nullified in matters that affect them directly. Only when the norms that reinforce adult privilege are exposed and the resulting social order is no longer considered inevitable can amendments be suggested.

CONCLUSION

Given the silencing of young people, their experiences of poverty, the racism that confronts certain segments, and the dislocation of girls in juvenile justice, we can safely conclude that there is no justice for youth. But what would *justice* look like? Given that those for whom justice remains elusive are subjugated, marginalized, and racialized populations, *justice*, broadly conceived, would imply an ethic of how to be *just* with/to the 'other'. The problem, however, is that universal pronouncements such as the Canadian Charter of Rights and Freedoms and the UN Convention on the Rights of the Child provide little guidance toward this end. We should therefore not be fully satisfied with such endeavours. Satisfaction with the application of conventions and charters reduces the language of justice to questions of rights and conceals the tyranny over the poor, the indigenous, the female, and the silent.

Canadians cannot be satisfied with contemporary action toward the 'other'—who are downtrodden, excluded, and intruded upon. But, you might say, these people have rights and the ability to exercise them, don't they? However, even if rights were the starting point and not the goal of a just relationship, very few youth understand what rights are bestowed on them and, more important, how to exercise them. There must be something more. Indeed, there is but one answer, which is to 'listen to the unspoken demand . . . [since] the beginning of all evil is to plug one's ears' (Bauman 2001). Let there be no mistake: listening to the 'other' is just an opening. Hearing and acting ethically toward the other is something altogether different. Thus giving voice to the voiceless demand is a necessary initial foray into being just—but not its infallible guarantee.

Questions to Consider ————————————————————————————————
1. What understanding(s) of 'justice' does the author suggest pervade the con-temporary Canadian scene? What examples does he use to illustrate this?
2. To what does the author attribute burgeoning rates of poverty experienced in an era of opulence? Why are youth affected most?
3. In your view, what political processes silence youth? How is one group of Edmonton youth challenging this condition?
4. Are girls offered a different form of 'youth justice' in Canada?

Chapter 13

Should Policing Be Privatized?

Curtis Clarke

INTRODUCTION

> Any understanding of contemporary developments in policing requires recognition of its indivisibility: the fact that public and private forms, far from being distinct, are increasingly connected. More and more, policing is undertaken by a complex and diverse network of public, private and hybrid agencies (Johnston 1996, 54).

Policing in Canada, as in most Western societies, has entered an era of transition wherein the governance and operationalization of security and policing has become multi-layered. In societies dominated by neo-liberal values and global market pressures, governments have had to rationalize public services such as policing. From an organizational and tactical perspective, this has meant shifting, sharing, and privatizing various aspects of policing (Murphy and Clarke 2005). Recent quantitative and structural changes in the nature of security have realigned the operational prominence of public policing and blurred the boundary between private and public providers. As Ian Loader points out, this fragmentation of providers has ushered in a 'plethora of agencies and agents, each with particular kinds of responsibility for the delivery of policing and security services and technologies' (2000, 323).

The resulting transformation raises numerous questions with respect to the role of the state, the assurance of accountable policing, and whether or not the public interest/good can be effectively protected by the emerging network of providers. The question we should be asking is not whether policing should be privatized but whether the state will remain a focal point in the provision and accountability of policing. A corresponding question would centre on how the state might formulate its connection to policing, given the contemporary conditions of diverse providers (Loader and Walker 2001). While these are important questions to ask, formulating an effective response is not so simple. In order to do, so we must understand how the current landscape of policing has been transformed. To begin, let us briefly outline what we mean by policing.

POLICING: A BRIEF EXPLANATION

The activity of policing is closely aligned with the previously discussed term 'governance' (see Chapters 9 and 11). Policing is a process of regulating and ordering contemporary societies and individuals. Governance and the activity of policing are thus used as terms to 'denote governmental strategies originating from inside and outside the state' (Jones 2003, 605). This notion of governance has been woven into much of the current analysis of policing, and it expresses a broad function within a system of formal regulation and promotion of security (Jones and Newburn 1998; Loader 2000; Jones 2003; Murphy and Clarke 2005). A corresponding layer of analysis focuses on the institution or specific state agency tasked with order maintenance, law enforcement, and public safety. In this analysis, our attention is drawn to the formal structure and organizational practices of these agencies, not to the broad function of social control. In this context policing refers to:

> those forms of order maintenance, peacekeeping, rule or law enforcement, crime investigation and prevention and other forms of investigation and associated information-brokering; which may involve a conscious exercise of coercive power; undertaken by individuals or organizations, where such activities are viewed by them and/or others as a central or key defining part of their purpose (Jones and Newburn 1998, 18).

Traditionally, many of these tasks and functions were considered the sole purview of the public police. And yet in the current era of transformation, these very tasks and functions have become the foothold of the private sector's perceived encroachment on public policing authority. These regulatory, investigative, and enforcement activities are, in fact, the site of intense debate with respect to the public/private nexus of policing, the crux of which rests on the issue of public accountability. As Burbidge notes:

> While the public police are governed by and accountable to democratically elected governmental authority and to the public, private police officers, even when performing the same policing functions as their public counterparts, are not subject to the same form of democratic governance and accountability (2005, 67).

Although the issue of accountability remains a central theme, it is essential to note that private providers do indeed offer similar services to those provided by the public police. The fundamental concern is: how did public policing shed many of these tasks, thus creating an opportunity for private providers to assume a level of prominence?[1] As the following section argues, the transformation was the result of broad neo-liberal governance policies and a perceived crisis of ineffective order maintenance.

THE CURRENT LANDSCAPE OF POLICING

In this era of public service rationalization, the public police have adopted various strategies of managerial and organizational reform. Operationally, this has meant 'eliminating, re-engineering, decentralizing, and privatizing' various types of police services. The resulting elimination or downloading of some traditional police services, coupled with an inability or reluctance to meet new policing and security demands, has created a new market for services previously provided by public police. In addition, the rapid growth of private mass property and space, as well as new modes of business and technology, has created a range of new policing and security needs that cannot be satisfied by the public police (Shearing and Stenning 1982).

As a result of this unmet demand, a mix of public and private sources are increasingly providing alternative policing and security services. In the public domain, individual citizens, community groups, agencies, and police-sponsored or 'partnered' community policing groups are adopting various modes of policing and protection. Governments, private companies, and citizens who want more personalized and/or sophisticated policing/security are increasingly creating their own in-house police and security services or are contracting with an expanding number of private security or hybrid public/private policing services. The fragmentation and transfer of police services is a consequence of neo-liberal strategies of fiscal restraint and decentralized governance. It signals a shift from expensive and expansive government or 'state'-based crime control (Garland 1996) to a more commodified, market-driven, and diversified security and risk management environment (Ericson and Haggerty 1997), an environment in which the centrality and nature of the public police role is increasingly called into question.

The rationalization of public services like health, education, and policing is often made easier by the use of mystifying reform rhetoric that both legitimates and masks shifts and reductions in traditional service, promoting them as progressive improvements. The ambiguous but powerful rhetoric of community policing/integrated policing has been particularly effective, offering both a critique of the modern full-service model of professional public policing as unresponsive and ineffective and a rationale for a more limited model of public policing (Murphy 1998, 9).

The realignment of policing under neo-liberal policies has required a rapid adaptation from a service that 'until relatively recently, still bore many of the structural characteristics of its organizational (and operational) origins in the nineteenth century' (Savage and Charman 1996, 39). Reform has been stoked by diminished confidence in the adequacy of public police services to achieve the outcomes desired of a modern police service and a growing demand for police services to adapt to the changing political economy of governance.

For more than a decade, police practitioners and researchers have confronted the need for a new model of policing (Bayley 1994; Sparrow, Moore, and Kennedy 1990; Kennedy and Moore 1997; Pelfry 1998; Peak and Glensor 1996). Bayley and Shearing argue that police services, 'no longer confident that they are either effective or efficient in controlling crime, . . . are anxiously examining every aspect of performance—objectives, strategies, organization, management, discipline and accountability' (1998, 393). Core changes such as 'the restructuring and relocation of policing authority and responsibility, the reconceptualization and commodification of public policing and the economic and ideological rationalization of public and private policing' have orchestrated a shift from the traditional reliance on public providers of policing (Murphy 1998, ii). Certainly, in a political environment influenced by a neo-liberal ideology, the public provider monopoly is regarded as theoretically incompatible with and unable to address current dilemmas of crime control, governance restructuring, and fiscal restraint.

From a neo-liberal perspective, single-provider policing models are considered as inefficient and wasteful as other government institutions (Stenson 1993). Palmer argues that 'police are under pressure to satisfy governments that they are cost effective and achieving the required results. Limited resources have already substantially impacted upon policing as governments apply funding cuts' (cited in O'Malley 1996, 23). Police managers have been forced to achieve considerable savings through more stringent and controlled use of finance and other resources. 'Lean and mean' has been the emphasis at the management levels when addressing this demand to provide policing services at a considerably reduced cost.

The neo-liberal doctrine of greater fiscal responsibility place police services 'under enormous pressures to economize and rationalize local police services' (Murphy 1998, 5). Public policing's viability is further undermined by the accusation that it supports a culture of dependence and learned helplessness—that communities have become dependent on the police to solve the problem of order, a reliance that has proven unrealistic, ineffective, and inefficient. The current rhetoric of policing, particularly within a neo-liberal paradigm, 'admonishes the community for its reliance on the police and declares the need for communities and individuals to accept their responsibilities and actively participate in policing their own communities in the fight against crime' (Murphy 1998, 9). One can detect the neo-liberal opposition to this level of dependence in the rhetoric of the mobilized, responsible, and self-governing citizen. Neo-liberal commitments to decentralization and individual/community empowerment challenge policing structures that support a culture of dependence. From a neo-liberal perspective, the monopoly of public policing represents a strategy of inefficiency, ineffectiveness, and lack of accountability. These alleged failings are cited to stress the need to rework or reconceptualize the police function in ways that would redefine the essential nature and scope of public police service. This critique has forced policing to grapple with the need to re-examine its role, its structure, and how it is to be judged. Unfortunately, the result of this re-examination has been a further blurring between private and public policing functions.

As one can see, the realm of public policing is moulded by influential political, economic, and ideological forces. This is not to suggest that the current transformation has resulted in detrimental operational and organizational outcomes. On the contrary, many public police services are now more effective and efficient with respect to their designated mandate of order maintenance and law enforcement. Unfortunately, the focus of this transformation has stifled the debate surrounding the issue of policing as a public good—because the objective of the realignment has been the elimination, re-engineering, decentralizing, and privatizing of various types of police services, not the assurance that policing would remain a public good.

A Question of Public Good

Ian Loader (2000) suggests that the provision and supervision of policing is secured through government, beyond government, and below government. Within these sites one notes alternative models to the previously accepted state-centred responsibility of dispensing and governing security. In this context, the traditional nexus between the state and police is replaced with a model that connects both state and non-state nodes in the process of governance (Shearing and Wood 2003; Johnston and Shearing 2003). However, the question still remains as to whether or not a diversity of security providers can be responsive to the concept of policing as public good.

For centuries, security and the state have been synonymous. Adam Smith, the dean of classical liberalism, is famous for stating that protecting citizens from harm is a duty of the government: it is a service that government must provide. Karl Marx argued that 'security is the supreme social concept of civil society' (cited in Jones and Newburn 1998, 33). Unfortunately, the backdrop to the current era of transition in policing is a governance trend toward a fragmented and pluralized network of security in which citizens may not broadly share security interests or achieve equal levels of security. This trend has undermined the importance of state-coordinated security as a fundamental public good. The provision of security has been couched in the economic rhetoric of efficiency, effectiveness, and creation of private goods rather than in terms of the public good.

Furthermore, it affirmed the importance of private interest and the pursuit of specific, self-defined 'security requirements without reference to any conception of the common good' (Loader 2000, 386). The state, with varying degrees of enthusiasm, had turned to business and the market as mechanisms to provide public goods such as education and health care. In the realm of public security and policing, the private sector was given responsibilities that in some settings effectively made it the key provider of perhaps the most basic public good: public safety. Thus the move toward satisfying self-defined security requirements did little in the way of ensuring that the private agencies performing more and more state actions were upholding any measure of democratic accountability (Valverde 1999).

In a post-9/11 world, the question we now grapple with is how the state might (re)formulate principles of accountability and regulation in order to address not only broadly shared security interests but also the governance of a disparate multi-organizational security and policing landscape. And while the emergence of this question may indicate a potential shift in governance, it does not suggest that the dichotomy between private and public interests no longer exists—nor is there a renewed appetite for a heavy-handed regime to ensure public security. What it does suggest is an evolving governance environment in which the provision of goods (i.e., public safety) may be achieved through the cooperative actions of multiple stakeholders.

Although the provision of a secure environment depends on the joint actions of various players, it also relies on the state's ability to coordinate the organizational apparatus of the integrated, multi-functional security and policing providers. Moreover, it is incumbent on the state to 'bring reflexive coherence and forms of democratic accountability to the inter-organizational networks and multi-level political configurations within which security and policing are situated' (Loader and Walker 2001, 27). One alternative would be to replace the previously accepted state-centred responsibility of dispensing and governing security with a model that connects both state and non-state nodes in the process of governance (Shearing and Wood 2003; Johnston and Shearing 2003). 'Within this conception of governance no set of nodes is given conceptual priority', and the level of contribution of each node is developed through negotiation or collaborative processes (Johnston and Shearing 2003, 147). Johnston and Shearing argue that 'by emphasizing that the state is no longer a stable locus of government, the nodal model defines governance as the property of networks rather than as the product of any single centre of action' (2003, 148). Moreover, governance is then considered the practice of shifting alliances as opposed to the 'product of state-led steering and rowing strategies' (ibid.). The issue that these models raise is whether we have any assurances that they may serve the desired outcome of enhanced security and policing—or whether they merely represent a theoretical framework that has little operational value.

A RECONFIGURED CONNECTION BETWEEN STATE AND POLICING

As noted previously, some people would contend that the reformulation of the state's central position has been undermined by the downloading of responsibility to corporations, municipalities, and citizens. In other words, how can the state expect to articulate a position of prominence when in fact it has previously reduced its significance in the realm of policing? This is indeed a critical concern, one that is both echoed and supported by Johnston and Shearing's (2003) assertion. And yet I would argue that the current realignment of policing actually strengthens the state's grip on the tiller. It is a realignment that 'flows from an appreciation of the status of policing as a public good' (Loader and Walker 2001, 11).

Jones and Newburn (1998) argue that it is the existence of a diverse network of providers that has forced the state to refocus its efforts to steer policing and security. Loader and Walker further argue that a 'positive (rather than pejorative) connection between policing and the state can be (re)formulated and defended under contemporary conditions' (2001, 11).

This differs from Johnston and Shearing's (2003) perception in that the state does play a central role both in coordinating collaborative alliances and in assuring accountability. Here, the joint actions of various players are both connected and coordinated by the state through reconstructed positions of governance. Within this formulation of governance, the state continues to maintain a primacy in the negotiation and collaborative processes involved in providing the public good of policing. This perspective is effectively presented in the following passage:

> Within the normative framework of the liberal democratic society, it is only the state or national government (and not the private sector) that has the capacity to mobilize all of the ingredients that, together, provide policing serv-

ices that ensure the security and safety of the community. The state, as the embodiment of the values of society, is uniquely capable of ensuring public security, characterized by a monopoly of the legitimate use of force, coordin- ated governance, collective provision and communities of attachment (Bur- bidge 2005, 66).

To illustrate the central prominence of the state and its capacity to mobilize a range of stakeholders, let us examine two points of connection at which the state formulates the principles of accountability, regulation, and civic coordination: the monopoly of legitimate coercion and the collective provision of policing.

Legitimate coercion

While the services provided both by private and by public policing providers may seem indivisible, there remain distinct differences, differences that are overlooked if we merely compare tasks and functions. As the following statement notes, sta- tus alone is no longer a clear determinant of difference:

> Where the public police and private security are performing functions that are to all appearances the same, their differing status becomes even more difficult to appreciate (Police Futures Group 2005, 3).

This debate over differences is most keenly argued with respect to the author- ity and legitimacy of the use of force: the monopoly of legitimate coercion. And while the use of legitimate force is indeed a site of contention, it also serves as a mechanism by which the state reinforces its governance prominence. Since it is the state that both grants and regulates the legitimate use of force, it therefore has the capacity to impose a range of regulatory parameters on all providers of polic- ing and security.[2] Max Weber argued that 'the right to use physical force is ascribed to other institutions or individuals only to the extent which the state per- mits it. The state is considered the sole source of the right to use force' (1948, 78). One understanding of Weber's claim would suggest that as representatives of the state, the police are legitimately 'empowered to use force if force is necessary' (Bit- tner 1990, 239). It is the police who are 'equipped, entitled, and required to deal with every exigency in which force may have to be used, to meet it' (256). Reiner (1993) argues, 'the police are the specialist carriers of the state's bedrock power: the monopoly of the legitimate use of power. How and for what this is used speaks to the very heart of the condition of political order' (cited in Jones and Newburn 1998, 35). Ker expands on this by arguing that a police officer's 'authority consists of a legal license to coerce others to refrain from using illegitimate coercion. Soci- ety licenses police officers to kill, hurt, confine and otherwise victimize non- policemen who would illegally kill, hurt, confine and victimize others whom policemen are charged to protect' (1977, 44).

These interpretations suggest that only the state has the right to deliver legit- imate violence and thus can limit the capacity of private policing providers to offer the full range of security and enforcement. The distinction to be made is that 'private security has no powers delegated by government, other than those pos-sessed by any citizen, the scope of their activities is necessarily limited to civil mat-ters ... it has the powers and protections granted all citizens in the Criminal Code and the delegated rights of clients who are property owners under provincial tres-pass and landlord tenant acts' (Police Futures Group 2005, 4).

But regardless of the limited statutory powers granted to private security providers, they do 'perform many of the functions hitherto regarded as the pre-rogative of the public police' (Burbidge 2005, 68). Loader and Walker argue that while the monopoly of legitimate coercion is indeed a central point of authority, it continues to be a 'somewhat limited basis for establishing the state-police nexus and it is in numerous ways being further undone by the contemporary fragmen-tation of policing and state forms' (Loader and Walker 2001, 13).

The concern that this raises has to do with the accountability of the private sector (especially regarding the use of force) since private policing is not gov-erned by the same oversight structures as the public police are. The reality is that 'while the public police are governed by and accountable to democratically elected governmental authority and to the public, private police officers, even when performing the same policing functions as their public counterparts, are not subject to the same form of democratic governance and accountability' (Bur-bidge 2005, 67).

It is within this context that the state has both the responsibility and the authority to address the current governance deficit. From a public good perspec-tive, the state must exercise a regimen in which private policing is regulated and audited and the objective of public good is ensured. Some (but not all) private security providers want more legal police powers, such as the powers of search and seizure and arrest, the use of force, and greater access to police intelligence information. However, this desire is tempered by a reluctance to become subject to the constraints and limits of public accountability, liability, and the courts. Most private security executives recognize that by having a more limited role, with limited public and legal responsibilities, they actually may have more operational freedom than public police.

While the granting of expanded legal powers to private security is a complex public policy question, one cannot ignore the implications of not moving to impose broad regulatory frameworks.[3] As the landscape of policing and security evolves, 'so should the governance and accountability arrangements with respect to the exercise of police powers that impinge on the rights and freedoms of citi-zens' (Burbidge 2005, 73). Examples of this policy shift can be noted in gover-nance changes flowing from the *Report of the Independent Commission on Policing for Northern Ireland* (Patten 1999); Bill 88, An Act to Amend the Private Investi-gators and Security Guards Act (Ontario 2004); and the *Government MLA review of the Private Investigators and Security Guards Act* (Alberta 2005). The challenge confronting each of these initiatives has been to achieve an appropriate balance between those who argue for a state-interventionist approach and those who sup-port the minimalist-government approach. In other words, can the providers of policing be effectively held accountable through market mechanisms, or can accountability be achieved only through the regulatory mechanisms of the state (Burbidge 2005)? A more important consideration is how these governance frameworks might ensure 'the protection and vindication of the human rights of all' (Patten 1999, 18) and 'promote an explicit set of democratic values' (Jones 2003, 623). It is precisely because of these considerations that the state cannot relinquish its regulatory capacity or its ability to steer the provision of policing.

Integrated policing, the responsible citizen: Civic coordination

In the current transformation of policing and security, policy-makers have adopted community participation and the rhetoric of partnership in their engagement with the imperatives of post-welfare crime prevention. These new imperatives suggest that the state respond to crime and disorder not in the traditional direct manner but indirectly through the resources and actions of individuals (Garland 1996). In the context of this arrangement, the role of an integrated policing model is to 'uncouple policing and police so that policing becomes everybody's business rather than exclusively or primarily the business of police' (Shearing 1997, 71). Phrased in a somewhat different manner but echoing a similar sentiment, Sheptycki suggests that through integrated policing we restore 'a balance between citizen and police responsibilities that reflects a more accurate assessment of actual capacities and acknowledges that effective social control cannot possibly be achieved by hired hands alone' (1998, 492).

Philosophically and operationally integrated policing encourages 'communities to recognize that the brunt of the task of policing a free society does not lie with the police but with citizens themselves' (Eggers and O'Leary, cited in Shearing 1997, 70). In the devolution of crime prevention, the discourse of partnership, the multi-agency approach, activating communities, and creating active citizens punctuates the strategies of prevention (Garland 1997). Evidence of this emphasis on citizen participation is strongly suggested in the following UK Home Office policy circular that states that 'Every individual citizen and all those agencies whose policies and practices can influence the extent of crime should make their contribution. Preventing crime is a task for the whole community' (cited in Gilling 1996, 106).

Further support for the shift toward renewed community responsibility is offered in a summary of police-originated commentaries examined by Palmer and O'Malley, which states:

> It is destructive . . . to attempt to pass over to the police the obligation and duties associated with the prevention of crime and the preservation of public tranquility. These are the obligations and duties of the public, aided by the police and not the police occasionally aided by some public spirited citizens (1996, 143).

Certainly, the overarching message woven throughout this discourse is that crime control and prevention are not the sole responsibilities of the police. In fact, the community must be made to 'recognize that they too have a responsibility in this regard, and must be persuaded to change their practices in order to reduce criminal opportunities and increase informal controls' (Garland 1997, 451). In other words, and in accordance with the general prescriptions of community empowerment, crime management is now to be shared with the empowered community—the partners in prevention.

While the optics of this devolution of responsibility suggests a diminished role for the police, it in fact increases the influence and range of surveillance. Shearing (1997) argues that downloading responsibility and streamlining government have shifted the role of policing to proactive leadership guiding community partners in the task of crime control and order management while supporting greater access to community surveillance, organization and intelligence-gathering. Further, 'responsibilization' sets in place a process in which the police 'take on a new set of co-ordinating and activating roles, which, in time, develop into new structures of support, funding, information exchange or co-operation' (Garland 1997, 452).

Community partnerships

> Community policing represents a re-negotiation of the social contract between the police and society (Bayley 1994, 120).

Underlying the renegotiated social contract of an integrated policing model is the central strategic principle of seeking a 'full partnership between the community and their police' (Leighton 1991, 487). In the context of this social contract, full partnership assumes that the community is an active negotiator, not a passive receptor of police policy. Full partnership, understood in these terms, is meant to 'empower the community to bring it onto a more equal footing with the police in terms of joint ownership of local crime and disorder problems and as co-producers of peace, order and security at the local level' (Normandeau and Leighton 1990, 49).

The emphasis on partnership sets the parameters for a new contractual relationship between police and community. It does so first by constructing an alternate identity of community, countering the image of dependence and helplessness as perpetuated by the professional model. Second, partnership forces a realignment of responsibility and authority, which in turn creates a network of alliances between communities and police. Third, it sets criteria of measurement and effectiveness based on the successful inclusion of community in the process of problem-solving—not based on arrest and clearance rates, which reflect a narrow mandate of law enforcement.

Integrated policing displaces the community's reliance on police services to resolve all issues of crime control, and by doing so it requires a shift in the roles of both the community and the police. This has meant a realignment of both the responsibility and the role the police are to take in the production of order—a new role frequently characterized by signifiers such as 'knowledge brokers, expert advisers and security managers' (Ericson 1994, 164). In terms of the community, its new responsibility is to apprise the police 'of the services it requires in its specific locale' and 'to advise its police on what are locally regarded as problems of order and security', as well as to 'stress a correlative adaptability and accountability of police to local communities' (Palmer and O'Malley 1996, 142).

While integrated policing models displace the public police as sole initiators of action, it does not necessarily undermine their locus of control. They continue to possess the attributes (resources and knowledge) required to resolve identified problems (Shearing 1996). Though they remain a locus of control, there is a need to alter their role from that of the reactive agent responding to criminal events to one that reflects what O'Malley refers to as 'a proactive leadership role' (1996, 18). O'Malley goes on to suggest that this leadership role is that of an 'accountable professional practitioner . . . a community leader harnessing community resources to tackle the problems which give rise to crime and disorder' (ibid.). In this designation, policing becomes not only a crime prevention resource but also a catalyst for neighbourhoods and communities to take the initiative for problem-solving (Trojanowicz and Bucqueroux 1990; Ericson 1994). In the role of proactive manager, the public police must not only spend time on resolving the determinants of crime but more important, they must engage the community to address these issues as well. For as Bayley suggests, 'Crime prevention is not a service people are given; it is an activity people must engage in. The public must become co-producers of public safety' (1994, 102). Therefore, the task of the police as proactive managers is to facilitate the activity of crime prevention and help communities help themselves.

From an operational stance, citizen empowerment is to be achieved through a consultative process. Consultation sets in place a mechanism whereby the police can discuss priorities and formulate strategies with the community they serve; it 'creates a sense of shared accountability for community vitality and quality of life' (Campbell and Wright 1993, 14). Consultation further serves as a platform from which the police may establish their proactive leadership in managing the required resources of crime prevention. Finally, a consultative process 'assists community representatives to set their agenda for safety and security in the area and to better understand the problems associated with public policing' (Normandeau and Leighton 1990, 44). Consultation therefore represents a means by which the community can become engaged and motivated, while the police simultaneously act as service providers managing the commodity of crime prevention. More important, consultation builds a process of interaction that imposes a level of accountability and develops partnerships. Through this process, the public police are able to impart the need for partnerships, for the sharing of resources, and for community responsibility.

Policing that is integrated both strategically and operationally works to develop a cooperative, reciprocal relationship that links both police and community actions. The development of civic partnerships not only strengthens the state's capacity to mobilize multiple stakeholders but also facilitates a collective provision of policing. Without the coordination of civic partners, it would be difficult to guide a coherent and consistent response to public security. It is in that guiding role that we see the importance of the state's function within the nodal network of police providers.

CONCLUSION

We began this chapter by asking the question 'should policing be privatized?' but then quickly discarded it for another set of questions. It is not that the question of whether we should privatize policing is unimportant; rather, it is just that in reality we are already there to a certain extent. While we did not directly respond to the initial question, we teased out corresponding concerns associated with the issues of accountability, assurances of the public good, and the function of the state in steering diverse providers. These are the issues that have monumental implications for how we as a society are governed and protected, and thus we must be constantly mindful of them. Whether or not we embrace a privatized, public, or hybrid model of policing, the critical question remains: can the public good of policing be maintained? The answer to this question lies in the capacity of the state to steer the process of policing and ensure that the diverse providers are held accountable to the principle of policing as a public good.

Questions to Consider

1. Why has policing undergone the changes described in this chapter?
2. What do you make of the distinction that Shearing makes between the 'police' and 'policing'?
3. In your view, can a hybrid version of public and private models of policing effectively protect the public? What are the potential dangers of such a model?
4. If the state is no longer the exclusive policing authority, what is the relationship between policing and democracy?
5. What institutions of accountability do you think might be appropriate for the emerging policing arrangements?

Notes

1. For example, in Ontario the number of licensed private investigators and security guards grew from approximately 4,600 in 1967 to about 28,000 in 2002 (Ontario 2003, 3), while a Statistics Canada report (*Police resources in Canada, 2004*) indicated that there were 23,214 municipal and provincial police officers in the province in 2004 (Statistics Canada 2004). The most recent national survey of private policing in Canada showed a substantial difference in the number of private security personnel and that of public police officers (82,010 private security versus 59,090 public police) (Swol 1998).
2. Criminal Code of Canada section 25(1) *Protection of persons acting under authority* states: 'Every one who is required or authorized by law to do anything in the administration or enforcement of the law a) as a private person, b) as a peace officer or public officer, c) in aid of a peace officer or public officer, or d) by virtue of his office, is, if he acts on reasonable grounds, justified in doing what he is required or authorized to do and in using as much force as is necessary for that purpose.' Section 27, *Use of force to prevent commission of offence*, is also of interest with respect to the authority to use force and the differentiation between public police and citizens (i.e., police/private security).

3. 'Across Canada and other jurisdictions, such as the United Kingdom, there is a growing awareness that the legislation governing the private security industry needs to be modernized . . . In order to enhance public safety and increase the efficiency and effectiveness of the industry, these jurisdictions have focused on amendments to licensing, training and equipment . . . Events such as Sept. 11, 2001, have reinforced the need to reform the current legislative and regulatory framework of the private security industry' (Ontario 2003, 5).

Chapter 14

Do Women's Bodies Matter in Prison?

Sylvie Frigon

INTRODUCTION

Some 15 years ago, a task force was established with a mandate 'to examine the *correctional management of federally sentenced women from the commencement of sentence to the date of warrant expiry and to develop a plan which will guide and direct the process in a manner that is responsive to the unique and special needs of this group'* (Correctional Service of Canada 1990; emphasis in original). We might ponder the plight of women incarcerated in Canada since then and the impact of any transformations on them. How are women governed and disciplined in prison? How are the new programs articulated in the new penal regime? How are the bodies of women central to the socio-politics of confinement? What is the future for women's prisons?

This chapter invites you to think critically about the oft-touted 'transformations' of the penal regimes for federally sentenced women and their associated benefits for women. It is divided into three sections. First, I offer a profile of imprisoned women in Canada. Second, given its centrality in the development of a new penal regime for women, I will revisit the recommendations of the task force in its report, *Creating choices*, and offer an assessment of its effects on both federally and provincially sentenced women. The third section examines how women are governed through corrective powers directed to their bodies. My analysis shows the ways in which the body is pivotal to the politics of confinement in institutions and the power of which directly or indirectly involves subjections associated with political techniques directed to the body.

WOMEN IN PRISON: A PROFILE

Women in custody are often overlooked in sociological and criminological accounts, sometimes viewed as a 'social inconvenience', at other times as 'too few to count'.[1] In 1990 provincially sentenced women (two years or less) represented 7 per cent of the Canadian prison population; federally sentenced women (two years or more) represented only 4 per cent of the entire federally sentenced population (Correctional Service of Canada 2006). Until 1996 the Kingston Prison for Women (P4W) was the only penitentiary for women in Canada as compared to more than 40 institutions for men, with some federal/provincial exchange of services that permits women to 'do their time' in provincial institutions near their families (Faith 1993, 138). Statistics from September 1995 indicate that 619 women were then serving a federal sentence; more than half (322) were in detention while others were carrying out commmunity sentences. Forty-two per cent of the women were at the Prison for Women and half of those in the prairie region were indigenous (Arbour 1996). Between 1990 (the year that *Creating choices* was published) and 2006, the number of federally sentenced women in custody increased by more than 75 per cent: from 210 to 401.[2] In March 2004, there were 810 federally sentenced women of whom 48 per cent were incarcerated and the rest (52 per cent) were serving their sentences in the community. Of the 810 women, 172 were indigenous of whom 60 per cent were incarcerated and 40 per cent were serving sentences in the community. As of March 2006, there were 909 federally sentenced women either incarcerated or on conditional release (Correctional Service of Canada 2006).

The growing number of women in prison has to be seen alongside the existence until very recently of only one penitentiary for women. This had several adverse effects on women, particularly in terms of the lack of programming, classification issues (all women housed in a maximum security setting), and geographical dislocation (imprisonment far from their communities and children). Such failings are particularly acute when one considers that two-thirds of the women in 2004 were mothers and 70 per cent were the sole caregivers to children. In contrast, most male prisoners are not primary caregivers to children while in prison. In addition, one might note the number of suicides in the Kingston Prison for Women, which according to unofficial sources numbered about 12 (eight of which were suicides by First Nations women) between 1977 and 1991 (Faith 1993, 139). Self-mutilation and self-injurious behaviour[3] has also been noted. Moreover, the plight of indigenous women has raised many issues surrounding their treatment and overrepresentation in the prison system as well as concerns that there may even be systemic racism in the criminal justice system (Jaccoud 1992; Monture-Angus 2001). Suicides and self-destructive behaviours have remained important issues for both federally and provincially sentenced women (Daigle, Alarie, and Lefebvre 1999; Frigon 2002).[4]

CREATING CHOICES REVISITED[5]

In 1990 *Creating choices* recommended the closure of the Kingston Prison for Women and the construction of five new regional facilities.[6] The closure of this institution was actually recommended soon after its opening in 1934. Since then, more than a dozen commissions, committees, and inquiries have identified the serious limitations in the resources provided to women there.[7] However, much less attention has been paid to provincially sentenced women even though they constitute the vast majority of incarcerated women in Canada.[8]

Creating choices represents a unique and significant moment in the history of federally sentenced women. By participating in the task force, feminist reformers and indigenous representatives helped to shape the development of a new neo-liberal mode of governance. They proposed a women-centred approach guided by five principles: empowerment, meaningful and responsible choices, respect and dignity, supportive environment, and shared responsibility. They sought and delivered new facilities that are architecturally innovative. Although the design might vary slightly from one institution to another, each prison was originally intended to offer residential-style houses for six to 10 women and a central core building for programs and administration.

The construction of the new regional facilities aimed to alleviate the various difficulties inherent in the old system that we noted earlier. To some extent, these difficulties have been addressed. As well, in the new regional facilities women now have access to a multiplicity of programs. These programs include living skills (cognitive, anger management), overcoming substance abuse, literacy and continuous learning, aid to survivors of abuse and trauma, and mother/child programs. Depending on the individual facility, other programs may include multicultural studies, recreation and leisure, vocational and educational training, peer support teams, employment strategies (including canine training and grooming), and health, including mental (*structured-living environment* and *dialectical behaviour therapy*) and physical health programs. There are also enhanced units for maximum-security and structured-living environments (for women with significant mental health issues), which are now in operation in most of the regional facilities.

However, the task force and its effects were not without critics.[9] Some felt that even though the task force included some radical voices—a few even advocating the abolition of prisons—a reformist logic triumphed during the committee work of the group. This led at least one incarcerated woman to regard their work as

> an exercise in frustration and futility . . . Women [task force members] with good hearts and well meaning attitudes came to visit with us this morning. We wanted to talk about improving this institution. They wanted to talk about building more prisons. We should all be talking about the abolition of prisons! (A Lifer at Prison for Women, cited in Correctional Service of Canada 1990, 12–13).

Various incidents, including self-injury, attempted suicides, assaults on staff, a homicide of a prisoner by another prisoner, and escapes at the Edmonton Institution for Women led to stricter parameters of security. This development significantly altered the vision of *Creating choices*, as has the notion that particular kinds of *needs* are automatically identified as *risks*. The hybrid notion needs/risks, as Hannah-Moffat (2001) coined it, becomes a new form of control premised on self-regulation and strategies of governing-at-a-distance (Rose 1989).

Another major fundamental concept that needs to be addressed is that of *empowerment*, which is central to this new penal philosophy. The strategy of empowerment coincides with both the feminist objectives of the reformers and those of the correctional representatives:

Under a new, self-governing regime of empowerment, the authorities can regulate women through the decisions the women themselves make, without resorting to overt expressions of power. The new technologies steer choices and prevent misbehaviour, instead of deterring through punishment (Hannah-Moffat 2001, 173).

According to Hannah-Moffat, the 'empowering-responsibilizating strategy' leaves the state with more power and '[i]ronically, it can be argued that women are now being sent to prison, and being kept longer in prison, with the goal of empowering them!' (175).

Tied to 'empowerment', the confessional genre has also formed a central component in the ever-expanding governmental technologies of the self in modern prisons for women (see Chapters 1, 5, and 11). The preoccupation with the self has not only been unprecedented in society in general but has gained considerable attention and momentum in prison and particularly women's prisons:

> Practices of self-help are thus connected to the management and government of populations. Governing psychologized subjectivities through liberal political choice, freedom and autonomy ensures that norms of obligation, accountability and responsibility continually turn the subject back on itself. This form of political rule shifts the necessity for social responsibilities to the domain for hyper-individual responsibility (Rimke 2000, 72).

Can these new forms of therapy, treatment, and programs be 'punishment in disguise'? With the emergence and development of very sophisticated programming agendas, it appears that we cannot be critical of imprisonment or the prison system. Moreover, '[b]ecause new strategies of responsibilization seem less intrusive and less regulatory, few contest them' (Hannah-Moffat 2001, 172). However, I argue that these new technologies of the self are both intrusive and regulatory. Despite the changes in the modalities of incarceration for imprisoned women, women's bodies are still marked by incarceration. By taking the body as a pivotal concept, we will now examine how the body is subjugated by but also resists the politics of confinement.

GOVERNING BODIES

At the dawn of the twenty-first century, the *body*, both men's and women's, has increasingly become a central part of rethinking theory and practice in many disciplines, including sociology, psychology, medicine, anthropology, geography, history, law, psychiatry, and criminology.

In this section, I will explore the simultaneous construction of bodies as *sites of control* and as *sites of resistance* as well as the notions of *dangerous bodies* and *bodies in danger* in order to uncover how the (re)production of 'docile bodies' operates and is constructed, specifically in criminological knowledge and practices. The thrust of the argument is constructed around the premise that criminology and law have probed, marked, measured, explained, and treated the deviant body, and this has taken many shapes and forms in criminal justice throughout history.[10] Moreover, the concern for the 'deviant' body rests on the assumption of a 'normal' one' (Terry and Urla 1995). We will also examine more particularly how confinement marks the body, how penal laws are imprinted onto it, and how governance is achieved through it. In order to undertake this task, we will use the pivotal concept *body*[11] as a parameter in exploring gendered practices of subjection. The key power is directed at the body—it involves new 'political technologies' that shape the body (Foucault 1975b, 1977b; for a more in-depth analysis of gender, body, and imprisonment, see Frigon 2003).

This section examines the politics of confinement through various mechanisms that are deployed to govern women's bodies. The discussion will, I hope, point to the double construction of the body as a *site of control* and as a *site of resistance* (see chapter 2). The final part of the section explores women's own lived experiences of the body in prison. At the end of our journey, this discussion of the experiences of corporality will have provided you with an example of *governing women in prison through the body*.

The interplay between gendered bodies and criminology

The question of the body is an important one in criminological and penal practices but has rarely been theorized very thoroughly.[12] However, the emerging links between the body and crime—the body as a site of explanation of deviance, marginality, and criminality—emerged well before the nineteenth century. They can be traced back to the work of early philosophers (Aristotle, Plato, Montesquieu, Bossuet, Rousseau).[13] In the sixteenth and seventeenth centuries, for example, various body parts (the face, the brain) were taken as explanations for and signs of deviance and criminality. In the nineteenth century, the Darwinian debate certainly contributed to the development of an emerging field known as criminal anthropology. In this historical context, Lombroso and Ferrero (1991 [1895]) produced the anatomy of the criminal in which a whole hierarchy of the body of the criminal emerges.

We have seen with the work of Michel Foucault and others that historically, the body of the condemned was supervised, controlled, tortured, and so on (see Chapters 9 and 11). However, at the beginning of the nineteenth century, punishment-as-spectacle (see for example van Dülmen 1990) was replaced by prison, and a 'micro-physics of power' emerged. Consequently, torture was replaced, and according to Foucault (1977b, 8), 'the gloomy festival of punishment was dying out.' We witnessed '[p]unishment of a less immediately physical kind, a certain discretion in the art of inflicting pain' (1977b, 8). Again according to Foucault, 'the body as the major target of penal repression disappeared' (1977b, 8). In this logic, the body now served as an instrument. In imprisonment, confinement, penal servitude:

> the body, according to this penalty, is caught up in a system of constraints and privations, obligations and prohibitions. Physical pain, the pain of the body itself, is no longer the constituent element of the penalty. From being an art of

unbearable sensations punishment has become an economy of suspended rights (1977b, 11).

As a result, 'a whole army of technicians took over from the executioner, the immediate anatomist of pain: warders, doctors, chaplains, psychiatrists, educationalists . . . they reassure it that the body and pain are not the ultimate objects of its punitive action' (1977b, 11). I might add that all these specialists take hold of different body parts in this so-called 'non-corporal penality'. The modern rituals of execution (e.g., lethal injection in the US) also attest to this dual process: the disappearance of the spectacle and the elimination of pain.[14] Nonetheless, certain modern forms of punishment certainly concern the body itself: rationing of food, sexual deprivation, loss of freedom, corporal punishment, solitary confinement, strip searches, body cavity searches, and segregation, to name a few.

The body remains, as it were, central to the penality: 'it is always the body that is at issue—the body and its forces, their utility and their docility, their distribution and their submission' (Foucault 1977b, 25). According to Foucault, we must analyze punishment as a complex social function and as a political tactic, for the body is invested, trained, marked, and tortured. Furthermore, in this penality, the body is both a *productive* body and a *subjected* body. This is the culminating point of disciplinary normalization. In fact, bodies are thus 'malleable under power' (Grosz 1992). How is this disciplinary normalization being projected or deployed onto women's bodies? On this, Foucault and others have remained silent. But feminist scholars' contributions have been central to redefining, reshaping, and gendering the practice.[15]

Women and the embodiment of deviance

Lombroso measured, observed, and classified the female body and delivered a typology of female criminality derived from evolutionary and degeneracy theories of the second half of the nineteenth century. According to Lombroso, the female criminal was much more terrible than the male criminal because her deviance was 'double': she transgressed law, but more important, she transgressed her role as woman, wife, and mother (see Chapters 2 and 3). In fact, she was viewed as a 'monster' (Lombroso and Ferrero 1991 [1895]). In this tradition, traits of degeneracy were attributed to women's bodies. Therefore, criminal women's biological constitution was viewed as pathological, a view that helped develop typologies of offenders (for both men and women) as well as philosophies of intervention in penal institutions for women. According to Dobash et al., Maudsley appears to be the first British doctor to identify the 'normal functionings of women's bodies as a cause of insanity and deviance, arguing that normal menstruation, pregnancy and lactation could form part of a pathological condition' (Dobash et al. 1986, 113–14; see also Maudsley 1863). He then concluded that sexual deviations in women were the product of the 'irritation of the ovaries or uterus—a disease by which the chaste and modest woman is transformed into a raging fury of lust' (quoted in Dobash et al. 1986, 114). Havelock Ellis (1891), for his part, argued that women found guilty of infanticide were 'endowed with excessive down in their faces, that female thieves went grey more quickly, were uglier, and exhibited more signs of degeneracy (especially of the sexual organs) than ordinary women' (see also Zedner 1991, 337).

Understandings of women's bodies as potentially deviant bodies are important in the politics of incarceration and highlight how the body is positioned, marked, and controlled. As we will show, the body is still present as a site and target of surveillance in the ideology and politics of confinement.

Body talk: Chronicles of women's bodies in prison

Power works directly on the body because power requires knowledge of the body and behaviour in order to maintain its efficiency and stability. There are various *dispositifs*, or 'grids', that make the world intelligible to subjects and serve to control and correct the behaviour of bodies. How does confinement produce knowledge of and work to change the body? How is the body invested? How is it controlled? How does confinement (en)gender deviant female bodies? How is the body pushed to its last trench? How is the body simultaneously *dangerous* and *in danger*? How is the body simultaneously a *site of control* and a *site of resistance*? In this section, I argue that women's bodies in prison are marked and alienated, yet despite their bodies as a *site of control*, women's bodies are also a *site of resistance*.

Marking and alienating the body

At different times, in different societies, the marking of the body is achieved in a variety of ways: tattoos, genital mutilation, circumcision, aesthetic surgery, and many more. In the context of incarceration, the processing of women inmates constitutes 'degradation ceremonies' that may result in a loss of identity (Garfinkel 1956; Goffman 1961). As Hamelin notes, women (as well as men) are stripped of their identity as subjects, and the mechanisms by which this is achieved include having to undress in front of strangers, taking their showers with a disinfectant, and other such requirements (1989, 60). For Nicole, an incarcerated woman, the goal of these mechanisms is humiliation (128–9). Ève, interviewed in the context of our research, recalls that she felt that they were treated as though they were 'lepers'. For Louise, 'Sometimes, I look at myself in the mirror and I find myself frightful' (my translation).

Women also speak about the humiliation they experienced when they were subjected to strip searches and body cavity searches. These searches may be carried out when women enter prison but also throughout their entire stay in an institution. For Laurence and other women, the searches are not understood as searches for contraband substances (because they are not effective as such) but rather are geared only to humiliating the prisoner (Hamelin 1989, 130). In a study conducted with women at the Fleury-Mérogis prison in Paris, Ginsberg recounts women's feelings of humiliation when they have to show a bloody sanitary napkins during a body cavity search (1992, 148). The protecteur du citoyen (ombudsman) of the province of Quebec has said that body searches are always humiliating (Protecteur du citoyen 1985). According to many women interviewed in our research, the strip search and body cavity search are breaches of their intimacy. Ève recalls:

> Lift your breasts, spread your legs, lift your hair, open your mouth, lift your tongue . . . I hate, it's humiliating.

For Nikita, 'being naked is humiliating for me because I am fat, it's very difficult.' For Isabelle, the search is also humiliating, as she recalled when she had to go to court, 'you get undressed and you remove a sanitary napkin, you put it in a tissue, they give you another one and they watch all the time you do this, there really has to be blood in the sanitary napkin.'

The processing, the strip searches, the body cavity searches—all take part in marking the body and a mortification process that leads to a loss of status and identity. Women do not see themselves as women anymore but rather as criminals. Many women feel changed, as this testimony from an incarcerated woman shows:

> I look at myself in the mirror. I am not the same person. Now, my eyes are hard, dark; my cheeks are rounder . . . I am heavier but I look thinner. Progressively, I become a hermit. I have the colours of the prison painted on my skin. I am pale. My hair is dry and dull (Gagnon 1997, 112; my translation).

These *dispositifs* produce the political technology for the body, which creates docility, obedience, submission, and production. Crucially though, it serves to create the 'responsible prisoner'. The marking of the body leads to the alienation and even disappearance of the body. As one medical doctor stated, 'The prison works in such a way that it empties you progressively. It is the logic of incarceration to get to your skeleton' (Dr Gonin, quoted in Ginsberg 1992; my translation). Confinement is all-pervasive, extending even to the senses. This sensorial confinement is expressed by Gayle Horii, an ex-inmate at the Prison for Women, in this way: 'Grey days and black nights are the colors of precisioned function— the colors of punishment' (Horii 1994, 6). She adds:

> The fragrance of flowers, of incense, of jasmine tea, the scent of your lover's skin—all are displaced with the odour of disinfectant, of mould, of foul-smelling water and stale food, of dusty paper and institutional soap which permeates your nostrils. The only sequence is dislocation (7).

The body is also alienated because intimate relationships with other women are not tolerated. In the Fleury-Mérogis prison in Paris until 1984, lesbian women were segregated in a special unit, known as the 'tomboy unit' (Ginsberg 1992, 156; my translation). Other mechanisms are deployed that also participate in producing the alienated body. For example, the bodies of pregnant incarcerated women are perceived as inferior to law-abiding bodies:

The body of the imprisoned woman however, is not only inferior in relation to that of the 'normal body' but also in relation to the conceptualization of the 'good' woman. A positivistic, scientific view of the body denotes 'criminal' bodies as ontologically inferior to 'law' abiding bodies. Under such an ideological position, pregnant imprisoned women possess bodies that reflect a qualitative and quantitative multiplication of levels of inferiority by virtue of their criminal 'abnormality' or 'atavism' and feminine inferiority (Finateri 1999).

The victimized body

The body is also marked through sickness and victimization. Lifestyles before incarceration have often marked women's bodies: health problems, often chronic, reappear. For example, sleeping and eating disorders, medical and dental problems, social isolation, gynecological infections, and HIV/AIDS linked to prostitution and addiction are linked with the poverty and marginalization that many of these women have experienced. Whatever illnesses women had before are often exacerbated by confinement (Robert, Frigon, and Belzile, forthcoming). As well, various psychosomatic illnesses tend to appear among female prisoners, often tied to the stresses of trials, incarceration, children, intimate relationships, and financial difficulties. These illnesses may include insomnia, hypertension, headaches, skin rashes, hair loss, vertigo, and vision problems as well as anorexia or bulimia (Ginsberg 1992, 118). For women who have to share a toilet with their cell-mate, serious, often chronic constipation problems occur. According to *Creating choices*, imprisoned women feel that they have lost their control over their own bodies and do not have access to essential medical advice and medication (Correctional Service of Canada 1990).

For many women, the victimization they experience in prison is an extension of the victimization they experienced 'on the outside'. Many women have histories of abuse before they enter prison. According to *Creating choices*, between 60 to 90 per cent of federally sentenced women had been abused at one time in their lives or even throughout their lives (i.e., sexual abuse, incest, domestic violence). For some, this abuse is linked to racism, sexism, and economic marginalization. And for many, the prison system reproduces and perpetuates the violence. This institutionalized violence (Faith 1993; *Journal of Prisoners on Prison* 1994) highlights how *victimization* might be linked to the process of *criminalization*.[16]

Remarkably, it is possible to encounter women for whom incarceration becomes a time to reconstruct themselves physically and mentally. Some recall that they are now in a position to eat three meals a day, sleep, and receive medical attention while being protected from the abuse outside (e.g., domestic violence or pimps' violence) as well as from economic and racial marginalization. That incarceration itself may be seen as a welcome reprieve is strong evidence of the systematic degradation experienced by many of these women before they were incarcerated.

The resistant/subversive body

Bodies may also *struggle against* surveillance and victimization. Women deploy various strategies, particularly tied to the body and body image, as a means of resisting. These resistance strategies may include make-up, clothes, tattoos, body-piercing, exercise, intimate relations, eating, or starvation. They may, of course, also be damaging to the incarcerated (or non-incarcerated) body. For example, self-mutilation occurs at a higher rate in women's prisons than in men's. Men in general direct their anger at others, while women turn it on themselves.[17] In 1979 an Ontario study conducted with provincially sentenced women found that 86 per cent of the women had mutilated themselves (Ross and McKay 1979, cited in Faith 1993, 243). Ten years later, Jan Heney (1990) conducted interviews with 44 federally sentenced women: 59 per cent had mutilated themselves and 92 per cent had cut their veins, while others had struck their heads or burned themselves.

For certain women, this is a way to mark their bodies, to reclaim control. That is, the women decide when to slash, where to slash, when to stop, and how far they go, in contrast to the lack of control they experience while incarcerated. According to Heney (1993), self-mutilation may be a survival strategy. Pollack (1993) considers that it can be a strategy to separate oneself from one's body, to dissociate the body from the spirit. For one indigenous woman:

> It is no wonder that so many of us cut our throats, lacerate our bodies, hang ourselves. It is no wonder that we need to identify our pain onto our physical bodies because our whole lives have been filled with incredible pain and traumatizing experiences—psychic pain, physical pain, spiritual pain (Ms Cree 1994).

Other female prisoners articulate how the frustration brought on by the restraints of confinement may also pave the way to self-mutilation and produce in return a sense of relief:

> I remember how they cut my temporary absence because my papers were badly done. The system had 'fucked up'. I worked so hard for this to happen, to get there, and they tell me this before Christmas. My son tells me, 'I thought you were my Christmas gift?' I went crazy. I went to my cell. I had to do something. I had rage inside of me. It had to come out. There was too much pain inside and I cut myself open for the first time. It felt like 'whoosh', like a 'release', as if I had released the tension inside of me. It scared me because it felt like such a good 'release' (Sara).

> I was in my cell, my razor was still there. It was razor day. I took my razor and I cut myself open (Lyne).

> I did it with a can of pop . . . I was angry with my mother because my mother does not love me (Eve).

In this process of self-destruction or self-injury, many women literally recount their lives with the traces of lacerations. Each laceration tells a story of isolation, desperation, and loneliness related to being separated from the children, missing their first day of school, grieving the death of a mother, or being in prison at Christmas. This behaviour illustrates to what extent women feel powerless, and their powerlessness reduces them to feel 'alive' through self-injurious behaviour.

However, women have other strategies to make them feel 'alive' and reconstruct a sense of self and a form of resistance to carceral logic and structure that helps them to self-govern or empower themselves. Through art and creativity, women unmask the link between their oppression and their bodies. During workshops in prison, women create masks, drawings, sculptures, pottery, and poetry. The Prison Arts Foundation encourages the personal development of convicted offenders through their involvement in arts. For example, with the support of the institution and Correctional Service of Canada, women prisoners in the Joliette facility in Quebec created a comic book to help demystify the issues of HIV and AIDS. Published in 2000, this comic book entitled *From darkness to light* illustrates the potential of growth through expression. At la Maison Tanguay in Montreal, choreographer Claire Jenny from the dance company Point Virgule in Paris designed and animated 50 hours of dance workshops with four incarcerated women, which culminated in a public presentation in the prison on 18 October 2004. More than a decade earlier, Claire Jenny had begun offering workshops for women prisoners in France.

Their sufferings, desires, alienation, and pleasures are 'engraved' on their bodies[18] and mediated through their multiple creative works (drawings, writings, theatre, dance) within the few interstices of freedom.

Women's bodies are then at times marked, alienated, sickened, victimized, and mutilated in prison. But they also resist. Thus to the body as a *site of control* is juxtaposed a body as *a site of resistance*. This exploration of the female confined body has been inspired by governmentality literature in the sense that it allows for a more complex reading of the interrelations between state power and other modalities of governance, multiple expressions of the regulation of citizens in prison.

BACK TO THE FUTURE?

Despite more humanistic discourses, task forces, new rationalities, architectural designs, and increased funding,[19] a prison remains a prison. And despite recent changes in detention practices, notably those stimulated by concerns over human rights and the needs of prisoners, the carceral institution still needs and produces docile bodies. Many difficulties remain (Martel 1999; Hannah-Moffat and Shaw 2000; Frigon 2000, 2001, 2002). Among the difficulties are the continuing high levels of suicide and self-destruction behaviours in both provincial and federal institutions, gaps in employment programs (Frigon, Strimelle, and Renière 2003), relations with children, the recourse to segregation and enhanced units, the erosion of indigenous principles in the governance of the Healing Lodge, the question of health in prison (Robert, Belzile, and Frigon, forthcoming; Robert and Frigon, in press) and community programming yet to be deployed. The 2003 report of the Auditor General of Canada revealed that further challenges remain. The concerns highlighted by the Auditor General centred around several issues, including classification instuments, case management, substance abuse programming, release mechanisms, employment training, accommodations, and community programs (Squires 2004, 7–8). The same year, the Canadian Human Rights Commission presented a critique of the situation of federally sentenced women, and in February 2004 a complaint of discrimination was filed with the commission.

Moreover, there may be a reconfiguration of the penal logic, but it maintains the same focus: on control. The control appears to be 'softer', but it remains nonetheless and is all the more powerful because of its diffusion. During our visits to Joliette and Kitchener in the winter of 2001, we were struck by the transformations in the space, the language, and the appearance. The *space* of punishment had been transformed, with small houses surrounded by lawns and gardens. The *face* of punishment had undergone a major lift: the guards are no longer 'correctional officers' but 'primary care workers'. They do not wear official correctional suits.[20] These cosmetic transformations have been accompanied by deeper changes, as we have seen, in terms of programs and philosophies. 'Custody by relationships' has replaced 'static security' rationalities. While we welcome some of these changes, the institution remains and its logic and mechanisms are not questioned. We join Kelly Hannah-Moffat in her caution:

> well-intentioned benevolent efforts to improve the conditions for women prisoners and to create a penal regime that addresses historically specific understandings of women's needs reproduces and obscures complex and ambiguous relations of power, and further, that prisons are remarkably flexible institutions that absorb, adapt, and accommodate a variety of competing and sometimes contradictory rationalities (2001, 5).

Questions to Consider

1. *Creating choices* was pivotal in the transformation of the penal regime for federally sentenced women in Canada. Present the recommendations and changes that occurred since 1990.
2. Name some of the challenges and/or difficulties remaining post-*Creating choices*.
3. How is the body central to the criminal justice system, both in the past and in the present?
4. How are women's bodies potentially deviant bodies and translated in the politics of incarceration?
5. How can women's bodies in prison be simultaneously sites of control and sites of resistance? Illustrate.

Notes

1. Referring to two titles: Berzins and Carrière (1979); Adelberg and Currie (1987).
2. Danielle Laberge (1991) has rightly pointed out that it can be misleading to rely solely on percentage increase given the relatively small absolute numbers of offenders referred to. For example, a 100 per cent increase may reflect an increase from five to 10 inmates.
3. For a discussion of self-injurious behaviour among Aboriginal women, see Dell (2001).

4. It is worth mentioning that according to various actors in the correctional services, statistics on suicide attempts and self-mutilation are not available for the new regional facilities.

5. For some overall critiques of *Creating choices*, see most notably Hannah-Moffat and Shaw (2000); Frigon (2002; 2003; 2005).

6. The new regional facilities are: Okimaw Ohci Healing Lodge for indigenous women in Maple Creek, SK; Nova Institution in Truro, NS; Edmonton Institution for Women in Edmonton, AB; Grand Valley Institution in Kitchener, ON; Joliette Institution in Joliette, QC; and Fraser Valley Institution in Abbotsford, BC.

7. As early as 1938, the Archambault Royal Commission recommended the closure of P4W. For a history of *Creating choices*, see Hannah-Moffat (2001); Robert and Frigon (in press).

8. For example, between April and December 1996, when la Maison Tanguay (a provincial prison in Montreal) still housed federally sentenced women, there were 2,031 admissions. The number of women incarcerated in this institution has not decreased. In fact, in 1998–9 there were 1,849 admissions even though federally sentenced women were no longer incarcerated there. During the same period, the facility housed approximately 120 women on any given day. In the fall of 2005, information from la Maison Tanguay indicated that 180 women were incarcerated there on any given day.

9. In fact, the initial vision embraced during the work of the group would be transformed by changes in the guiding principles and goals. For example, it has been reported anecdotally that various people adopting a more critical approach or even an abolitionist approach were dismissed from the group. Moreover, given the various difficulties experienced during the implementation phase in Edmonton, for example (Watson 2004, 4), the new regional facilities' security parameters were highlighted. Finally, *Creating choices* was originally designed to aim strongly at community strategy, which had just begun to take shape in 2002, at least on paper.

10. For a historical look, see for example Conrad and Schneider (1992). One can think of past practices such as lobotomies, massive electric shock therapy, castration, and witchburning, to name a few, and more recent practices such as electronic monitoring, chemical treatment of deviance through pharmacology, and profiling.

11. I will refer to the 'body' in the singular form since we are referring to a pivotal concept, but it should be noted that the term is meant to cover many different bodies.

12. For notable exceptions, see Foucault (1975b; 1977b) and Feinman (1992) on the criminalization of motherhood (abortion, pregnancy, contract motherhood, and maternity); Labadie (1995) on the history of the emergence of the body in criminology; Frigon (1995) for a genealogy of the representations of women as embodying deviance and criminality; Frigon and Kérisit (2000) on the construction of 'deviant' female bodies in various disciplines, including history, sociology, criminology, social work, and psychiatry; and Frigon (2001; 2002; 2003) on the control and resistance of women through their bodies in a prison setting.

13. See Michel Porret (1998) for a discussion of these early conceptualizations of the body.

14. This ethic of sobriety in punishment and execution is sometimes breached. The media attention around the execution of Karla Fay Tucker on 3 February 1998 in Texas is a case in point.

15. See for example Bartky (1990); Bordo (1993); Butler (1993); Beausoleil (1994); Frigon and Kérisit (2000). More specifically in the field of criminology, see Ginsberg (1992);

Faith (1993); Howe (1994); Frigon (1994; 1996; 1999; and 2000).

16. On this issue, it is interesting to note the major conference organized by the Canadian Association of Elizabeth Fry Societies and the Canadian Association of Sexual Assault Centres, 'Women's Resistance: From Victimization to Criminalization', Ottawa, 1–3 October 2001.

17. This is well-documented. See for example Faith (1993) and Kendall (1993).

18. See for example the sculptures created by Gayle Horii, which use the body as a medium to address women's oppression (*Journal of Prisoners on Prison* 1994).

19. It is worth noting that it costs a minimum of $150,000 annually for each woman incarcerated in a new regional facility.

20. At the time of writing, this policy was under review.

Chapter 15

What Is Sovereignty for Indigenous People?

Patricia Monture

INTRODUCTION

First Nations made agreements with settlers about sharing the land. These agreements are recorded in both the oral history and the Western written historical record. Primarily in the prairie region (Alberta, Saskatchewan, and Manitoba) but also covering significant parts of Ontario and extending into the Northwest Territories and British Columbia, the agreements are known as the numbered treaties (from one to 11). They were signed over a 50-year period commencing in 1871 and ending in 1921, and—in view of the time frame—are often referred to as post-Confederation treaties (Brown and Maquire 1979; Burrell et al. 1975). It is important to study these agreements because they provide a way to understand the laws and governance structures of First Nations while remembering that 'change is constant and diversity is everywhere within First Nations and dominant culture communities' (LeBaron 2004, 13). Acknowledging the diversity of First Nations means understanding that the concept of indigenous sovereignty is not homogeneous but entails a multiplicity of sovereignties.

An analysis of indigenous sovereignties often begins with a discussion of the 1982 repatriation of Canada's constitution and the inclusion of section 35(1). Section 35(1) is the most comprehensive recognition of indigenous sovereignty included in the repatriation, and it 'recognizes and affirms' the 'existing' Aboriginal and treaty rights of the Aboriginal peoples of Canada. Political science scholar Kiera Ladner (Cree) explains the trouble with this approach:

> By most accounts, Aboriginal peoples became interested in federalism circa 1982 when they became uninvited participants in Canada's constitution process. Canada's constitutional orthodoxy typically portrays Aboriginal peoples as 'constitutional outsiders' who became participants in Canadian federalism and modern constitutionalism as a result of the emergence of 'charter politics' or 'constitutional minoritarianism' (2003, 167).

Ladner argues that this view of federalism is bound to the idea that Canada comprises the provinces, the territories, and the federal government exclusively. Consequently, Aboriginal peoples are typically ignored by those who study Canadian federalism. She points out that the problem with constitutional orthodoxy and reliance on Canada's 'official history' ignores the fact that the history of federalism on this continent predates European arrival on the shores of the Americas (2003, 167–9). For this reason, the constitutional events of 1982 and the protection of Aboriginal and treaty rights in section 35(1) of Canada's constitution are not the focus of this chapter. Rather, it approaches indigenous sovereignties in an historical way that respects the length of the relationship between Canada and First Peoples.

The numbered treaties are just one example of the agreements between Onkwehon:we ('indigenous peoples' in the language of the Kanien'kehaka—the Mohawk) and the Crown in the territory that is now known as Canada. Across the country, the agreements entered into did not only or always involve land. In the east, the focus was most often on peace and friendship. Treaty-making in Canada follows the pattern of colonial settlement from east to west, with the earliest agreements having been signed in the east. It should also be remembered that not all First Nations have signed treaty agreements with the Crown.[1] Treaties are not just historical documents: in British Columbia, modern-day treaty negotiation talks have been only recently established.

At the time of signing the treaties, the Crown recognized that indigenous peoples had the right to negotiate agreements with other nations, including both the settler governments and other indigenous nations (Ladner 2003, 175–8). This constituted an express recognition of indigenous sovereignty(ies), which is to acknowledgement that First Nations had their own distinctive laws, governance structures, and social orders. Thus treaties were not the source of First Nations governance authorities. First Nations already held these rights and responsibilities at the time of treaty signing. As Ladner explains:

> the treaty was an agreement between two independent powers that recognized the autonomy of each nation and the ability of each to determine their political status vis-à-vis the other. It was an agreement that 'created shared responsibilities rather than supreme powers' (i.e., neither government was subordinate to the other), shared as well as exclusive territories (i.e., reserves) and two classes of 'British subjects' (2003, 178).

This understanding of the treaty sees the Crown's rights as derivative and acknowledges that any right not delegated by First Nations remains with them.

Aboriginal title and Aboriginal rights (including treaty rights) are Creator-given rights, as the Elders of many nations have explained. Detailed understandings of the authority to govern First Nations can only be gained by studying specific First Nations such as the Nehiowè (Cree), Kanien'kehaka (Mohawk), Dene or Anishnabe (Ojibwe), and so on. Speaking of the Nehiowè traditions of Treaty Six, the late Harold Cardinal (Cree) and Walter Hildebrandt explain:

> '*Miyo-wîcêhtowin*' is a Cree word meaning 'having or possessing good relations'. It is a concept that arises from one of the core doctrines or values of the

Cree nation. The term outlines the nature of relationships that Cree peoples are required to establish. It asks, directs, admonishes, or requires Cree peoples as individuals and as a nation to conduct themselves in a manner such that they create positive or good relations in all relationships, be it individually or collectively with other peoples. '*Miyo-wîcêhtowin*' as a concept and a term originates in the laws and relationships that their nation has with the Creator (2000, 14).

Miyo-wîcêhtowin is just one example of the laws governing the conduct of Nehiowè people, and it is common to a number of First Nations. Haudenosaunee (Iroquois) people are taught about the 'great law of peace' or the 'ways to most live most nicely together' (Monture-Angus 1995, 1999). Anishnabe (Ojibwe) people are taught about the principles of the 'good life'. These teachings influence the ways in which indigenous peoples understand the meaning of sovereignty (Benton Banai 1979; Solomon 1990). In their 2005 report on the recognition and implementation of First Nations governments, the Assembly of First Nations affirmed this position on the nature of indigenous sovereignties when they wrote:

> In many First Nations languages, the concept of government means 'our way of life' or simply 'our life'. There are differences in First Nation and non-Aboriginal understandings of the concept of government. While some Canadians tend to see government as remote, divorced from the people and everyday life, First Nations people generally view government in a more holistic way, as inseparable from the totality of communal practices that make up a way of life. Unlike non-Aboriginal governments, First Nation governments involve relationships between families, clans and tribes rather than a relationship of strangers governing strangers (34).

Approaching the study of indigenous sovereignty from the treaty paradigm allows one to highlight several important issues. From the standpoint of indigenous knowledge, all parties to a treaty are assumed to have prior rights. This means that it is not just First Nations who have treaty rights and responsibilities. Various Crowns, including the British, Dutch, French, and Canadian, as well as the United States government, were also a party to those treaties and were accorded both rights and obligations under various treaties. This means that non-indigenous people, who follow the Crown, also have treaty rights. It is important to examine why we only hear about First Nations having treaty rights. We mostly hear about First Nations fighting for those rights, especially hunting and fishing rights. If you were to research the rights of non-indigenous people under a given treaty, you would probably not find a single article in the library. If nothing else, this demonstrates the degree to which power is an essential variable in the analysis of both historical and present-day First Nations relationships with the Crown and its citizens.

Let us take an example. In the case of Treaty Six, non-indigenous people have the right to share the land up to the depth of a plow (about six inches) (Cardinal and Hildebrandt 2000). Hence, non-First Nations have the right to their own agricultural practices. As well, non-indigenous people would also have the right to their government, language, and religious and educational practices. It is of course revealing that we do not hear about non-indigenous peoples fighting to exercise these rights (or more important, fighting to demonstrate that they possess them). This is because non-indigenous peoples exercise those rights every day, as easily as they breathe. Non-indigenous people do not even have to be aware that they have those rights in order to exercise them. Furthermore, why do students studying Treaty Six (or any other treaty territory, I suspect) come to their university classes without any background in this topic? And what does the discipline of sociology have to offer in the political, legal, social, and economic debates about indigenous sovereignty, including reconciliation with the state?

The study of Aboriginal nations in the discipline of sociology is a relatively new phenomenon. In 1974 James S. Frideres published a book titled *Canada's Indians: Contemporary conflicts*. It was followed by the work of Rick Ponting and Roger Gibbins in 1980. Much of the early work in sociology focused on one of the following ideas or concepts: demography, Aboriginal persons and nations as 'issues', social conflict, deviance, or race and ethnicity (including the study of discrimination). As Vic Satzewich and Terry Wotherspoon conclude:

> Somewhat ironically, Canadian sociologists have not kept pace with these other disciplines in the study of aboriginal peoples. While there was a flurry of sociological and anthropological studies of aboriginal peoples in the early 1970s, particularly in the context of Indian urbanization, the issue of aboriginal/non-aboriginal relations has been placed on the so-called 'backburner' by sociologists (1993, xii).

These categorizations have unfortunately limited the knowledge base of sociologists interested in understanding the relationship between Canada and First Peoples (see Agocs 2000; Steckley 2003). Writing in 1981, anthropologist John A. Price noted that he was critical of sociologists' practice of placing their knowledge of indigenous peoples within the sub-discipline of ethnic studies rather than creating a new sub-discipline of 'North American Indian sociology' (1981, 353).

As sociologists (both students and scholars) begin to consider the idea of an indigenous sociology, several important factors should be considered. First, in the preceding passage, all of the scholars cited (and this is representative of the authors who completed the early work) are men with the exception of Carol Agocs (a feminist and political scientist). But sovereign traditions among First Nations do not necessary reflect the same gendering of society that we are accustomed to studying in university. Second, it is not that such issues as discrimination, social conflict, and the overrepresentation of Aboriginal persons in the criminal justice system are not important to consider—they are. It is just that the approaches usually adopted are insufficient. These approaches have tended to view Aboriginal peoples as 'social problems' (Steckley 2003). They cast their gaze at individual explanations, not structural ones. As Frideres explains:

> For too long, social scientists have viewed Aboriginal-White relations through
> a micro model, focusing exclusively on individual actions, e.g., prejudice and
> discrimination. Not surprisingly, these models see solutions to the problems
> Aboriginal people face as being brought about through individual action, e.g.,
> individual enhancement and individual entrepreneurship. We wish to
> approach the problem from a different perspective—structural (1998, 2).

Without discussions and developing understandings of indigenous sovereignty
and governance, the studies cannot reflect who and what Aboriginal persons
believe they are.

We can expect that the recent inclusion of indigenous scholars in the field of
sociology in Canada will change the way in which Aboriginal nations are studied
within the discipline. It is important to note that until four decades ago, Indians
who earned university degrees were forced to give up their status under the Indian
Act. This in part explains why indigenous scholars only began to enter academia
as faculty members in the late 1980s. Of course, poverty among First Nations people and lack of success in educational systems (especially since the first exposure
to formal education often came in residential or industrial schools) have also had
a profound impact on the ability of First Nations peoples to succeed in the university setting. The result is indisputable: no 'Native sociology' has yet to emerge
(Steckley 2003)

CHALLENGING MYTHS, STEREOTYPES, AND DISCRIMINATION

A number of myths and stereotypes about Aboriginal people must be corrected
before we can engage in a discussion about indigenous sovereignties. Most people
are now aware of the historical stereotyping that cast Aboriginal peoples as less
civilized and less intelligent and their societies as less advanced. Historian John
Tobias has studied the colonization of the Plains Cree and provides this example
of how stereotypes of inferiority provided justification for the actions taken
against the Cree nation by the Crown:

> The Plains Indians, and particularly the Plains Cree, are said to be a primitive
> people adhering to an inflexible system of traditions and customs, seeking to
> protect themselves against the advance of civilization, and taking up arms in
> rejection of the reserve system and an agricultural way of life. This traditional
> interpretation distorts the roles of both the Cree and the Canadian govern-
> ment, for the Cree were both flexible and active in promoting their own inter-
> ests, and willing to accommodate themselves to a new way of life, while the
> Canadian government was neither as far-sighted nor as just as tradition main-
> tains. Canada's principal concern in the relationship with the Plains Cree was
> to establish control over them, and Canadian authorities were willing to and
> did wage war upon the Cree in order to achieve this control (1998, 150).

Both pronouncing and perpetuating stereotypes, as well as acting on those stereotypes, requires power over those stereotyped. In this discussion, it is important to

note that 'power is always a factor that shapes whose cultural values are seen as legitimate, whose values are accommodated and how' (LeBaron 2004, 14).

Many people do not acknowledge how stereotypes have evolved and remain embedded in Canadian society. For this reason, the past is not the past (see Chapter 8). One current example of the problem with embedded stereotypes can be found in common political discourse, fed by both the media and conservative ideologues. Consider the view on the part of one segment of the population that the special rights of Aboriginal peoples are an affront to Canadian unity (Cairns 2000). However, these so-called special rights are entrenched in Canada's constitution (hence making them 'merely' constitutional rights, similar to the distinct rights held by francophones). Thus this view is a denigration of the constitutional rights held by Aboriginal nations and people. Such political stereotyping follows patterns common through all historical periods, particularly when it comes to inferiorizing anything indigenous.

The Elders teach that one has to know where one has come from to know where one is going (Solomon 1990). Historian Ken Coates notes that

> Canadians have gradually, and grudgingly, come to accept that the First Nations occupied the land now known as Canada as much as 15,000 years ago and that a series of complex, sophisticated societies lived in the area for thousands of years. Only thirty years ago, the prevailing image was less favourable, suggesting that a tiny population of Indigenous people scratched out a meager living in a land that Europeans would subsequently prove to be rich in potential. This image served the interests of the dominant society very well, for it justified a history of conquest, occupation, and land confiscation; it also 'explained' the relative inability of First Nations people to join the Canadian economic and social mainstream. First Nations, though battered by decades of assimilationist programming, resented the unflattering portrait and struggled to highlight the richness and diversity of the Indigenous experience. Gradually, the message was heard, at least in part (1999, 142).

The prevalence of stereotypes rather than the development of knowledge about indigenous understandings of sovereignty and developing intercultural competencies emphasizes the degree to which power has been a key variable in governance relations between First Nations and the Crown (LeBaron 2004).

The first of these embedded stereotypes is the problem of naming Aboriginal persons and nations. The Canadian constitution names the Aboriginal peoples of Canada as the 'Indian, Inuit and Métis'. No further definitions are found in the constitution. To this list we can add the names 'Native' or 'Native peoples', 'First Nations', and 'indigenous peoples'. The major problem with each of these names is that it collapses all Aboriginal peoples into a single category and creates a stereotype of sameness. In fact, Aboriginal nations are diverse groupings with unique languages, cultures, traditions, institutions (including governing structures), and laws. Since these names all result from colonial imposition, none of them is a good choice for referring to Aboriginal persons and nations.

Each of the names that has been applied to Aboriginal nations and persons is part of the colonial process. As I explained elsewhere:

> I tell this story about naming because it is symbolic. Growing up 'Indian' in this country is very much about not having the power to define yourself or your reality. It is being denied the right to say, 'I am!'—instead, always finding yourself saying, 'I am not!' (Monture-Angus 1995, 3).

The stereotypes, both historical and present-day, have profound impacts on Aboriginal persons, and it is important to acknowledge this in any sociological analysis.

The naming conundrum may be answered by deferring to Canada's constitution and adopting the term 'Aboriginal peoples'. 'Indigenous peoples' is the term generally used when the focus is international, and it is used in this chapter to refer to all persons of Aboriginal ancestry who reside around the globe. Most often, this chapter uses the term 'First Nations' instead of 'Indian'. However, 'Indian' is used when the reference is to the Indian Act, which applies only to those persons entitled to be registered (also called 'status' Indians).

The second of these embedded stereotypes is the idea that real 'Indians' come from reserves. Reserves, however, are not a good 'Indian' idea but rather a result of Canadian laws and the imposition of the Indian Act. Reserves are a colonial idea, intended to separate 'Indians' from the rest of society. Reserves have also had an internal impact on indigenous nations in that the communities' small size and defined membership, coupled with the inability to easily transfer membership from reserve to reserve, frustrates the ability of indigenous citizens to participate in the nation as a nation and not just a small community called a reserve. The reserve policy was justified through paternalism or the belief that assimilation was the best policy. Paternal ideas suggested that 'Indians' needed the protection of the state until such time as they were able to fit into the larger society growing around them. For 'Indian' people, it is much more accurate to think in terms of the territories that First Nations, Métis, and Inuit occupied. Hence, one thinks in terms of Nehiowè territory, Kanien'kehaka territory, Mi'kmaq territory, and so on.

The early belief was that Aboriginal persons in the prairies were nomadic, hunters and gathers, simple agriculturalists—or simply inferior to settlers. These ideas have been demonstrated to be false. The people who used to be thought of as inhabiting territory in a nomadic fashion are now known to have occupied those territories through their vast knowledge of seasonal and animal life cycles. Indeed, the advanced agricultural practices of many First Nations are only now being discovered. For example, Haudenosaunee women grew corn, beans, and squash in a mound. Today we understand that growing these three plants together, known to the Haudenosaunee as the three sisters, contributes to a balanced soil. Historical records have overemphasized male roles in providing sustenance for the people, often in tales of the big game hunters. More recently, the contributions of indigenous women to the people's sustenance by hunting small animals, harvesting, and agriculture have been acknowledged (Carter 1990, 28, 176–80; Peers 1996, 39–50).

The problem of stereotypes must be understood from within a much larger paradigm. Not only do stereotypes lead to both prejudice and discrimination but they are cumulatively part of a larger process known as colonialism. Colonization entails a series of complex process and actions that begins with a forced intrusion into the territories of indigenous peoples, quickly followed by land takeover. This in turn is followed by actions that deny the validity of the political, economic, legal, and religious systems of First Peoples. Later stages of the process include attacks on indigenous languages and denials of indigenous legal systems, social structures (including educational systems), and cultural beliefs and practices. The end product is dependency in multiple forms (Frideres 1998, 3–5). Writing on the impact of colonialism on present-day Aboriginal lives, I have noted:

> As I struggled with the pain in my life and in the lives of those I am close to, I became more and more determined to understand the process of colonialism and colonization. If colonialism brought our nations to this point, then undoing the damage of colonialism must be the answer. I now understand this thinking to be much too linear . . . to be helpful. It is not just the colonial relations that must be undone but all of the consequences (addictions, loss of language, loss of parenting skills, loss of self-respect, abuse and violence, and so on). Colonialism is no longer a linear, vertical relationship—colonizer does to colonized—it is a horizontal and entangled relationship (like a spider web) (Monture-Angus 1999, 10–11).

Gender has often been the vehicle by which colonial strategies have been delivered upon First Nations (Jaimes 1992, 11; Acoose 1995, 56). For instance, another historical misinterpretation is the view that First Nations women were servants of their men and indeed 'drudges' (Acoose 1995, 39). Janice Acoose (Nehiowè-Métis and Nahkawè) wrote:

> Moreover, the women in my family fit none of the white stereotypes of Indigenous women. As extremely powerful, resourceful, and dynamic women who vitally contributed to the survival of my family, communities, and nations (1995, 11).

Stereotypes of indigenous women rooted in the larger practice of 'inferiorizing' all things indigenous continue to have devastating consequences. In 1991 the Aboriginal Justice Inquiry of Manitoba concluded that the murder of Helen Betty Osborne was based on both race and gender. Commissioners Hamilton and Sinclair wrote:

> It is clear that Betty Osborne would not have been killed if she had not been Aboriginal. The four men who took her to her death from the streets of The Pas that night had gone looking for an Aboriginal girl with whom to 'party.' They found Betty Osborne. When she refused to party she was driven out of town and murdered. Those who abducted her showed a total lack of regard for her

person or her rights as an individual. Those who stood by while the physical assault took place, while sexual advances were made and while she was being beaten to death showed their own racism, sexism and indifference. Those who knew the story and remained silent must share their guilt (1991, 98).

More recently, the Sisters in Spirit Campaign launched by the Native Women's Association of Canada has estimated that 500 Aboriginal women in this country are missing and murdered (2005). Amnesty International examined this situation and in a report titled *Stolen sisters* concluded that 'this intersection of sexism and racism contributes to the assumption on the part of perpetrators of violence against indigenous women that their actions are justifiable or condoned by society' (2004, 17). Gender discrimination, both historical and current, has an enormous impact on the lives of Aboriginal women and interferes with our abilities to live in a sovereign way.

Understanding sovereignty from the position of indigenous people requires the ambitious challenging of history's misinterpretations and the stereotypes about indigenous nations and their citizens that have become embedded in what we think is objective or neutral knowledges. This challenging can be an unsettling experience for both indigenous people and the descendants of the settler nations. Indigenous people must confront an often-traumatic past (Thomas 2005, 238), while the descendants of settlers must confront both guilt and disbelief.

SOCIOLOGICAL UNDERSTANDINGS OF INDIGENOUS SOVEREIGNTY

Contrary to common belief, indigenous peoples have had a significant influence on the social structures of the world. In introducing his book *Forgotten founders: How the American Indian helped shape democracy*, Johansen, a former journalist, writes of first learning about the influence of the Iroquois on the evolution of American democracy and constitutionalism from a student at Evergreen State College in Washington:

> The idea struck me as disingenuous. I considered myself decently educated in American history, and to the best of my knowledge, government for and by the people had been invented by white men in powdered wigs. I asked the young woman where she had come by her information. 'My grandmother told me,' she said. That was hardly the kind of source I could use for a newspaper story. I asked whether she knew of any other sources. 'You're the investigative reporter,' she said. 'You find them' (1982, xi–xii).

The issue is not that indigenous ideas have not had influence; it is that the source of those ideas has not been accurately credited (see also Venables 1992, 77–8; Thornton 1998, 91–4). This can be said not only about the agricultural practices of First Nations but also about the influence of indigenous thinking on the ideas of Marx and Engels (see Engels 1972, 734).

The influence of the Haudenosaunee (Iroquois) on Karl Marx and Friedrich

Engels is particularly worthy of further comment. It originated with Lewis Henry Morgan, an anthropologist who was a close friend of Ely Parker, a Seneca (one of the six Iroquoian nations). His first book was about the Iroquois (1851), followed by *Ancient society* (1985), which Karl Marx read. The Iroquois intrigued Marx because of their democratic political organization and the way that they achieved economic equality without coercion. After Marx's death, Engels received his notes on Morgan's work and subsequently wrote his well-received essay on family, private property, and the state (Johansen 1982, 122). Engels described the Iroquoian state in this way:

> Everything runs smoothly without soldiers, gendarmes, or police, without nobles, kings, governors, prefects or judges; without prisons, without trials. All quarrels and disputes are settled by the whole body of those concerned. . . . The household is run communistically by a number of families; the land is tribal property, only the small gardens being temporarily assigned to the households—still, not a bit of our extensive and complicated machinery of administration is required. . . . There are no poor and needy. The communistic household and the gens know their responsibility toward the aged, the sick and the disabled in war. All are free and equal—including the women (cited in Johansen 1982, 123).

Despite the influence on these founding fathers of sociology, the relationship between First Nations and Western intellectual traditions receded into the background. This is a common pattern: indigenous practices—their foods, their intellectual traditions, even images appropriated as 'team mascots' by the colonizing nations (Weatherford 1988)—have their origins denied.

Sociological study soon focused on industrialized societies, and the study of 'primitive' societies was left to anthropology (Thornton 1998, 92). As time passed, academic boundaries continued to be drawn without indigenous influence. These boundaries began to be challenged as the numbers of indigenous students attending post-secondary institutions increased in the 1970s, a trend that continues today (Thornton 1998, 87). The demands of indigenous students on Canadian academia led to the development of a number of Native studies programs across the country (Price 1981, 354). For sociologists, the demand led to the development of some issues-based courses such as 'Native peoples in urban areas' and 'Native peoples and social welfare'. As indigenous sociologists joined the faculty ranks in Canada (of whom I now count six), courses that examine the nature of indigenous justice systems, institutional racism, collective questions of identity, and the structure of First Nations governance traditions are being formed. Students of sociology will soon have greater opportunity to access indigenous understandings of the world, including indigenous sovereignties.

What we know as sociologists about indigenous sovereignties is limited not only by the history of our discipline but by other significant factors as well. Language sets the parameters through which humans amass knowledge, and language is bound by culture (Sapir 1929, 1949; Whorf 1956). Post-modernists point to the multiple ways in which language can be used to silence the voices of those whose lives are located at the margins (Kovach 2005, 25; Meyer 2001). In order to examine the definitions of sovereignty without being ethnocentric, it is important to consider the different structure of indigenous languages. Leroy Little Bear (Blood of the Blackfoot Confederacy) explains:

> It can be generally said that Euro-languages such as English are very noun-oriented. English is a good language for dichotomies, categorizations, and reductionist specificity. In its dichotomy mode, it manifests polarized, binary thinking: good and bad; saint and sinner; black and white; old and new; and so on. Aboriginal languages generally can be said to be action-oriented. Everything is about process, actions, happenings. It can be said that constant flux manifests itself in the language. The noun-orientation of English and the action-orientation of Aboriginal languages have led to different relational expectations, especially as regards relationships to land and treaty making (2005, 29).

The differences in the structure of the languages of indigenous peoples and Europeans reflect the differences in the way people think about themselves in the world (Cajete 1999). Language is an excellent position from which to contemplate difference.

Care must be taken with language and concepts discussed only in English since they may not mean the same thing across cultures—and sovereignty (also referred to as self-government or self-determination) is just one example. Again, this emphasizes the need to consider power:

> When Aboriginal Peoples discuss the meaning of self-government and/or self-determination, we are forced to do it in a language that is not our own. We must express our ideas in English or in French, both of which epitomize our colonial experiences. It is almost solely Aboriginal energy that fosters the accommodations that are required to carry on both the political and legal dialogues in either of the Canadian colonial languages. This is a particular experience of colonial oppression. At the same time, the languages that were brought to our territories have benefited Aboriginal people, as we are able to more fully share our ideas beyond Indigenous boundaries (Monture Angus 1999, 22).

Not all indigenous scholars agree (Alfred 1999, 55–60) on the best language to use from the list of possibilities, which includes self-government, self-determination, First Nations governance, or indigenous sovereignty. My preference is for a governance structure that provides First Nations with the opportunity for economic, social, legal, and spiritual independence. Choosing 'sovereignty' as the word to describe the goal prevents further degradation or inferiorizing of indigenous peoples and ways, thus disrupting the historically embedded pattern of oppression.

From many Aboriginal understandings, sovereignty (including the practice of good governance) focuses on community and relationships. In my language, there is no precise translation for the word self-government. Kanien'kehaka (Mohawk) people would say tewatatha:wi. This word best translates into 'I or we carry ourselves' (Monture-Angus 1999, 36). It is governance that requires both personal and collective responsibility for living right. Haudenosaunee scholar and traditional leader Oren Lyons explained at the Montreal Conference on Indian Government in 1979:

> Sovereignty—it's a political word. It's not a legal word. Sovereignty is the act. Sovereignty is the do. You act. You don't ask. There is no limitation on sovereignty. You are not semi-sovereign. You either are or aren't. It's simple (cited in Hill 1992, 175).

First Nations are beginning to acknowledge that waiting for federal acknowledgement of their rights is a long and frustrating experience. The message of many traditional leaders, such as the hereditary chief and former Assembly of First Nations BC vice-chief Satsan (Herb George), is that we do not just have rights but the responsibility to act (2005).

In a Western sense, statehood is identified when governments possess characteristics such as the ability to use coercive force (both militarily and legally), have defined boundaries and control over their territory, and command recognition from their population as well as from the international community. Alongside these characteristics, states have absolute authority over their citizens, are hierarchical, and often have an identifiable ruling elite. States require compliance with their decisions, and this is often the role that law plays in their social systems. States are sovereign nations. These are not the concepts used when an indigenous person describes indigenous sovereignty. But does this mean that indigenous peoples are not sovereign? Or does it mean that the definition of sovereignty has been inaccurately and overly narrowly defined? The result of the incomplete international definition of sovereignty is the inability to be inclusive of all peoples and states.

For Canada, indigenous scholars agree that the structural solution is not really so difficult. The Canadian state is built on the tradition of federalism—shared sovereignty between the federal and provincial governments. It includes a plural legal tradition combining both civil and common law systems. To this, indigenous scholars remind us of the agreements between the Crown and First Nations and argue for the implementation of treaty federalism (Henderson 1994a, 1994b; Ladner 2003). According to both Ladner and James (Sakej) Henderson, the treaties are the 'foundational law of Canada' (Ladner 2003, 173). It was the treaties that allowed settlers to establish governments in this territory now known as Canada. The solution lies in implementing the true order of Canadian governance and recognizing the third order, that of the First Peoples (or the treaties; see Henderson 1994a; 1994b, 60).

The study of social structures, including political systems, has been a core area of study for sociologists such as Marx, Weber, and Durkheim. Regarding state functions, these three sociologists studied power and authority, capitalism, legiti-macy, bureaucracy, and labour. According to Weber, 'power is the business of gov-ernment, a formal organization that directs the political life of a society' (Macionis and Gerber 2005, 411). Not often recognized in the study of social the-ory concepts such as 'democracy, nationalisms, individualism, liberty, rights and freedoms' (Brandon 1986; Ladner 2000, 35) is that these were also core concepts in indigenous knowledge systems, demonstrating that the birth of sociology truly predates the work of its founding fathers.

In the 1960s and 1970s in both Canada and the United States, Aboriginal peo-ple became more militant in asserting their rights (Cornell 1998; Mercredi and Turpel 1993; Warrior 1996). There is no reason to believe that Aboriginal peoples will cease this struggle. The Assembly of First Nations recognizes that the 'inter-national and domestic scholars and independent experts have confirmed the link between the right of people to choose how to be governed and successful devel-opment' (2005, 12). In Canada, the Supreme Court in 1997 clearly recognized Aboriginal title in the landmark Delgamuukw and Gisday'wa decision. Legal recognition must be followed by continued political evolution on the part of the Canadian state toward supporting Aboriginal peoples' journey away from the consequences of colonialism.

Questions to Consider

1. How might indigenous knowledge be used to analyze Canadian society?
2. Does the notion of governmentality speak to questions of sovereignty?
3. Discuss the different definitions of sovereignty presented in this chapter.
4. Describe the kinds of rights that Aboriginal peoples possess in Canadian law.
5. How have sociologists contributed to the study of the relationship between Aboriginal nations and Canada?

Notes

1. Because the focus of this chapter is on treaty relationships, the discussion focuses on the sovereign experiences of First Nations, not Métis or Inuit.

Chapter 16

What Is Sovereignty in Quebec?

Philippe Couton

INTRODUCTION

There are three simple and divergent answers to the question asked in the title of this chapter. The first is provided by proponents of sovereignty: they argue that Quebec has long suffered oppression at the hand of the British Empire and its successor state, Canada, and would be better off as an independent country. That account emphasizes the fact that Quebec has experienced a series of humiliations—from the conquest of 1760 to repression of various uprisings, to a political and cultural domination of anglophone elites (even within Quebec), and to an ongoing lack of recognition of Quebec society's uniqueness within Canada (see Bourque 2001). Second, opponents of sovereignty who insist on the negative aspects of the movement provide the opposite answer. They describe what they often call 'separatism' as a product of narrow nationalism that seeks to protect and defend a particular ethnic group at the expense of both the larger Canadian society and the minorities within Quebec. They further argue that it is democratically illegitimate, violates international law, and goes against the global trend for greater diversity and pluralism.

A third, less ideologically charged answer, often provided by social scientists, points out that as a historically and culturally distinct community within the larger Canadian political entity, Quebec lacks what most other such communities in the world enjoy: full political control over its own destiny. As a result, the sovereignty movement seeks to obtain independence in order to achieve this control, protect the distinctiveness of Quebec culture, and pursue social and political objectives with tools that are currently in the hands of the federal government. This quest for independence simply follows a global process that has seen the world divided into more or less clearly defined cultural units (nations) endowed with their own sovereign political institutions (states). Where this process has not come to completion for historical reasons (conquest, colonialism, etc.) in many other parts of the world (Scotland and Kurdistan, for example), groups similarly seek to achieve sovereignty by either peaceful or violent means. Like these other communities, Quebec has developed into a thriving, unique society that now wishes to achieve the last stage of a fully mature social and political entity: independence (see Venne 2001).

All three answers contain elements of truth. Preference for one depends on a variety of personal, cultural, and intellectual factors. There is certainly no right or wrong answer since each reflects particular political inclinations not amenable to simple right/wrong determinations. In any case, the point of this chapter is not to lend support to any particular viewpoint but to help disentangle the assumptions that underlie all three answers and that often remain underanalyzed. Only once these considerations are better understood can a person make a fully informed, critically minded choice about Quebec sovereignty. To this effect, the rest of this chapter provides a discussion of the following key assumptions: the 'naturalness' of political independence; the concept of nation; independence as the endpoint of an evolutionary process; nationalism as an ideology; and the idea of sovereignty itself.

(Un)natural Independence

The first of these assumptions is the idea that the natural condition for any significant social group is political independence (synonymous with sovereignty). This is not always the case, although political independence remains a strong and durable aspect of modern social and political life throughout the world. A first argument against the presumed naturalness of independence is the clear lack of 'fit' between state and nation, which is a near universal dimension of most of the countries existing in the world today. Few states can legitimately claim to be the home of a single, culturally homogenous nation (Keating 2004). That is, few political entities (states) govern a single, culturally homogenous population (a nation), and conversely a very large number of culturally distinct groups do not enjoy a state entirely of their own. Canada is certainly one of the best examples of this as a true multinational state and one of the most diverse places in the world (Laczko 2000). Quebec itself is of course just as diverse, with large Aboriginal groups, linguistic minorities, and rising immigration levels. Even some of the oldest nation-states in the world are home to sizeable culturally distinct minority groups, including France, China, and many others (a few exceptions exist, notably Japan). And many of the oldest cultural groups in the world do not live in states of their own (nearly all Aboriginal peoples in the Americas, for instance). If language is one measure of the expression of a distinct culture, there are several thousand languages in the world today but only about 200 independent states.

The 'naturalness' of the nation-state is therefore more myth than reality; moreover, it is a potentially dangerous myth at that. One of the legacies of Western political history is the notion that states should encourage cultural uniformity within their populations, that they should mould the nations over which they rule in order to obtain a fit between state and nation. As Rae (2002) puts it, states are typically nation-forming states, and this process has very often been based—even before the advent of nationalism on a world scale—on 'pathological homogenization': on the imposition of a single culture on the entire population. Quebec and other parts of Canada have periodically suffered from efforts at eradicating French as well as other non-English cultural traditions. The idea that most Western democracies have been and continue to be ethnically neutral (i.e., that they tend not to favour a particular ethnic group) is therefore simply untrue (Kymlicka 2000). All have and continue to promote one (sometimes more) culture that is believed to be that of the nation the state governs. What nevertheless remains true is that a number of nation-states are home to several large cultural groups that coexist in relative harmony (Canada, Switzerland, and India are examples). Yet the norm remains that most nation-states tend to be the home of one dominant group from which comes the notion that political independence is the natural condition of culturally distinct communities (Italy is for Italians, Brazil for Brazilians, etc.).

In the case of Quebec, the argument is easily extended to say that Quebec should become a 'normal' country with the attributes of these other nation-states, although even strong proponents of Quebec sovereignty agree that Quebec has become less a single, homogenous community and more a 'community of national communities', as Bourque (2001) puts it. No proper attempt to understand Quebec sovereignty can therefore rely on the putative naturalness of political independence. Quebec is not exceptional in having to share sovereignty with a larger entity. *Some* fit between state and nation is common in most countries, which does lend some support to the assumption, but even that is changing as some of the discussion below shows. On the other hand, most other existing states have been relatively free to promote a specific culture (through educational, cultural, and other policies), and Quebec understandably also wants to have this de facto aspect of nation-states at its disposal.

WHAT IS A NATION?

The previous discussion touches on the question of the concept of nation itself, the second assumption that needs to be analyzed in order to better understand Quebec sovereignty. If Quebec is to achieve independence in the name of the dominant nation that resides on its territory (Québécois, French-speaking Quebecers), what is this nation? Nations have attracted considerable attention from social scientists, historians, philosophers, and others, generating a large literature, including a number of classic works (e.g., Gellner 1997; Anderson 1991). There is little agreement on exactly how to define a nation, but major parameters of the discussion have emerged. First is the question of whether nations have always existed or are a fairly recent product of modern social life (or the constructionism/primordialism debate, as it is often termed). A loose consensus has emerged that sees nations as we understand them—large communities, territorially bound, sharing a common language and culture—as historically fairly recent. France, for instance, although one of the oldest countries in the world, has only truly shared a common language for the past century or so, and parts of its territory were disputed even during the twentieth century.

Likewise, the current territory of Quebec was only finalized in the early twentieth century, and Aboriginals, who have national claims of their own, populate very large parts of it. People within Quebec have only been identifying themselves as members of the Quebec nation (Québécois) since the middle of the twentieth century. Prior to this point, the dominant identity was French-Canadian or simply Canadian. But this is not very different from what has happened elsewhere in the world. Before the development of mass public education, mass media, and other aspects of modernity, most countries were marked by a high level of linguistic and cultural diversity, and most still are. The transition to greater national homogeneity is facilitated by various administrative instruments, including censuses, representative politics, mass education, and so on (Anderson 1998, 43; Laczko 2000). The process of nation-making is not unproblematic. Some have described it as the serialization or homogenization of individuals into largely constructed communities. Most national categories are, after all, the product of institutions and administrations. Quebec fits this general pattern and has only recently become a relatively unified society. Basing one's opposition to sovereignty on the recentness of Quebec nationhood is therefore not very helpful. Very few nations have any solid claims to ancient histories as homogenous cultural entities.

One thing is clear, however: despite their relative newness, nations are tremendously resilient. Several ideological currents of the past predicted that nations would disappear. Liberals were hoping that a global, peaceful culture would emerge, while Marxists thought that classes would replace nations as the predominant form of social and political identity. Currently, a number of commentators claim that globalization is eradicating national borders and that we are about to enter a post-national world (Cohen 1996). The reality is, however, that a number of 'new' nations are emerging and a number of old ones are making new claims to autonomy. For instance, Aboriginal peoples in Canada, including in Quebec, and in other parts of the world are positioning themselves as nations and demanding some measure of self-determination. Another striking example of the resilience of ethno-national identity is its resurgence after the collapse of the Soviet Union in 1989 (Laitin 1998). Despite the best efforts of the regime to repress or remove national minority groups for over 70 years, they resurfaced and sought their independence in the wake of the disappearance of the Soviet Union. Quebec, in other words, is certainly not alone in wanting sovereignty as a nation, and there is little reason to believe that claim is irrelevant to today's world.

Evolution toward Independence?

A third and related dimension to be considered is whether or not societies, and Quebec in particular, follow a slow, evolutionary development that necessarily ends in political independence. As some of the above indicates, there is some truth to this view. The world seems to have evolved from fairly simple human groupings to large empires (Roman, Greek, then British, French, etc.), almost all of which eventually split into sovereign states, some very recently. This phenomenon would also address the issue raised above: if so many cultural and linguistic groups have not reached sovereignty, it is simply because they have not yet experienced the full evolutionary process that leads to sovereignty. In some cases, the process is still unfolding, and this could be the case in Quebec as well as in Scotland, Kurdistan, and many other nations.

The history of Quebec is well-known and only needs to be briefly summarized here to further illustrate the point (see Dickinson and Young 2000 for details). Quebec emerged as Canada's second largest and sole majority-franco-phone province over the past two and a half centuries. Once a French colonial possession, what is now Quebec was conquered by the British in 1760. Only about 60,000 French colonists lived in New France at that time. Over the following decades, inflows of English-speaking immigrants from the newly independent United States and from the British Isles came to outnumber francophones in British North America. New provinces emerged east and west of Quebec, most of them almost entirely anglophone. But despite these forces (conquest, English-speaking immigration), Quebec managed to survive and indeed thrive under British institutions. By the early twentieth century, thanks to a high birth rate, Quebec was more than holding its own demographically. And thanks to strong institutions both religious (the Catholic church) and secular (growing political institutions), it managed to preserve its culture and identity. By the 1960s, Mon-treal was emerging as one of the world's great cities (with the consecration of Expo 67 and later the 1976 Olympic Games), and Quebec was undergoing mas-sive social and political change: the role of the church declined, while the provin-cial government took a more active role in a number of areas, including education, culture, health care, and so on. During this period, political parties promoting Quebec independence emerged and were successful at the polls. The logical outcome of this long history might seem to be some form of independence for Quebec, just as other countries have formed and developed elsewhere in the world, building their institutions, creating a unique culture, and achieving full independence. Quebec is in many ways in a similar position: long included in the British Empire, then in Canada, it has been attempting to evolve into a fully inde-pendent nation-state.

But leaving the argument at this level would miss several important points. First, the idea that Quebec should become an independent country is not new. Jules-Paul Tardivel, for instance, was an early proponent of Quebec independ-ence. His 1895 novel, *Pour la patrie*, summarized his political position, which failed to generate much support during his lifetime. Nationalists of various stripes have argued and struggled for independence over the past two centuries. Lord Durham's infamous 1839 report aptly summarized the situation as 'Two nations warring in the bosom of a single state'. But the debate between sover-eignty and federalism was not always as stark as it is today (Meunier and Warren 1998). A number of early French-Canadian nationalists were also staunch feder-alists. Earlier versions of Quebec nationalism included the work produced dur-ing the interwar period by Lionel Groulx, whose organic, traditional view of the nation was decidedly anti-liberal (Boily 2004). The notion of sovereignty only became a central aspect of Quebec and by extension Canadian politics in the 1960s, culminating in the first referendum on sovereignty in 1980. It was only during that period that the Quebec provincial government slowly constructed a large bureaucracy able to challenge some of the power of the federal government, particularly during the 1960s and 1970s, a period known as the Quiet Revolu-tion. But in that sense, the Quebec nation is actually the product of Canadian federalism, forcing a large number of Canada's francophones to identify with the

Quebec territory and later with its institutions (Bourque 2001). Yet this might still seem to support the evolutionary view of Quebec sovereignty: only once its institutions were fully developed did the population of Quebec express strong support for independence.

There are, however, other explanations for the timing of the rise of the sovereignty movement. One is the influence of global anti-colonial struggles, and French-Canadian nationalism was reinterpreted through this prism during the 1950s and 1960s. French-speaking Canadians had long struggled for some measure of self-determination and against Anglo domination (from the uprising of the late 1830s to resistance to conscription during the two world wars), but only in the second half of the twentieth century did this struggle become a full-fledged independentist movement centred on Quebec. This new dimension of the fight drew direct inspiration from similar struggles in Algeria, Vietnam, and Cuba, among others. A second explanation is simply the emergence of a new class of politicians and public servants who had a significant stake in the developing Quebec institutions. They formed the backbone of the sovereigntist movement.

Another, more clearly supported explanation points to the tremendous influence of political events on the sovereignty movement, especially during the period that followed the first referendum. Quebec's position within Canada has been ambiguous and hybrid for at least 50 years: neither sovereign nor completely integrated (Laforest 2001, 299). But the recent nationalist movement has been particularly affected by the patriation of the constitution in 1982 and by the events that followed it. In brief, for historical reasons the process of amending the 1867 constitution of Canada had been left in the hands of the British government. Prime Minister Pierre Trudeau decided to 'patriate' the constitution, meaning to bring full control over the constitution from the UK to Canada. At the same time, Trudeau decided to add a charter of rights and freedoms to it and to provide for court-based enforcement of its provisions. This proved to be a divisive process, and Quebec felt cheated both by the way it unfolded and by the substance of the Charter, which failed to clearly recognize that Canada consisted of two founding societies. Two agreements were attempted, the Meech Lake and Charlottetown accords, both of which failed, only adding fuel to the fire. To this day a number of politicians and commentators feel that the entire process was illegitimate, possibly in breach of legal principles, and that the basic principle on which Canada had been founded was broken (Laforest 2001). The Charter was perceived to be a centralizing document that recognized a range of individual and collective rights but distinctly failed to recognize Quebec as such. It was seen as undermining provincial autonomy and weakening the ability of Quebec to be a nation (Kymlicka 1998). One of the consequences of this protracted process was dramatically increased support for sovereignty in Quebec, leading to the election of a Parti Québécois government in Quebec in 1994, a strong showing by the Bloc Québécois in federal elections, and near victory for the 'yes' side in the 1995 referendum.

The role of this divisive political process confirms that support for sovereignty does not follow a steady evolutionary path but is strongly influenced by political events. A large proportion of Quebecers, sovereigntists and federalists alike, were angered by the constitutional process and further inflamed by the bungled agreements. Support for sovereignty receded significantly in later years to the point that the Parti Québécois lost the province to the Liberals in the 2003 election. This would tend to confirm that although there might be an evolutionary component to sovereignty (the development of institutions, etc.), the way the issue is handled at the political level continues to matter a great deal.

IS NATIONALISM AN IDEOLOGY?

The fourth key assumption of the sovereignty question is the circumstances under which nations emerge and the claims that are most commonly made in their name. In other words, what is the nature of nationalism, and how does this apply to Quebec? Historians have long pointed out that nations are a product of the rise of democratic ideals. Nations are in that sense very similar to the 'people' that putatively govern in a democracy. The beginning of democracy, in revolutions and reform movements in Europe and North America, occurred in the name of the people or the nation in opposition to the ruling class (see Hobsbawm 1992). It is only fairly recently that nationalism has become associated with destructive and politically extreme political ideologies and movements (e.g., Nazism, the wars that ravaged parts of the former communist Europe in the 1990s). No single ideology is clearly and uniquely associated with nationalism, which has been a force of both emancipation and oppression—even genocide—in recent history. Simply equating the quest for national independence with narrow tribalism or claiming it is purely a liberation movement is therefore inaccurate. Just as elsewhere in the world, the movement for Quebec sovereignty has had its share of extremists (but far fewer than in, for example, Ireland; see Cormier and Couton 2004), although it has been thoroughly democratic and peaceful in recent decades.

A related and important aspect of the question is usually presented as a tension between liberal individualism and communitarianism—or to put it differently, between the idea that the ultimate source of freedom and autonomy resides in the individual and the idea that it resides in the community. This issue emerges in a number of debates, not only about Quebec sovereignty but about the rights and objectives of a range of minority communities the world over (similar national minorities in Belgium, Spain, Indonesia, and parts of Africa; immigrant groups in many Western countries; Native communities in former European colonies). Debates on the issue tend to present most nationalist movements as primarily communitarian and thus as posing a threat to the core value of Western democracies: individual liberty. However, this is usually not the case and clearly not as far as Quebec is concerned (see Kymlicka 1998; 2000). There is no evidence to indicate that Quebec's aspiration to sovereignty is based on a stronger commitment to collective values than to individual autonomy. There is in fact substantial evidence that Quebecers tend to be more liberal and individualistic in their attitudes and behaviour than English-speaking Canadians—for example, in terms of respect for traditional institutions like marriage and religion. Sovereigntist parties and individuals have embraced many of these liberal attitudes. On the other hand, there is some evidence that Quebecers are more attached to their collective culture (with higher rates of domestic cultural consumption, for instance). It would therefore be inaccurate to characterize the Quebec sovereignty movement as ideologically homogenous and either good or bad. Like most other political movements, it contains several often contradictory trends and tensions.

SOVEREIGNTY TO POST-SOVEREIGNTY

The final issue that needs to be fully unpacked in order to better understand the question of Quebec's independence is the concept of sovereignty itself. We have just seen that neither nations, nation-states, nor nationalism are easily defined and understood. This is also the case with sovereignty. On the one hand, it is a key feature of the world today. We take it so much for granted that we rarely stop to think about it: the world is divided into a finite number of sovereign, independent countries over which no greater power exists. But this too is undergoing profound changes. The trend toward 'post-sovereignty'—that is, toward forms of governance that do not rely exclusively on the traditional statehood—is only in its infancy, but it is slowly unfolding (Keating 2004). A range of processes is challenging the traditional understanding of sovereignty, including international organizations. The European Union, for instance, is weakening the traditional power of the individual state to the point at which a number of movements in Europe are mobilizing around a more regionalist perspective than around simple nationhood (Keating 2004). In other words, what is happening in Europe is a slow but profound reshaping of the nature and location of political authority. This is also happening on a more modest scale in North America where part of the sovereign authority of states has been delegated to the institutions of the North American Free Trade Agreement (NAFTA). Quebec in fact has confirmed several times that it intends to remain in NAFTA in the event that it achieves sovereignty. Some have even argued that NAFTA may actually facilitate the transition to sovereignty by providing a level of political and economic stability above and beyond Canada.

Other processes are challenging the traditional sovereignty of states as well, including multinational corporations, transnational actors (immigrant groups, for instance), and global technological changes (states can do little to stop the flow of information). In a number of countries, including Canada, competing groups and institutions dispute sovereignty. Quebec is the most significant contender in Canada, but First Nations come a close second, with a number of less important groups making occasional claims (proponents of western Canadian separatism, for instance).

The most provocative conclusion of this line of reasoning is that state sovereignty no longer really matters. Whether or not Quebec achieves sovereignty will not change many of the processes mentioned above. Quebec will still be part of global networks of trade, migration, and information flows, just as Canada minus Quebec will remain connected to them. Yet this too would be an exaggeration. Both the federal and provincial governments in Canada have tremendous powers and responsibilities as yet unequalled by non-state actors. In fact, many see the state as the last barrier against the homogenizing forces of globalization, and some argue that Quebec would be better able to be a successful member of a glob-alizing world as a sovereign nation-state (see Venne 2001). Others point out that remaining in a larger multinational entity is the best way for Quebec, and fran-cophones throughout Canada, to stave off the threat of globalization.

CONCLUSION

How does the foregoing discussion help to answer the question heading this chap-ter? Quebec's quest for sovereignty remains high on anyone's list of the critical, unresolved issues facing Canada. After two referendums—1980 and 1995—and several decades of active political mobilization, including electoral victories by nationalist parties provincially and federally, the question of Quebec sovereignty remains unresolved. The choice is largely but not solely in the hands of Quebe-cers. What matters most is that we understand all the issues at stake and how best to address them.

First, it is clear that portraying Quebec sovereignty and its associated move-ment and ideas as simplistic oppositions (nationalism against pluralism, etc.) is at best unhelpful and at worst politically dangerous. The movement is obviously part of a much greater global story in which nation-states have emerged as the basic unit of political reference. But there is nothing inevitable to that story in the world in general, as the trend towards post-nationalism and post-sovereignty illustrates, or in Quebec, as the ebb and flow of the sovereignty movement con-firms. A range of historical administrative and political factors has influenced it. It cannot merely be characterized as a simple yearning for national homogeneity or in opposition to federalism or diversity. Neither is it simply a liberation move-ment: by many measures, Quebecers enjoy very similar social and political condi-tions as in the rest of Canada and do not suffer from any significant level of oppression.

And Quebec itself is changing rapidly. The province is becoming increasingly diverse, although it has always maintained a conflicted relationship with immi-gration and cultural diversity. Immigrants have historically gravitated towards English North American culture, leaving many in Quebec unsure about the con-sequences of immigration—to the point where some have accused governmental institutions of fostering the subordination of immigrant communities in the name of maintaining a fictitious national unity (Fontaine 1993). This accusation does not entirely reflect Quebec's recent success in the field of immigration. The province has secured nearly full control over immigration from the federal gov-ernment and has been attracting more and more francophone newcomers. In 2002 nearly half of the immigrants to Montreal spoke some French as opposed to only about 2 per cent of those moving to Toronto and Vancouver (Canada. Citi-zenship and Immigration 2002).[1] Partly as a result, Quebec culture is becoming increasingly diverse—to the point that an important intellectual current within Quebec literature and social sciences identifies Quebec as marked by its American character: it is a 'new world' society, more influenced by North American than by European cultural practices (Theriault 2002). Similarly, others have pointed out that Quebec culture is moving away from a sharp distinction between nationalism and cosmopolitanism, finding instead a more complex mode of belonging somewhere in between (Maclure 2003). The strong attachment of most Quebecers to their culture is beyond doubt. But it is also clear that today as well as in the past, sovereignty has been viewed as only one of the many options available to ensure the development of this culture.

The debate over Quebec sovereignty may take several routes in years and decades to come. Some have argued that a gradual evolution is unfolding, particularly in Europe, away from locating political authority simply at the level of the national state, and that a kind of 'third way' of handling the desire for national sovereignty is emerging (Keating 2004). Quebec may very well embrace this new trend and become one of the many places in the world that sit somewhere between traditional sovereignty and its current, already hybrid status. Canada may also follow a similar route, further sharing its sovereignty with multinational institutions and sub-state communities (Aboriginals, provinces other than Quebec, etc.). In that sense, both Quebec and Canada may follow what some have identified as two contradictory global trends: one towards increasing pluralism and multiplicity and one towards 'unmixing' and consolidation (Cornell and Hartmann 1998). On the one hand, migration and ethno-cultural diversity is on the rise in much of the world, but on the other hand, nationalist movements seeking independence from larger political units have also dramatically strengthened (Quebec, but also eastern Europe, parts of Asia, etc.). How these forces will play out to decide the future of Quebec and Canada is for history one day to decide.

Questions to Consider

1. Why does a significant part of Quebec's population want political independence?
2. Is Quebec already sovereign?
3. Should all nations have the right to become sovereign?
4. Is a nation necessarily a sovereign nation?
5. Is Canada a sovereign nation?

Notes

1. Canada received about 230,000 immigrants in 2002, the majority from Asia. See Canada, Citizenship and Immigration (2002) for details.

Chapter 17

Will the Call Centre Industry Revitalize Maritime Economies?

Jennifer Jarman

INTRODUCTION

Maritime Canada consists of three provinces, New Brunswick, Prince Edward Island, and Nova Scotia, situated on Canada's East Coast. It was first populated by immigrants from Asia who crossed the land bridge between Siberia and Alaska about 30,000 years ago and then gradually made their way across the North American continent, arriving in the Atlantic region some 10,000 years ago, according to archaeological evidence. Nomadic Vikings may have wandered through in the eleventh century (a 'runic stone' remains at the Yarmouth Museum in Nova Scotia). In 1497 a European explorer, John Cabot, dropped anchor in Cape Breton and claimed it for England. Throughout the seventeenth century, French, English, Portuguese, and Spanish fishing people used Maritime shores to dry their fish. Over time, European communities developed alongside the pre-existing Mi'kmaq communities. All of these diverse peoples found a location that was well forested, with a temperate climate (for Canada), and oceans with some of the richest fishing grounds in the world. The subsequent interactions, engagements, and conflicts among these communities form the early history of the country we call Canada.

Early relations among these diverse peoples fluctuated between periods of peaceful cooperation and periods of intense conflict. General Cornwallis did offer and pay British money for Indian scalps (Boucher 2004 [1906]), and European diseases did sweep through the Mi'kmaq communities with devastating consequences for its population (Miller 1982). But there were also long periods of peaceful co-existence and intermarriage, especially between the Mi'kmaq community and the French community. However, the 1755 deportation of the French settlers (Acadians), who had laboured hard to build an extensive system of dikes and establish fields in the Annapolis Valley, resulted in thousands of deaths in that community as a result of disease, shipwreck, and poverty, as well as the complete loss of lands, homes, farms, and livestock for the survivors (Griffiths 1992). Those deemed loyal to the English Crown reaped the benefits of the Acadians' labours. The landscape of dikes that the Acadians had built to claim land from the Fundy tides can still be seen today.

The early English and French communities used African slaves (slavery was abolished in the British Empire in 1834). In 1784 approximately 3,000 free black Loyalists arrived in Nova Scotia and established a community, Birchtown, which for a time was the largest settlement of free black people in North America. Other black communities were also established throughout the provinces.[1] Despite their free status, these communities have suffered racism throughout their existence. During the eighteenth and nineteenth centuries, the colonies became bustling trade and commercial centres. In fact, when the possibility of confederation was discussed in 1864, eventually leading to a Canada binding together diverse British colonies, the venue chosen for the conference was Charlottetown, Prince Edward Island. This was an indication that Prince Edward Island was not a marginal place known for potato farms, or later *Anne of Green Gables*, but a part of a bustling eastern Canadian economy.

Contemporary Maritime Canadian society is thus partly a product of colonial rule and colonial rivalries as well as a settlement of land that had a population established long before European contact. Conflicts between two major European powers, England and France, had important consequences for the composition of the population as both powers competed to create communities in order to secure access to the region's resources as well as maintain strategic military advantage. These struggles created opportunities for some and serious repercussions for others. By the nineteenth century, most of the communities that exist today had been established, with a diverse population drawn from several different cultures and linguistic traditions.

Over the course of the twentieth century, however, the fortunes of the three Maritime provinces declined. The region's economy was originally rooted deeply in the resources of the region—fish, timber, agriculture, and coal. Its geographical location was highly favourable for business and trade from the Americas to Britain, Africa, and the Caribbean. These advantages, however, have been eclipsed by the growth of powerful economies and communities in the central and western part of the North American continent. Halifax, a port that the British originally created because it had the advantage of a huge natural harbour that was ice-free year-round, has declined in stature. Many of the rail lines that were built to move goods from the Atlantic seaboard to central Canada have disappeared—some have had the rails removed and are being used as hiking trails. No longer languishing but totally dead is the steel industry in Cape Breton, which was established to manufacture the rails used to construct the railway tracks in Canada; the coal mining industry established to supply the steel industry is virtually gone too. Thus the nineteenth-century transportation network of ports and railways has been all but rendered obsolete by economic shifts.

The Maritime provinces now have some of the highest levels of unemployment and underemployment in Canada (see Table 1). As in many places with economies that are natural resource or agriculture-based, many jobs in Maritime Canada are seasonal—the fishing industry, agriculture, and the tourism industry, for example. The consequence is that employment alternates between high-intensity work and long periods of unemployment. Thus the unemployment

Table 1. Provincial Unemployment Rates and Levels

Province	Unemployment rate %	Unemployment '000s	Total labour force '000s
Newfoundland	15.2	38.4	252.5
Prince Edward Island	10.8	8.3	76.5
Nova Scotia	8.4	40.8	483.9
New Brunswick	9.7	37.7	388.2
Quebec	8.3	335.4	4,052.7
Ontario	6.6	451.3	6,849.1
Manitoba	4.8	29.1	609.4
Saskatchewan	5.1	25.9	509.4
Alberta	3.9	73.1	1,857.5
British Columbia	5.9	132.9	2,263.4

Source: Statistics Canada. 2005. 'Labour force, employed and unemployed, numbers and rates, by province'. *Labour force survey.* CANSIM, Table 282-002.

insurance system, or employment insurance as it has been optimistically renamed, became the backbone of many families' survival strategies (Butler and Smith 1983).

EDUCATION LEVELS

Over the past 30 years, higher education has expanded in almost every country around the world, and the Maritime region has also become increasingly educated. Table 2 shows, however, that the Maritime provinces still have lower levels of education than the Canadian population as a whole. This pattern may be partly due to the fact that the average age in the Maritimes is higher than in the rest of Canada and older people tend to have lower levels of formal education because a few decades ago, formal qualifications were not as important as they are now for labour market entrance. Nova Scotia emerges with slightly higher levels than the other two provinces, but Table 3 shows that all three Maritime provinces rank

Table 2. Education Levels in Canada and in the Maritime Provinces, Population Aged 15 and over by Highest Level of Schooling

	Canada	% of pop.	PEI	% of pop.	NS	% of pop.	NB	% of pop.
Total	23,901,360		106,690		732,370		589,370	
Elementary/secondary	10,844,795	45.4	52,255	49.0	330,365	45.1	306,975	52.1
College only	6,047,085	25.3	25,780	24.2	183,675	25.1	133,825	22.7
University	6,173,225	25.8	25,175	23.6	191,860	26.2	129,815	22.0

Source: Statistics Canada. 2001b. *Population 15 years and over by highest level of schooling, by provinces and territories, census of the population 2001.*

Table 3. Education Levels in Canada and in the Maritime Provinces: Breakdown by University Degree

	Canada	% of pop.	PEI	% of pop.	NS	% of pop.	NB	% of pop.
Total	23,901,360		106,690		732,370		589,370	
With bachelor's or first degree	2,534,010	10.6	8,995	8.4	71,470	9.6	48,415	8.2
With university certificate above bachelor's level	382,955	1.6	1,095	1.1	10,065	1.4	5,855	1.0
With master's degree	642,055	10.4	1,750	7.0	17,465	9.1	10,260	7.9
With earned doctorate	128,625	2.1	350	1.4	3,655	1.9	2,090	1.6

Source: Statistics Canada. 2001b. *Population 15 years and over by highest level of schooling, by provinces and territories, census of the population 2001.*

below the national average in terms of the highest level of qualifications—master's and PhD degrees.

Today's young Maritimers do not aspire to agricultural, resource-based, or manufacturing careers (Thiessen and Blasius 2002). Thiessen and Blasius's analysis of the aspirations of young people in urban Hamilton, Ontario, and rural and urban Nova Scotia shows that both boys and girls—those in rural areas and those in urban areas, those whose parents were professional workers as well as those whose parents were working-class—are 'remarkably homogeneous' in their aspirations to 'middle-class male' careers—in other words, to service sector work. This explains the turn to higher education: faced with uncertain futures in the occupations their parents chose, young people are pursuing formal education instead.

THE BRAIN DRAIN AND MARITIME COMMUNITIES

One of the longstanding problems in the region has been the retention of its own human capital. This process has sometimes been described as stopping the 'brain drain' or migration of workers, especially those who are skilled and educated, out of the region. Ross Finnie has shown that high provincial unemployment rates, high rates of collection of employment insurance benefits, and absence of employment income induce people to migrate to provinces where opportunities are better. Further, he shows that young people with higher educational qualifications are more likely to move than older people with weaker qualification profiles (Finnie 2000). Maurice Beaudin and Sébastien Breau report that data for 1995 show New Brunswick and Prince Edward Island losing large numbers of their new graduates; Nova Scotia actually increased its number of new graduates but not enough to compensate for the overall loss of human capital (Beaudin and Breau 2001).

For provincial governments then, the continued departure of young educated people poses a problem. Education budgets are one of the largest categories of expenditure for provincial governments. How do they legitimize continued expenditure for students who leave the province as soon as they graduate when they must fund other areas of need, such as health care, for those who remain? If they do not invest in education, they do not build the type of labour force capable of supporting higher-level industries. If they do invest in higher education but do not have any way of retaining labour, then the investment in higher education is a loss to the region. The departure of young people creates problems for the reproduction of stable communities. When young people move thousands of miles away in search of jobs, who looks after the older people? Even with extensive air transport networks, electronic communication, and cheap telephone rates, family support becomes very difficult when people are thousands of miles away. Human capital retention, particularly of young educated people, thus becomes a very important priority for both communities and governments.

A NEW ECONOMY?

Many people in the rest of Canada puzzle at the reasons for the low levels of economic growth in this part of the country. The perception of Maritimers as somehow backward persists, and the self-deprecating humour of East Coast comedians who engage the Canadian imaginary with depictions of local folk on *The Red Green show* or *This hour has 22 minutes* probably does more to reinforce the impression than to change it. Over the past few decades, there have been a series of attempts to find a new base for the economy. One research group in Canada has summarized the situation as follows:

> the region's provinces have competed among themselves and with hinterlands of other advanced industrial societies for carpet mills, electronic assembly operations and with other low wage, labour intensive industries with the usual result being a waste of public funds (Jarman et al. 1997).

In the past few years, however, there has been an important sign of change that could finally be the beginning of a significant turnaround. The call centre industry, an unlikely saviour, has crept into the Maritimes almost unnoticed. As one government official recently told the author: 'We don't know how it got here—it just grew up.'[2] In fact, Maritime Canada is now home to 25 per cent of the Canadian share of the 'business services' industry (Akyeampong 2005, 6).

The remainder of this chapter develops a sociological perspective on the rise of this industry and its consequences for work, life, and community in twenty-first-century Maritime Canada. Some of the details and factors that are important in understanding this new site of job growth are unique to the Maritimes. This chapter focuses on two related questions: What is the nature of the new call centre jobs? And what can the industry contribute to long-term growth and development in the region? To answer these questions, we must understand both how it changes the lives of those who work in the industry and the broader question of how it affects the capacity of the larger communities to sustain themselves. We must go beyond what we think we know—our preconceived understandings or what some sociologists have called our 'common sense' understandings—to arrive at a reasoned and informed understanding based both on empirical facts and on theoretically informed analysis of those facts. Finally, we must situate our understanding of the industry with research knowledge drawn from the region in order to understand its impact in this place and at this time.

FIELD STUDY METHODOLOGY AND SOURCES OF DATA

The research on which this chapter is based was conducted between 1996 and 2005 in a series of projects[3] the goals of which were to conduct a comprehensive examination of the nature of the call centre industry. In these projects, viewpoints were sought from participants ranging from call centre agents, technicians, supervisors, team leaders, and managers to government officials from economic development boards, as well as personnel from telecommunications companies and other suppliers. The aim was to understand the wide variation in the way the industry is viewed and draw on a full range of experiences within it. The reason for such a broad perspective is in keeping with the sociological understanding that different actors in a society have different experiences structured by their positions. Some have views and experiences that are directly contradictory to those of others, while some share attitudes and experiences.

Sociologists have taken different positions on the question of whether some positions are 'privileged'—that is, whether views from people at the top provide a better understanding than views from those located at the 'bottom' of structures (Smith 1987). This research found that senior managers in the industry provide different information from those working on the calling platforms. The information they provided varied substantially from firm to firm. Discrepancies between their views and those of people in junior positions were dependent on the sensitivity of individual managers to the needs of their employees. Those who have mobility through the industry (e.g., suppliers) and therefore have contacts with a broad range of players because they work inside many centres provided some of the most interesting perspectives.

This chapter draws upon the following sources of data:

1. Qualitative interviews with call centre employees. These employees were asked to describe their work history, their career goals and ambitions, 'a typical day at work', what they had learned from the job, what they did not like about the job, and how it compared to other jobs they had had. These interviews were taped and transcribed (see Jarman and Barkow 1999).

2. Site visits to 20 Maritime call centres over the period 1997 to 2005.[4] These centres ranged in size from a few small-scale operations ('nascent' operations of fewer than 10 seats with plans to grow but still at an early stage of business development) to operations employing hundreds or in one case thousands of workers. The majority were non-union shops, but several

were unionized because they were part of a larger organization. Some were 'in-house' operations, vertically integrated into a larger organization with career routes leading out of the centre. Others were freestanding operations. Some were 'outsourced' call centres that would bid on contracts from a number of firms. The site visits themselves were useful in that they gave the researcher insight into the diversity of employment situations and types of work available in this area as well as basic impressions and understandings of the nature of the labour process in the operations. Information from the site visits was also essential in preparing the researcher to talk comfortably about call centre experiences with a range of other people in the industry.

3.   Interviews with managers. One of the projects involved interviews with 25 call centre managers to obtain information such as the size of the business, the nature of its labour supply, its turnover rate, and its identification of its own successes and failures.

4.   A large set of government documents, government statistics, consultancy reports, newspaper clippings, annual reports, help wanted ads, and 'yellow pages'.

5.   A careful search of corporate and government websites for information about company start-ups, expansions, layoffs, and closures.

6.   Many individual conversations. These took place in call centres, offices, conference settings, government corridors, social gatherings, people's homes, and universities. With the growth of the call centre industry, many people have call centre experience and are keen to talk about and analyze that experience.

THE RISE OF THE CALL CENTRE INDUSTRY

Call centres began to arrive in the Maritimes in the early 1990s. Of the three Maritime provinces, New Brunswick had the most aggressive strategy for recruiting new firms to come to the region. Former Premier Frank McKenna's much heralded and much criticized strategy of making New Brunswick 'open for business' involved identifying the strengths of the New Brunswick labour force and attempting to develop an industrial mix that would capitalize on this strength. Because of the heritage of both the Acadian French and the English, one of the strengths identified was a labour force containing many bilingual people. Call centres, relying heavily as they do on communication and language skills, were identified as an appropriate industry for the province. So New Brunswick sent a team of recruiters into the United States to inform American firms of the opportunities available in New Brunswick and to help facilitate the location of operations to New Brunswick. The province thus had an 'active' campaign of recruitment. The result was the creation of some 6,000 new jobs by 1997 (Buchanan 2000).

The two other provinces, Nova Scotia and Prince Edward Island, developed their call centre strategies somewhat later. Nova Scotia, for example, on seeing the rise of the industry in neighbouring New Brunswick, set up a body called Connections Nova Scotia with a mandate to recruit call centre operations to the province. Nova Scotia never had as many recruiters on the road as New Brunswick did but tried to focus recruiting efforts on the 'higher' end of the call centre industry—firms paying higher wages. By 1998 at least 41 firms had set up operations in Nova Scotia. However, ambivalence about the call centre strategy remained. Connections Nova Scotia itself was a victim to budget cuts and was subsumed by the Department of Economic Development. The specific focus on call centre operations was lost, as was the active recruitment strategy of having personnel specifically asked to draw in call centre business to the province. The Department of Economic Development reverted to a passive strategy, simply providing information or facilitating the entrance of any firm that decided of its own accord to consider moving to the province. Even with a passive strategy, however, call centre operations have grown in the province. As of July 2005, there were at least 65 centres in the province with a total labour force of approximately 15,000. Existing operations such as Convergys have expanded their operations, growing from 800 employees in one centre to multiple centres with a total workforce of over 2,600. Tiny Prince Edward Island has adopted a similar passive strategy regarding call centre recruitment. Nonetheless, at least 11 call centres have opened their doors there with a total workforce of 1,192 in 2003 (MRSB Consulting Services 2003).

WHAT IS A CALL CENTRE?

So what exactly is a call centre? A call centre is a specialized workplace that provides service and/or information over the telephone. Increasingly, call centres also provide web support, including email handling, fax support, and online chat. Indeed, some are beginning to call themselves 'contact centres' to reflect the diversity of their methods of interacting with customers or clients. They typically handle a large volume of interactions every day. Depending on the nature of the service provided, calls can be very short—less than a minute long. Complicated calls can take up to 40 minutes, although occasionally they can be even lengthier. The work process is supported by computer hardware such as computerized call distribution systems that 'feed' calls to agents and software such as database management systems that help the agent to systematically record information from the customer. Most centres have advanced record-keeping systems; each call from a customer is linked with an existing file so that it is immediately available to the person who answers the telephone and s/he knows exactly what the customer has previously ordered or requested. This allows a service worker to see the client's history without having to start from scratch every time someone contacts the centre.

In previous generations, when service was conducted via face-to-face interactions, employees would often get to know regular customers. Therefore, much information about customer preferences would be part of their own knowledge. They would know, for example, that Mrs Lee usually comes to the bank on Fridays and withdraws $200, that she has a little house, and that she sometimes has trouble making the mortgage payments on time. Call centres change this relationship because transactions are done over the telephone and are mediated through voice or electronic interactions. Therefore, the job of knowing the background information needed to provide good service has been centralized and routinized instead of remaining embodied in the service worker.

Call centres now serve many different organizations in a range of industries. In the Maritimes, these organizations include banks, insurance companies, telecommunications companies, technical help desks, marketing firms, government services, pharmaceutical companies, customer service departments, parcel delivery firms, transportation companies, oil delivery operations, ambulance services, taxi companies, and funeral homes.[5]

A PROFILE OF EMPLOYMENT IN CALL CENTRES[6]

A number of specific occupations are emerging in the call centre industry, and 'teleservice representatives' make up the largest occupational group in the industry. The representatives are drawn from the local labour market, and the jobs are in demand (particularly at the high end of the spectrum). While educational credentials are not a hiring factor for some centres, a number of workers are high school and university students, particularly in the lower-paying centres. Those offering higher wages require a minimum of a university degree for entrance. Candidates who are gregarious and have strong people skills are typically chosen, and in many centres these personal qualities were rated as much more important than formal education. Formal education tends to be more important for call centres that serve as the 'intake' or entry level for a larger organization, so prospective employees are considered not merely for their ability to perform call centre work but also for their potential for promotion and advancement through the organization toward a more substantial career. Formal education is also required by firms where the work is more complicated. Insurance call centres, for example, often require insurance industry qualifications; some banking call centres require three-year BAs and will even fund further university commerce or accounting courses.

An added bonus of hiring English-speaking Atlantic Canadians, according to one large teleservice employer, is that they have an accent that is relatively indistinguishable across Canada and in the United States. Bilingual representatives are also highly prized. Managers report that because of their value, bilingual representatives tend to have a high turnover rate even in the high-end operations, often moving right out of the call centre industry for more lucrative positions.

Teleservice representatives in Maritime Canada have a varied demographic profile although they are generally young (typically in their 20s). While researchers elsewhere have described the industry as predominantly female, in this region the call service labour force has greater gender parity. There is a small but significant presence of members of visible minority groups and occasionally people reporting serious disabilities. The large firms that have received government subsidies in particular show an interest in hiring from the employment equity populations.

The teleservice representative's work process is intense, primarily consisting of two types of work: handling inbound calls from customers phoning the company and placing outbound calls, which involve the company calling the customer. The two types of calls are viewed as requiring different kinds of skills and making different demands on the worker. Inbound calls are viewed as less stressful even though callers can sometimes be disgruntled. Agents making outbound calls often deal with rude responses as people frequently react negatively to sales calls that they consider intrusive and unwanted. The pace is fast; as soon as one call finishes, representatives are immediately involved in the next call, which is automatically dialled and queued for them. In operations with direct dialling machines (all of the larger firms and many of the medium-sized firms), representatives have little control over the process and thus over the pace of their work.

The work performed by the teleservice representative involves judgment, maturity, and discretion, albeit to varying degrees depending on the precise nature of the teleservice transaction. In banking call centres, for example, representatives act effectively as bank tellers and are remunerated at a level slightly above bank tellers working in a branch bank. They give information about bank products and services (such as mortgages, credit cards, personal computer banking, and telephone banking) and customer account information. To protect the bank from legal proceedings, all telephone conversations are taped, and the tapes are stored in the event of conflicts arising from the transactions. These tapes are also regularly screened, and employee performance is assessed on the way they handle the calls.

Most of the firms conduct their own training. Some of the small firms merely have new employees sit next to experienced operators to learn the ropes. In the larger operations, however, training is formalized and ranges from one-day to six-week courses in which workers are instructed in the details of new products and trained in conducting complex transactions over the telephone. The firms with more sophisticated labour strategies emphasize continuous training as new products are brought on, and in these firms one employee (or more) is designated as a 'trainer' or 'coach'. Many firms place great emphasis on training, utilizing 'down' times in the call centre to retrain workers in classrooms that can be converted to take calls off the floor if demand in the centre suddenly and unexpectedly increases. Most establishments have workstations or company lounges where instructional videotapes can be screened and instructional software used. Despite this emphasis on training, most of the jobs can be learned in one to four months.

Another category of employee is the technician, and the presence or absence of technicians in a firm is directly related to its level of technology. Technicians can be found at the middle and high levels of the industry. They described their jobs as satisfying, exciting, and fast-paced, and they are confident of their ability to remain employed in the industry. More likely to be male than female, technicians are young (in their late 20s to mid-30s) but a little older than most of the teleservice representatives, who tend to be in their teens and 20s.

Both technicians and managers are sometimes from out-of-province, which indicates that the market for this kind of labour is national rather than local. They talked positively about the quality of life in the Maritimes—being able to drive to work and park conveniently, the availability of housing close to work, the friendliness of people on the East Coast, and the ease of transition in terms of making friends. While they seemed happy with life in the region, many also mentioned that career opportunities might take them out of the province or even into the growing call centre industry in the United States, which they saw as expanding particularly in Texas and the northeastern states.

Technicians are involved in tailoring software to particular types of calling situations and installing and maintaining computer equipment. Typically, these technicians have professional-level qualifications in engineering or computer science, but some have backgrounds in the social sciences with an emphasis on quantitative and statistical analysis. Some of the large service bureaus have workers who are employed by the telephone companies but work full-time in the call centres to ensure that the telephone lines remain operational and to run equipment that involved detailed monitoring of the destination of calls, call frequency, and so forth.

Above representatives and technicians are the managers, who perform very different tasks depending on the firm. In smaller firms, they tend to be 'masters/mistresses of all trades' and even participate in making calls when the need arises. In general, management functions include staffing, maintaining complex shift rotations that match the hourly demand for representatives with specific projects, maintaining complex record systems of work accomplished, soliciting work (which involves carefully estimated bids on work), budgeting, record-keeping, and general trouble-shooting.

As with technicians, there are significant opportunities for upward mobility for managers, with frequent opportunities to move, both within and outside the region. While it might be possible for a worker to move from the call centre floor to a managerial position as the industry matures, we found that managers have either moved from management positions in call centres outside the region or have been drawn from managerial positions in related industries such as retail sales, insurance, or banking. Surprisingly, supervisors and team leaders are much more likely to be women than men.

SERVICE SECTOR EMPLOYMENT VERSUS WORK IN TRADITIONAL INDUSTRIES

The new job growth is very much service sector work as opposed to the agricultural or industrial work traditional in the region for the past few hundred years. Above all, it is human resources that have drawn this industry to Maritime Canada. It makes no use of the natural resources available, nor is the region's geographical location particularly important. These centres could be located anywhere else in the world, given the possibilities that new telecommunications infrastructures create for firms, allowing them to connect instantly and cheaply to diverse locations around the globe.

The new job growth draws on a very different kind of skills and training than those required in the old economy. Although a small number of workers have made the transition from the old to the new economy, those in the industry are generally not people displaced from older industries. The fishers, foresters, farmers, miners, and steelworkers tend to be older males: they have low levels of formal education and live in rural areas.

The new industry has a different profile. Some of the call centre workers are indeed the children of the fishers and foresters, but they have had to make a significant transition in terms of upgrading their education from elementary to at least high school certification, and many centres require a university degree. While some call centres are in rural areas, the largest concentrations are in urban centres, which means that some workers have had to leave their communities to work elsewhere. Despite a popular image of call centre work as 'low-end' jobs, they demand higher educational levels than the jobs of previous generations did. Providing information, problem-solving, or making a sale in an environment that is strictly 'voice-to-voice' is a complicated social process—a fact that seems to receive relatively little recognition. Workers have none of the usual visual cues that have governed human interactions since our species first began to walk upright. The industry thus puts a premium on people with well-developed social skills. Most of the better call centres train heavily around such attributes as voice and phone manner as well as the ability to navigate computer databases quickly in order to obtain information pertinent to the inquiry. Literacy is also important in the call centre because the teleservice representative must access and record information accurately. One manager recently told me that it was surprisingly difficult to find employees who could spell properly. Misspelled and inaccurately recorded information can cause major mistakes—imagine, for example, dispatching an ambulance to Beech Street instead of Beach Street. Thus social skills, literacy skills, communication skills such as speech and listening, and computer competency are all essential in a call centre.

Another element of the contemporary call centre workplace that sets it apart from other types of workplace is that many centres operate in highly competitive environments. Most managers report that expectations for both the quality and the speed of service delivery have been rising steadily since the mid-1990s. Customers expect their calls to be answered on the fourth or fifth ring, hate to be placed in queues listening to music even for a minute, and want their questions answered efficiently without a second or third call-back. Increasingly, they expect the service to be available 24 hours a day, seven days a week.

Constant employee surveillance has become a feature of most call centre workplaces. The centres usually contain large databases of valuable information, ranging from business information to information governed by privacy and data protection and security laws. The banking, financial, and insurance industries have the highest security protections. Their databases routinely contain customer information that includes names, home addresses, salary details, investment holdings, personal assets, mortgage information, bank account numbers, and credit card numbers with dates of expiry as well as records of whether or not the customer has been approved or rejected for credit. Similarly, telepharmacy operations may have information about people's health care history, including information such as disease status and profile and medications prescribed, along with customer details such as home addresses. Not surprisingly, customers demand that extreme care be taken with such information. Recent breaches of credit card information in the United States and India[7] have been very badly received by the general public. Call centres involved in such breaches face lawsuits and loss of contracts. The call centre industry has responded with a range of measures from careful selection of employees to security cameras, the taping of all interactions, and regular 'listening in' on employee conversations. Some centres ban employees from bringing any recording devices—including pens, pencils, and cell phones—onto call centre platforms. Screening to prevent one employee from seeing the monitor of another employee may also be used. Outsourced call centres are sometimes required to set up separate rooms for each of their contracts to minimize the chance of information floating about. Many industries have been forced to create tighter and tighter surveillance and security procedures in recent years—and the call centre industry is certainly one of them, creating new challenges and strains for workers and managers alike.

Perhaps more problematically, the concern with high speed and high quality has persuaded a number of managers to start assessing the work of their employees on the basis of a battery of 'key performance indicators': service level, talk time, wrap-up time, first call resolution, 100 per cent attendance, and punctuality—some call centres even measure 'bathroom time'! As anyone who follows the career and statistics of a professional baseball or hockey player knows, careful measurement of employee output can be useful information. However, the indiscriminate and heavy-handed use of these statistics by some managers can turn a workplace into an unnecessarily stressful and driven environment full of workers insecure about whether their performance is adequate.

ASSESSING THE FIT OF THE INDUSTRY FOR THE MARITIME REGION

Most of the jobs created by the call centre industry are full-time permanent jobs—year-round rather than seasonal in nature as so many other Maritime jobs have been. According to Statistics Canada, 83.5 per cent of the jobs in the industry are full-time, the remaining 16.5 per cent being part-time jobs. This is a higher ratio than that in the rest of the service sector (77.3 per cent full-time and 22.7 per cent part-time) (Akyeampong 2005). Full-time year-round employment is precisely the kind of employment that the region needs if it is to break out of its reliance on the employment insurance system. Furthermore, year-round 'shore-based' work is a distinct improvement over patterns of work common in other industries in the Maritimes, such as fishing, the oil rig industry, or the navy or coast guard, which require people to be away for weeks or months at a time. Sociologists and anthropologists have amply documented the difficulties this creates for family life, both because of worries about dangerous work at sea and because of the difficulty of managing the intermittent presence of partners in the family environment (Binkley 1994; Harrison and Laliberte 1994).

Although the industry seems to have a clear preference for urban areas, job growth has occurred in rural areas where communities have been suffering badly from high unemployment levels. While call centres developed first in urban centres, as urban labour markets reached saturation they moved on to smaller towns and to rural locations, giving new hope to those who want to stay in the region and find jobs there. The number of jobs being created is significant. According to Statistics Canada, the 'technology-driven fast employment growth in business support services' has benefited Atlantic Canada more than any other Canadian region (Akyeampong 2005). Figures drawn from the diverse sources cited earlier in this chapter suggest that there are now tens of thousands of workers employed in the industry on the East Coast, which is important given its high unemployment levels compared to those of the rest of Canada.

While these jobs are not the highest-wage jobs in the economy, it could be argued that since there are reasonably large numbers of them, and given the lower educational profile of the Maritimes, they are a reasonably good fit. Akyeampong reports that in Canada as a whole, the average hourly wage rate in 2004 was $12.45 and average hours of work amounted to 35.2 per week (Akyeampong 2005, 3). This works out to an average wage of $23,788 for Canadian workers. While wage rates in the Maritimes may be lower than the Canadian average,[8] the jobs compare reasonably with other jobs available in the Maritime provinces. According to census figures, average annual earnings for Prince Edward Island were $22,303, for New Brunswick $24,971, and for Nova Scotia $26,632 (Statistics Canada 2001c). Wages for business services jobs appear to rank somewhere near the average wage in these provinces: they are not the lowest-level jobs, nor are they the highest-level jobs. Managers in general and people working in occupations requiring greater skills, such as natural and applied sciences and health care, do receive higher pay. But these fields employ people with above-average educational qualifications and experience, and workers are likely to be older than those employed in the business services industry. The average hourly wage for a person in the group aged 15 to 24, for example, was $10.81 in April 2005 (Statistics Canada 2006). So rather than seeing these jobs as offering 'low' wages as some have done, it seems more accurate to describe them as having 'lower middle' levels of pay. Additionally, many of the call centres provide significant benefit packages, with medical, dental, educational leave, and pension plans.

These jobs help retain human capital in the region, and furthermore they employ a group that has typically been footloose—young workers. The industry trains its employees constantly and thus plays a role in human capital development. One of the groups least likely to engage in lifelong learning or, in other words, to update their own skill sets is the group with the lowest educational qualifications to start with. Thus on-the-job training, as opposed to periods of credential upgrading outside the workplace available to those with some high school education, is likely one of the best ways for an individual to achieve improvements in skill and capability. Indeed, the industry's norms for training (optimum class size of 10 to 12 employees and one-to-one coaching) compare favourably with publicly funded institutions of higher education where staff/student ratios are much higher.

There is now a significant concentration of call centre operations in the region and a significant level of investment. As noted earlier, Statistics Canada reports that Maritime Canada now has 25 per cent of the Canadian share of business support services jobs (Akyeampong 2005, 6). This creates the possibility of economies of scale with respect to the purchase of hardware and software, telecommunications support, recruitment costs, and joint training ventures. It also creates opportunities for joint efforts to recruit new business contracts and the possibility of creating a strong base for industrial-level organizations and councils.

Despite concerns about the 'flighty' nature of the industry, the call centres have so far been remarkably stable in the region. There have been some failures, but on the whole the companies that were recruited have not only stayed in the region but expanded operations. Some have opened multiple centres (e.g., Convergys, Teletech, ICT, and Watts Communications). While some people have predicted that the advent of self-serve web portals would eliminate the need for call centres, the centres have so far simply added web support to their service provision. Far from disappearing, calls from people who fail to navigate websites successfully have become longer and more complex.

What are the issues that need to be faced in order to adequately understand this industry? First, call centres suffer from an image problem not only because they represent unwanted intrusions into dinnertime conversations but also because they are understood as a convenient symbol of repetitive, boring, and unpleasant work. The 'sweatshop' image persists in many quarters. The industry just does not seem exciting as those high-paying oil and gas jobs that may materialize if larger gas reserves are found off the North Atlantic coast. However, the offshore oil and gas industry has estimated that it needs a mere 1,880 employees, according to one recent study (Beaudin and Breau 2001). The cutting edge of modern scientific research and application has also been put forward as of major importance to the region because of its fast pace of development, its potential for revenue generation, and its spin-offs in complementary areas such as aquaculture. But how many people were needed in biotechnology in 2002? A total of just 990 (Beaudin and Breau 2001). Convergys call centres alone employ more people than these industries combined!

A strategy for regional economic development in a large and diverse region must include a range of solutions for different segments of its labour force. Certainly it is desirable to create $130,000-a-year jobs for oil and gas engineers, executives, and highly skilled tradespeople. The call centre industry, however, is an industry that provides jobs for people with high school degrees and bachelor's degrees. It employs several groups of workers who have traditionally had difficulty obtaining employment—namely, young people and those from rural populations.

CONCLUSION

This chapter started by exploring some of the early history of Maritime Canada. The legacy of this history is a population with two major linguistic competencies—English and French—and a number of strong communities with long-standing ties to this part of the world. Its economy was originally based on the region's natural resources and strategic position for international trade and commerce in eighteenth-and nineteenth-century world markets. The region has seen many transitions—some improving the health and quality of life of its diverse communities and others threatening its survival. Now it faces major problems as its economies try to reinvent themselves after the decline of a number of major industries.

The chapter then focused on a new industry—the call centre industry—that has started to provide stable employment to significant numbers of people in the Maritime region. This industry has often been branded as unstable and exploitative and not a good solution for a region with economic development problems. The chapter went on to describe different provincial government strategies with regard to attracting and supporting foreign and domestic firms. New Brunswick started earlier and engaged in an active campaign to recruit firms from other parts of Canada and the US. The other two provinces, Prince Edward Island and Nova Scotia, have been more passive in their approach, seeing their role as helping companies that contact them to make informed decision about suitable locations in the province—particularly trying to estimate whether a given area has reached saturation in terms of its labour supply's ability to support an incoming operation. None of the governments can offer substantial subsidies: subsidies are limited to payroll tax breaks that enable an operation to get off the ground, as well as some indirect subsidy in terms of provincially funded community college programs that act as feeders for some firms.

Despite some of the industry's problems, the chapter suggests that it provides entry-level jobs with pay levels ranging from minimum wage to salaries sufficient to support an adult lifestyle, with benefits including medical, dental, and pension plans. The jobs may be at the lower end of the service economy, but the Maritimes as a whole does not yet have as high an educational profile as that of other parts of the country where economies are more dynamic. The advantage of 'lower middle jobs' is that there are a lot of people with 'lower middle' levels of education and experience in the region. Its track record so far indicates that it has created tens of thousands of jobs for people with high school and bachelor's degrees. As Tables 2 and 3 show, between 70.2 and 74.8 per cent of the Maritime population aged 15 and over have only an elementary, secondary, or college-level education (as compared to 70.7 per cent of the Canadian population aged 15 and over).

It is highly unlikely that one industry can change the features of a regional economy dramatically. The question of what other industries might complement the skills and experience developed in the call centre industry remains a significant challenge for the region. Furthermore, communities around the world are beginning to recognize the scope of the job growth in call centres. In Canada, the number of jobs in the business support services industry increased by 447 per cent between 1987 and 2004; contrast this figure to the service sector as a whole in which employment grew by a mere 37 per cent (Akyeampong 2005). This growth pattern has been mirrored around the world. Not surprisingly, new entrants into the global call centre market are emerging. South Africa recently announced a major call centre drive, citing its English-speaking labour force and temperate location as desirable factors. The quality, maturity, and discipline of Asian labour forces is increasingly recognized, and significant pools of highly qualified information technology professionals reside in India, Pakistan, Bangladesh, Malaysia, and China. Their skills, combined with those of experienced and aggressive Asian business entrepreneurs with access to large pools of capital, are now emerging on the global market. The Maritime region will have to work hard to keep the industry thriving.

It is clear that some of the advantages that first induced people to settle in the region can no longer support communities. The fishing industry has been plagued with problems because of a combination of over-fishing and climatic change. The restructuring of Canada's rail industry tolled the bell for the coal and steel industries. Trade and commerce has shifted westward over the past 100 years. Yet there remains a vibrancy and richness of culture on Canada's East Coast. The current challenge is to stem the brain drain and generate a new economy capable of employing those who want to live in the region. Here the much-maligned call centre industry has entered the picture. While most emphasize its disadvantages, sociology trains us to consider an object in its context. In the context of the Maritimes' developmental problems, this industry has a number of advantages, particularly for those who work at the lower end of the labour market, providing much-needed jobs, work experience, and skill development.

It might be most appropriate then to think of the industry as a bridging industry. It builds bridges for young people as they move through those difficult first few years in the labour market when their aspirations are jolted into line with their actual skills and abilities and when they gain valuable knowledge about their own likes and dislikes, strengths, weaknesses, and career possibilities as well as the demands of work in contemporary workplaces. Similarly, the industry builds bridges for rural areas attempting to replace older, dying, or dead industries with newer sources of economic livelihood. And it bridges past and future as it provides a window of opportunity for some of the oldest communities on the North American continent to retain their working-age populations and young people.

Questions to Consider

1. How does the 'brain drain' affect the Maritime provinces? What dilemmas does this pose for those who make decisions about the allocation of provincial spending priorities?
2. Did the call centre industry develop the same way in the three Maritime provinces?
3. What skills are needed for jobs in the old economy and how are they different from jobs in the new economy?
4. Discuss the advantages and disadvantages of the growth of the call centre industry for the development of Maritime Canada.
5. Discuss the strengths and weaknesses of the methodology and data sources

used in this chapter in relation to helping the author to develop a contextual framework in which to understand change and development in this region of Canada.

Notes

1. This information was obtained from the Library and Archives Canada website, funded by the Canadian Culture Online Program: www.collectionscanada.ca/confederation.
2. Interview with government official, July 2005.
3. Jarman (2004); Clairmont, Jarman, Butler, and Barkow (1999); Jarman and Barkow (1998); Clairmont, Butler, and Jarman (1997).
4. The author has subsequently visited another 40 call centres in Singapore, Malaysia, India, Hong Kong, and China, giving her a comparative perspective on what she observed on Canada's East Coast.
5. This profile is drawn from a database of Maritime call centres compiled painstakingly over the years from a number of sources, including newspapers, yellow pages, government listings, web searches, and information provided by employees.
6. This section is an updated version of a section of a paper that the author wrote for a joint conference. See Jarman et al. (1997).
7. In April 2005 workers at a call centre named MphasiS based in India were involved in a $400,000 online credit card fraud. In June 2005 MasterCard International in the US experienced a breach in security resulting in 40 million accounts being exposed.
8. Akyeampong's analysis does not include provincial breakdowns.

Chapter 18

How Do Migrants Become Canadian Citizens?

Randy Lippert

INTRODUCTION

A few blocks from where I sit writing this chapter in my university office is one end of the massive international Ambassador Bridge that spans the Detroit River from Windsor, Ontario, to Detroit, Michigan. Forming a key seam in the 'NAFTA[1] superhighway' that runs back and forth through Canada's industrial manufacturing heartland in Quebec and southern Ontario, the entire north–south expanse of the continental US, and into Mexico, the bridge permits countless semi truckloads of goods to move along the superhighway. The sheer volume of goods passing daily over this bridge makes it the busiest international border crossing in the world. Yet the bridge also serves as a major port of entry that funnels immigrants and other migrants from the US and distant nations into Canada to live. Some of these migrants later become Canadian citizens.

Immigration and citizenship are intimately intertwined. Though discussions of citizenship do not necessarily turn on immigration—obviously some persons are citizens by birth, descent, or adoption—immigration nevertheless tends to lead to citizenship. But how do these processes work? How do migrants enter Canada's immigration streams and then settle to begin exercising a newly acquired citizenship? The answers to these questions have particular significance for Canada, which is commonly thought of as a settler society, meaning that historically much of its citizenry has migrated from abroad. Canada is in the company of the US, Australia, and New Zealand in this respect but also societies such as Taiwan and Brazil. How migrants become citizens is a key question for those trying to understand such societies, including critical sociologists who seek to understand governance, moral regulation, and related dimensions of social life.

In this chapter, I first briefly discuss the sociology of immigration as well as the sociology of governance and moral regulation. I then focus on some ways of being and becoming first a migrant and then a citizen in Canada. Persons living outside Canada do not simply become migrants; they are selected and processed as such, and once in Canada they do not automatically or 'naturally' become citizens. Rather, some of these migrants undergo what is variously called settlement, establishment, adjustment, integration, or incorporation, part of which can involve formal procedures of obtaining legal citizenship. Other migrants, however, enter Canada on a temporary basis and are not intended within Canadian policies to become citizens. Finally, I discuss resistance to these processes, mostly by focusing on the recent rise of sanctuary incidents in Canada. But in this chapter I am especially interested in the transition from migrant to citizen. In considering this shift, I wish to cast doubt on some taken-for-granted assumptions about immigration and citizenship and to make the following interrelated points. First, there are several migrant and citizen categories and identities in Canada, not one of each. Second, while immigration and to a lesser extent citizenship processes are often assumed to be about ethnicity and labour markets, they are also about governance and moral regulation. Third, these processes are thus not only more complex than typically acknowledged but are fraught with inequalities and stimulate forms of resistance. As far as immigration and citizenship processes are concerned, we could focus on virtually any Canadian region to illustrate these points. In this chapter, I use Windsor and the surrounding region of southwestern Ontario—not because they are special but because I know them better than other Canadian regions.

THE SOCIOLOGY OF IMMIGRATION

Immigration is a realm of longstanding sociological interest, and related research is easily found in sociology's annals. That said, the sociology of immigration is not a clearly defined field of inquiry. Attention to immigration is also evident in other disciplines, including anthropology, demography, geography, economics, history, law, and political science. The main research questions and levels of analysis in these disciplines vary, but at certain points they overlap with those of sociology. Perhaps one way to distinguish sociology's interest in immigration is that it has tended to focus on the receiving end of the migration process—that is, what happens to migrants on entering a settler or host society.

Rather than provide an extensive review, as sociologists usually like to do, let me briefly mention a few approaches. Much research on immigration in Canada has focused on ethnicity and has seen ethnicity and race as the result of 'unequal relationships produced and maintained by differential power between a dominant and subordinate group' (Li 1990). Ethnicity and race are relational concepts, and both are thought to be social constructions with boundaries that vary over time. Marxist accounts suggest that 'racialization' and unequal ethnic relations emerge within the development of capitalism (Satzewich 1990). These approaches range from structuralist Marxist accounts that emphasize the role of race in the working of capitalism (Bolaria and Li 1988) to those that see how working-class divisions (known as split labour markets) bring about racialization (e.g., Calliste 1987). The emphasis is on immigrants as workers. Other research has incorporated feminist understandings of how race and class intersect with gender in the context of immigration processes (e.g., Stasiulus 1990). Still other studies have focused on the content of ethnicity and race (Driedger 1996) and approach them as fixed rather than constructed or relational. These latter studies have resulted in extensive measurable data on ethnic groups in Canada but ignore the workings of power in the creation of ethnicity and race in the first place.

Several models of immigrant integration have been suggested in this research, some of which correspond to actually existing policies. Recently, features of the labour market have been studied to see the effects on migrants' adaptation (Reitz 2003). But one of the main questions stemming from this research is how immigrants' ethnic identity (with 'immigrant' and 'ethnic' often used interchangeably) is diluted or strengthened (Li 1990) in the course of settlement. One major effort in this regard is the work of Driedger (1996) who presents a comprehensive schematic model to explain ethnic change and persistence among immigrants. Driedger suggests a five-cell model that brings together a 'conformity–pluralism' continuum with a 'voluntary–involuntary' continuum, thereby classifying existing theories of immigration integration and predicting which types of integration will develop under certain conditions.

I do not wish to deny or diminish the importance of these well-established areas of sociological study or their contributions to understanding immigration processes in Canada. Yet I want to say that our specific, key question—*how* migrants become citizens—is not usually addressed there. Instead, it is often taken for granted, in part because immigration integration models are usually distinguished from citizenship policies and practices (Castles and Miller 1998, 238–43). Indeed, sociology has traditionally paid much less attention to citizenship than to immigration. However, recent years have witnessed an emerging citizenship literature (e.g., Isin 2002), with some studies carried out by sociologists. This small body of work includes groundbreaking work on immigrant civic engagement in Canada (Siemiatycki and Isin 1998)—that is, the varied ways in which immigrants practise citizenship. One thrust of this newer but relatively petite literature is to suggest that citizenship is not limited to the formal legal kind but refers to a much broader set of practices and ways of being. It is beginning to focus on how migrants become citizens of various types.

A relevant and recent sociological perspective is called the sociology of governance (see Hunt 1999 and Chapters 1, 9, and 11 in this book). As noted, it draws heavily from the later work of philosopher and historian Michel Foucault on 'governmentality' and tends to be of a critical variety. Here 'governance' means 'any attempt to control or manage any known object' (Hunt and Wickham 1994, 78). This broad concept includes laws, policies, and practices of the municipal, provincial, and federal levels of the state but also the efforts of private authorities and organizations as well as those of new forms that do not always easily fit into public or private categories. It also refers to how individuals govern themselves. Most often in this research, governance is equated to the conduct of conduct—that is, governance is about how human behaviour or action is directed or guided.

Aspects of moral regulation are present in all governing practices (Hunt 1999, 6), and indeed governing practices in the realm of immigration and citizenship take the form of moral regulation. The 'moral' in moral regulation refers to normative judgments (those judgments involving 'should') that a particular form of conduct or behaviour is essentially or inherently wrong or bad (Hunt 1999, 7). An emphasis in these studies is on language and forms of knowledge (e.g., formal and informal) and technology (understood in the broadest sense) that make governing conduct possible. Here such elements are seen to shape and in a sense bring objects and corresponding identities into being—or, put simply, to 'constitute' or 'make' them. Such a perspective brings to light aspects of immigration and citizenship policies and practices that might otherwise be ignored. One of the features of this approach is to focus on aspects of policies that seem at first to be self-evident but that on closer examination begin to be problematized or to seem themselves in need of explanation. When taken together, this perspective can begin to make something as seemingly simple and automatic as migrants becoming citizens look more contingent, more complex, and perhaps more amenable to change. Such a sociology can potentially lend insight into how citizens are 'made' from migrants.

BECOMING A MIGRANT

Immigration to Canada—that is, becoming a migrant—is non-random. It is a structured process, shaped mainly by Canadian immigration and refugee policies. Such policies presume eventual citizenship for immigrants. Immigration law and policy that regulates permanent residency may be more significant in influencing who becomes a citizen than citizenship law itself. Immigration law and policy is therefore potentially the principal barrier to achieving citizenship and is therefore worthy of attention.

The history of Canada's immigration policy shows the exclusion of potential migrants on the basis of ethnicity and race—including the infamous Chinese 'head tax'. Following the building of the Canadian Pacific Railway by thousands of Chinese migrants, a 'head tax' was implemented to discourage immigration, reaching $500 by 1904 (equivalent to a full year's wages for full-time work). By 1923 the Chinese Immigration Act had passed in the federal Parliament, thereby virtually ending Chinese immigration to Canada. When Chinese labour had been required for massive construction projects like the railway, they had been permitted to enter; when other labour later became available, Chinese migrants were excluded (Li 1998). The Canadian state also instituted a 'continuous journey' provision in 1908 to prevent the arrival of East Indian migrants in Canada (Bolaria and Li 1988, 171). Canada's systematic exclusion of Jewish refugees fleeing the tyranny of Nazi Germany during the 1930s and 1940s is also well-documented (Abella and Troper 1982). Potential immigrants from 'less preferred' nations, usually groups considered 'non-white', were similarly excluded in the past (Kelley and Trebilcock 1998).

With the creation of a 'points system' in 1967, federal immigration regulations for the first time laid out in detail how immigrants were to be selected. This system was intended to end the explicitly racist practice of selecting immigrants from 'preferred' nations. It used a grid to assign applicants a number of points (to a maximum of 100) for education, age, training, demand for their occupational skills, English or French proficiency, personal qualities, the presence of relatives in Canada, prearranged employment, and employment opportunities (Kelley and Trebilcock 1998, 358–9). This obviously reduced discretion on the part of state immigration officers, though they could still assign anywhere from 0–15 points in the personal quality category and with approval of a senior immigration officer could override the point process altogether in individual cases (358–9). The reduction of discretion associated with this development was nevertheless widely heralded as a major turning point in Canadian immigration policy. This key shift has helped to bring about the result that recent immigrants—including those arriving in Canada over the past decade—are now more likely to have come from nations in Asia, especially China, India, and the Philippines, whereas the migrants who came before the 1960s were more likely to come from Europe, particularly the United Kingdom, Germany, and Italy (Tran, Kustec, and Chui 2005, 11).

The point system, adjusted over the years and now up to 110 points, remains in place. A critical sociology would be less than sanguine about this system, in part because there is certainly room for racism, sexism, and other forms of discrimination to enter the picture (see Thobani 2000). For example, points are given for occupational skill in paid work, but non-paid and domestic work, more often the responsibility of women, does not count as skilled work (Fincher et al. 1994). But a critical sociology also approaches such a system with reservation because of what it ostensibly is—a device to assess who would make the 'best' immigrants and eventual citizens and a means to determine the risk that those allowed into Canada permanently would be other than 'good' immigrants and citizens. Those found wanting are systematically excluded. The point system and immigrant selection more generally have a definite moral aspect to them. They entail moral regulation and are of interest for this reason.

Currently, potential immigrants pay a nominal administrative fee (ranging from $550 to $1,050 depending on the immigrant category) to the state to apply from a consulate or embassy abroad through an often lengthy bureaucratic process. For example, for skilled workers applying through visa offices abroad, only 30 per cent of their applications are finalized within two years and only 80 per cent by 46 months or nearly four years (Canada. Citizenship and Immigration 2005e). In the hope of eventually becoming landed immigrants (also known as 'permanent residents'), applicants must also pass medical and security screening. If successful, they will then travel to Canada (paying an additional $975 fee) and be officially 'landed' on arrival at the Canadian end of the Ambassador Bridge or at some other port of entry such as Pearson International Airport in Toronto or Vancouver International Airport.

Yet there are several streams and categories (as well as several subcategories) of migrants imagined within Canadian immigration and refugee policies. The three basic categories are economic immigrants, refugees, and family class immigrants. Sociologists do not have easy access to statistics held by the Department of Citizenship and Immigration revealing who applies to immigrate to Canada or otherwise enters these streams. We only know 'who gets in' and some features of the immigration process they undergo. We know, for example, that in Canada during every year since 1993, between 174,000 and 250,000 persons became permanent residents (Canada, Citizenship and Immigration 2005c) and that in 2003 there were some 69,000 family class immigrants, 105,000 skilled workers, 26,000 refugees, 8,000 business immigrants, and 13,000 migrants falling into various other special categories for a total of approximately 221,000 landed immigrants (2005c).

We should note the key distinction between refugees and immigrants. Refugees are defined according to the United Nations (UN) Convention on Refugees, a 1951 international agreement to which Canada acceded in 1967.[2] A refugee is a person who

> owing to a well-founded fear of being persecuted for reasons of race, religion, nationality, membership of a particular social group or political opinion, is outside the country of his [sic] nationality, and is unable to or, owing to such fear, is unwilling to avail himself of the protection of that country or to return there, for fear of persecution.

There are two refugee streams. One stream includes refugees selected from camps and crisis situations who may or may not precisely fit the UN definition. The second stream includes persons who make refugee claims in Canada. These refugee claimants have been permitted to enter the country but then must undergo a lengthy process involving quasi-legal hearings before Canada's Immigration and Refugee Board to determine whether they are bona fide refugees. Those found to be refugees undergo further screening similar to that applied to immigrants, and if they are successful, they are eventually landed; those deemed not to be refugees are asked to leave and if necessary physically 'removed' or deported from Canada.

At first glance, the state appears stingy when it comes to immigrant selection since state immigration officers administer the point system to decide 'who gets in'. Indeed, the Canadian public tends to think of immigrants mostly as skilled workers who have undergone the screening, even though in 2003, for example, they represented less than half of all the migrants who became permanent residents. The remainder included refugee claimants, business immigrants, and family class immigrants. Since at least the mid-1980s, asylum-seekers have been depicted as 'spontaneously' arriving at ports of entry to make refugee claims. This characterization stems from the perspective of the Department of Citizenship and Immigration, even though these claimants would have planned their migration to Canada, in some cases for several months ahead of their arrival. Media attention and public concern have focused on the notion that these migrants have 'self-selected' (as though persecution or related oppression did not force them to flee to Canada) and therefore were not pre-screened by Canadian immigration authorities for their capacity to become citizens. Various restrictions, including interdiction abroad, have been implemented to reduce the numbers arriving (Lippert 1998). Yet what is generally overlooked is that other immigrants virtually 'self-select' in that they almost explicitly buy their way into Canada as business immigrants. For entry to Canada, business immigrant applicants are scored on a range of selection criteria, and the threshold for success is low: out of a maximum of 87 points across seven criteria, an entrepreneur or investor class aspirant who scores just 25 points is accepted as an immigrant (Ley 2003). A business class applicant can enter as an immigrant even if they have no post-secondary education and speak neither English nor French (Ley 2003, 428). Further, Ley (429) writes that 'the Canadian state has made it evident that prospective entrepreneurs do not require substantial financial resources, ownership experience, or a detailed business plan to qualify for the business immigration program.' Business immigrants' applications are also on average processed more quickly at visa offices abroad than, for example, those of skilled workers: 19 months compared to 24 (Canada, Citizenship and Immigration 2005e). In contrast to the 25-point requirement, skilled worker applicants must reach 70 of 110 points based on 10 criteria (Ley 2003, 428). 'Self-selection' by entering the refugee determination process is often seen as negative, on many occasions even depicted in mass media accounts as equal to the morally reprehensible practice of 'jumping the queue' (Lippert 1998), whereas 'self-selection' by way of the business immigrant process is apparently largely invisible or positive.

Thobani (2000) found similar distinctions among immigrant categories. In her analysis of the 1994 federal Immigration Policy Review, she found that in the discussion following public consultation, women and family class immigrants were deemed less desirable. In contrast, skilled workers and business immigrants were depicted as 'good', demonstrating the moralized nature of immigrant selection.

State bureaucratic processes involving entitlement, such as public medical care, public education, or welfare, inevitably involve some fraud among claimants. Immigration and refugee procedures are hardly unique in this regard. But it is interesting that the enforcement of fraud within streams also varies. 'Operation Shortstop' was implemented abroad to stop migrants who travel with fraudulent documents and destined for Canada as refugee claimants (Lippert 1998), and the vast majority of the thousands 'removed' from Canada every year, aided by significant enforcement efforts, are failed refugee claimants. Far fewer enforcement resources have been directed toward business immigrants engaged in fraud, in particular those who fall into the entrepreneur sub-category, a minority of whom never intend to or otherwise do not make investments in Canada as promised. Between 1994 and 1998, more than 7,000 entrepreneurs defaulted on the two-year deadline for opening a business in Canada—the reason they qualified to enter this stream in the first place. Fewer than 10 were deported as a consequence (Warner 1999). Many never reported to immigration officials as required after arriving in Canada. In 1998 alone, the visas of 753 expired, but only one was deported as a result (Warner 1999). Such inequality of enforcement and the related hierarchy of migrant categories are of interest to a critical sociology.

That becoming a migrant is complex and less than self-evident is further revealed when one considers how many different kinds of people are involved in the process besides the migrant. The process is mediated not only by state immigration officers who administer the program but also by immigration lawyers, consultants, and family and private sponsors. As the processes become more complex, many people now require consultants or lawyers to navigate the bureaucratic labyrinth that results. Many potential migrants cannot afford the services of such professionals or are without family or private sponsors, which points to an obvious inequality in the immigrant selection system.

It is important to understand that (im)migrant and citizen are both a bureaucratic/legal category and an identity. By identity I refer to a way of understanding and relating to ourselves and others. Law and bureaucratic categories within immigration and citizenship processes, including the Immigration and Refugee Protection Act and the Citizenship Act, contribute to the formation of such identities. For example, there is evidence that business immigrants to Canada actually self-identify as such (Ley 2003). Legal status and identity overlap of course, which is to say that law helps to constitute or 'make up' identities. The Citizenship Act, however, does not 'act' alone: citizenship laws in the West often go hand in hand with programs 'that encourage those identified as citizens to behave in particular ways, such as publicly celebrating their status, and even to conceive of their legal status as an integral aspect of their identity' (Galloway 2000, 83). In other words, it is not only citizenship law that makes citizens but much broader processes as well; law is one but not necessarily the most important source of these identities. An interesting puzzle for sociologists is how migrant identities shift to citizen identities—and this is partially what our key question is about. It is the various sources of both identities that is of interest to sociologists. In a recent literature review, Tastsoglou concludes by remarking about a

> conspicuous absence of historical and contemporary research on the impact of the institutional aspects of the immigration process—mainly settlement and multicultural policies—on collective and individual identities of Canada's ... immigrant minorities ... [and that] there is not a particular focus on, or link to, identities (2001, 29–30).

She notes the same lack of research regarding citizenship policies, including benefit distribution and its relation to identities (32).

The notion of *governing through* is gleaned from the sociology of governance discussed above: governing is seldom exclusively an instrumental effort to govern others' conduct (Hunt 1999, 6). Indeed, in this case, all manner of problems, processes, and conduct may be governed *through* immigration. This is evident, for example, in attempts to encourage economic growth through the introduction of the business immigrant program, the notion being that these immigrants will bring investment capital and entrepreneurial experience with them to Canada, thus fuelling the national economy. Consider two other examples: the tragic Tsunami disaster in Asia and its immediate aftermath and national and continental security following the events of 9/11 in the US.

One way that the Canadian government responded to the Tsunami disaster, encouraged by members of the public, was to expedite the existing immigrant applications of those with immediate family members in Canada and to waive new immigrant application processing fees as well as the $975 fee for potential migrants seriously and personally affected by the disaster (Canada, Citizenship and Immigration 2005b). The disaster's horrific effects on the region's human population were, in a sense, governed *through* immigration, which is to say that increasing immigration from the region was not the primary target of this policy shift; instead, the goal was to alleviate human suffering or at least to respond to the Canadian public's calls for the government to do so.

Similarly, since the terrorist attacks on 11 September 2001 in the US, Canada's immigration policy has changed to respond to the need for greater scrutiny and surveillance at its borders and stepped up screening of immigrant applicants (Adelman 2002). The recent introduction of the 'safe third country' provision renders Canadian policy more dependent on the fairness (or unfairness) of US refugee and immigration policies than before. This development is consistent with broader shifts evident in other world regions toward what is called the increasing 'securitization of migration' (Bigo 2002) or the notion of governing security *through* immigration. Since the early 1980s, many refugee claimants would enter the US at various points and then travel to the Canadian border, such as the Ambassador Bridge, to make refugee claims (the Canadian refugee determination system is generally seen as fairer or at least more open than that of the US). But the 'safe third country' provision forces refugee claimants to enter the US immigration system before they can enter Canada. Canada is obliged to do likewise with refugee claimants who first enter Canadian territory and seek status in the US. The suggestion here is that terrorism (mostly in the US) can be somehow better prevented by changing Canadian immigration policies in this way. The three targets—fostering national economic growth, reducing human misery resulting from natural disaster, and improving national or continental security— are all governed *through* immigration. The significance of these examples is simply that studying immigration (and citizenship) processes in this way is important to understanding how aspects of society that appear to have little to do with immigration at first glance are governed.

OTHER MIGRANTS: SEX-TRADE AND AGRICULTURAL MIGRANT WORKERS

Many migrants in Canada are not immigrants or 'permanent residents' and will never have the opportunity to become so. These migrants are in Canada legally but temporarily (Basok 2002), which is to say that they are not imagined within Canadian policies as *potential* citizens.

Several blocks upriver from the Ambassador Bridge, closer to where the Detroit River meets Lake St Clair, is Windsor's downtown area. Like any downtown, it serves the needs of Windsor's residents, but it also serves their desires and those of visiting American residents who come across the bridge or through the Detroit/Windsor tunnel that connects the two downtown cores. Perhaps needless to say, US visitors are the most temporary of migrants, coming across for a couple of hours, a day, or a weekend, mostly to shop, drink, gamble, or purchase sexual services, and they do not usually seek eventual Canadian citizenship. Until very recently, a huge building-high 'Canadian Club' (whiskey) sign was installed at the nearby Hiram-Walker distillery, easily visible only from downtown Detroit, and a bit closer to Windsor's downtown, an equally massive and similarly positioned 'Casino Windsor' sign has been affixed atop the new casino since the mid-1990s—both plainly set up to attract would-be US visitors. On Windsor's main street strip are shops that sell Cuban cigars (illegal in the US, which by itself makes them a more attractive commodity), and there are several massage parlours within or very close to the core. For its size, Windsor's downtown core also has a disproportionately large bar district that reflects in part the lower legal drinking age in Ontario compared to that of adjacent Michigan. On any given weekend, throngs of young American adults spill onto Windsor's downtown streets to 'bar-hop' and consume (sometimes large quantities of) alcohol. Several of the more well-known licensed establishments are strip clubs that employ temporary migrant sex-trade workers, mostly from nations in eastern Europe and Asia, as 'exotic dancers'.

Special policy provisions permit migrants to enter Canada to work temporarily as 'exotic dancers'. At many strip clubs here and elsewhere in Canada, these sex-trade workers are required to pay daily fees to the club and the disc jockey and sometimes special fees for the use of cubicles. In some cases, the women are not even paid by the establishment itself but are instead expected to charge patrons for lap dances, table dances, or sexual acts in the cubicles or 'VIP rooms' (Macklin 2003). The workers often feel pressured to charge patrons in part because of the significant fees they must pay but also because of (other) forms of coercion. The result is that these workers are particularly susceptible to sexually transmitted diseases and other physical harm. Agents play a role in demanding additional fees and may force these temporary migrant workers to give up their earnings in order that they be 'safely' deposited in a bank account in the woman's home country (Macklin 2003). Many of the temporary workers speak little English, and they are instructed by their agents not to speak to anyone in case that person is from the government (Macklin 2003).

It was noted earlier that our key question is often about moral regulation. The fact that sex workers' work permits are temporary is highly relevant. A rationale that employers and the Canadian state use to justify the program is that there are not enough Canadian women willing to work as 'exotic dancers' in Canada. But as Macklin astutely notes:

> At no point in the evolution of policy responses did the government or employers contemplate that the solution to the allegedly chronic labor shortage of Canadian strippers would be to facilitate the permanent immigration of qualified and experienced strippers. Here, economic objectives operate in tandem with morality to reinforce the exclusion of sex-trade workers from permanent residence. Club owners' interest is in retaining a pool of women who have no legal option but to work for them, which would be defeated if the women were granted permanent resident status (permanent residents are entitled to work in the occupation of their choice). In the sphere of morality, the silence of government officials and club owners alike also expresses the shared but unarticulated consensus that these women are not suitable candi-

dates for membership in the Canadian nation-state. After all, Canadian sex-trade workers live on the margins of social citizenship (2003, 481).

Beyond the Detroit River, past where it meets Lake Erie, and around the shoreline toward Pelee Point, the southern-most mainland point in Canada—about a 50-km drive from Windsor—is Leamington, Ontario. It is dubbed the 'Tomato Capital of Canada' because of the Heinz processing plant that dominates the city's centre and the large-scale production of tomatoes surrounding the city. As a result of another special program, some 4,000 workers migrate to this region of Canada every year, primarily from Mexico but also from Caribbean nations. They migrate to work harvesting vegetables and fruit in the rapidly growing greenhouse industry, which is now the largest of its kind in North America (Basok 2002).

Paid minimum wage of about $7 per hour, these workers are required to work 10 hours per day, seven days a week, without overtime pay. Employment insurance premiums and Canada Pension Plan contributions are deducted from their pay even though these migrants will never be permitted to draw on these benefits should they become unemployed or upon their return to their home nations. Should they want to move from one greenhouse employer to another, they need permission from the Canadian government to do so (Basok 2002). These workers experience deplorable living conditions, exposure to dangerous pesticides, and uncertainty about workers' compensation coverage should they have a work accident (Basok 2002).

A recent in-depth study revealed that these workers are seen by employers as temporary, cheap, and reliable labour (Basok 2002). It is precisely their 'unfreedom'—their lack of capacity to choose whether and where to work—that renders them valuable to the greenhouse industry. They cannot voice their concerns about, for example, pesticide dangers without risking losing their place in the program for which they had been selected, a predicament augmented by high unemployment and low wages in Mexico and the Caribbean. Basok's study reveals that local growers are not so much interested in cheap labour—of which these migrants are a form—but in workers willing to work during the brief period when a vegetable is at its optimum for picking—during Canadians' traditional leisure time at night, on holidays, and on weekends. Many of these migrants return year after year. The irony is that it is conceivable that some migrants will actually spend more days of their lives working in Canada than some Canadian citizens.

Some of these migrants *could* become citizens. But a critical sociology would be interested in how these temporary sex-trade and agricultural migrants are prevented from doing so—prevented from leaving their assigned places of work, going underground to work and live illegally in Canada, and later surfacing to gain legal status and become Canadian citizens. Of interest are the techniques used to govern or police these migrants to bar them from citizenship. As far as temporary sex-trade workers are concerned, once in Canada these women are governed not so much by Canadian immigration officers as by their private agents:

Once in Canada, agents routinely and unlawfully seize the women's passports and visas, confine the women's movements and interactions, restrict their ability to interact with Canadians (other than customers), and intimidate them through physical and sexual violence, retaliation against family members in the home country, or by warning the women that they can have them jailed and/or deported by Canadian authorities. The women do not speak English, do not know what Canadian law permits, and are multiply stigmatized as foreigners and as sex-trade workers (Macklin 2003, 14).

These workers are prevented from accessing the resources that would allow them to go underground or gain permanent legal status through regular means. For agricultural workers, one policing technique is ensuring that these migrants are selected according to certain criteria: male, married, with families in Mexico highly dependent on their incomes. The program imagines that these individuals will be highly unlikely to risk losing their regular incomes by going underground or somehow gaining status by entering the refugee determination process, waiting out a general amnesty, or using fraudulent means, because they have a strong reason to work for their designated employer and dutifully return to Mexico every year. The strategy is not to seek out those migrants who will make 'good' immigrants and later citizens but those migrants who will desist from seeking permanent residence and citizenship while they work in Canada.

FROM MIGRANT TO CITIZEN

Citizenship refers to a shared sense of belonging and is one way of being political (Isin 2002, 30). The notion of citizen is present in Roman law and is also associated with the French Revolution (Valverde et al. 1999). Isin (2002) defines citizenship broadly as:

> that kind of identity within a city or state that certain agents constitute as virtuous, good, righteous, and superior, and differentiate it from strangers, outsiders, and aliens who they constitute as their alterity via various solidaristic, agonistic, and alienating strategies and technologies.

In other words, citizenship may well be dependent on the notion of migrants, and the latter helps to constitute or 'make up' the former. Isin (2002) notes: 'The alterity of citizenship, therefore, does not preexist, but is made possible by it.' Migrant categories may well be generated within citizenship processes.

There are competing kinds of citizenship in Canada. With renewed interest in citizenship has come the suggestion that there are forms of citizenship beyond the national kind. The development of the European Union, for example, has led to European citizenship. This is also referred to as 'post-national' citizenship that is no longer limited to the borders of a nation-state (Soysal 2000), consistent with the onset of globalization and transnationalism. Despite NAFTA (and the NAFTA superhighway), however, no corresponding North American citizenship (yet) exists or at least not one that is fast replacing Canadian citizenship. It is probably best to think of competing citizenships, but ultimately the way that people exercise and understand citizenship and the shifting categories they embrace and that shape their lives is a problem that sociologists can explore empirically.

Though challenged, there is no doubt that national citizenship is still in the running. But just what kind of citizenship is national citizenship? National citizenship obviously refers to allegiance to a nation rather than to some other form of community. In Canada many rights of citizenship are defined in the Canadian Charter of Rights and Freedoms, which is part of Canada's constitution. The Charter legally stipulates the basic rights and freedoms of everyone in Canada, including the right to a trial, equality rights, mobility rights such as the right to live and work anywhere in Canada, and Aboriginal peoples' rights, as well as basic freedoms, such as freedom of thought, speech, religion, and peaceful assembly. Under the Charter, Canadian citizens can run as candidates and vote in federal, provincial, and territorial elections, receive either French or English education, and freely enter and exit Canada. It is clear that as we have moved away from social citizenship with its corresponding benefits associated with a welfare state, national citizenship is becoming less social and more individualistic.

Discussing the transition from migrant to Canadian citizen as a one-way journey is a bit misleading. The vast majority of migrants in Canada are already citizens of at least one nation, so to suggest that they develop into citizens is seeing them only from a Canadian perspective. That said, once migrants are accepted as landed immigrants and if they are 18 years or older, have lived in Canada for three of the four years prior to applying, and speak either English or French, they can submit an application to the Department of Citizenship and Immigration to become citizens. Like immigration, this process currently takes a long time—estimated at 15 to 18 months in 2005 (Canada, Citizenship and Immigration 2005d)—during which officials check applicants' landed immigrant status and whether they have a criminal record. The applicants are then required to pass a standardized (either written or oral) citizenship test that includes questions pertaining to Canada's history, geography, and system of government as well as the citizenship rights and responsibilities mentioned above (2005a).

We know some characteristics of the process of migrants legally becoming Canadian citizens. It is known that 95 per cent of persons residing in Canada are Canadian citizens—81 per cent became citizens by birth, and 14 per cent first migrated to Canada (Tran, Kustec, and Chui 2005, 9). It is also clear that the decision to become a citizen occurs shortly after entering Canada. As well, more than nine in 10 immigrants who came to Canada between October 2000 and September 2001 indicated their intention to become Canada citizens, which is to say that seeking citizenship is part of the immigrant identity.

The latest census data (2001) indicates that the percentage of immigrants who are legally entitled to become citizens and who choose to do so (84 per cent) is higher than in other Western societies. In Australia the percentage is 75 per cent; for the UK it is only 56 per cent; and for the foreign-born in the US it is only 40 per cent (Tran, Kustec, and Chui 2005, 10). In other words, eligible migrants are more likely to become citizens in Canada than in similar societies, and our key question therefore may be more relevant here than elsewhere.

It is also true that younger immigrants are more likely than older immigrants to become citizens in Canada. Younger immigrants have more time to settle and are also more likely to be active in the labour market. It may be that they wish to pursue occupations available only to citizens (Tran, Kustec, and Chui 2005, 10). At the same time, older immigrants may be less likely to become citizens because they will have less time to enjoy the benefits it promises. However, the difference is not extreme—85 per cent of those under 20 at the time of their arrival and 72 per cent of those 70 and over upon entry became citizens (10).

The longer that immigrants are in Canada, the greater the likelihood that they will become legal citizens. Of the migrants in Canada for two to five years, 79 per cent had become citizens. After 30 years, some 90 per cent had gained that status. If achieving legal citizenship is a measure of the outcome of the social process of migrants becoming citizens, this means that 'establishment' for some migrants can take several years. But the process is speeding up. For recent migrants, less time elapses before they become citizens than for migrants who came prior to 1981 (56 per cent compared to 42 per cent) (Tran, Kustec, and Chui 2005, 10–11).

As noted earlier, immigrants to Canada increasingly come from Asia. Newly eligible immigrants from that region, as well as from Africa, are much more likely to become citizens than their recent counterparts from European nations and the US (Tran, Kustec, and Chui 2005, 11). For example, 90 per cent of the immigrants from China had become citizens after six to 10 years in Canada. In contrast, only 50 per cent of eligible immigrants from the US had become citizens by 2001 after six to 10 years of residence (11).

What is not often recognized is that, historically, immigration to Canada has been coupled with emigration, or persons leaving Canada. Between 1951 and 1991, for example, while 12.5 million persons immigrated to Canada, almost eight million left (McKie 1994). Migrants who become citizens in Canada (as well as other Canadians citizens) emigrate, and if legally required in their new host society, they may eventually renounce their Canadian citizenship to initiate citizenship there. The vast majority (84 per cent) of the Canadian citizens who left during that period went to the US. The next largest number of citizens emigrated to the UK. Hence some migrants, after legally becoming Canadian citizens, give up that status—that is, they leave Canada, never to return. This is rarely acknowledged, much less studied, perhaps because it is contrary to the widely held view that Canada is a desirable, *permanent* destination for immigrants and, consistent with this view, that Canadian citizens would not contemplate or choose emigration. Of course, not all those leaving Canada are citizens; some are landed immigrants who hold citizenship elsewhere. Why some migrants *do not* become citizens is apparently related to this fact. Laws in some source countries, such as the US and Japan, prohibit dual citizenship. A lack of knowledge about the process of becoming a citizen may also be a factor, as undoubtedly is the cost of doing so ($200). And migrants' language ability is yet another feature (Tran, Kustec, and Chui 2005, 11) since this is one criterion of eligibility.

Some emigration from Canada is forced—it takes the form of state deportation (Pratt 2005). Thus some migrants never get a chance to become citizens because they are forcibly deported from Canada (citizens have a right to enter and reside in Canada and cannot be legally deported). This was true in Canada historically (Roberts 1994), and thousands of migrants continue to be 'removed' every year, thus raising the further question of how this happens or, to put it another way, how some migrants *do not* become citizens. As will be seen later in this chapter, some migrants resist state attempts at their removal.

In summary, most 'Canadians'—usually assumed to include both landed immigrants and citizens—are citizens; most immigrants to Canada want to, and most eventually do, become citizens. Younger migrants and those in Canada for longer periods are more likely than others to secure citizenship. But a critical sociology recognizes that these numbers and related trends will not suffice; they do not reveal *how* migrants become citizens but only some features of those who do and of one process (i.e., the legal process) they undergo. The fact that so many migrants appear to become citizens is somewhat misleading because these numbers refer only to *immigrants* becoming legal citizens. As already shown, there are other migrants in Canada who are here temporarily and are not permitted to become citizens through regular or at least official means. Becoming a legal citizen can be seen only as a marker of a migrant's integration: 'Moving from permanent resident status to Canadian citizen may be interpreted as an indicator of integration into society in general and the labour market in particular' (Tran, Kustec, and Chui 2005, 11). For migrants, receiving legal citizenship may be perceived as the end of the migration process, but whether it is equivalent to full incorporation is doubtful if research in other settler societies is any indication (Ip, Inglis, and Wu 1997). Citizenship is therefore more than legal citizenship.

Becoming a legal citizen is sometimes called 'naturalization'. Yet this term suggests that there is something non-social about the process of migrants becoming citizens—that it is automatic, 'naturally' occurring, and therefore of little interest to sociologists. Critical sociologists are typically inclined to investigate further any process widely claimed to be 'natural'. With the gradual demise of social citizenship, the movement from migrant to citizen is increasingly understood in the broad sense of gradually installing a capacity to exercise choice. In settlement, migrants' active capacities are to be nurtured and promoted. Far from being assumed to adapt 'naturally' after arriving in Canada, migrants are thought to require considerable care and moral investment—the inculcation of skills to develop into virtuous self-governing entities that exercise choice. Settlement programs thus seek to change individuals drawn from distant locales, remote refugee camps, or crisis situations into self-regulating citizens. This involves the conversion of entities lacking a capacity for choice when they enter Canadian society's conceptual margins to citizens freely exercising choice at its centre. Settlement programs have long involved financial assistance and special services that promise to foster such change.

WAYS OF MAKING CITIZENS: TECHNOLOGIES OF CITIZENSHIP

For critical sociologists, what is interesting is how the transition from migrant to citizen happens—that is, the technologies and knowledges of settlement and establishment, of 'migrating' from migrant to citizen. The ways of making citizens of migrants vary. Ethnic pluralism or Canada's policy of multiculturalism is one strategy of citizenship that has been much discussed and debated. An eclectic but by no means exhaustive list of these strategies would include multiculturalism but also the less discussed citizenship tests, host programs, and passports.

We noted earlier that citizenship tests are part of the process. These tests include questions such as:

> What are the three main groups of Aboriginal peoples?
> When did settlers from France first establish communities on the St Lawrence
> River?
> Which four provinces first formed Confederation?
> List three ways in which you can protect the environment.
> Where does the name 'Canada' come from?
> Which region covers more than one-third of Canada?
> In what industry do most Canadians work?
> What is Canada's system of government called?

The irony is that many present citizens—including me—do not readily know the answers to all or even most of these questions.

The test is also intended to determine whether a landed immigrant has acquired an adequate knowledge of French or English. If successful, applicants can then participate in a ceremony in which they take the oath of citizenship:

> I swear (or affirm) that I will be faithful and bear true allegiance to Her
> Majesty Queen Elizabeth the Second, Queen of Canada, Her Heirs and Successors, and that I will faithfully observe the laws of Canada and fulfil my
> duties as a Canadian citizen.

During this ritual, migrants sign the oath form and receive a Canadian citizenship certificate indicating citizenship status. This practice encourages would-be citizens to think of themselves as ideal citizens. The examination and oath-swearing practices are on the more obvious end of the spectrum of technologies of citizenship in that they clearly identify their aim as instilling citizenship.

Like becoming a migrant, becoming a citizen is a process that involves agents besides the eligible migrant. The best known form is probably the counsellor working in state-funded immigrant settlement organizations found in communities across Canada. Perhaps less known is the volunteer host associated with the 'host program' (Canada. Citizenship and Immigration 2004). A national pilot host program for refugee resettlement was launched in Canadian cities in 1985 (Lanphier 1993). This program anticipated volunteers aligned with private groups and organizations becoming involved with state-sponsored refugees (Lanphier 1993, 255). It foresaw the transfer of state funds to cover costs and a coordinator recruiting hosts, matching them with newly arrived individual refugees or refugee families, and then overseeing the hosts' subsequent resettlement practices, which were to include teaching English or French and helping refugees secure employment. Besides reducing costs and state counsellors' workloads, this program sought to effect 'more rapid adaptation to community life in Canada' (Canada, Employment and Immigration 1987, 2). Refugees were to be resettled within and through communities. The host program was later extended to 10 cities in six provinces, and in 1990 it was announced that the pilot host plan would be made permanent and expanded to target immigrants as well (Canada, Employment and Immigration 1990, 15). Of course, similar hosting took place before there was an explicit state-sponsored program. But now the key issues are framed in moral terms. Mariana Valverde, writing about sexual purity and immigration policy in early twentieth-century Canada, notes the importance of 'sanitation' among church missionaries working with new immigrants:

> The term 'sanitation' referred primarily to physical hygiene, but since in the minds of social reformers soap and water were spiritual as well as physical cleansers, sex hygiene and moral uplift were also intended. The degree of impurity affecting immigrants, however, was a hotly debated point. Some reformers thought immigrants were basically healthy and only needed some training in the English language, self-control, and self-government to become good Canadians, while others saw 'foreign' immigrants as inherently degenerate in body and spirit (1991, 116).

Canadians crossing international borders—other than at the Ambassador Bridge or elsewhere on the US/Canada border—know that the passport represents the effort of nation-states, including Canada, to control the legal means of movement (Torpey 2000, 159). Torpey writes:

> The passport vouchsafes the issuing state's guarantee of aid and succor to the bearer while in the jurisdiction of other states. Possession of a passport thus [is] . . . evidence of a legitimate claim on the resources and services of the embassies or consulates of the issuing state . . . Modern passports . . . facilitate movement into and out of spaces controlled by others than one's own sovereign (2000, 160).

Yet as mundane as they may appear, a national passport is more than this. Citizens' passports and immigrants' identity cards (often known as 'green cards' in the US because of their colour, which was at one time green) can be taken more literally. With photographs and personal information about their holders as well as a compact form that permits them to be carried on the holder's person, they are person(al) documents *par excellence* (Lippert 1999). Their issuance encourages holders to think of themselves as citizens of particular nations.

Metropolis

Governance demands knowledge of its objects (Rose and Miller 1992). To that end, Canada created Metropolis in the 1990s—a massive, internationally networked, knowledge-producing machine about integration and settlement (Metropolis 2005). The introduction of the various categories and identities noted earlier has been accompanied by greater production of expert knowledge about the various categories. For example, the new immigration economists (e.g., De Voretz 1995) who rose to greater prominence during this period have identified the refugee category as risky to the national economy compared to other categories (e.g., business, independent, and to a lesser extent family class). The goal of Metropolis is 'to improve policies for managing migration and cultural diversity in major cities' (Metropolis 2005). Rarely stated explicitly, its central focus, put simply, is *how to select 'better' migrants and how to 'better' transform these migrants into citizens.* This project, funded mainly by the federal Department of Citizenship and Immigration and other federal government departments, provides research grant monies to university-based economists, geographers, psychologists, and sociologists. Metropolis's central assumption is that major cities are the foremost destination of migrants (it is true that most recent immigrants and refugees reside in Canada's three largest cities: Vancouver, Montreal, and Toronto). Metropolis affords an opportunity to see an important difference between such policy-oriented research and more critical issues. While Metropolis presumes that cities are the principal places where migrants will establish themselves and therefore assumes that this is where research about settlement needs to concentrate (hence the project's name), a critical sociology would be inclined to ask other questions. For example, such a sociology could ask: How are Canadian cities *deployed* to incorporate migrants, or how are urban spaces and ethnic enclaves strategically *used* to assemble citizens from migrants? How does the knowledge produced in Metropolis allow this to happen? In other words, a critical sociology would not take the settlement of migrants in Canadian cities for granted; it would approach it as a research problem to be investigated.

RESISTANCE AND SANCTUARY

At this point in the chapter, it may seem as though things go pretty much according to plan. Migrants pay their fees and dutifully either enter the various immigration streams or, if they are deemed not to measure up in point systems and other assessments, simply give up or are 'removed' from Canada. Ten blocks from my university office, farther down the bank of the Detroit River from the Ambassador Bridge, is Sandwich First Baptist Church in historic Sandwich Towne, now part of the City of Windsor. This nineteenth-century church formed part of the famous 'underground railroad'. Within it can still be found a trap door leading to a passageway beneath the church floor in which migrants of African descent, fleeing the tyranny of slavery in the US, hid from authorities after crossing the Detroit River (Molnar 1997). Some of these migrants later settled permanently in what is now Canada: many became citizens. Even today, there remain numerous unorthodox and unofficial ways to migrate to and otherwise remain permanently in Canada. Migrants have adopted many different strategies to resist the official channels and the various bureaucratic categories that although embraced by and helping to form the identities of some are imposed on and resisted by others. These strategies include using fraudulent passports and other identity documents, often with the help of those engaged in human trafficking and smuggling (Matas 2005). Over the past 20 years in Canada, hunger strikes have become a desperate but nonetheless common tactic of anti-deportation resistance (see for example Catteneo 1983). Another current strategy is sanctuary, which is worth a closer look.

A strange event occurred in August 1998 in London, Ontario, less than a two-hour drive northeast of Windsor on the NAFTA superhighway. An Iranian migrant family facing deportation took sanctuary in an Anglican cathedral. The clergy and the broader community held a press conference on the steps of the cathedral and said that they were prepared to be arrested and jailed before they would permit this migrant family to be 'removed' by immigration officials. Thirteen days later, the federal minister of immigration suddenly announced that the family had been given permission to stay in Canada on 'humanitarian and compassionate' grounds.

A recent study reveals that similar incidents have occurred in Vancouver, Winnipeg, Calgary, Toronto, Edmonton, Ottawa, Saint John, London, Dieppe, Kingston, and Halifax (Lippert 2005). Since a December 1983 case in Montreal, churches and communities across Canada have provided sanctuary to migrants exhausted of legal appeals and threatened with deportation. The typical Canadian sanctuary incident occurs in a large city; involves a single migrant or migrant family; receives support from major Christian denominations, the broader community, and local political authorities; lasts on average five months; and yields positive outcomes for migrants (Lippert 2005). In these instances, immigration authorities avoid entering the church to make arrests (Lippert 2005). Sanctuary incidents have been limited to specific communities, and to date no distinctive Canadian national sanctuary movement or network has emerged. Nine of 36 incidents involved migrants leaving sanctuary after a time to be deported, to return whence they came, or to enter the US or another nation illegally. However, excluding incidents involving mixed and undecided outcomes, 70 per cent (21 of 30) yielded legal status for the migrants concerned. The making of citizens did not begin when the migrants walked out of the church door. Rather, sanctuary providers at the churches gave them language instruction and other training while they lived in sanctuary.

Sanctuary is about resistance to the regular channels and creation of new ones that make it possible for migrants to become citizens. It was noted earlier that the state is stingy about who can become members of our society. Self-selection is discouraged and so is sanctuary, which amounts to sovereign intervention by church and community groups on migrants' behalf. This may be why on 5 March 2004 Quebec City police entered St Pierre United Church to arrest Mohamed Cherfi. Living in sanctuary for several days, Cherfi was an Algerian migrant faced with deportation who, like most sanctuary recipients before him, had failed to gain status through the refugee determination process. He was quickly deported to the US to await a hearing to determine whether he will be further removed to Algeria.

The means to permanent legal status or long-term permission to remain in Canada differed significantly across sanctuary incidents. In 11 incidents, sanctuary recipients were required to temporarily and 'voluntarily' leave sanctuary (and Canada), to legally enter other nations (including the US, Mexico, and Peru), to reapply for immigrant status from abroad, or to re-enter the refugee determination process after a designated period consistent with Canada's immigration regulations. In these instances, this was usually accomplished through promises of special or expedited consideration of their independent immigrant applications. These promises usually remained unofficial so that immigration and political authorities could avoid declarations tantamount to a general amnesty or establish legal precedent affecting other migrants in similar dire situations. Other cases ended with the granting of a ministerial permit or a federal court ruling. So even if we limit our attention to the 36 sanctuary incidents, which at first glance appear to have much in common, the means to securing legal status in these cases also turns out to be varied and complex.

The increasing prevalence of sanctuary is undoubtedly linked to Canadian immigration and refugee policies that have become increasingly restrictive since the early 1980s and through the 1990s (Lippert 1998; Razack 1999). It is significant that the Refugee Appeals Division mandated in the new Immigration and Protection Act, which came into effect in 2002 and would permit appeals on the merits of a refugee claim, has yet to be implemented after three years (Lippert 2005, 54, 177). This is an appeal process that refugee advocacy groups have been calling for since the early 1980s. Across the 36 incidents, sanctuary providers consistently pointed to its absence in the new system and more recently to a failure to implement it as promised as a key reason that migrants have been forced to seek sanctuary (Lippert 2005).

CONCLUSION

My chief aim in this chapter has been to try to provide answers to the question of how migrants become citizens. The question turns out to be more complex than it first appeared, in part because there are a range of categories of migrants and citizens and ways of becoming such. As indicated by the selection of temporary migrants and their subsequent control once in Canada, as well as deportation and emigration, there are also ways of *not* becoming citizens. I have of course not fully answered the question, but I hope to have demonstrated that it is one that encourages investigation of other questions that may seem at first to have little to do with immigration and citizenship. A critical sociology provides insights into the myriad inequalities that the operation of these processes engender, the forms of resistance that recognition of such inequalities encourage, and the workings of governance and moral regulation that shape and make these processes possible. It may also reveal alternative categories and identities beyond those of migrant and citizen and that entail fewer inequalities among them. This chapter has also tried to suggest that immigration and citizenship are processes distant neither from the daily lives of 'Canadians' nor from where I sit writing this chapter in my university office.

Questions to Consider

1. Would allowing more discretion in immigration officers' decision-making be beneficial to applicants and permit humanitarian needs to be considered to a greater degree, or would increased discretion lead only to increased discrimination and inequality? Are there alternatives to using a rigid point system to decide which potential immigrants will be allowed to enter Canadian society to live permanently?
2. What other social problems and processes appear to be governed *through* immigration in Canadian society?
3. How important is national citizenship compared to other kinds of citizenship in the daily lives of Canadians? Given the continuing far-reaching effects of NAFTA on Canadian society, will a corresponding North American citizenship soon become more prevalent?
4. Why are some migrants, while deemed good enough to work in Canada, not imagined to be good enough to become Canadian citizens within current immigration and citizenship policies? To what extent are these policies moral in nature?
5. Do you think the formation of migrant identities is logically necessary for the formation of citizen identities? Are the various migrant identities the 'alterity' of national citizenship, or do they represent an identity/category that lies somewhere between citizens and outsiders?

Notes

1. The North American Free Trade Agreement, a trade agreement among Canada, the US, and Mexico with the aim of increasing the flow of goods among the three nations, came into effect in 1994.
2. 28 July 1951, 189 U.N.T.S. 137; 31 January 1967, 606 U.N.T.S. 267.

List of Contributors

Adam, Barry D. Professor, Department of Sociology and Anthropology, University of Windsor, Windsor, ON.

Beamish, Rob Associate Professor, Department of Sociology, Queen's University, Kingston, ON.

Burfoot, Annette Associate Professor, Department of Sociology, Queen's University, Kingston, ON.

Clarke, Curtis Associate Professor and Program Coordinator, Criminal Justice, Centre for State and Legal Studies, Athabasca University, Athabasca, AB.

Couton, Philippe Assistant Professor, Department of Sociology, University of Ottawa, Ottawa, ON.

Currie, Dawn H. Professor, Department of Sociology, University of British Columbia, Vancouver, BC.

Doran, Nob Professor, Department of Social Studies, University of New Brunswick Saint John, Saint John, NB.

Frigon, Sylvie Professor and Chair, Department of Criminology, University of Ottawa, Ottawa, ON.

Harder, Lois Associate Professor, Department of Political Science, University of Alberta, Edmonton, AB.

Hird, Myra J. Professor, Department of Sociology, Queen's University, Kingston, ON.

Hogeveen, Bryan Assistant Professor, Department of Sociology, University of Alberta, Edmonton, AB.

Jarman, Jennifer Associate Professor, Department of Sociology, Dalhousie University, Halifax, NS.

Katz, Stephen Professor, Department of Sociology, Trent University, Peterborough, ON.

Kelly, Deirdre M.   Professor, Department of Educational Studies, University of British Columbia, Vancouver, BC.

Lippert, Randy   Associate Professor (Sociology), Department of Sociology and Anthropology, University of Windsor, Windsor, ON.

Monture, Patricia   Professor, Department of Sociology, University of Saskatchewan, Saskatoon, SK.

Moore, Dawn   Assistant Professor of Legal Studies, Department of Law, Carleton University, Ottawa, ON.

Pavlich, George C.   Professor of Law and Sociology University of Alberta, Edmonton, AB.

Sydie, R.A.   Professor and Chair, Department of Sociology, University of Alberta, Edmonton, AB.

Glossary

Anatamo-politics: One of the two poles of Michel Foucault's power/knowledge concept, anatamo-politics involves amassing knowledge about the human body itself (in contrast to the second pole, bio-politics, which focuses on gathering knowledge about the 'social body'). Such knowledge is then used to exercise power over individuals.

Anomie: A condition in modern life identified by Émile Durkheim in which individuals are not provided with any norms by which to live their lives, which leads to alienation and confusion. The remedy, in Durkheim's view, is to allow society's structures to develop spontaneously in response to individuals' natural capacities.

Bio-politics: The second of two poles in Michel Foucault's power/knowledge concept, bio-politics focuses on gathering knowledge about the 'social body', as opposed to anatamo-politics, which concentrates on amassing knowledge about the body itself. This knowledge is used to exercise power over society.

Critical sociology: A sociological approach that seeks to understand the injustices in given situations and find ways of eliminating them through incremental or even revolutionary social change.

Codification: The transformation or reinterpretation of an existing culture, often by the statistical sciences, in such a way as to make that culture appear nonsensical to the individuals who share it.

Emphasized femininity: The idea that women should accept subordination to men and seek to accommodate the interests and desires of men in terms of their physical appearance, behaviour, and dedication to the home.

Essentialism: The belief that inherent and inescapable characteristics govern a given condition (e.g., being female), which lie beyond the individual's control and make it impossible to transcend the condition in any meaningful way.

Ethnomethodology: A sociological approach initiated by Harold Garfinkel that focuses on and analyzes the methods by which individual people interpret and create sense and meaning in the ever-changing social environments in which they live. Society itself is thus shaped by the collective free choices that individuals make in specific contexts, and the social world can only be understood from within.

Existentialism: The theory that human beings are inescapably free—indeed, condemned to freedom—which causes great anguish as they confront having to make choices and bear the responsibility for those choices in a world that is ultimately meaningless, never knowing whether the choices they make are the right ones.

Existential sociology: Emerging in the 1970s, this school of thought is based on the assumption that individuals are free to choose their own social meanings. It explores the collective patterns generated by the anxiety people feel as they try to give their lives meaning in a meaningless world.

Foucauldian sociology: Challenging liberal sociology, this school of thought holds that individuals are not naturally free—or even 'free' when they manage to successfully challenge the power that others hold over them. Instead, Michel Foucault argues that power is essential to freedom: power not only shapes individuals but also creates the freedoms within society. Indeed, freedom itself cannot exist without power, and a 'free' society is in fact structured by power.

Governmentality: The art of governing—i.e., how states and other agents of authority govern human subjects through the application of accepted principles and the production of the subjects to be governed. For example, neo-liberal states today encourage their subjects to govern themselves in such a way that they become consumers and entrepreneurs, which serves the ends of the state.

Hermeneutic tradition: Challenges positivism in arguing that sociology cannot effectively use scientific methods to understand society but must devise and use its own means of interpretation because individuals (unlike physical phenomena) can exercise free choice.

Ideology: The socio-political organization of ideas, or more specifically in Marxist thinking, the way that class consciousness is obscured for the benefit of the ruling class. Ideology is used by the dominant class as a means of indirectly controlling social institutions and therefore the subordinate classes.

Imaginary: A shared vision of social life and values within a given nation-state, usually as articulated and promoted by the state itself.

Instrumental rationality: Using the power of reason to determine the most effective means of achieving a goal, without regard to the broader impact of such actions.

Interaction order: Erving Goffman's approach to the study of the self, involving analysis of the interaction among people in terms of forms of speech, body language, etc., in face-to-face situations.

Keynesian economics: Propounded by John Maynard Keynes after the Second World War, this school of thought holds that societies are vulnerable to recession/depression when consumer demand in the marketplace drops. Therefore, government should increase taxes in prosperous times and spend to the point of deficit during economic downturns to bolster people's spending power, while always providing an economic safety net through such programs as unemployment insurance, family allowances, and old age pensions.

Liberal sociology: An early school of sociological thought holding that human beings are free by nature and can only live according to their true nature when they inhabit free societies where the state's power is held in check.

Micro-sociology: A view of society as a complex of individual interaction, reciprocity, and activity, with individual participation and everyday life as the bases of society.

Neo-conservatism: Similar to neo-liberalism in its focus on the individual and the market economy, neo-conservatism differs in its approach to moral issues, contending that the state should, for example, uphold traditional notions of the family and disallow such practices as abortion.

Neo-liberalism: An extension of classical eighteenth-century liberal thought, neo-liberalism focuses on the individual and individual rights as opposed to collective rights and responsibilities. Its tenets include minimal state intervention in individuals' lives, fiscal responsibility, and the efficacy of free markets to achieve economic well-being.

Positivist sociology: An early incarnation of sociology originating with Auguste Comte in the mid-nineteen century, positivism is dedicated to the notion that the empirical methods of inquiry used in the natural sciences can also be used to discover the true nature of society. Positivism holds that like 'scientific facts', 'social facts' are governed by their own natural, absolute laws.

Post-modernity: Questions the very basis of 'modernity'—that society is governed by absolute laws, ruled by unalterable structures, and that knowledge about these 'truths' can lead to freedom and fulfillment for the individual. But in a post-modern world, knowledge can never be absolute but rather is contingent on the circumstances of any given society.

Post-structuralism: Challenges structuralism in that it holds that 'social structures' do not themselves exist in any absolute way but rather are the product of unpredictable and constantly changing historical contexts. Thus the individuals that such structures create are not absolute but ever-changing.

Power: As theorized by Michel Foucault, power is a changing set of techniques and tools exercised by a 'subject' (an individual or a group) on the actions of another 'subject'. Taken together, these exercises of power pervade society and ultimately determine its shape at any given moment as well as the nature of any given individual.

Reflexive modernity: The way that individuals monitor their aspirations and behaviour in response to the ongoing flow of social life in the world today—a time when the proliferation of communication technology has vastly expanded their ability to orient themselves in the social world. The result is a continual self-reinvention, in contrast to the passive acceptance of one's pre-ordained role as defined by convention.

Semiology: The study of signs and symbols or images and their connection to deeper or embedded meanings in a culture.

Sociological imagination: A 'quality of mind' that enables sociologists to connect the personal/individual to the general structures that shape a given society by allowing them to suspend their everyday understandings and reflect on the broader social context.

Sociology: A discipline involved in naming, understanding, critically evaluating, and/or seeking to change the collective patterns and groupings in which people live their lives.

State formation: Scholars who study state formation focus on the state's power to produce consensus among its citizens through a kind of moral regulation, which produces a constantly evolving national culture.

Structuralism: The theory that systematic inquiry can uncover regular, recurring, and ordered patterns of social behaviour (termed 'social structures') that lead to the creation of individual human beings.

Structuration: The view that human agency (the power of individuals to act) and social structures are mutually dependent: the structures give individuals the means to act, but individuals' actions in turn shape the social structure.

Symbolic interactionism: Originating with George Herbert Mead, symbolic interactionism sees the development of the self as a result of interaction with others in the socialization process. The self thus emerges not only through self-definition but also through the ways that an individual is defined by others.

Technoculture (or technoscience): A branch of cultural studies that focuses on the relationship between new technologies (e.g., the internet, biotechnology, genetic engineering, virtual reality) and individuals/society.

Visual culture: A branch of cultural studies that focuses on images rather than the written word on the assumption that society is now largely image-based.

Bibliography

Abella, I., and H. Troper. 1982. *None is too many*. Toronto: Lester and Orpen Dennys.

Abercrombie, Nicholas, Stephen Hill, and Bryan S. Turner. 1984. *Dictionary of sociology*. London: Penguin.

Acoose, Janice. 1995. *Iskewewak kah'ki yaw ni wahkoma kaak: Neither Indian princesses nor easy squaws*. Toronto: Women's Press.

Adam, Barry D. 1978. *The survival of domination*. New York: Elsevier/Greenwood.

———. 1985. 'Age, structure and sexuality'. *Journal of Homosexuality* 11 (3/4):19–33.

———. 1995. *The rise of a gay and lesbian movement*. New York: Twayne.

———. 1996. 'Structural foundations of the gay world'. In S. Seidman (Ed.), *Queer theory/sociology*. Cambridge, MA: Blackwell.

———. 1998. 'Theorizing homophobia'. *Sexualities* 1 (4):387–404.

———. 2004. 'Care, intimacy, and samesex partnership in the 21st century'. *Current Sociology* 52 (2):265–79.

———. 2006. 'Relationship innovation in male relationships'. *Sexualities* 9 (1):5–26.

Adelman, H. 2002. 'Canadian borders and immigration post 9/11'. *International Migration Review* 36 (1):15–28.

———, and C. Currie. 1987. *Too few to count: Canadian women in conflict with the law*. Vancouver: Press Gang Publishers.

Adkins, Lisa. 2002. *Revisions: Gender and sexuality in late modernity*. Buckingham, UK: Open University Press.

Adorno, Theodor, and Max Horkheimer. 1979 [1947]. 'The culture industry: Enlightenment as mass deception'. In *Dialectic of enlightenment*. London: Verso.

Agger, Ben. 1991. *A critical theory of public life*. London: Falmer Press.

Agocs, Carol. 2000. 'Race and ethnic relations'. In J. Teevan and W.E. Hewitt (Eds), *Introduction to sociology: A Canadian focus*. Scarborough: Prentice Hall.

Aikenhead, S. 2004. 'Youth justice?' *Halifax Daily News* 1 February: 6.

Akyeampong, E.B. 2005. 'Business support services'. *Perspectives on Labour and Income* 6 (5):5–9.

Alberta. 2001. *A framework for reform: A report of the Premier's Advisory Council on Health for Albertans*. Edmonton.

———. 2005. *Government MLA review of the Private Investigators and Security Guards Act*. Edmonton: Alberta Solicitor General and Public Security.

Alfred, Taiaiake. 1999. *Peace, power and righteousness: An indigenous manifesto*. Toronto: Oxford University Press.

Alphonso, Caroline. 2004. 'A coast-to-coast cover-up: The Britney generation refuses to be overdressed, but schools across Canada are drawing a line at the classroom door'. *The Globe and Mail* 3 April: F2.

Althusser, Louis. 1971. 'Ideology and ideological state apparatuses'. In *Lenin and philosophy and other essays* (Ben Brewster, trans.). New York: Monthly Review Press.

Amadiume, Ifi. 1980. *Male daughters, female husbands*. Toronto: DEC.

Amnesty International. 2004. *Stolen sisters—A human rights response to discrimination and violence against indigenous women in Canada*. www.amnesty.ca/resource_centre/reports.

Anderson, Benedict. 1991. *Imagined communities: Reflections on the origin and spread of nationalism*. New York: Verso.

———. 1998. *The spectre of comparisons: Nationalism, Southeast Asia and the world*. London: Verso.

Anderson, C. 1999. 'Governing Aboriginal justice in Canada: Constructing responsible individuals and communities through tradition'. *Crime, Law and Social Change* 31 (2): 303–26.

Arbour, Louise. 1996. *Commission of Inquiry into Certain Events at the Prison for Women in Kingston*. Ottawa: Public Works and Government Services Canada.

Armstrong, Frank. 2004. 'Officer says he feared for his life'. *Kingston Whig Standard* 2 September: 1.

Armstrong, P. 1996. 'The feminization of the labor force: Harmonizing down in a global economy'. In I. Bakker (Ed.), *Rethinking restructuring: Gender and change in Canada*. Toronto: University of Toronto Press.

Arnold, Mathew. 1990 [1875]. *Culture and anarchy*. Cambridge, UK: Cambridge University Press.

Atkinson, J.M. 1971. 'Societal reactions to suicide: The role of coroners' definitions'. In S. Cohen (Ed.), *Images of deviance*. Harmondsworth, UK: Penguin.

———. 1982. *Discovering suicide: Studies in the social organization of sudden death*. London: Macmillan.

Bakan, Abigail, and Audrey Kobayashi. 2000. *Employment equity policy in Canada: An interprovincial comparison*. Ottawa: Status of Women Canada.

Banner, David. 2005. *Ain't got nothing*. US.

Bargh, John A., Katelyn Y.A. McKenna, and Grainne M. Fitzsimons. 2002. 'Can you see the real me? Activation and expression of the "true self" on the internet'. *Journal of Social Issues* 58:33–48.

Barney, R.K., S.R. Wenn, and S.G. Martyn. 2002. *Selling the five rings: The International Olympics Committee and the rise of Olympic commercialism*. Salt Lake City: University of Utah Press.

Barris, Stephen. 2005. 'How long will lesbian, gay, bisexual and transgender rights be ignored at the UN?' *Bulletin of the International Gay and Lesbian Rights Association* 117:22–5.

Barthes, Roland. 1972. *Mythologies*. London: Jonathon Cape.

Bartky, Sandra Lee. 1990. *Femininity and domination*. New York: Routledge.

———. 1997. 'On psychological oppression'. In Mary F. Rogers (Ed.), *Contemporary feminist theory: A text/reader*. Boston: McGraw-Hill.

Basok, T. 2002. *Tortillas and tomatoes: Trans-migrant Mexican harvesters in Canada*. Montreal: McGill-Queen's University Press.

Basting, Anne Davis. 2001. '"God Is a Talking Horse": Dementia and the performance of self'. *The Drama Review* 45:78–94.

Battle, K. 1999. 'The National Child Benefit: Best thing since medicare or new poor law?' In D. Durst (Ed.), *Canada's National Child Benefit: Phoenix or fizzle?* Halifax: Fernwood.

Baudrillard, Jean. 1983a. *Simulations*. New York: Semiotext(e)

———. 1983b. *In the shadow of the silent majorities or 'the death of the social'*. New York: Semiotext(e).

Bauman, Zygmunt. 1987. *Legislators and interpreters*. Cambridge, UK: Polity Press.

———. 1988. *Freedom*. Minneapolis: University of Minnesota Press.

———. 1990. *Thinking sociologically*. Oxford, UK: Basil Blackwell.

———. 1992. *Intimations of postmodernity*. London: Routledge.

———. 1997. *Postmodernity and its discontents*. New York: New York University Press.

———. 2000. 'Sociological enlightenment—For whom, about what?' *Theory, Culture and Society* 17 (2):71–81.

———. 2001. *Globalization: The human consequences*. New York: Columbia University Press.

Bayley, David. 1994. *Police for the future*. Oxford, UK: Oxford University Press.

———, and Clifford Shearing. 1998. 'The future of policing'. In G. Albert and A. Piquero (Eds), *Community policing: Contemporary readings*. Prospect Heights, IL: Waveland Press.

Beaman, Lori G. (Ed.). 2000. *New perspectives on deviance: The construction of deviance in everyday life*. Scarborough, ON: Prentice Hall Canada.

Beamish, R. 1993. 'Labor relations in sport: Central issues in their emergence and structure in high performance sport'. In A. Ingham and J. Loy (Eds), *Sport in social development: Traditions, transitions, and transformations*. Champaign, IL: Human Kinetics.

———, and J. Borowy. 1989. *Q: What do you do for a living? A: I'm an athlete*. Kingston, ON: Sport Research Group.

———, and I. Ritchie. 2004. 'From chivalrous brothers-in-arms to the eligible athlete: Changed principles and the IOC's banned substance list'. *International Review for the Sociology of Sport*. 39:355–71.

Beasley, Chris. 1999. *What is feminism? An introduction to feminist theory*. London: Sage.

Beaudin, M., and S. Breau. 2001. 'Employment, skills and the knowledge economy in Atlantic Canada'. *Maritime Series Monographs*. Moncton: Institut canadien de recherche sur le développement regional/The Canadian Institute for Research on Regional Development.

Beausoleil, Natalie. 1994. 'Makeup in everyday life: An inquiry into the practices of urban American women of diverse backgrounds'. In Nicole Sault (Ed.), *Many mirrors: Body image and social relations*. New Brunswick, NJ: Rutgers University Press.

Bendelow, Gillian, and Simon J. Williams (Eds). 1998. *Emotions in social life: Critical themes and contemporary issues*. London and New York: Routledge.

Benjamin, Walter. 1968. 'The work of art in the age of mechanical reproduction'. In *Illuminations* (Harry Zohn, trans.). New York: New Left.

Bennett, Andy. 2001. 'Contemporary youth music and "risk" lifestyles'. In Joel Best (Ed.), *How claims spread*, 169–84. Hawthorne, NY: Aldine de Gruyter.

Benton Banai, Edward. 1979. *The Mishomis book: The voice of the Ojibway*. St. Paul, MN: Indian Country Press.

Berger, Peter. 1973. *An invitation to sociology: A humanist approach*. Harmondsworth, UK: Penguin.

———, and Brigitte Berger. 1976. *Sociology: A biographical approach*. Harmondsworth, UK: Penguin.

Bernard, J. (Ed.). 1961. *Teen-age culture*. Special edition of *Annals of the American Academy of Political Social Sciences* v. 338.

Berzins, L., and Renée Colette Carrière. 1979. 'Les femmes en prison: un inconvénient social.' *Santé mentale au Québec* 4 (2):87–103.

Bette, K.-H. 1984. *Strukturelle aspekte des hochleistungssports in der Bundesrepublik* [Structural aspects of high performance sport in the Federal Republic]. Sankt Augustin, Germany: Verlag Hans Richarz.

Bettie, Julie. 2003. *Women without class: Girls, race, and identity*. Berkeley: University of California Press.

Bierly, Margaret. 1985. 'Prejudice toward contemporary outgroups as a generalized attitude'. *Journal of Applied Social Psychology* 15 (2):189–99.

Biggs, Simon. 1997. 'Choosing not to be old? Masks, bodies, and identity management in later life'. *Ageing and Society* 17:553–70.

Bigo, D. 2002. 'Security and immigration: Toward a critique of the governmentality of unease'. *Alternatives* 27:63–92.

Billings, D., and T. Urban. 1982. 'The socio-medical construction of transsexualism: An interpretation and critique'. *Social Problems* 29:266–82.

Bindel, Julie. 2004. 'Gender benders, beware'. *Guardian Unlimited* 31 January. http://www.guardian.co.uk/weekend/story/0,3605,1134099,00.html.

Binkley, M. 1994. *Voices from offshore: Narratives of risk and danger in the Nova Scotia deep sea fishery*. St John's, NF: Iser Books.

Birke, Lynda. 2000. *Feminism and the biological body*. Piscataway, NJ: Rutgers University Press.

Bittner, Egon. 1990. *Aspects of police work*. Boston: Northeastern University Press.

Blackstock, C. 2003. 'Same country, same land, 78 countries apart'. Unpublished paper.

Blumer, Herbert. 1969. *Symbolic interaction: Perspective and method*. Englewood Cliffs, NJ: Prentice Hall.

Boily, Frédéric. 2004. 'Lionel Groulx et l'esprit du libéralisme'. *Recherches sociographiques* 45:239–57.

Bolaria, B.S., and P. Li. 1988. *Racial oppression in Canada*. 2nd edn. Toronto: Garamond.

Bolin, A. 1994. 'Transcending and transgendering: Male-to-female transsexuals, dichotomy and diversity'. In G. Herdt (Ed.), *Third sex, third gender*. New York: Zone Books.

Bordo, Susan. 1993. *Unbearable weight: Feminism, Western culture, and the body.* Berkeley: University of California Press.

Boswell, John. 1994. *Samesex unions in premodern Europe.* New York: Villard.

Boucher, J. N. 2004 [1906]. *History of Westmoreland County.* New York: Lewis Publishing.

Bourdieu, P. 1977. *Outline of a theory of practice.* Cambridge, UK: Cambridge University Press.

————. 1998. *Acts of resistance: Against the tyranny of the market.* New York: New Press.

Bourque, Gilles. 2001. 'Between nations and society'. In Michel Venne (Ed.), *Vive Quebec! New thinking and new approaches to the Quebec nation.* Toronto: Lorimer.

Boychuk, G. 2001. 'Aiming for the middle: Challenges to federal income maintenance policy'. In Leslie Pal (Ed.), *How Ottawa spends 2001–2002.* Toronto: Oxford University Press.

————. 2004. 'The Chrétien non-legacy: The federal role in health care ten years on...1993–2003'. In S. Patten and L. Harder (Eds), *Review of Constitutional Studies: Special Issue on the Chrétien Legacy* 9 (1/2):221–40.

Brake, Mike. 1980. *The sociology of youth cultures and youth subcultures.* New York: Routledge and Kegan Paul.

Brandon, William. 1986. *New worlds for old: Reports from the New World and their effect on the development of social thought in Europe.* Athens, OH: Ohio University Press.

Bray, Alan. 1982. 'Homosexuality and the signs of male friendship in Elizabethan England'. *History Workshop* 29:1–19.

Britton, Dana. 1990. 'Developmental origins of antihomosexual prejudice in heterosexual men and women'. *Clinical Social Work Journal* 19:163–75.

Brodie, J. 2002. 'An elusive search for community: Globalization and the Canadian national identities'. *Review of Constitutional Studies* 7 (1/2):155–78.

Brown, George, and Ron Maguire. 1979. *Indian treaties in historical perspective.* Ottawa: Department of Indian Affairs.

Brown, Lyn Mikel. 1998. *Raising their voices: The politics of girls' anger.* Cambridge, MA: Harvard University Press.

Brown, W.M. 2001. 'As American as gatorade and apple pie: Performance drugs and sports'. In W.J. Morgan, K.V. Meier, and A.J. Schneider (Eds), *Ethics in sport,* 142–68. Champaign, IL: Human Kinetics.

Brumberg, Joan Jacobs. 1997. *The body project: An intimate history of American girls.* New York: Vintage.

Brym, Robert J., and Cynthis Lins Hamlin. 2004. 'Culture, Durkheim's *Suicide,* and the Guarani-Kaiowa'. *Theory: Newsletter of the Research Committee of Sociological Theory* Fall:8–11.

Buchanan, R. 2000. '1-800 New Brunswick: Economic development strategies, firm restructuring and the local production of "global" services'. In. J. Jenson and B.d.S. Santos (Eds), *Globalizing institutions, Case studies in regulation and innovation,* 53–80. Aldershot, UK: Ashgate.

Bullough, V. 1975. 'Transsexualism in history'. *Archives of Sexual Behavior* 4:561–71.

Burbidge, S. 2005. 'The governance deficit: Reflections on the future of public and private policing in Canada'. *Canadian Journal of Criminology and Criminal Justice* 47 (1):64–85.

Burchell, G., C. Gordon, and P. Miller (Eds). 1991. *The Foucault effect.* Chicago: University of Chicago Press.

Burfoot, Annette. Forthcoming. 'Pearls and gore: The spectacle of woman as arbiter of life and death'. In Annette Burfoot and Susan Lord (Eds), *Killing women: The visual culture of gender and violence.* Waterloo, ON: Wilfred Laurier University Press.

Burke, P. 1996. *Gender shock: Exploding the myths of male and female.* New York: Anchor.

Burns, Tom. 1992. *Erving Goffman.* London: Routledge.

Burrell, Gordon, Robert Young, and Richard Price. 1975. *Indian treaties and the law: An interpretation for laymen.* Edmonton: Indian Association of Alberta.Butler, Judith. 1990. *Gender trouble: Feminism and the subversion of identity.* London: Routledge.

———. 1993a. *Bodies that matter: On the discursive limits of 'sex'.* New York: Routledge.

———. 1993b. 'Critically Queer'. *GLQ* 1 (1):17–32.

Butler, P.M., and R. Smith. 1983. 'The worker, the workplace and the need for unemployment insurance'. *Canadian Review of Sociology and Anthropology* 20 (4):393–412.

Byrne, Bridget. 2003. 'Reciting the self: Narrative representations of the self in qualitative interviews'. *Feminist Theory* 4 (1):29–49.

Cairns, Alan C. 2000. *Citizens plus: Aboriginal peoples and the Canadian state.* Vancouver: University of British Columbia Press.

Cajete, Gregory. 1999. *Native science: Natural laws of interdependence.* Santa Fe, NM: Clear Light Publishers.

Calhoun, Craig. 1995. *Critical social theory.* London: Blackwell.

Calliste, A. 1987. 'Sleeping car porters in Canada: An ethnically submerged split labour market'. *Canadian Ethnic Studies* 19:1–15.

Campbell, Peter, and Susan Wright. 1993. *Leadership in turbulent times.* Ottawa: Solicitor General of Canada.

Camus, Albert. 1991. *The plague.* New York: Vintage.

Canada. 1982. *Canadian Charter of Rights and Freedoms.* Ottawa: Government Printer.

———. 2004. 'Canada Child Tax Benefit for July 2004–July 2005'. www.nationalchild benefit.ca/ncb/govtofcan4.html.

Canada, Citizenship and Immigration Canada. 2004. 'Be a host to a newcomer, 2003'. http://www.cic.gc.ca/english/newcomer/involve/canadian-host.html.

———. 2005a. 'Citizenship'. http://www.cic.gc.ca/english/citizen/look/look-19e.html.

———. 2005b. 'Tsunami and earthquake disaster response'. http://www.cic.gc.ca/eng lish/tsunami/index.html.

———. 2005c. 'Facts and figures 2003: Immigration overview: Permanent and tempo rary residents'. www.cic.gc.ca/english/pub/facts2003/overview/1.html.

———. 2005d. 'Applications processed outside of Canada'. http://www.cic.gc.ca/eng lish/department/times-int/index.html.

———. 2005e. 'Statistical information: Applications processed at Canadian visa offices'. www.cic.gc.ca/english/department/times-int/03a-business-fed.html.

Canada, Employment and Immigration. 1987. *Employment and immigration, Host Family Program: Summary report.* Ottawa: Employment and Immigration Canada.
———. 1990. *Annual report to Parliament: Immigration plan for 1991–1995.* Ottawa: Employment and Immigration Canada.
Canadian Council on Social Development. 2003a. *Campaign 2000: Report card on child poverty in Canada.* Ottawa: Canadian Council on Social Development.
———. 2003b. *Aboriginal children in poverty in urban communities.* http://www.ccsd.ca/pr/2003/aboriginal.htm.
———. 2004. *Percentage change in welfare benefits in Canada.* http://www.ccsd.ca/fact sheet/fs_96wel.htm (retrieved 7 December 2004).
Cancian, Francesca M. 1986. 'The feminization of love'. *Signs* 11:692–709.
Cardinal, Harold, and Walter Hildebrandt. 2000. *Treaty elders of Saskatchewan: Our dream is that our peoples will one day be clearly recognized as nations.* Calgary: University of Calgary Press.
Carnoy, M. 1984. *The state and political theory.* Princeton, NJ: Princeton University Press.
Carrington, P., and J. Schulenberg. 2004. 'Introduction: The Youth Criminal Justice Act: A new era in Canadian juvenile justice?' *Canadian Journal of Criminology and Criminal Justice* 46 (2):219–23.
Carter, Sarah. 1990. *Lost harvests: Prairie Indian reserve farmers and government policy.* Montreal: McGill-Queen's University Press.
Castles, S., and M. Miller. 1998. *The age of migration.* 2nd edn. New York: Guilford.
Cattaneo, Claudia. 1983. 'Hunger strikes unite Romanian families'. *Montreal Gazette* 4 January.
CBC (Canadian Broadcasting Corporation). 2005. 'Running off track: The Ben Johnson story'. http://archives.cbc.ca/IDD-1-41-1392/sports/ben_johnson/.
Charest, J. 2003. 'Le défi de la santé dans un contexte électoral: redonner aux Québécois un système public de santé à la hauteur de leurs attentes'. *Policy Options* 24 (2):54–6.
Chase, C. 1998. 'Affronting reason'. In D. Atkins (Ed.), *Looking queer,* 205–20. New York: Harrington Park Press.
Ciara (Ciara feat) and Missy Elliot. 2005. *1,2, step.* US.
Cicourel, A.V. 1967. 'Fertility, family planning and the social organization of family life: Some methodological issues'. *Journal of Social Issues* 23 (4):57–81.
———. 1968. *The social organization of juvenile justice.* New York: John Wiley and Sons.
———. 1973. *Theory and method in a study of Argentine fertility.* New York: John Wiley and Sons.
———, and J.I. Kitsuse. 1963. *The educational decision-makers.* Indianapolis, IN: Bobbs-Merrill.
Clairmont, D., P.M. Butler, and J. Jarman. 1997. 'Sweatshops and teleprofessionalism: An investigation of life and work in the teleservice industry in the Maritimes'. Dalhousie University Research Development Fund Award.
———, J. Jarman, P.M. Butler, and J. Barkow. 1999. *The call centre industry in Nova Scotia.* Connections Nova Scotia.
Clanton, Gordon. 1989. 'Jealousy in American culture, 1945–1985'. In David D. Franks

and E. Doyle McCarthy (Eds), *The sociology of the emotions: Original essays and research papers*, 157–66. Greenich, CT: JAI Press.

Clark, T. 1997. *Art and propaganda in the twentieth century.* New York: Calmann and King.

CLC (Canadian Labour Congress). 2003. 'Submission in response to Finance Canada's EI premium rate-setting mechanism consultation online'. www.fin.gc.ca/consul tresp/eiratesResp_2e.html.

Coates, Ken. 1999. 'The "gentle" occupation: The settlement of Canada and the dispossession of the First Nations'. In Paul Havemann (Ed.), *Indigenous peoples rights in Australia, Canada and New Zealand*, 141–61. Auckland, NZ: Oxford University Press.

Cohen, Robin. 1996. 'Diasporas and the nation-state: From victims to challengers'. *International Affairs* 72 (3):507–20.

Colapinto, J. 2000. *As nature made him: The boy who was raised as a girl.* Toronto: HarperCollins.

Coleman, James S. 1961. *Adolescent society: The social life of the teenager and its impact on education.* New York: Free Press of Glencoe.

Comte, Auguste. 1853. *The positivist philosophy of Auguste Comte.* (Harriet Martineau, trans.). New York: Calvin Blanchard.

———. 1975. *Auguste Comte and positivism: The essential writings.* Gertrude Lenzer, Ed. Chicago: University of Chicago Press.

Connell, R.W. 1987. *Gender and power.* Stanford, CA: Stanford University Press.

———. 2000. *Men and the boys.* Cambridge, UK: Polity Press in association with Blackwell.

———. 2004. 'Encounters with structure'. *International Journal of Qualitative Studies in Education* 17 (1):11–28.

Connolly, P. 1989. 'Hearings on steroids in amateur and professional sports: The medical and social costs of steroid abuse'. Testimony before the United States Senate Committee on the Judiciary. 101st Congress, 1st session, 3 April, 9 May.

Conrad, P., and J.W. Schneider. 1992. *Deviance and medicalization: From badness to madness.* 2nd edn. St. Louis, MO: Mosby.

Cormier, Jeffrey, and Philippe Couton. 2004. 'Civil society, mobilization and communal violence: Quebec and Ireland, 1890–1920'. *Sociological Quarterly* 45 (3):487–508.

Cornell, Stephen E. 1998. *The return of the Native: American Indian political resurgence.* New York: Oxford University Press.

———, and Douglas Hartmann. 1998. *Ethnicity and race.* Thousand Oaks, CA: Pine Forge Press.

Correctional Service of Canada. 1990. *Creating choices: The report of the Task Force on Federally Sentenced Women.* Ottawa: Correctional Service of Canada.

———. 2006. *Ten-year status report on women's corrections.* Ottawa: Correctional Service of Canada.

Corrigan, Philip, and Derek Sayer. 1985. *The great arch: English state formation as cultural revolution.* Oxford, UK: Basil Blackwell.

Cossman, Brenda, Shannon Bell, Lise Gotell, and Becki Ross. 1997. *Bad attitudes on trial.* Toronto: University of Toronto Press.

Coubertin, Pierre de. 2000. *Olympism: Selected writings.* Lausanne, Switzerland: International Olympic Committee.

Covell, K., and B. Howe. 2001. *The challenge of children's rights for Canada.* Waterloo, ON: Wilfred Laurier University Press.

Cupach, William R., and Sandra Metts. 1994. 'Face management in interpersonal relationships and embarrassing predicaments'. In *Facework*, 1–33. Thousand Oaks, CA: Sage.

Currie, Dawn H., Deirdre Kelly, and Shauna Pomerantz. In press. '"The geeks shall inherit the earth": Girls' agency, subjectivity and empowerment'. *Journal of Youth Studies* 9 (4).

Curtis, B. 1995. 'Taking the state back out: Rose and Miller on political power'. *British Journal of Sociology* 46 (4):575–97.

———. 2001. *The politics of population.* Toronto: University of Toronto Press.

Dahrendorf, Ralph. 1973. *Homo sociologicus.* London: Routledge and Kegan Paul.

Daigle, Marc, Mylène Alarie, and Patrick Lefebvre. 1999. 'La problématique suicidaire chez les femmes incarcérées'. *Forum* 11 (3):41–5.

Daston, L., and K. Park. 1998. *Wonders and the order of nature.* New York: Zone Books.

Dean, A. 2004. *Locking them up to keep them 'safe': Criminalized girls in British Columbia.* Vancouver: Justice for Girls.

de Beauvoir, Simone. 1961. *The second sex.* (H.M. Parshley, trans.). New York: Bantam.

Deber, R. 2003. 'Health care reform: Lessons from Canada'. *American Journal of Public Health* 93 (1):20–4.

Deleuze, Gilles. 1988. *Michel Foucault.* (Paul Bové, trans.). Minneapolis, MN: University of Minnesota Press.

———. 1993. *The fold: Leibniz and the baroque.* (Tom Conley, trans.). Minneapolis, MN: University of Minnesota Press.

Dell, Colleen Anne. 2001. *Correctional Service of Canada ideology and 'violent' Aboriginal female offenders.* Ph.D. dissertation. Ottawa: Carleton University.

Della-Mattia, E. 2004. 'Martin fingers Liberals for child benefit clawback'. *Sault Star* 22 November: A4.

Delphy, C. 1994. 'Changing women in a changing Europe'. *Women's Studies International Forum* 17:187–201.

Denny, D. (Ed.). 1998. *Current concepts in transgender identity.* New York: Garland.

Denov, M. 2004. 'Children's rights, juvenile justice, and the UN Convention on the Child: Implications for Canada'. In K. Campbell (Ed.), *Understanding youth justice in Canada.* Toronto: Pearson.

Derrida, Jacques. 1976. *Of grammatology.* Baltimore, MD: Johns Hopkins University Press.

Devon (Devon Martin). 1990. 'Mr. Metro'. Canada.

De Voretz, D. 1995. *Diminishing returns: The economics of Canada's immigration policy.* Vancouver: C.D. Howe Institute and Laurier Institution.

Dewhurst, C., and R. Gordon. 1969. *The intersexual disorders.* London: Balliere, Tindall and Cassell.

Diamond, M. 1982. 'Sexual identity, monozygotic twins reared in discordant sex roles and a BBC follow-up'. *Archives of Sexual Behavior* 11 (2):181–5.

———, and H. Sigmundson. 1997. 'Sex reassignment at birth: A long term review and clinical implications'. *Archives of Paediatrics and Adolescent Medicine* 151:298–304.

Dickinson, John A., and Brian Young. 2000. *A short history of Quebec*. Montreal and Kingston: McGill-Queen's University Press.

Doane, Mary Anne. 1982. 'Film and the masquerade: Theorizing the female spectator'. *Screen* 23 (3/4):81.

Dobash, Russell P., R. Emerson Dobash, and Sue Gutteridge. 1986. *The imprisonment of women*. Oxford, UK: Basil Blackwell.

Dobrowolsky, A. 2004. 'The Chrétien legacy and women: Changing policy priorities with little cause for celebration'. In S. Patten and L. Harder (Eds), *Review of Constitutional Studies: Special Issue on the Chrétien Legacy* 9 (1/2):171–98.

Donzelot, J. 1984. *L'invention du social*. Paris: Fayard.

———. 1988. 'The promotion of the social'. *Economy and Society* 17 (3):394–427.

Doob, A., and C. Cesaroni. 2004. *Responding to youth crime in Canada*. Toronto: University of Toronto Press.

Doran, N. [C. Doran]. 1986. *Calculated risks: An alternative history of workers' compensation*. Unpublished doctoral dissertation. Calgary: University of Calgary.

———. 1994a. 'Codifying women's bodies? Towards a genealogy of British victimology'. *Women and Criminal Justice* 5 (2):45–70.

———. 'Maintaining the simulation model in the era of the 'social': The inquiry system of workers' compensation, 1914–84. *Canadian Review of Sociology and Anthropology* 31 (4):446–69.

———. 1996. 'From embodied "health" to official "accidents": Class, codification and the early British factory legislation, 1831–1844'. *Social and Legal Studies* 5 (4):523–46.

———. 1999. 'Growing up under suspicion: The problematization of youth in recent criminologies'. In L. Beaman (Ed.), *New perspectives on deviance: The construction of deviance in everyday life*. Toronto: Prentice Hall.

———. 2004. 'Re-writing the social, re-writing sociology: Donzelot, genealogy and working class bodies'. *Canadian Journal of Sociology* 29 (3):333–57.

———. Forthcoming. 'Decoding "encoding" in a cultural studies' classic: Moral panics, media portrayals and Marxist presuppositions'. *Theoretical Criminology*.

Douglas, Jack. 1967. *The social meaning of suicide*. Princeton, NJ: Princeton University Press.

———. 1970. 'Understanding everyday life'. In J. Douglas (Ed.), *Understanding everyday life: Toward the reconstruction of sociological knowledge*, 3–44. Chicago: Aldine.

———, and John Johnson. 1977. *Existential sociology*. New York: Cambridge University Press.

Douglas, M. 2002. 'Neediest children feel sting'. *Kamloops Daily News* 22 April: A1.

Dover, K.J. 1978. *Greek homosexuality*. New York: Vintage.

Driedger, L. 1996. *Multi-ethnic Canada: Identities and inequalities*. Toronto: Oxford University Press.

Driscoll, Catherine. 2002. *Girls: Feminine adolescence in popular culture and cultural theory*. New York: Columbia University Press.

Dubin, C. 1990. *Commission of Inquiry into the Use of Drugs and Banned Practices Intended to Increase Athletic Performance*. Ottawa: Canadian Government Publishing Centre.

Durkheim, Émile. 1895. *The rules of sociological method*. George G. Catlin, Ed. (Sarah A. Solovay and John H. Mueller, trans.). New York: Free Press.

———. 1952 [1897]. *Suicide: A study in sociology*. London: Routledge and Kegan Paul.

———. 1984 [1893]. *The division of labour in society*. (W.D. Halls, trans.). London: Macmillan.

Egan and Nesbitt v. Canada. 1995 (4th) 609 (SCC).

Ekins, R., and D. King (Eds). 1996. *Blending genders*. New York: Routledge.

Ellis, Havelock. 1891. *The criminal*. London: W. Scott.

Engels, Friedrich. 1972. 'The origin of the family, private property, and the state'. In Robert C. Tucker (Ed.), *The Marx-Engels reader*, 2nd edn, 734–59. New York: Norton.

Enloe, C. 1990. *Bananas, beaches and bases: Making feminist sense out of international politics*. Berkeley: University of California Press.

Ericson, Richard. 1994. 'The division of expert knowledge in policing and security'. *The British Journal of Sociology* 45 (2):134–50.

———, and Kevin Haggerty. 1997. *Policing the risk society*. Toronto: University of Toronto Press.

Erikson, E.H. 1968. *Identity: Youth and crisis*. New York: Norton.

Fabolous. 2004. 'Breathe'. US.

Faith, Karlene. 1993. *Unruly women. The politics of confinement and resistance*. Vancouver: Press Gang Publishers.

Faludi, Susan. 1999. *Stiffed*. New York: Morrow.

Featherstone, Mike. 1988. 'In pursuit of the postmodern: An introduction'. *Theory, Culture and Society* 5 (2/3):195–216.

———, and Mike Hepworth. 1991. 'The mask of ageing and the postmodern life course'. In Mike Featherstone, Mike Hepworth, and Bryan S. Turner (Eds), *The body: Social process and cultural theory*, 371–89. London: Sage.

Feinberg, L. 1996. *Transgender warriors*. Boston: Beacon

Feinman, C. (Ed.). 1992. *The criminalization of a woman's body*. New York: Haworth.

Feld, B. 2000. '"Juveniles" waiver of legal rights: Confessions, Miranda, and the right to counsel'. In T. Grisso and R.G. Schwartz (Eds), *Youth on trial: A developmental perspective on juvenile justice*. Chicago: University of Chicago Press.

Finateri, Lisa. 1999. 'The paradox of pregnancy in prison: Resistance, control, and the body'. *Canadian Woman Studies/Les cahiers de la femme* 19 (1/2):136–44.

Fincher, R., L. Foster, W. Giles, and V. Preston. 1994. 'Gender and migration policy'. In H. Adelman, A. Borowski, M. Burstein, and L. Foster (Eds), *Immigration and refugee policy: Australia and Canada compared*, v. 1, 149–84. Toronto: University of Toronto Press.

Finnie, R. 2000. *Who moves? A panel logit model analysis of inter-provincial migration in Canada*. Ottawa: Business and Labour Market Analytical Division, Statistics

Canada.

Fiske, John. 1989. *Understanding popular culture*. London: Routledge.

Fontaine, Louise. 1993. *Un labyrinthe carré comme un cercle; Enquête sur le ministère des communautés culturelles et de l'immigration et sur ses acteurs réels et imaginés*. Montréal: L'Étincelle.

Foucault, Michel. 1973. *The order of things*. New York: Vintage.

———. 1975a. *The birth of the clinic*. New York: Vintage.

———. 1975b. *Surveiller et punir : La naissance de la prison*. Paris: Gallimard.

———. 1977a. *Madness and civilization: A history of insanity in the Age of Reason*. London: Tavistock.

———. 1977b. *Discipline and punish: The birth of the prison*. (A. Sheridan, trans.) New York: Pantheon.

———. 1978. *The history of sexuality*. New York: Pantheon.

———. 1980a. *Power/knowledge: Selected interviews and other writings, 1972-1977*. New York: Pantheon.

———. 1980b. 'Two lectures'. In C. Gordon (Ed.), *Power/knowledge: Selected interviews and other writings, 1972–1977*, 78–108. New York: Pantheon.

———. 1982. 'The subject and power'. In Hubert Dreyfus and Paul Rabinow, *Michel Foucault: Beyond structuralism and hermeneutics*. Chicago: University of Chicago Press.

———. 1989 [1984]. 'The return of morality'. In Sylvère Lotringer (Ed.), *Foucault live*, 317–31. New York: Semiotext(e).

———. 1991. *Remarks on Marx, conversations with Duccio Trombador*. (R. James Goldstein and James Cascaito, trans.). New York: Semiotext(e).

Fox, Adam. 2002. 'The wrong result'. *The Guardian* 18 July.

Francis, C. 1990. *Speed trap: Inside the biggest scandal in Olympic history*. Toronto: Lester and Orpen Dennys.

Francis, D., and S. Hester. 2004. *An invitation to ethnomethodology*. London: Sage.

Franke, W.F., and B. Berendonk. 1997. 'Hormonal doping and androgenization of athletes: A secret program of the German Democratic Republic government'. *Clinical Chemistry* 43 (7):1262–79.

Freud, Sigmund. 1966 [1916]. 'The dream work'. In *Introductory lectures on psychoanalysis* (James Strachey, trans.). New York: Norton.

Frideres, James S. 1974. *Canada's Indians: Contemporary conflicts*. Scarborough, ON: Prentice Hall.

———. 1998. *Aboriginal peoples in Canada: Contemporary conflicts*. Scarborough, ON: Prentice Hall Allyn and Bacon Canada.

Friedan, Betty. 1963. *The feminine mystique*. New York: Dell.

Frigon, Sylvie. 1994. 'Femmes, hérésies et contrôle social : des sages-femmes et au-delà'. *Revue femmes et droit/Canadian Journal of Women and the Law* 7 (1):133–55.

———. 1995. 'A genealogy of women's madness'. In R.E. Dobash and L. Noaks (Eds), *Gender and crime*, 20–48. Cardiff: University of Wales Press.

———. 1996. 'A gallery of portraits: Women and the embodiment of difference, deviance and criminality'. In Thomas O'Reilly-Fleming (Ed.), *Post-critical criminology*, 78–110. Scarborough, ON: Prentice Hall.

———. 1999. 'Une radioscopie des événements survenus à la Prison des femmes : la construction d'un *corps dangereux* et d'un *corps en danger*'. *Canadian Woman Studies/Les cahiers de la femme* 19 (1/2):154–60.

———. 2000. 'Corps, féminité et dangerosité : de la production de « corps dociles » en criminology'. In Sylvie Frigon and Michèle Kérisit (Eds), *Du corps des femmes : Contrôle, surveillance et résistance*, 127–64. Ottawa: Les Presses de l'Université d'Ottawa.

———. 2001. 'Femmes et emprisonnement : le marquage du corps et l'automutilation'. *Criminologie* 34 (2):31–56.

——— (Ed.). 2002. 'L'enfermement des femmes au Canada : Une décennie de réformes'. *Criminologie* 35 (1).

———. 2003. *L'homicide conjugal au féminin : D'hier à aujourd'hui*. Montréal : Les éditions du Remue-ménage.

———. 2005. 'Transformations de la philosophie et de la gestion pénale des femmes justiciables au Canada : Trois cas de figure'. *Revue femmes et droit/Canadian Journal of Women and the Law* 16 (2).

———, and Michèle Kérisit (Eds). 2000. *Du corps des femmes : Contrôle, surveillance et résistance*. Ottawa: Les Presses de l'Université d'Ottawa.

———, V. Strimelle, and C. Renière. 2003 [translation, summer 2005]. *Job entry and retention for women offenders in Québec*. Québec: Comité aviseur pour la clientele judiciarisée—adulte et Emploi Québec, juin.

Frisby, David. 1992. *Simmel and since: Essays on Georg Simmel's social theory*. London: Routledge.

Fudge, Judy. 2002. 'From segregation to privatization: Equality, the law and women public servants 1908–2001'. In Brenda Cossman and Judy Fudge (Eds), *Privatization, law and the challenge to feminism*, 86–127. Toronto: University of Toronto Press.

Gagné, P., and R. Tewksbury. 1998. 'Conformity pressures and gender resistance among transgendered individuals'. *Social Problems* 45:81–101.

Gagnon, Marie. 1997. *Bienvenue dans mon cauchemar*. Montréal: VLB éditeurs.

Galloway, D. 2000. 'The dilemmas of Canadian citizenship law'. In T.A. Aleinikoff and D. Klusmeyer (Eds), *From migrants to citizens: Membership in a changing world*. Washington: Carnegie Endowment for International Peace.

Garfinkel, Harold. 1956. 'Conditions of successful degradation ceremonies'. *The American Journal of Sociology* 61 (5):420–4.

———. 1963. 'A conception of and experiments with "trust" as a condition of concerted stable actions'. In O.J. Harvey (Ed.), *Motivation and social interaction*, 220–35. New York: Ronald Press.

———, in collaboration with R. Stoller. 1967. *Studies in ethnomethodology*. Cambridge, UK: Polity Press.

———. 1974. 'The origins of the term "ethnomethodology"'. In R. Turner (Ed.), *Ethnomethodology*, 15–18. Harmondsworth, UK: Penguin.

———. 1986. *Ethnomethodological studies of work*. New York: Routledge and Kegan Paul.

Garland, D. 1985. *Punishment and welfare*. London: Gower.

———. 1996. 'The limits of the sovereign state: Strategies of crime control in contemporary society'. *British Journal of Criminology* 36 (4):445–72.

———. 1997. 'Governmentality and the problem of crime: Foucault, criminology, sociology'. *Theoretical Criminology* 1 (2):173–214.

Gee, Ellen M., and Gloria M. Gutman (Eds). 2000. *The overselling of population aging: Apocalyptic demography, intergenerational challenges, and social policy.* Don Mills, ON: Oxford University Press.

Gee, James Paul. 2000–1. 'Identity as an analytic lens for research in education'. *Review of Research in Education* 25:99–125.

———. 2002. *An introduction to discourse analysis: Theory and methods.* London: Routledge.

Gellner, Ernest. 1997. *Nationalism.* New York: New York University Press.

George, Nelson. 1998. *Hip hop America.* New York: Penguin.

Gergen, Kenneth J. 1991. *The saturated self: Dilemmas of identity in contemporary life.* New York: Basic Books.

German Sport Association. 2003. *Sport in Deutschland* [Sport in Germany]. http://www.dsb.de/fileadmin/fm-dsb/arbeitsfelder/wiss-ges/Dateien/Sport_in_Deutschland.pdf.

Giddens, Anthony. 1984. *The constitution of society.* Berkeley: University of California Press.

———. 1987. *Sociology: A brief but critical introduction.* New York: Harcourt, Brace and Jovanovich.

Gieseler, K-H. 1980. 'Das freie Spiel der Kräfte. Spitzensport in der Industriegesellschaft [The free play of powers. High-performance sport in industrial society]'. In R. Andresen (Ed.), *Schneller, Höher, Stärker... Chancen und Risiken im Leistungssport* [Faster, higher, stronger... Opportunities and risks in high-performance sport], 24–37. Niedernhausen, Germany: Golling, Schors-Verlag.

Gilbert, D. 1980. *The miracle machine.* New York: Coward, McCann and Geoghegan.

Gilling, Daniel. 1996. 'Policing, crime prevention and partnerships'. In Frank Leishman, Barry Loveday, and Stephen Savage (Eds), *Core issues in policing.* London: Longman.

Gillis, John R. 1988. 'From ritual to romance: Toward an alternative history of love'. In Peter N. Stearns, and Carol Zisowitz Stearns (Eds), *Emotion and social change: Toward a new psychohistory,* 87–121. New York: Holmes and Meier.

Ginsberg, Gisèle. 1992. *Des prisons et des femmes.* Paris: Éditions Ramsay.

Gleeson, Kate, and Hannah Frith. 2004. 'Pretty in pink: Young women presenting mature sexual identities'. In Anita Harris (Ed.), *All about the girl: Culture, power and identity.* New York: Routledge.

Globe and Mail. 2005a. Toronto. 26 March.

Globe and Mail. 2005b. Toronto. 30 March.

Goffman, Erving. 1961. *Asylums.* London: Penguin.

———. 1967. 'On face-work'. In *Interaction ritual: Essays on face-to-face behavior,* 5–45. Garden City, NY: Doubleday, Anchor Books.

———. 1971 [1959]. *The presentation of self in everyday life.* Harmondsworth, UK: Penguin.

———. 1974. *Frame analysis: An essay on the organization of experience.* New York: Harper and Row.

———. 1976. *Gender advertisements.* London: Macmillan.

———. 1983. 'The interaction order'. *American Sociological Review* 48:1–17.

Goldman, B. 1984. *Death in the locker room: Steroids and sports.* South Bend, IN: Icarus.

Goldthorpe, J., D. Lockwood, F. Bechhofer, and J. Platt. 1968a. *The affluent worker: Industrial attitudes and behaviour.* Cambridge, UK: Cambridge University Press.

———. 1968b. *The affluent worker: Political attitudes and behaviour.* Cambridge, UK: Cambridge University Press.

———. 1969. *The affluent worker in the class structure.* Cambridge, UK: Cambridge University Press.

Gordon, Avery. 1997. *Ghostly matters.* Minneapolis, MN: University of Minnesota Press.

Gould, Stephen Jay. 1977. 'The child a man's real father'. In *Ever since Darwin*, 63–9. New York: Norton.

Gouldner, A. 1970. *The coming crisis of Western sociology.* New York: Basic Books.

Gramsci, Antonio. 1971. *Selections from the prison notebooks.* Q. Hoare and G.N. Smith (Eds and trans.). New York: International Publishers.

Grandin, Temple. 1995. *Thinking in pictures: And other reports from my life with autism.* New York: Doubleday.

———, and Catherine Johnson. 2004. *Animals in translation: Using the mysteries of autism to decode animal behavior.* Riverside, NJ: Scribner.

———, and Margaret M. Scariano. 1986. *Emergence, labeled autistic.* Novato, CA: Arena Press.

Green, J. 1999. 'Look! Don't! The visibility dilemma for transsexual men'. In K. More and S. Whittle (Eds), *Reclaiming genders.* London: Cassell.

Green, M., and B. Oakley. 2001. 'Elite sport development systems and playing to win: Uniformity and diversity in international approaches'. *Leisure Studies* 20:247–67.

Green, R. 1978. 'Sexual identity of 37 children raised by homosexual or transsexual parents'. *American Journal of Psychiatry* 135 (6):692–7

Greenberg, David. 1988. *The construction of homosexuality.* Chicago: University of Chicago Press.

Griffin, J.E., and J.D. Wilson. 1992. 'Disorders of sexual differentiation'. In P.C. Walsh, A.B. Retik, T.A. Stamey, and E.D. Vaughan (Eds), *Campbell's urology*, 1509–37. Philadelphia: Saunders.

Griffiths, N.E.S. 1992. *The contexts of Acadian history, 1686–1784.* Pawtucket, RI: Quintin.

Grosz, Elizabeth. 1992. 'Le corps et les connaissances. Le féminisme et la crise de la raison'. *Sociologies et sociétés* 24 (1):47–66.

Gubrium, Jaber F., and James A. Holstein. 1998. 'Narrative practice and the coherence of personal stories'. *Sociological Quarterly* 39:163–87.

Guttmann, A. 2002. *The Olympics: A history of the modern Games.* Urbana and Chicago: University of Illinois Press.

Habermas, Jürgen. 1971. *Towards a rational society: Student protest, science and politics.*

Boston: Beacon.

———. 1975. *Legitimation crisis*. (T. McCarthy, trans.). Boston: Beacon.

Hacking, I. 1982. 'Biopower and the avalanche of printed numbers'. *Humanities in Society* 5 (1):279–95.

Hall, G. Stanley. 1904. *Adolescence: Its psychology and its relations to physiology, anthropology, sociology, sex, crime, religion and education*. New York: Appleton.

Hall, Kira. 1995. 'Lip service on the fantasy lines'. In Kira Hall and Mary Buchotz (Eds), *Gender articulated: Language and the socially constructed self*, 183–216. London and New York: Routledge.

Hall, Stuart. 1959. 'Deviance, politics and the media'. In P. Rock and M. McIntosh (Eds), *Deviance and social control*. London: Tavistock.

———. 1981. 'Notes on deconstructing the popular'. In Raphael Samuel (Ed.), *People's history and socialist theory*. London: Routledge and Kegan Paul.

———, and Paddy Whannel. 1998 [1964]. 'The young audience'. In John Storey (Ed.), *Cultural theory and popular culture*. 2nd edn. Hemel Hampstead, UK: Prentice Hall.

Halperin, David. 1990. *One hundred years of homosexuality*. New York: Routledge.

———. 1995. *Saint Foucault*. New York: Oxford University Press.

———. 2002. *How to do the history of homosexuality*. Chicago: University of Chicago Press.

Hamelin, Monique. 1989. *Femmes et prison*. Montréal: Éditions du Méridien.

Hamilton, R. 2004. *Gendering the vertical mosaic: Feminist perspectives on Canadian society*. 2nd edn. Toronto: Pearson.

Hammarberg, T. 1990. 'The UN Convention on the Rights of the Child and how to make it work'. *Human Rights Quarterly* 12 (1):97–105.

Hannah-Moffat, K. 2001. *Punishment in disguise: Penal governance and federal imprisonment of women in Canada*. Toronto: University of Toronto Press.

———, and M. Shaw. 2000. *An ideal prison? Critical essays on women's imprisonment in Canada*. Halifax: Fernwood.

Hansen, D. 1976. *An invitation to critical sociology*. New York and London: Free Press.

Haraway, Donna. 1985. 'Manifesto for cyborgs: Science, technology, and socialist feminism in the 1980s'. *Socialist Review* 80:65–108.

———. 1988. 'Situated knowledges: The science question in feminism and the privilege of partial perspective'. *Feminist Studies* 14 (3):575–99.

Harding, J. 1996. 'Sex and control: The hormonal body'. *Body and Society* 2 (1):99–111.

Harding, S. 1986. *The science question in feminism*. Ithaca, NY: Cornell University Press.

Hareven, Tamara K. 1995. 'The discovery of old age and the social construction of the life course'. In Cornelia Hummel and Christian J. Lalive D'Epinay (Eds), *Images of aging in Western societies*, 13–38. Geneva: Centre for Interdisciplinary Gerontology, University of Geneva.

Harré, Rom, and Robert Finlay-Jones. 1986. 'Emotion talk across times'. In Rom Harré (Ed.), *The social construction of emotions*, 220–33. Oxford, UK: Basil Blackwell.

Harrison, D., and L. Laliberte. 1994. *No life like it*. Toronto: Lorimer.

Hartley, John. 2003. *A short history of cultural studies*. Thousand Oaks, CA: Sage.

Hartsock, N. 1987. 'Rethinking modernism: Minority vs. majority theories'. *Cultural*

Critique 7:187–206.

Hausman, B. 1995. *Changing sex: Transsexualism technology and the idea of gender*. Durham, NC: Duke University Press.

Hayles, Katherine. 1999. *How we became posthuman: Virtual bodies in cybernetics, literature and informatics*. Chicago: University of Chicago Press.

Hebdige, Dick. 1979. *Subculture: The meaning of style*. London: Methuen.

Hemmings, C. 1996. 'Hausman's horror'. *Radical Deviance: A Journal of Transgendered Politics* 2 (2):59–60.

Henderson, James (Sakej). 1994a. 'Empowering treaty federalism'. *Saskatchewan Law Review* 58:269.

———. 1994b. 'Implementing the treaty order'. In Richard Gosse, James Youngblood Henderson, and Roger Carter (Eds), *Continuing Poundmaker's and Riel's quest: Presentations made at a conference on Aboriginal peoples and justice*. Saskatoon: Purich.

Henley, Nancy, and Fred Pincus. 1978. 'Interrelationship of sexist, racist and antihomosexual attitudes'. *Psychological Reports* 42 (1):83–90.

Heney, Jan. 1990. *Report on self-injurious behaviour in the Kingston Prison for Women*. Ottawa: Correctional Service of Canada.

Hennessy, Rosemary. 1995. 'Queer visibility in commodity culture'. In L. Nicholson and S. Seidman (Eds), *Social postmodernism: Beyond identity politics*. Cambridge, UK: Cambridge University Press.

Herdt, Gilbert. 1984. *Ritualized homosexuality in Melanesia*. Berkeley: University of California Press.

Herek, Gregory. 1988. 'Heterosexuals' attitudes toward lesbians and gay men'. *Journal of Sex Research* 25 (4):451–77.

Hermer, Joe, and Janet Mosher. 2002. *Disorderly people: Law and the politics of exclusion in Ontario*. Halifax: Fernwood.

Hewitt, John P. 1998. *The myth of self-esteem: Finding happiness and solving problems in America*. New York: St. Martin's.

Hey, Valerie. 1997. *The company she keeps: An ethnography of girls' friendships*. Buckingham, UK: Open University Press.

Hilbert, Richard. 1992. *The classical roots of ethnomethodology: Durkheim, Weber and Garfinkel*. Chapel Hill: University of North Carolina Press.

Hill, Richard. 1992. 'Continuity of Haudenosaunee government'. In Jose Barreiro (Ed.), *Indian roots of American democracy*. Ithaca, NY: Akwe:don Press, Cornell University.

Hird, M.J. 2000. 'Gender's nature: Intersexuals, transsexualism and the "sex"/"gender" binary'. *Feminist Theory* 1 (3):347–64.

———. 2004. *Sex, gender and science*. Basingstoke, UK: Palgrave Macmillan.

———, and K. Abshoff. 2000. 'Women without children: A contradiction in terms?' *Canadian Journal of Comparative Family Studies* 31 (3):347–66.

———, and J. Germon. 1998. 'Women on the edge of a dyke-otomy: Confronting subjectivity'. *Journal of Lesbian Studies* 3:103–11.

———. 2001. 'The intersexual body and the medical regulation of gender'. In K. Backett-Milburn and L. McKie (Eds), *Constructing gendered bodies*, 162–78. London: Palgrave.

Hobbes, Thomas. 1989. *The leviathan.* Belmont, CA: Wadsworth.

Hoberman, J. 1984. *Sport and political ideology.* Austin: University of Texas Press.

———. 2001. 'How drug testing fails: The politics of doping control'. In W. Wilson and E. Derse (Eds), *Doping in elite sport: The politics of drugs in the Olympic movement*, 241–74. Champaign, IL: Human Kinetics.

Hobsbawm, Eric J. 1992. *Nations and nationalism since 1780: Programme, myth, reality.* Cambridge, UK: Cambridge University Press.

Hochschild, Arlie Russell. 1983. *The managed heart: The commercialization of human feeling.* Berkeley: University of California Press.

———. 1990. *The second shift: Working parents and the revolution at home.* New York: Viking.

———. 1998. 'The sociology of emotion as a way of seeing'. In Gillian Bendelow and Simon J. Williams (Eds), *Emotions in social life: Critical themes and contemporary issues*, 5–15. London and New York: Routledge.

———. 2003. *The commercialization of intimate life: Notes from home and work.* Berkeley: University of California Press.

Hogeveen, B. 1999. 'An intrusive and corrective government: Political rationalities and the governance of Plains Aboriginals 1870–1890'. In R. Smandych (Ed.), *Governable places: Readings on governmentality and crime control.* Aldershot, UK: Dartmouth.

———. 2002. 'Mentally defective and feeble-minded juvenile offenders: Psychiatric discourse and the Toronto juvenile court 1910–1930'. *Canadian Bulletin of Medical History* 20 (1):43–74.

———. 2005. '"If we are tough on crime, if we punish crime, then people get the message": Constructing and governing the punishable young offender in Canada during the late 1990s'. *Punishment and Society* 7 (1):73–89.

Hollingshead, A.B. 1949. *Elmtown's youth: The impact of social classes on adolescents.* New York: John Wiley and Sons.

Hood-Williams, John. 1996. 'Goodbye to sex and gender'. *Sociological Review* 49 (1):1–16.

hooks, bell. 2001. 'Eating the other'. In Meenakshi Gigi Durham and Douglas M. Kellner (Eds), *Media and cultural studies: Key works.* Malden, MA: Blackwell.

Horii, Gayle. 1994. 'The art in/of survival'. *Journal of Prisoners on Prisons* 5 (2):10–23.

Howe, Adrian. 1994. *Punish and critique: Towards a feminist analysis of penalty.* London: Routledge.

Hudson, B. 2003. *Understanding justice: An introduction to ideas, perspectives, and controversies in modern penal theory.* Philadelphia: Open University Press.

Human Rights Watch. 2001. *Hatred in the hallways.* Washington: Human Rights Watch.

Hunt, Alan. 1999. *Governing morals: A social history of moral regulation.* Cambridge, UK: Cambridge University Press.

———, and Gary Wickham. 1994. *Foucault and the law: Towards a sociology of law as governance.* London: Pluto.

Iacovetta, F. 1999. 'Gossip, contest and power in the making of suburban bad girls: Toronto, 1945–60'. *Canadian Historical Review* 80 (4):585–623.

International Olympic Committee. 1989. *The Olympic Charter: 1989*. Lausanne, Switzerland.

Ip, D., C. Inglis, and C. Wu. 1997. 'Concepts of citizenship and identity among recent Asian immigrants in Australia'. *Asian and Pacific Migration Journal* 6:363–84.

Isin, E. 2002. *Being political: Genealogies of citizenship*. Minneapolis: University of Minnesota Press.

Ivison, Duncan. 1997. *The self at liberty: Political liberty and the arts of government*. Ithaca, NY: Cornell University Press.

Jaccoud, Mylène. 1992. 'Les femmes autochtones et la justice pénale'. *Criminologie* 25 (1):65–85.

Jackson, C. 2000. 'Waste and whiteness: Zora Neale Hurston and the politics of eugenics'. *African American Review* 34 (Winter):639–60.

Jackson, M. 1989. 'Locking up Natives in Canada'. *University of British Columbia Law Review* 23 (special issue):213–40.

Jacobs, Sue Ellen, Wesley Thomas, and Sabine Lang. 1997. *Twospirit people*. Urbana: University of Illinois Press.

Jaggar, Alison M., and Paula S. Rothenberg (Eds). 1993. *Feminist frameworks: Alternative theoretical accounts of the relations between women and men*. 3rd edn. New York: McGraw-Hill.

Jagger, Elizabeth. 2001. 'Marketing Molly and Melville: Dating in a postmodern, consumer society'. *Sociology* 35:39–57.

Jaimes, M. Annette (Ed.). 1992. *The state of Native America: Genocide, colonization and resistance*. Boston: South End Press.

Jarman, Jennifer. 2004. 'Backshops in the global economy, Singapore, India and Canada'. National University of Singapore.

———, and J. Barkow. 1998. *Telework and the construction of self in Nova Scotian call centres*. Research Development Grant, Dalhousie University.

———. 1999. 'Worker identity in the call centre industry'. Canadian sociology and anthropology meetings, Edmonton.

———, Peter Butler, and Donald Clairmont. 1997. 'Sweatshops and teleprofessionalism: An investigation of life and work in the teleservice industry'. Paper presented at the Second International Telework Conference, Building Actions on Ideas, Amsterdam.

Jeffreys, S. 1990. *Anticlimax*. London: Women's Press.

———. 2003. *Unpacking queer politics: A lesbian feminist perspective*. Oxford, UK: Polity Press.

Jenson, J. 1989. 'Different but not "exceptional": Canada's permeable Fordism'. *Canadian Review of Sociology and Anthropology* 26 (1):69–94.

———, and M. Sineau. 2001. *Who cares? Women's work, childcare and welfare state redesign*. Toronto: University of Toronto Press.

Johannson, Thomas. 2000. 'Georg Simmel: The psychologist of social life'. In *Social psychology and modernity*, 19–38. Buckingham, UK: Open University Press.

Johansen, Bruce E. 1982. *Forgotten founders: How the American Indian helped shape democracy*. Boston: Harvard Common Press.

Johnsrude, L. 1999. 'Budget restraints hurt children'. *Edmonton Journal* 7 August: A3.

Johnston, Les. 1996. 'Policing diversity: The impact of the public-private complex in policing'. In F. Leishman, B. Loveday, and S. Savage (Eds), *Core issues in policing*. London: Longman.

———, and Clifford Shearing. 2003. *Governing security: Explorations in policing and justice*. London: Routledge.

Jones, Alison. 1993. 'Becoming a "girl": Post-structuralist suggestions for educational research'. *Gender and Education* 5 (2):157–67.

Jones, T. 2003. 'The governance and accountability of policing'. In Tim Newburn (Ed.), *Handbook of policing*. Collompton, UK: Willan.

———, and T. Newburn. 1998. *Private security and public policing*. Oxford, UK: Police Studies Institute, Clarendon.

Jordan, Mark. 1997. *The invention of sodomy in Christian theology*. Chicago: University of Chicago Press.

Jordison, S., and D. Kieran (Eds). 2004. *Crap towns II*. London: Boxtree.

Journal of Prisoners on Prisons. 1994. Special issue 5 (2).

Karp, David A., William C. Yoels, and Barbara H. Vann. 2004. *Sociology in everyday life*. 3rd edn. Long Grove, IL: Waveland Press.

Kashima, Yoshihisa, and Margaret Foddy. 2002. 'Time and self: The historical construction of the self'. In Yoshihisa Kashima, Margaret Foddy, and Michael Platon (Eds), *Self and identity: Personal, social, and symbolic*, 180–206. Mahwah, NJ: Lawrence Erlbaum Associates.

Katz, Stephen. 2001. 'Growing older without aging? Positive aging, anti-ageism, and anti-aging'. *Generations* 25:27–32.

———, and Barbara L. Marshall. 2003. 'New sex for old: Lifestyle, consumerism and the ethics of aging well'. *Journal of Aging Studies* 17:3–16.

Keating, Michael. 2004. 'European integration and the nationalities question'. *Politics and Society* 32:367–88.

Kelley, N., and M. Trebilcock. 1998. *The making of the mosaic: A history of Canadian immigration policy*. Toronto: University of Toronto Press.

Kelly, Deirdre M., Shauna Pomerantz, and Dawn H. Currie. 2005. 'Skater girlhood and emphasized femininity: "You can't land an ollie properly in heels"'. *Gender and Education* 17 (3):129–48.

Kember, Sarah. 2003. *Cyberfeminism and artificial life*. London and New York: Routledge.

Kendall, Kathleen. 1993. *Evaluation des services thérapeutiques offerts à la Prison des femmes*. Ottawa: Service correctionnel du Canada.

Kenway, J., S. Willis, J. Blackmore, and L. Rennie. 1998. *Answering back: Girls, boys and feminism in schools*. New York: Routledge.

Kenyon, Gary, Phillip Clark, and Brian de Vries (Eds). 2001. *Narrative gerontology: Theory, research and practice*. New York: Springer.

Ker, Muir. 1977. *Police: Street corner politicians*. Chicago: University of Chicago Press.

Kessler, S. 1990. 'The medical construction of gender: Case management of intersexed infants'. *Signs: Journal of Women in Culture and Society* 16:3–26.

Killanin, L. 1976. 'Eligibility and amateurism'. In L. Killanin and J. Rodda (Eds), *The Olympic Games: 80 years of people, events and records*. Don Mills, ON: Collier

Macmillan.

Kinsman, Gary. 1996. *The regulation of desire*. Montreal: Black Rose.

Kitwood, Tom. 1997. *Dementia reconsidered: The person comes first*. Buckingham, UK: Open University Press.

Klein, Naomi. 2000. *No logo*. Toronto: Knopf.

Kontos, Pia. 2004. 'Ethnographic reflections on selfhood, embodiment and Alzheimer's Disease'. *Ageing and Society* 24:829–49.

Kovach, Margaret. 2005. 'Emerging from the margins: Indigenous methodologies'. In Leslie Brown and Susan Strega (Eds), *Research as resistance: Critical, indigenous and anti-oppressive approaches*. Toronto: Canadian Scholars Press.

Kymlicka, Will. 1998. *Finding our way: Rethinking ethnocultural relations in Canada*. Toronto: Oxford University Press.

———. 2000. 'Nation-building and minority rights: Comparing west and east'. *Journal of Ethnic and Migration Studies* 26:183–212.

Labadie, J.-M. 1995. 'Corps et crime : De Lavater (1775) à Lombroso (1876)'. In C. Debuyst, F. Digneffe, J.-M. Labadie, A. Pires (Eds), *Histoire des savoirs sur le crime et la peine; 1. Des savoirs diffus à la notion de criminel-né*, 295–345. Montréal, Ottawa, Bruxelles : Les Presses de l'Université de Montréal, Les Presses de l'Université d'Ottawa, DeBoeck Université.

Laberge, Danielle. 1991. 'Women's criminality, criminal women, criminalized women? Questions in and for a feminist perspective'. *Journal of Human Justice* 2 (2):37–56.

Laczko, Leslie S. 2000. 'Canada's linguistic and ethnic dynamics in an evolving world-system'. In Thomas D. Hall (Ed.), *A world-systems reader: New perspectives on gender, urbanism, cultures, indigenous peoples, and ecology*, 131–42. Lanham, MD: Rowman and Littlefield.

Ladner, Kiera. 2000. 'Women and Blackfoot nationalism'. *Journal of Canadian Studies* 35 (2):35–62.

———. 2003. 'Treaty federalism: An indigenous view of Canadian federalisms'. In François Rocher and Miriam Smith (Eds), *New trends in Canadian federalism*, 2nd edn, 167–94. Peterborough, ON: Broadview.

Laforest, Guy. 2001. 'The true nature of sovereignty: Reply to my critics concerning Trudeau and the end of a Canadian dream'. In Ronald Beiner and Wayne Norman (Eds), *Canadian political philosophy*. Don Mills, ON: Oxford University Press.

Lahey, K. 2000. *The benefit/penalty unit in income tax policy: Diversity and reform*. Ottawa: Law Commission of Canada.

Laidman, J. 2000. 'Reproduction a touch-and-go thing for fungus'. *Nature* 24 July: 1–3.

Laitin, David D. 1998. *Identity in formation: The Russian-speaking populations in the near abroad*. Ithaca, NY: Cornell University Press.

Lang, Sabine. 1998. *Men as women, women as men*. Austin: University of Texas Press.

Lanphier, M. 1993. 'Host groups: Public meets private'. In V. Robinson (Ed.), *The international refugee crisis: British and Canadian responses*, 255–73. London: Macmillan.

Laqueur, T. 1990. *Making sex*. Cambridge, MA: Harvard University Press.

Larsen, Knud, Rodney Cate, and Michael Reed. 1983. 'Antiblack attitudes, religious orthodoxy, permissiveness and sexual information'. *Journal of Sex Research* 19:105–18.

Leavis, F.R. 1999 [1930]. *Mass civilisation and minority culture*. Cambridge, UK: Minority Press.

LeBaron, Michelle. 2004. 'Learning new dances: Finding effective ways to address intercultural disputes'. In Catherine Bell and David Kahane (Eds), *Intercultural dispute resolution*. Vancouver: University of British Columbia Press.

Lee, Jennifer. 2005. 'The man date'. *New York Times* 10 April: 1.

Lee, K., and C. Engler. 2000. *A profile of poverty*. Ottawa: Canadian Council on Social Development.

Lefebvre, Pierre, and Philip Merrigan. 2003. 'Assessing family policy in Canada: A new deal for families and children'. *Choices* 9 (5). Montreal: Institute for Research on Public Policy.

Lehnertz, K. 1979. *Berufliche Entwicklung der Amateurspitzensportler in der Bundesrepublik Deutschland* [Occupational development of amateur elite athletes in the Federal Republic of Germany]. Schorndorf, Germany: Karl Hofmann Verlag.

Lévesque, A. 2002. 'Le travail des femmes à l'heure de la mondialization néo-libérale'. *Canadian Woman Studies/Les cahiers de la femme* 21/22 (4/1):151–5.

Lewins, F. 1995. *Transsexualism in society*. Melbourne: Macmillan.

Lewis, J. 2001. 'Legitimizing care work and the issue of gender equality'. In M. Daly (Ed.), *Care work: The quest for security*. Geneva: International Labour Office.

Ley, C. 1996. *The rise and fall of development theory*. London: James Currey.

———. 2003. 'Seeking homo economicus: The Canadian state and the strange story of the Business Immigration Program'. *Annals of the Association of American Geographers* 93 (2):426–41.

Li, P. 1990. 'Race and ethnicity'. In P. Li (Ed.), *Race and ethnic relations in Canada*, 3–20. Toronto: Oxford University Press.

———. 1998. *The Chinese in Canada*. 2nd edn. Toronto: Oxford University Press.

Lippert, R. 1998. 'Canadian refugee determination and advanced liberal government'. *Canadian Journal of Law and Society* 13:177–207.

———. 1999. 'Governing refugees: The relevance of governmentality to understanding the international refugee regime'. *Alternatives* 24 (3):295–328.

———. 2005. *Sanctuary, sovereignty, sacrifice: Canadian sanctuary incidents, power, and law*. Vancouver: University of British Columbia Press.

Lister, R. 2004. *Poverty*. Cambridge, UK: Polity Press.

Little, M., and I. Morrison. 1999. 'The pecker detectors are back: Regulation of the family form in Ontario welfare policy'. *Journal of Canadian Studies* 34 (Summer):110–36.

Little Bear, Leroy. 2004. 'Aboriginal paradigms: Implications for relations to land and treaty making'. In Kerry Wilkins (Ed.), *Advancing Aboriginal claims: Visions, strategies, directions*, 26–8. Saskatoon: Purich.

Loader, I. 2000. 'Plural policing and democratic governance'. *Social and Legal Studies* 9 (3):323–45.

————, and N. Walker. 2001. 'Policing as a public good: Reconstituting the connection between policing and the state'. *Theoretical Criminology* 5 (1):9–35.

Lombroso, Cesare. 1911. *Crime: Its causes and remedies.* (H.P. Horton, trans.). Boston: Little, Brown.

————, and G. Ferrero. 1991 [1895]. *La femme criminelle et la prostituée.* Grenoble: Éditions Jérôme Million.

Lorber, Judith. 2005. *Gender inequality: Feminist theories and politics.* 3rd edn. Los Angeles: Roxbury.

Lupton, Deborah. 1998. *The emotional self.* London: Sage.

Lyotard, J.F. 1988. 'An interview'. *Theory, Culture and Society* 5 (2/3):277–309.

M. v. H. 1996 31 OR (3d) 417 (CA).

McClellan, David. 1971. *The thought of Karl Marx: An introduction.* London: Macmillan.

McCreary Centre. 2001. *Time out: A profile of BC youth in custody.* Vancouver: McCreary.

MacDonald, A.P., Jr, J. Huggins, S. Young, and R.A. Swanson. 1973. 'Attitudes toward homosexuality'. *Journal of Consulting and Clinical Psychology* 40 (1):161.

Macionis, John J., and Linda M. Gerber. 2005. *Sociology.* 5th edn. Toronto: Prentice Hall.

MacKay, R. 1974. 'Standardised tests: Objective/objectified measures of "competence"'. In A.V. Cicourel, K.H. Jennings, S.H. Jennings, K.C. Leiter, R. MacKay, H. Mehan, and D.R. Roth (Eds), *Language use and school performance*, 218–47. New York: Academic Press.

MacKenzie, G. 1994. *Transgender nation.* Bowling Green, OH: State University Popular Press.

McKie, C. 1994. 'A history of emigration from Canada'. *Canadian Social Trends* 35 (Winter):26–9. Statistics Canada catalogue 11-008E.

Macklin, A. 2003. 'Dancing across borders: "Exotic dancers," trafficking, and Canadian immigration policy'. *International Migration Review* 37 (1):464–500.

McLuhan, Marshall. 1994 [1964]. *Understanding media: The extensions of man.* Cambridge, MA: MIT Press.

Maclure, Jocelyn. 2003. *Quebec identity: The challenge of pluralism.* Montreal and Kingston: McGill-Queen's University Press.

McMahon, Tamsin. 2005. 'Chief's apology too little, too late for Wallen'. *Kingston Whig Standard* 28 May.

————, and Frank Armstrong. 2005. 'Police chief "sorry" for racial profiling'. *Kingston Whig Standard* 27 May.

McNay, Lois. 1992. *Foucault and feminism: Power, gender and self.* Oxford, UK: Polity Press.

————. 1994. *Foucault: A critical introduction.* New York: Continuum Publishers.

————. 2004. 'Situated intersubjectivity'. In B.L. Marshall and A. Witz (Eds), *Engendering the social: Feminist encounters with sociological theory.* New York: Open University Press.

McRobbie, A. 1980. 'Settling accounts with subcultures: A feminist critique'. *Screen Education* 34:37–49.

Madonna and Patrick Leonard. 1989. 'Like a prayer'. US.

———— and Shep Pettibone. 1990. 'Vogue'. US.

Maestro Fresh Wes. 1994. 'Naaah dis kid can't be from Canada'. US.

Maioni, Antonia. 2003. 'Romanow—A defence of public health care, but is there a map for the road ahead?' *Policy Options* 24 (2):50–3.

Mandell, Nancy (Ed.). 2005. *Feminist issues: Race, class and sexuality*. 4th edn. Toronto: Prentice Hall.

Mandell, R. 1971. *The Nazi Olympics*. New York: Macmillan.

Mannheim, Karl. 1952. 'The problem of generations'. In P. Kecskemeti (Ed.), *Essays on the sociology of knowledge*. New York: Routledge and Kegan Paul.

Marshall, Barbara L. 2000. *Configuring gender: Explorations in theory and politics*. Peterborough, ON: Broadview.

Marshall, T. 1996. 'The evolution of restorative justice in Britain'. *European Journal on Criminal Policy and Research* 4 (4):21–43.

Martel, J. 1999. *Solitude and cold storage: Women's journeys of endurance in segregation*. Edmonton: Elizabeth Fry Society of Edmonton.

Martineau, Harriet. 1983 [1869]. *Autobiography*. London: Virago.

Martino, W., and B. Meyenn (Eds). 2001. *What about the boys? Issues of masculinity in schools*. Buckingham, UK: Open University Press.

————, and M. Pallotta-Chiarolli. 2001. *'So what's a boy?' Addressing the issues of masculinity and schooling*. Buckingham, UK: Open University Press.

Marx, Karl. 1947. *The German ideology*. New York: International Publishers.

————. 1970. *A contribution to the critique of political economy*. M. Dobb, Ed. (S.W. Ryazanskaya, trans.). Moscow: Progress Publishers.

————. 1973. *Grundrisse*. (M. Nicolaus, trans.). Harmondsworth, UK: Penguin.

————. 1975 [1852]. 'The 18th Brumaire of Louis Bonaparte'. In *Karl Marx, Friedrich Engels: Collected works*, 11:99–197. London: Lawrence and Wishart.

————. 1976 [1867]. *Capital*. v. 1. Harmondsworth, UK: Penguin.

————, and Friedrich Engels. 1948. *Manifesto of the Communist party*. New York: International Publishers.

————, and ————. 1970. *The German ideology*. New York: International Publishers.

Matas, R. 2005. 'Vancouver man charged with human trafficking'. *Globe and Mail* 14 April: S3.

Mathews, H. 2001. 'Citizenship, youth councils and young people's participation'. *Journal of Youth Studies* 4 (3):299–318.

Maudsley, Henry. 1863. 'Review of female life in prison'. *Journal of Mental Science* 9:69–87.

Mead, George Herbert. 1934. *Mind, self, and society*. Chicago: University of Chicago Press.

Mercredi, Ovide, and Mary Ellen Tupel. 1993. *In the rapids: Navigating the future of First Nations*. Toronto: Viking.

Metropolis. 2005. 'General information: Overview'. www.canada.metropolis.net/gener alinfo/index_e.html.

Meunier, E. Martin, and Jean-Philippe Warren. 1998. 'De la question sociale à la question nationale: La revue *Cité libre* (1950–1963)'. *Recherches sociographiques* 39:291–316.

Meyer, Manu Aluli. 2001. 'Acultural assumptions of empiricism: A Native Hawaiian critique'. *Canadian Journal of Native Education* 24 (2):188–98.

Miller, David. 1991. *Liberty*. Oxford, UK: Oxford University Press.

———. 1999. *Principles of social justice*. Cambridge, MA: Harvard University Press.

Miller, V. 1982. 'The decline of Nova Scotia Micmac population A.D. 1600–1850'. *Culture* 2 (3):107–18.

Mills, C. Wright. 1959. *The sociological imagination*. Oxford, UK: Oxford University Press.

———. 1963. *Power, politics and people: The collected essays of C. Wright Mills*. Introduction by Irving Louis Horowitz (Ed.). New York: Oxford University Press.

———. 2004 [1959]. 'The promise of sociology'. In John J. Macionis, Nijole V. Benokraitis, and Bruce Ravelli (Eds), *Seeing ourselves: Classic, contemporary, and cross-cultural readings in sociology*, Canadian edition, 1–4. Toronto: Pearson.

Mills, D. 2002. 'Children will be protected despite cutbacks'. *National Post* 3 October.

Milner, Murray, Jr. 2004. *Freaks, geeks, and cool kids: American teenagers, schools, and the culture of consumption*. London: Routledge.

Mitchell, Wendy, Robin Bunton, and Eileen Green (Eds). 2004. *Young people, risk and leisure: Constructing identities in everyday life*. Basingstoke, UK: Palgrave Macmillan.

Mitchell, W.O. 1990. *Roses are difficult here*. Toronto: McClelland and Stewart.

Moi, T. 1991. 'Appropriating Bourdieu: Feminist theory and Pierre Bourdieu's sociology of culture'. *New Literary History* 22 (4):1017–49.

Molnar, D. 1997. 'Remembering the past'. *Windsor Star* 12 July: E2.

Money, J. 1985. 'The conceptual neutering of gender and the criminalisation of sex'. *Archives of Sexual Behaviour* 14:279–91.

Monture-Angus, Patricia. 1995. *Thunder in my soul: A Mohawk woman speaks*. Halifax: Fernwood.

———. 1999. *Journeying forward: Dreaming First Nations independence*. Halifax: Fernwood.

———. 2001. 'Aboriginal women and correctional practice: Reflections on the Task Force on Federally Sentenced Women'. In Kelly Hannah-Moffat and Margaret Shaw (Eds), *An ideal prison? Critical essays on women's imprisonment in Canada*, 52–60. Halifax: Fernwood.

Moore, B. 1966. *The social origins of dictatorship and democracy*. Boston: Beacon.

More, K., and S. Whittle. 1999. 'Reclaiming genders'. London: Cassell.

Morgan, Lewis Henry. 1851. *The League of the Ho-dé-no-sau-nee*. Rochester, NY: Sage.

———. 1985. *Ancient society*. Foreword by Elisabeth Tooker. Tucson: University of Arizona Press.

Morin, Stephen, and Ellen Garfinkle. 1978. 'Male homophobia'. *Journal of Social Issues* 34 (1):29–47.

Morrison, T. 1992. *Playing in the dark: Whiteness and the literary imagination*. New York: Vintage.

Moss, Jeremy. 1988. *The later Foucault*. London: Sage.

MRSB Consulting Services. 2003. 'PEI urban call centre labour market profile'. Charlottetown, PE: PEI Labour Market Development Agreement, Human Resources Development Canada and PEI Department of Development and Technology.

Ms Cree. 1994. 'Entrenched social catastrophe'. *Journal of Prisoners on Prisons* 5 (2):45–8.

Muir Edwards et al. v. Canada (A.G.) [1930] AC 124 (JCPC).

Mulvey, Laura. 1975. 'Visual pleasure and narrative cinema'. *Screen* 16 (3):6–18.

Murphy, C. 1998. 'Policing postmodern Canada'. *Canadian Journal of Law and Society* 13 (2):1–28.

———, and C. Clarke. 2005. 'Policing communities and communities of policing: A comparative study of policing and security in two Canadian communities'. In Dennis Cooley (Ed.), *Re-imagining policing in Canada*. Toronto: University of Toronto Press.

Murray, Stephen. 2000. *Homosexualities*. Chicago: University of Chicago Press.

Namaste, V. 2005. *Sex change, social change: Reflections on identity, institutions and imperialism*. London: Women's Press.

Nash, Jeffrey E., and James N. Calonico. 1996. *The meaning of social interaction*. Dix Hills, NY: General Hall.

Nataf, Z. 1998. 'Whatever I feel…' *New Internationalist* April: 22–5.

Nelson, Lise. 1999. 'Bodies (and spaces) do matter: The limits of performativity'. *Gender, Place and Culture* 6 (4):331–53.

Normandeau, A., and B. Leighton. 1990. *A vision of the future of policing in Canada: Police Challenge 2000*. Ottawa: Solicitor General of Canada.

O'Brien, N. 2004. 'Youth "justice" a joke'. *Peterborough Examiner* 4 October: A4.

Olympia. 1938. Leni Riefenstahl, producer and director. Germany.

O'Malley, P. 1996. 'Policing, politics and postmodernity'. Paper delivered at the Centre Of Criminology, University of Toronto, November.

Ontario. 2003. *Private Investigators and Security Guards Act: Discussion paper*. Toronto: Ontario Ministry of Public Safety and Security. June.

———. 2004. Bill 88: An Act to Amend the Private Investigators and Public Security Guards Act. Toronto: Legislative Assembly of Ontario. June.

Oudshoorn, N. 1994. *Beyond the natural body: An archaeology of sex hormones*. London and New York: Routledge.

Pagon, R.A. 1987. 'Diagnostic approach to the newborn with ambiguous genitalia'. *Pediatric Clinics of North America* 34:1019–31.

Palmer, D., and P. O'Malley. 1996. 'Post-Keynesian policing'. *Economy and Society* 25 (2):137–55.

Paris is burning. 1990. Jennie Livingston, director. US.

Patten, Christopher. 1999. 'The Report of the Independent Commission on Policing in Northern Ireland'. London: HMSO.

Pavlich, George C. 2000. *Critique and radical discourses on crime*. Aldershot, UK: Ashgate.

———. 2005. 'Experiencing critique'. *Law and critique* 16:95–112.

Peak, Kenneth, and Ronald Glensor. 1996. *Community policing and problem solving: Strategies and practices*. Englewood Cliffs, NJ: Prentice Hall.

Peck, J. 2001. *Workfare states*. New York: Guilford.

Peers, Laura. 1996. 'Subsistence, secondary literature and gender bias: The Saulteaux'. In Christine Miller, Patricia Chuchryk, Marla Smallface Marule, Brenda Manyfingers, and Cheryl Deering (Eds), *Women of the First Nations: Power, wisdom and strength.* Winnipeg: University of Manitoba Press.

Pelfry, William. 1998. 'Precipitating factors of paradigmatic shift in policing: The origin of the community policing era'. In Geoffrey Alpert and Alex Piquero (Eds), *Community policing: Contemporary readings.* Prospect Heights, IL: Waveland Press.

Perlmutter, A.D., and M.D. Reitelman. 1992. 'Surgical management of intersexuality'. In P.C. Walsh, A.B. Retik, T.A. Stamey, and E.D. Vaughan (Eds), *Campbell's urology,* 1951–66. Philadelphia: Saunders.

Peterson-Badali, M., and R. Abramovich. 1992. 'Children's knowledge of the legal system: Are they competent to instruct legal counsel?' *Canadian Journal of Criminology* 34 (2):139–60.

Pfetsch, F., P. Beutel, H.-M. Stork, and G. Treutlein. 1975. *Leistungssport und Gesellschaftssystem: Sozio-politische Faktoren im Leistungssport* [Performance sport and the social system: Socio-political factors in performance sport]. Schorndorf, Germany: Karl Hofmann Verlag.

Phoenix, Ann, Stephen Frosh, and Rob Pattman. 2003. 'Producing contradictory masculine subject positions'. *Journal of Social Issues* 59 (1):179–95.

Pipher, Mary. 1994. *Reviving Ophelia: Saving the selves of adolescent girls.* New York: Ballantine.

Police Futures Group. 2005. 'Private policing'. www.policefutures.org/docs/PFG_Private_Policing.

Pollak, Shoshana. 1993. *Opening the window on a very dark day: A program evaluation of the peer support team at the Kingston Prison for Women.* Unpublished master's thesis. Ottawa: Carleton University.

Pollner, Melvin. 1967. 'Sociological and common-sense models of the labelling process'. In Roy Turner (Ed.), *Ethnomethodology,* 27–40. Harmondsworth, UK: Penguin.

Pomerantz, Shauna, Dawn H. Currie, and Deirdre M. Kelly. 2004. 'Sk8er girls: Skateboarders, girlhood and feminism in motion'. *Women's Studies International Forum* 27 (5/6):547–57.

Ponting, J. Rick, and Roger Gibbins. 1980. *Out of irrelevance: A socio-political introduction to Indian affairs in Canada.* Scarborough, ON: Butterworth.

Porret, Michel. 1998. *Le corps violenté: Du geste à la parole.* Genève: Librairie Drosz S.A.

Potter, Russell A. 1995. *Spectacular vernaculars: Hip hop and the politics of postmodernism.* New York: SUNY Press.

Prasad, A. 2005. 'Reconsidering the socio-scientific construction of sexual difference: The case of Kimberly Nixon'. *Canadian Woman Studies* 24 (2/3).

Pratt, A. 2005. *Securing borders: Deportation and detention in Canada.* Vancouver: University of British Columbia Press.

Premiers' Council on Canadian Health Awareness. 2004. 'Premiers launch new public awareness campaign on health care funding'. www.premiersforhealth.ca/newsroom.php.

Prentice, A., P. Bourne, G. Cuthbert Brandt, B. Light, W. Mitchinson, and N. Black. 1988. *Canadian women: A history*. Toronto: Harcourt, Brace and Jovanovich.

Price, John A. 1981. 'Native studies in Canadian universities and colleges'. *Canadian Journal of Native Studies* 2 (1):349–61.

Prince, M. 1999. 'From health and welfare to stealth and farewell: Federal social policy, 1980–2000'. In L. Pal (Ed.), *How Ottawa spends, 1999–2000: Shape shifting: Canadian governance toward the 21st century*. Toronto: Oxford University Press.

Prosser, J. 1998. *Second skins*. New York: Columbia University Press.

Putnam, R. 2000. *Bowling alone: The collapse and revival of American community*. New York: Simon and Schuster.

Québec. Protecteur du citoyen. 1985. *Le respect des droits des personnes incarcérées*. Québec: Protecteur du citoyen.

R. v. Keegstra [1990] 3 S.C.R.

R. v. Latimer [2001] 1 S.C.R. 3.

R. v. Morgentaler [1993] 3 S.C.R. 463.

R. v. Parker [2000] 49 09 3d 481.

Rae, Heather. 2002. *State identities and the homogenisation of peoples*. Cambridge, UK: Cambridge University Press.

Ramsay, Richard, and Pierre Tremblay. 2005. 'Bisexual, gay, queer male suicidality'. University of Calgary. http://www.fsw.ucalgary.ca/ramsay/homosexualitysuicide/(retrieved 23 April 2005).

Raymond, J. 1994. *The transsexual empire*. New York: Teachers College Press.

Razack, S. 1999. 'Making Canada white: Law and the policing of bodies of colour in the 1990s'. *Canadian Journal of Law and Society* 14 (1):159–85.

Rebel without a cause. 1955. Nicholas Ray, director. US.

Reiman, J. 1979. *The rich get richer and the poor get prison: Ideology, class and criminal justice*. New York: Wiley.

Reitsma-Street, M. 1999. 'Justice for Canadian girls: A 1990s update'. *Canadian Journal of Criminology* 41 (3):335–58.

Reitz, J. (Ed.). 2003. *Host societies and the reception of immigrants*. San Diego: Center for Comparative Immigration Research, University of California.

Renold, E. 2004. '"Other" boys: Negotiating non-hegemonic masculinities in the primary school'. *Gender and Education* 16 (2):247–66.

Rich, Adrienne. 1989. 'Compulsory heterosexuality and lesbian existence'. In L. Richardson and V. Taylor (Eds), *Feminist frontiers II*. New York: Random House.

Rimke, Heidi Marie. 2000. 'Governing citizens through self-help literature'. *Cultural Studies* 14 (1):61–78.

Riordan, J. 1977. *Sport in Soviet society*. Cambridge, UK: Cambridge University Press.

Ritzer, George (Ed.). 2002. *McDonaldization: The reader*. Thousand Oaks, CA: Pine Forge Press.

Robert, Dominique, Renée Belzile, and Sylvie Frigon. Forthcoming. 'Women, embodiment of health and carceral space'. In C. Setna (Ed.), *Body talk*. Ottawa: Les Presses de l'Université d'Ottawa.

———, and Sylvie Frigon. In press. 'La santé comme mirage des transformations carcérales'. *Déviance et societé* automne 2006

Roberts, B. 1994. 'Shovelling out the "mutinous": Political deportation from Canada before 1936'. In G. Tulchinsky (Ed.), *Immigration in Canada: Historical perspectives*, 265–96. Toronto: Copp Clark Longman.

Roberts, J., and R. Melchers. 2003. 'The incarceration of Aboriginal offenders'. *Canadian Journal of Criminology* 45 (2):170–89.

Robertson, Ann. 1990. 'The politics of Alzheimer's Disease: A case study in apocalyptic demography'. *International Journal of Health Services* 20:429–42.

Robertson, Roland. 1990. 'After nostalgia? Willful nostalgia and the phases of globalization'. In Bryan S. Turner (Ed.), *Theories of modernity and postmodernity*. London: Sage.

Röder, H. 2002. *Von der 1. zur 3. Förderstufe* [From the first to the third level for advancement]. http://www.sport-ddr-roeder.de/kapitel_10_0.htm.

Roediger, D. 1991. *Wages of whiteness: Race and the making of the American working-class*. New York: Verso.

Rose, N. 1989. *Governing the soul: The shaping of the private self*. London: Routledge.

———. 1999. *Powers of freedom*. Cambridge, UK: Cambridge University Press.

———, and P. Miller. 1992. 'Political power beyond the state: Problematics of government'. *British Journal of Sociology* 43:173–205.

Rose, Tricia. 1994. *Black noise: Rap music and black culture in contemporary America*. Middletown, CT: Wesleyan University Press.

Ross, Robert Robertson, and Hugh Bryan McKay. 1979. *Self-mutilation*. Toronto: Lexington.

Rothblatt, M. 1995. *The apartheid of sex*. New York: Crown.

Rousseau, Jean-Jacques. 1983. *The social contract and discourses*. London: J.M. Dent and Sons.

Royal Commission on Aboriginal Peoples. 1993. *Aboriginal peoples and the justice system*. Ottawa: Minister of Supply and Services.

Royal Commission on Aboriginal Peoples. 1996. *Bridging the cultural divide: A report on Aboriginal peoples and criminal justice in Canada*. Ottawa: Minister of Supply and Services.

Rubin, Gayle. 1975. 'The traffic in women'. In R. Reiter (Ed.), *Toward an anthropology of women*. New York: Monthly Review.

Ryan, A.J. 1976. 'Athletics'. In C. Kochakian (Ed.) *Anabolic-androgenic steroids. Handbook of experimental pharmacology*, v. 43. New York: Springer-Verlag.

Sacks, Oliver. 1995. 'An anthropologist on Mars'. In *An anthropologist on Mars: Seven Paradoxical Tales*, 244–96. Toronto: Random House Canada.

Sagan, D. 1992. 'Metametazoa: Biology and multiplicity'. In J. Crary and S. Kwinter (Eds), *Incorporations*, 362–85. New York: Urzone.

Sagarin E. 1978. 'Transsexualism: Legitimization, amplification and exploitation of deviance by scientists and mass media'. In C. Winick (Ed.), *Deviance and mass media*. Beverly Hills, CA: Sage.

Saint-Simon, Henri de. 1814. 'The reorganization of Europe'. In F.M.H. Markham (Ed.), *Henri Comte de Saint-Simon: Selected writings*. Oxford: Basil Blackwell.

Sanders, Clinton R. 1990. 'Excusing tactics: Social responses to the public misbehavior of companion dogs'. *Anthrozoös* 4:82–90.

———. 1993. 'Understanding dogs: Caretakers' attributions of mindedness in canine-human relationships'. *Journal of Contemporary Ethnography* 22:205–26.

Sanger, T. 2006. 'Desiring difference? Transpeople's intimate partnerships and the cultural construction of gender and sexuality'. Ph.D. thesis, Queen's University, Belfast.

Sapir, Edward. 1929. 'The status of linguistics as a science'. *Language* 5:207–14.

———. 1949. *Selected writings of Edward Sapir in language, culture, and personality.* David Mandelbaum (Ed.). Berkeley: University of California Press.

Sartre, Jean-Paul. 1964. *Nausea.* (L. Alexander, trans.). New York: Penguin.

———. 1970. 'An existentialist's view of freedom'. In R. Dewey and J. Gould (Eds), *Freedom, its history, nature and varieties'.* London: Macmillan.

Satsan (Herb George). 2005. National Centre for First Nations Governance website, www.fngovernance.org.

Satzewich, Vic. 1990. 'The political economy of race and ethnicity'. In P. Li (Ed.), *Race and ethnic relations in Canada,* 251–68. Toronto: Oxford University Press.

———, and Terry Wotherspoon. 1993. *First Nations: Race, class and gender relations.* Toronto: Nelson.

Saussure, Ferdinand. 1983 [1916]. *Course in general linguistics.* London: Duckworth.

Savage, S., and S. Chapman. 1996. 'Managing change'. In F. Leishman, B. Loveday, and S. Savage (Eds), *Core issues in policing.* London: Longman.

Schiebinger, L. 1993. *Nature's body.* London: Pandora.

Schutz, Alfred. 1962. *Collected papers, volume 1.* The Hague: Martinus Nijhoff.

———. 1967. *The phenomenology of the social world.* Evanston, IL: Northwestern University.

———, and Helmut Wagner. *On phenomenology and social relations: Selected essays.* Chicago: University of Chicago Press.

Scott, Wilbur, and Sandra Stanley. 1994. *Gays and lesbians in the military.* Hawthorne, NY: Aldine de Gruyter.

Sedgwick, Eve. 1990. *Epistemology of the closet.* Berkeley: University of California.

Seidman, Steven. 1991. 'Postmodern anxiety: The politics of epistemology'. *Sociological Theory* 9 (2):180–90.

———. 1998. *Contested knowledges: Social theory in the postmodern era.* London, Blackwell.

Seltzer, Richard. 1992. 'The social location of those holding antihomosexual attitudes'. *Sex Roles* 26 (9/10):391–8.

Senn, A. 1999. *Power, politics and the Olympic Games.* Champaign, IL: Human Kinetics.

Sennett, Richard. 1992. *The fall of public man.* New York: Norton.

Settersten, Richard A., Jr (Ed.). 2003. *Invitation to the life course: Toward new understandings of later life.* Amityville, NY: Baywood.

Sharrock, W., and B. Anderson. 1986. *The ethnomethodologists.* London: Tavistock.

Shearing, C. 1996. 'Reinventing policing: Policing as governance'. In O. Marewin (Ed.), *Policing change, changing police, international perspectives.* New York: Garland.

———. 1997. 'The reinvention of community policing'. In T. Thomas (Ed.), *The politics of the city.* Toronto: Nelson.

————, and P. Stenning. 1982. *Private security and private justice: The challenge of the eighties*. Montreal: Institute for Research on Public Policy.

————, and Jennifer Wood. 2003. 'Nodal governance, democracy and new denizens'. *Journal of Law and Society* 30 (3):400–19.

Sheptycki, J.W. 1998. 'Policing, postmodernism and transnationalization'. *British Journal of Criminology* 38 (3):485–503.

Shilling, C. 1993. *The body and social theory*. London: Sage.

Siemiatycki, M., and E. Isin. 1998. 'Immigration, diversity and urban citizenship in Toronto'. *Canadian Journal of Regional Science* 20:73–102.

Simmel, Georg. 1968 [1918]. *The conflict of modern culture*. (K. Peter Etzhorn, trans.). New York: Teachers College Press.

————. 1971. *On individuality and social forms*. Donald N. Levine (Ed.). Chicago: University of Chicago Press.

————. 1990 [1900]. *The philosophy of money*. David Frisby (Ed.). (Tom Bottomore and David Frisby, trans.). London and New York: Routledge.

Simpson, Mark. 1994. *Male impersonators*. London: Cassell.

Sisters in Spirit. 2005. http://www.sistersinspirit.ca/enghome.htm.

Smart, B. 1985. *Michel Foucault*. London: Tavistock.

Smart, C. 1976. *Women, crime and criminology*. London: Routledge and Kegan Paul.

————. 1989. *Feminism and the power of law*. London: Routledge.

Smith, Adam. 1976 [1776]. *An inquiry into the nature and causes of the wealth of nations*. R.H. Campbell and A.S. Skinner (Eds). Oxford, UK: Clarendon Press.

Smith, D. 1974a. 'The ideological practice of sociology'. *Catalyst* 2:39–54.

————. 1974b. 'The social construction of documentary reality'. *Sociological Inquiry* 44 (4):257–68.

————. 1975. 'The statistics on mental illness: What they will not tell us about women and why'. In D. Smith and S. David (Eds), *Women look at psychiatry*, 73–119. Vancouver: Press Gang Publishers.

————. 1978. '"K is mentally ill": The anatomy of a factual account'. *Sociology* 12 (1):25–53.

————. 1987. *The everyday world as problematic: A feminist sociology*. Toronto: University of Toronto Press.

————. 1990a. 'The statistics on women and mental illness: The relations of ruling they conceal'. In *The conceptual practices of power*, 107–38. Toronto: University of Toronto Press.

————. 1990b. 'No one commits suicide: Textual analyses of ideological practices'. In *The Conceptual Practices of Power*, 140–73. Toronto: University of Toronto Press.

————. 1992. 'Sociology from women's experience: A reaffirmation'. *Sociological Theory* 10:88–98.

————. 1999. *Writing the social: Critique, theory and investigations*. Toronto: University of Toronto Press.

Snider, L. 2004. 'Female punishment: From punishment to backlash'. In C. Sumner (Ed.), *The Blackwell companion to criminology*. Malden, MA: Blackwell.

Socarides, C. 1970. 'A psychoanalytic study of the desire for sexual transformation: The plaster-of-Paris man'. *International Journal of Psychoanalysis* 51:341–49.

Society for the Promotion of the Olympic Idea (Ed.). 1972. *Spiele der XX. Olympiade, München 1972* [Games of the 20ᵗʰ Olympiad, Munich 1972]. East Berlin: German Democratic Republic.

Solomon, Arthur, with Michael Posluns. 1990. *Songs for the people: Teachings on the natural way.* Toronto: NC Press.

Sontag, S. 1980. 'Fascinating fascism'. In *Under the sign of Saturn*, 73–105. New York: Farrar, Straus and Girous.

Soysal, Y. 2000. 'Citizenship and identity: Living in diasporas in post-war Europe?' *Ethnic and Racial Studies* 23:1–15.

Sparrow, Malcolm, Mark Moore, and David Kennedy. 1990. *Beyond 911: A new era for policing.* New York: Basic Books.

Speer, A. 1969. *Erinnerungen* [Memoirs]. Berlin: Verlag Ullstein.

Spitzer, G., H.-J. Teichler, and K. Reinartz (Eds). 1998 [1952]. 'Das Staatliche Komitee für Körperkultur und Sport übernimmt die wesentlichen Funktionen des Sportausschusses [The State Committee for Physical Culture and Sport takes over the essential functions of the Sport Committee]'. In *Schlüsseldokumente zum DDR-Sport. Ein sporthistorischer Überblick in Originalquellen. Schriftenreihe: Sportentwicklungen in Deutschland [Key documents in GDR Sport. A historical overview of sport through original sources: Sport development in Germany]*, v. 4. Aachen, Germany: Meyer & Meyer Verlag.

Squires, Judith. 2000. *Gender in political theory.* Cambridge, UK: Cambridge University Press.

Squires, K. 2004. 'Nouvel établissement correctionnel pour délinquantes'. *Actualités-justice* 19 (2):11–12.

Stasiulis, D. 1990. 'Theorizing connections: Gender, race, ethnicity and class'. In P. Li (Ed.), *Race and ethnic relations in Canada*, 3–20. Toronto: Oxford University Press.

Statistics Canada. 2000. *Youth in custody and community services in Canada, 1998–9.* Ottawa: Centre for Justice Statistics.

———. 2001a. *A profile of criminal victimization: Results of the 1999 General Social Survey.* Ottawa: Statistics Canada.

———. 2001b. *Population 15 years and over by highest level of schooling, by provinces and territories, census of population 2001.* http://www40.statcan.ca/101/cst01/educ43a.htm.

———. 2001c. *Average earnings of the population 15 years and over by highest level of schooling, by province and territory, census of population 2001.* http://www40.statcan.ca/101/cst01/labor50a.htm.

———. 2004. *Police resources in Canada, 2004.* Ottawa: Canadian Centre for Justice Statistics. http://dsp-psd.pwgsc.gc.ca/Collection-R/Statcan/85-225XIE/0000485-225-XIE.pdf.

———. 2005. 'Labour force, employed and unemployed, numbers and rates, by province'. *Labour force survey 2005.* http://www40.statcan.ca/101/cst01/labor07a.htm.

———. 2006. 'Average hourly wages of employees by selected characteristics and profession, unadjusted data, by province'. *Labour force survey, April 2005.* http://www40.statcan.ca/101/cst01/laabor69a.htm.

Steckley, John. 2003. *Aboriginal voices and the politics of representation in Canadian introductory sociology books.* Toronto: Canadian Scholars Press.

Steinberg, Shirley R., and Joe L. Kincheloe. 1997. *Kinderculture: The corporate construction of childhood.* Boulder, CO: Westview.

Stenson, Kevin. 1993. 'Community policing as a governmental technology'. *Economy and Society* 22 (3):373–89.

Stone, S. 1991. 'The empire strikes back: A post-transsexual manifesto'. In J. Epstein and K. Straub (Eds), *Body guards: The cultural politics of gender ambiguity,* 280–304. New York: Routledge.

Stryker, S. 1994. 'My words to Victor Frankenstein above the village of Chamounix'. GLQ 1 (3):237–54.

———. 1995. 'Transsexuality: The postmodern body and/as technology'. *Exposure* 30 (1/2):38–50.

Stychin, Carl. 1998. *A nation by rights.* Philadelphia: Temple University Press.

Sudnow, D. 1967. *Passing on: The social organization of dying.* Englewood Cliffs, NJ: Prentice Hall.

Szasz, T. 1990. *Sex by prescription.* Syracuse, NY: Syracuse University Press.

Tanner, J. 1996. *Teenage troubles: Youth and deviance in Canada.* Scarborough, ON: Nelson.

Tastsoglou, E. 2001. 'Re-appraising immigration and identities'. Report commissioned by the Department of Canadian Heritage for the Ethno-cultural, Racial, Religious and Linguistic Diversity and Identity Seminar, Halifax, 1–2 November.

Taylor, J. 1995. 'The third sex'. *Esquire* 123 (4):102–12.

Teeter, Brad. 2005. 'Court slams BC bullying'. *Xtra!* 534:22.

Teichler, H.-J. 1975. 'Berlin 1936—ein sieg der NS-propaganda? [Berlin 1936—A victory for Nazi propaganda?]'. *Stadion* 2:265–306.

———. 1982. 'Coubertin und das Dritte Reich [Coubertin and the Third Reich]'. *Sportwissenschaft* 12:18–55.

Terry, Jennifer, and Jacqueline Urla (Eds). 1995. *Deviant bodies. Critical perspectives on difference in science and popular culture.* Bloomington: Indiana University Press.

Theriault, Joseph-Yvon. 2002. *Critique de l'américanité.* Montréal: Éditions Québec-Amérique.

Thiessen, V., and J. Blasius. 2002. 'The social distribution of youth's images to work'. *Canadian Review of Sociology and Anthropology* 39 (1):49–78.

Thobani, S. 2000. 'Closing ranks: Racisms and sexism in Canada's immigration policy'. *Race and Class* 42:35–55.

Thomas, L. 1974. *The lives of a cell.* New York: Viking.

Thomas, Robina. 2005. 'Honouring the oral traditions of my ancestors through storytelling'. In Leslie Brown and Susan Strega (Eds), *Research as resistance: Critical, indigenous and anti-oppressive approaches.* Toronto: Canadian Scholars Press.

Thornton, Russell. 1998. 'Institutional and intellectual histories of Native American studies'. In Russell Thornton (Ed.), *Studying Native America: Problems and prospects*. Madison: University of Wisconsin Press.

Titus, J. J. 2004. 'Boy trouble: Rhetorical framing of boys' underachievement'. *Discourse: Studies in the Cultural Politics of Education* 25 (2):145–69.

Tobias, John L. 1998. 'Canada's subjugation of the Plains Cree, 1879–1885'. In Ken Coates and Robin Fisher (Eds), *Out of the background: Readings on Canadian Native history*. 2nd edn, 150–76. Toronto: Irwin.

Todd, J., and T. Todd. 2001. 'Significant events in the history of drug testing and the Olympic movement: 1960–1999'. In W. Wilson and E. Derse (Eds), *Doping in elite sport: The politics of drugs in the Olympic movement*. Champaign, IL: Human Kinetics.

Todd, T. 1987. 'Anabolic steroids: The gremlins of sport'. *Journal of Sport History* 14 (1):87–107.

Torpey, J. 2000. *The invention of the passport: Surveillance, citizenship and the state*. Cambridge, UK: Cambridge University Press.

Tran, K., S. Kustec, and T. Chui. 2005. 'Becoming Canadian: Intent, process, and outcome'. *Canadian Social Trends*. Statistics Canada catalogue no. 11-008.

Triumph of the will. 1935. Leni Riefenstahl, producer and director. Germany.

Trojanowicz, R., and B. Bucqueroux. 1990. *Community policing: A contemporary perspective*. Cincinnati: Anderson.

Turner, Bryan S. 1990. 'Periodization and politics in the postmodern'. In Bryan S. Turner (Ed.), *Theories of modernity and postmodernity*. London: Sage.

Turner, R. 1974. 'Words, utterances and activities'. In R. Turner (Ed.), *Ethnomethodology*, 197–215. Harmondsworth, UK: Penguin.

Valverde, M. 1991. *The age of light, soap, and water: Moral reform in English Canada, 1885–1925*. Toronto: McClelland and Stewart.

———. 1999. 'Democracy in governance: Socio-legal framework'. Report for the Law Commission of Canada, University of Toronto.

———, Ron Levi, Clifford Shearing, Mary Condon, and Pat O'Malley. 1999. *Democracy in governance: A socio-legal framework*. Ottawa: Law Commission of Canada.

van Dülmen, Richard. 1990. *Theatre of horror: Crime and punishment in early modern Germany*. Cambridge, UK: Polity Press.

Venables, Robert W. 1992. 'American Indian influences on the America of the founding fathers'. In Oren Lyons (Ed.), *Exiled in the land of the free: Democracy, Indian nations, and the U.S. Constitution*, 74–124. Sante Fe, NM: Clear Light Publishers.

Venne, Michel. 2001. *Vive Quebec! New thinking and new approaches to the Quebec nation*. Toronto: Lorimer.

Vicinus, Martha. 1992. 'They wonder to which sex I belong'. *Feminist Studies* 18 (3):467–97.

Voy, R. 1991. *Drugs, sports and politics*. Champaign, IL: Leisure Press.

Vriend v. Alberta [1998] 156 DLR (4th) 385 (SCC).

Wacquant, L. 1999. 'Urban marginality in the coming millennium'. *Urban Studies* 36 (10):1639–47.

———. 2001. 'Deadly symbiosis: When ghetto and prison mesh'. *Punishment and Society* 3 (1):95–134.

Walcott, Rinaldo. 2000. *Rude: Contemporary black Canadian cultural criticism.* Toronto: Insomniac Press.

Warner, C. 1999. 'Failed business immigrants free to stay in Canada'. *National Post* 11 October.

Warrior, Robert. 1996. *Like a hurricane: The Indian movement from Alcatraz to Wounded Knee.* New York: New Press.

Watson, Lisa. 2004. 'Managing maximum security women in federal corrections 1989–2004'. *Forum* 16 (1):3–6.

Weatherford, Jack. 1988. *Indian givers: How the Indians of the Americas transformed the world.* New York: Fawcett Columbine.

Weber, Max. 1904–5. *The Protestant ethic and the spirit of capitalism.* (Talcott Parsons, trans.). New York: Charles Scribner's Sons.

———. 1947. *The theory of social and economic organization.* Talcott Parsons (Ed.). New York: Free Press.

———. 1948. *From Max Weber: Essays in sociology.* H. Gerth and C. Wright Mills (Eds). London: Routledge and Kegan Paul.

———. 1962. *Basic concepts in sociology.* Secaucus, NJ: Citadel.

———. 1968. *Economy and society: An outline of interpretive sociology.* Guenther Roth and Claus Wittich (Eds). New York: Bedminster.

Weedon, Chris. 1999. *Feminism, theory and the politics of difference.* Malden, MA: Blackwell.

Weeks, Jeffrey. 1995. *Invented moralities.* New York: Columbia University Press.

———, Brian Heathy, and Catherine Donovan. 2001. *Same sex intimacies.* London: Routledge.

Weissman, Aerlyn. 2002. *Little Sisters vs. Big Brother.* Video.

West side story. 1961. Jerome Roberts and Robert Wise, directors. US.

White, Emily. 2002. *Fast girls: Teenage tribes and the myth of slut.* New York: Scribner.

Whittle, S. 1998. 'The trans-cyberian mail way'. *Social and Legal Studies* 7:389–408.

Whorf, Benjamin L. 1956. *Language, thought and reality: Selected writings.* John B. Caroll (Ed.). Cambridge, MA: Technology Press of Massachusetts Institute of Technology.

Wittgenstein, L. 1953. *Philosophical investigations.* Oxford, UK: Blackwell.

Wrong, Dennis. 1988. *Power: Its forms, bases and uses.* Oxford, UK: Blackwell.

Yesalis, C., and M. Bahrke. 2002. 'History of doping in sport'. *International Sports Studies* 24 (1):42–76.

Young, I.M. 1990. *Justice and the politics of difference.* Princeton, NJ: Princeton University Press.

Zedner, Lucia. 1991. 'Women, crime and penal responses: A historical account'. In M. Tonry (Ed.), *Crime and justice: A review of research.* Chicago: Chicago University Press.

Index